ROADSIDE GEOLOGY of SOUTHERN CALIFORNIA

ARTHUR GIBBS SYLVESTER

ILLUSTRATED BY
ELIZABETH O'BLACK GANS

2016
Mountain Press Publishing Company
Missoula, Montana

ROADSIDE GEOLOGY

**Roadside Geology is a registered trademark
of Mountain Press Publishing Company.**

Geological maps for the road guides are based on the 2010 *Geologic Map of California*, published by the California Geological Survey, and on maps published by the Dibblee Geological Foundation

All photos by Arthur Gibbs Sylvester unless otherwise credited.

Front cover photo: *Fine-grained aplite dikes of quartz and feldspar intruded this granite in Joshua Tree National Park.* —Tyson McKinney photo

Back cover photo: *Colorful Point Loma Formation conglomerate and mudstone on the west side of Point Loma cliffs.* —Arthur Gibbs Sylvester photo

Library of Congress Cataloging-in-Publication Data

Names: Sylvester, Arthur Gibbs. | O'Black Gans, Elizabeth, 1971-
Title: Roadside geology of southern California / Arthur Gibbs Sylvester and
  Elizabeth O'Black Gans.
Description: Missoula, Montana : Mountain Press Publishing Company, 2016.
  Series: Roadside geology series
Identifiers: LCCN 2015039518 | ISBN 9780878426539 (pbk. : alk. paper)
Subjects: LCSH: Geology—California, Southern—Guidebooks. | California,
  Southern—Guidebooks.
Classification: LCC QE89 .S95 2016 | DDC 557.94/9—dc23
LC record available at http://lccn.loc.gov/2015039518

PRINTED IN THE UNITED STATES BY VERSA PRESS, INC.

MP Mountain Press
PUBLISHING COMPANY

P.O. Box 2399 • Missoula, MT 59806 • 406-728-1900
800-234-5308 • info@mtnpress.com
www.mountain-press.com

ACKNOWLEDGMENTS

Much of this book was written with reference to an enormous geologic literature by hundreds of intrepid geologists, especially Thomas W. Dibblee, Jr., whose hundreds of geologic maps are published by the Dibblee Geological Foundation, and the support of the Santa Barbara Museum of Natural History. We thank the Dibblee Geological Foundation for permission to use parts of some of Tom's maps.

Chris Wills of the California Geological Survey provided digital files for the 2010 *Geologic Map of California*, which we used as a base for most of the book's geologic maps.

The extensive collection of South Coast Geological Society guidebooks contain a wealth of information that we could only abstract for this book. We thank Jeff Miller, the society's publications officer, for making the most recent volumes available to us.

Dave Kimbrough, Becky Dorsey, Egil Hauksson, and Tom Hopps gave us permission to modify and publish their maps and cross sections. John Barron, Gary Rasmussen, Richie Kurkewicz, Tyson McKinney, John Crowell, Warren Hamilton, John Veevaert of Trinity Mineral Company, Paul Valentich-Scott of the Santa Barbara Museum of Natural History, David M. Rib of Mitsubishi Cement Corporation, Phillip Colla of Oceanlight.com, J. R. Morgan, Andy Wyss, Bob Gray, Marli Miller, and Sophie Briggs graciously provided photographs and illustrations. Becky Dorsey, Tom Rockwell, Ray Ingersoll, Dave Kimbrough, Daryl Wold, Mark Kamerling, Eldon Gath, and Chris Henry spared us from some embarrassing mistakes through their counsel about selected topics. Craig Nicholson, Keith Howard, Bill Elliott, Jim Boles, and Jeff Miller read early versions of the manuscript and offered perfect suggestions for remedying its faults and smoothing kinks in the prose.

We spent a lot of time in the field with other geologists, learning about their areas of interest. Bob Webb and Bob Norris introduced us to the Mojave Desert and Salton Trough; John Crowell, Butch Brown, and Tor Nilsen shared their insights about sedimentation and tectonics of southern California Tertiary basins; Bill Wise and Dick Fisher taught us about Mojave and Hawaiian volcanoes; Perry Ehlig took us to study the Pelona Schist; Cliff Hopson shared his interpretations of Proterozoic metamorphic rocks of the Transverse Ranges; and Tanya Atwater and Craig Nicholson helped us understand the complexities of the plate tectonic evolution of southern California.

We owe special thanks to Mountain Press editor Jenn Carey, whose patience and reasoned, blue-pencil advice moved the manuscript smoothly from darkness to light, and to Chelsea Feeney for helping in a pinch with some of the illustrations.

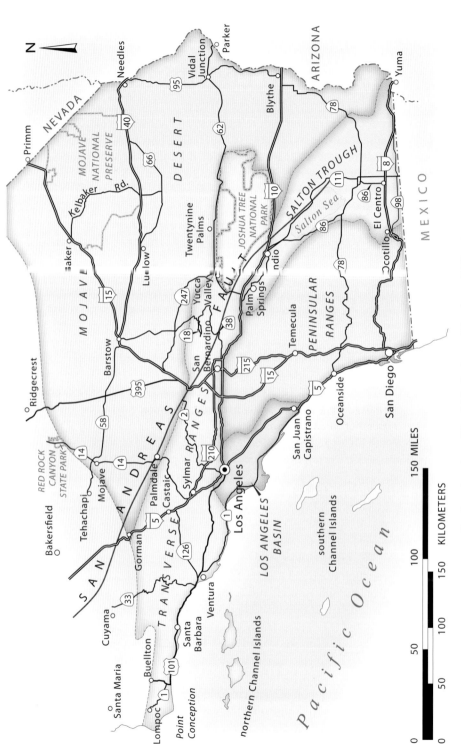

Roads and sections of **Roadside Geology of Southern California.**

CONTENTS

PREFACE   viii

INTRODUCTION   1
  UNDERSTANDING THE EARTH   3
    Rocks and Rock Formation   3
    Plate Tectonics   4
    Faults, Faulting, and Earthquakes   6
    Geologic Processes in Desert Environments   8
  GEOLOGIC EVOLUTION OF SOUTHERN CALIFORNIA   12
    PROTEROZOIC EON   12
      Gneissic Basement Rock   12
    PALEOZOIC ERA   13
      The Continental Shelf   13
    MESOZOIC ERA   13
      Subduction and Batholith Formation   13
    CENOZOIC ERA   16
      Crustal Breakup, Rift Volcanism, and Basin Sedimentation   16
      Development of the San Andreas Fault   17
      Rotation of the Western Transverse Ranges   20
      The Present   21

MOJAVE DESERT   25
  DETACHMENT FAULTS   28
  JOSHUA TREE NATIONAL PARK   28
  Road Guides for the Mojave Desert   34
    INTERSTATE 10: INDIO—BLYTHE   34
    INTERSTATE 15: CAJON SUMMIT—BARSTOW   39
    INTERSTATE 15: BARSTOW—BAKER   44
    INTERSTATE 15: BAKER—PRIMM, NEVADA   54
    INTERSTATE 40: BARSTOW—NEEDLES   59
    US 66: LUDLOW—FENNER   64
    US 95: BLYTHE—NEEDLES   70
    CA 14: PALMDALE—MOJAVE—RED ROCK CANYON   77
    CA 58: TEHACHAPI—BARSTOW   83
    CA 62: NORTH PALM SPRINGS—ARIZONA BORDER   89
    KELBAKER ROAD: INTERSTATE 40—BAKER   92
    CA 247: YUCCA VALLEY—BARSTOW   99

SALTON TROUGH 105

SALTON TROUGH EARTHQUAKES 108
LAKE CAHUILLA AND THE SALTON SEA 109
ALGODONES DUNES 110

WORLD-CLASS GEOLOGIC SITES 111
Mecca Hills: Box Canyon and Painted Canyon 111
Split Mountain Gorge 123

Road Guides for the Salton Trough 128
INTERSTATE 8 AND CA 98: OCOTILLO—YUMA, ARIZONA 128
INTERSTATE 10: BEAUMONT—INDIO 133
CA 86: COACHELLA—BRAWLEY 140
CA 111: CALEXICO—MECCA 144

PENINSULAR RANGES 153

PENINSULAR RANGES BATHOLITH 155
ELSINORE, SAN JACINTO, AND ROSE CANYON FAULTS 157
THE OLD EROSION SURFACE, PERRIS PLAIN, AND THE POWAY CONGLOMERATE 158
COASTAL TERRACES 161

Road Guides for the Peninsular Ranges 162
INTERSTATE 5: SAN YSIDRO—SAN CLEMENTE 162
INTERSTATE 8: OCEAN BEACH—OCOTILLO 171
INTERSTATE 10: LOS ANGELES—BEAUMONT 180
INTERSTATE 15: SAN DIEGO—CORONA 183
CA 78: CARLSBAD—OCOTILLO WELLS 194

LOS ANGELES BASIN 200

FORMATION OF THE BASIN 200
OIL FIELDS AND THE MONTEREY FORMATION 204
Long Beach Oil Field and Signal Hill 205
Baldwin Hills and Inglewood Oil Field 207
Huntington Beach Oil Field 208
Seal Beach Oil Field 209
Wilmington Oil Field 209
LOS ANGELES RIVER 210
LA BREA TAR PITS 212
SAN JUAN CAPISTRANO 213
COASTAL REGION OF THE BASIN 214
Dana Point 214
Laguna Beach 218
Crystal Cove State Park 218
Newport Bay 220
Marshes and Lagoons 221
Palos Verdes Hills 222
Redondo Submarine Canyon and Sand Dunes 223
Marina del Rey Breakwater 223

TRANSVERSE RANGES 224
  WESTERN TRANSVERSE RANGES 225
    Ventura Basin 225
    Conejo and Santa Cruz Island Volcanics 227
  EASTERN TRANSVERSE RANGES 228
    San Bernardino Mountains 228
    San Gabriel Mountains 229

  Road Guides for the Transverse Ranges 231
    INTERSTATE 5: SYLMAR—GRAPEVINE 231
    INTERSTATE 15 AND INTERSTATE 215: SAN BERNARDINO—CAJON SUMMIT 242
    INTERSTATE 210: SYLMAR—SAN BERNARDINO 249
    INTERSTATE 405: WEST LOS ANGELES—SYLMAR 255
    US 101: HOLLYWOOD—VENTURA 262
    US 101 AND CA 1: VENTURA—BUELLTON AND LOMPOC 267
    CA 1: SANTA MONICA—OXNARD 287
    CA 2: EAGLE ROCK—WRIGHTWOOD 296
    CA 14: SYLMAR—PALMDALE 305
    CA 33: VENTURA—CUYAMA 311
    CA 38 AND CA 18: REDLANDS—BIG BEAR CITY—LUCERNE VALLEY 320
    CA 126: VENTURA—SANTA CLARITA 331

CHANNEL ISLANDS 337
  SAN MIGUEL ISLAND 338
  SANTA ROSA ISLAND 339
  SANTA CRUZ ISLAND 340
  ANACAPA ISLAND 341
  SANTA BARBARA ISLAND 342
  SANTA CATALINA ISLAND 343
  SAN CLEMENTE ISLAND 344
  SAN NICOLAS ISLAND 345

**NATURAL HISTORY MUSEUMS AND
EXHIBITS IN SOUTHERN CALIFORNIA** 346

GLOSSARY 350

FURTHER READING AND REFERENCES 361

INDEX 371

PREFACE

The road must eventually lead to the whole world.

—Jack Kerouac, *On the Road*

This book is a practical touring guide to the rocks and geologic history of southern California. Our goal is to present information we have gleaned from many people, written sources, and our own field experiences over many years into a useful form for the interested motorist. No single book on this subject can possibly be encyclopedic, however. This one barely scratches the surface of the enormous amount of available information collected, compiled, and published about the region by hundreds of intrepid geologists since the 1850s. We borrow in no small measure from their prodigious work.

We were greatly tempted to drive as many southern California roads as possible to see as many geologic wonders as possible, but the number of its roads and their distances are daunting. The complexity of its geology, moreover, and our lack of infinite time, money, and space cause us to ruthlessly limit our purview to major highways at the expense of some incredible geologic sights along the region's many back roads and footpaths. The result of our narrative, or travelogue, is not anything that you should mistake for a comprehensive treatment. We recommend Bob Sharp and Allen Glazner's marvelous book *Geology Underfoot in Southern California* for more in-depth coverage of some of the places we merely touch upon in this book. Ruth Pittman's *Roadside History of California* provides a colorful companion to this book.

We've organized the road guides into six regions, each with its own unique geology, geologic history, cultural history, climate, and vegetation. Before setting out on any one of the book's tours, you should become familiar with the geologic evolution of California presented in the introduction and the relevant regional introductions in the beginning of the other chapters.

Most of the driving tours are point to point, with a few interesting side trips and byways for adventurous travelers to explore, but be forewarned: Some of the routes in desert areas are quite long and traverse some very lonely country lacking services. You must give particular thought to gasoline and food, perhaps even lodging, before setting out on some of these tours. Rest stops are few and far between. Desert temperatures can be extreme in summer, and snow may make mountain roads impassable in winter. Freeway traffic, especially around metropolitan Los Angeles, can be daunting, so enlist a passenger to read and navigate while you drive.

The southern California deserts abound with active and abandoned mines and prospects that are exceedingly dangerous and mostly on private land. Never attempt to visit any site without first ensuring that you have the permission of the land or mineral rights holders for access and that you are aware of all necessary safety precautions.

Guide to Highway Distances

Most California highways lack mileposts, so specific places in this book are referenced by post mile where possible and appropriate. Post miles give mileage on a per-county basis. Some counties place post mile signs only every mile, whereas other counties place them on virtually every construction feature along the route. Rarely are they posted in commercial or urbanized areas.

Post miles are used as a reference system for planning, design, construction, and operation of the state highway system. They start at 0 at the west or south boundary of a given county. Mileage increases eastward or northward and then restarts at 0 at the next county line. Their main drawback for the casual motorist is that they are rather small and hard to read at 65 miles per hour.

Driving California Freeways

Driving freeways in the greater Los Angeles metropolitan area is like swimming in a bait tank: You must go with the flow and pay close attention to other fish. Know well in advance where you wish to go, know what exit you expect to use, and look for it a mile or two before you get there to be positioned in the correct lane to exit. Some radio stations broadcast traffic alerts by highway number, so you need to know highway numbers to understand the alert: "Traffic is at a complete standstill on the 405 between the 10 and 101, so use Sepulveda as an alternative." In this particular example, you wouldn't want to be on the 405, one of the most heavily traveled freeways in the world.

Post mile sign and call box. On the white paddle, 101 is the highway number; SB is Santa Barbara County; 29.00 is highway mileage from the south boundary of the county. Post miles are also encoded on call boxes: thus 101 292. (34°26.4492N, 119°57.4800W)

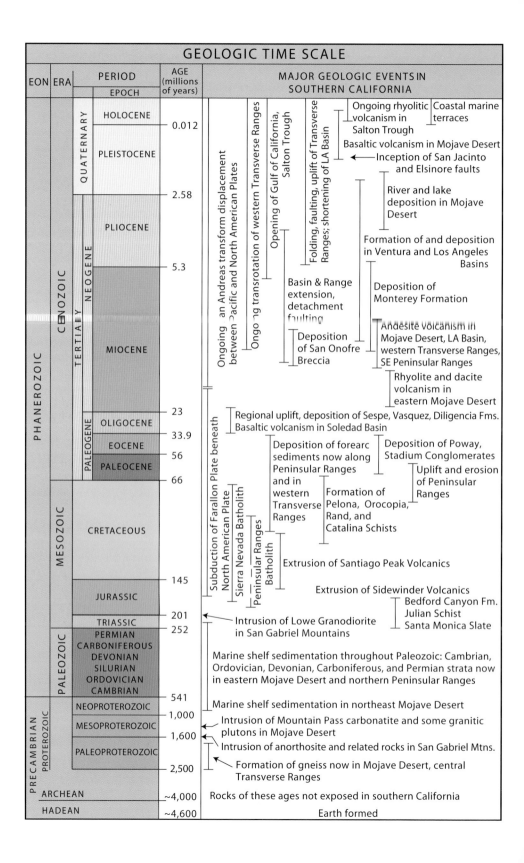

INTRODUCTION

Go as far as you can see; when you get there you'll be able to see farther.
—Thomas Carlyle, 1795–1881

Within an eight-hour drive of any point in southern California, you may view the results of almost every type of geologic process, from desert erosion to glaciation, from ancient to recent volcanism, and from giant prehistoric landslides to active earthquake faults. You may also find almost every age of rock, from 2.5-billion-year-old gneiss to 3,000-year-old volcanic cinders, and every type of rock, from rare plutonic and volcanic rocks to common sandstone and limestone, from high-grade metamorphic rocks to soupy sediments yet to harden into rock, and from precious gemstones to giant quarries of sand and gravel.

Southern California owes its marvelous geologic diversity to the complexity of tectonic processes operating over the eons, long before the form of California came anywhere close to taking the shape it has today. The relative motions of three great tectonic plates—Farallon, North American, and Pacific—have left indelible marks on southern California's geology.

Over the past 1,000 million years, five major tectonic settings have been layered upon one another to shape the present landscape and geologic structure of southern California. First, between 1,000 and 180 million years ago, there existed a stable continental margin, similar to the eastern US coast today. Sediments deposited along the margin now occur here and there as metamorphosed rocks in southern California. Second, between 180 to 20 million years ago, the Farallon Plate subducted beneath the North American Plate, leaving behind evidence of the subduction zone and its associated magmatic arc and fore-arc basin. Third, the San Andreas strike-slip system developed 23 million years ago and continues today, offsetting, shearing, and rotating rocks along it. Fourth, between 16 and 6 million years ago, a large area of the western North American Plate stretched apart, forming the Basin and Range in eastern California. Finally, during the last 2 to 1 million years and continuing today, the youngest mountains—the Transverse Ranges— were uplifted in a modern mountain building event known as the Pasadenan orogeny, caused by a projection of the Pacific Plate jamming into the edge of the North American Plate.

Each of the younger tectonic events must be figuratively peeled away to discern the older landscapes and structures. The geologic snapshots gained by this process are increasingly nebulous as we proceed backward through time, because rocks and their histories may have been eroded away. Working out a geologic history of a region is similar to interpreting a picture puzzle with only 10 percent of the pieces.

Two deserts and two mountains ranges constitute southern California's four major regions, or physiographic provinces, each of which has its own unified geologic history. The Mojave Desert, with average elevations between 2,000 and 3,000 feet, is higher than the Colorado Desert, which averages around 1,000 to 2,000 feet but dips below sea level in the Salton Trough. The mountainous Transverse Ranges trend east-west across the belly of California. The broad, uplifted, northwest-trending Peninsular Ranges extend from east of the Los Angeles area south to San Diego, continuing across the Mexican border into the Baja peninsula in Mexico. The Los Angeles Basin is a deep, sediment-filled trough between the Peninsular and Transverse Ranges. The northern Channel Islands are offshore extensions of the Transverse Ranges, whereas the southern Channel Islands are offshore fault blocks of a region geologists call the Continental Borderland.

Each of California's physiographic provinces has its own unique character and common geologic history.

The first part of this introduction will familiarize you with some basic information and terminology needed to understand southern California's complex geology. The second part is a brief synopsis of the regional geologic history, organized chronologically from the Proterozoic Eon to the present. See each chapter introduction for more specific history of each region.

UNDERSTANDING THE EARTH

Rocks and Rock Formation

Rocks are aggregates of minerals and are named according to the kind and proportions of minerals in them. Minerals are naturally occurring, inorganic compounds having an ordered internal crystal structure and a specific chemical composition. About four thousand minerals are known in and on the Earth, but just thirteen of them form 99 percent of all rocks on the Earth's surface. Southern California boasts some of the world's richest concentrations, not only of gem-grade pink tourmaline, once prized by the empress dowager of China, but also of borate and rare-earth minerals.

Rocks are classified first according to their origin, whether igneous, sedimentary, or metamorphic. The size, shape, and arrangement of their constituent grains or mineral crystals also enter into their names, as, for example, a quartz-muscovite-biotite-andalusite schist or a hornblende granite.

IGNEOUS ROCKS. Igneous rocks form by crystallization from a molten magma, when they either erupt upon the Earth's surface as volcanic rocks or intrude the Earth's crust as plutonic rocks. All volcanic rocks have their chemically similar plutonic equivalents. For example, basalt, which cools from lava erupted from volcanoes, has the same chemical composition as gabbro, which cools deep within the Earth's crust. Basaltic lava, such as you may have seen flowing on the surface in Hawaii, has a molten temperature around 2,500°F and may take several days or weeks to cool sufficiently to walk on it without getting burned. Geologists describe dark igneous rocks, such as basalt, as mafic, because they consist of *ma*gnesium- and iron-bearing minerals (iron referred to as *fe*rric), whereas they describe light-colored igneous rocks, such as granite, as felsic, meaning rock consisting of *fe*ldspar and other *si*lica-rich minerals.

Depending on the specific proportions of its constituent minerals, usually quartz, alkali feldspar, and plagioclase feldspar, granite may be classified more narrowly as quartz monzonite, granodiorite, quartz diorite, or even true granite. Their intrusion temperatures range from 1,000° to 1,600°F, and they may require thousands of years to cool underground. Because they cool so slowly, crystals in granitic rocks are typically large enough to see with the naked eye.

Granite is a common and widespread plutonic rock type in many southern California mountain ranges, especially in the Mojave Desert and Peninsular Ranges. It probably matters little whether it is a granodiorite or a quartz monzonite when you are whizzing along at 65 miles per hour. Just to know it is granitic rock should suffice in most cases.

SEDIMENTARY ROCKS. Mud, silt, sand, and gravel, the ingredients of sedimentary rocks, are the breakdown products of weathering of any kind of rock—igneous, metamorphic, or even other sedimentary rock. Individual particles or fragments of rock within sedimentary rocks are called clasts, and geologists commonly add the word *clastic* to rock descriptions. For example, a volcaniclastic rock is a rock made up of fragments of volcanic rock. When unconsolidated sediments are cemented together with silica, carbonate, or iron oxides, they harden into sedimentary rock.

Sedimentary rock names are derived from what the rock is made of: mud turns into mudstone or shale, silt becomes siltstone, sand becomes sandstone, and cobbles are cemented to form conglomerate. Some sedimentary rocks are made from precipitation of various salts and carbonates, such as sodium chloride and calcium carbonate, to make evaporate deposits and limestone.

METAMORPHIC ROCKS. Metamorphism is the process that converts rock—igneous, sedimentary, and even other metamorphic rocks—into other forms of rock by means of recrystallization of the minerals. The analogy might be the way a mound of dough with raisins is put in the oven and with heat and time is converted to a loaf of raisin bread. Rock metamorphism occurs via heat and pressure while the rock is still solid, mostly deep in the Earth's crust. Shale is metamorphosed to schist, limestone to marble, and sandstone to quartzite. The prefix *meta* is commonly attached to a rock name to indicate it has been metamorphosed: metavolcanic rock, metasedimentary rock, and metabasalt.

Plate Tectonics

According to the theory of plate tectonics, the Earth's brittle surface, known as the crust, is cracked like the shell of an egg into several huge plates that move relative to one another due to fluid motions in the Earth's mantle, or

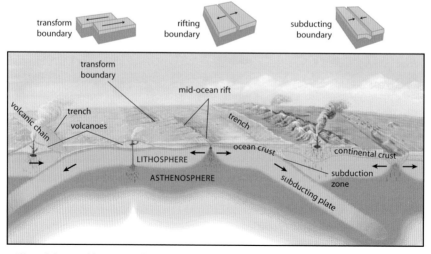

Slice of the Earth's crust and mantle showing how inner convection currents, driven by heat energy from the Earth's core, cause tectonic plates to converge, diverge, and slip parallel to one another.

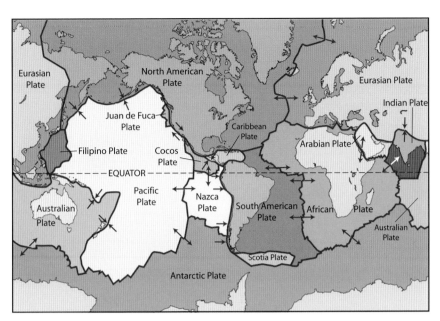

The Earth's crust is subdivided into seven major plates and several lesser ones. The red arrows indicate the motion of plates relative to one another.

asthenosphere. These tectonic plates interact by pushing against, pulling away from, and sliding past one another. Well-defined zones of earthquakes outline the plate boundaries at the global scale, and most of the Earth's volcanic activity is also confined to plate boundaries.

DIVERGENT PLATE BOUNDARIES. Some plates move away from one another across a spreading rift characterized by shallow, low- to moderate-magnitude earthquakes. Spreading at the Mid-Atlantic Ridge causes the North American and Eurasian Plates to diverge from one another. Magma from the Earth's interior typically wells up along the rift, hardens into rock, and heals the crack, forming new ocean floor, only to break anew during continued spreading. The North American and the Pacific Plates are moving away from each other across the East Pacific Rise in the Gulf of California.

CONVERGENT PLATE BOUNDARIES. In plate convergence, one plate typically overrides the other along long, arc-shaped zones called subduction zones. If the overridden plate is an oceanic plate, it dives or subducts beneath the continental plate along the subduction zone into the upper mantle. Downward slippage along a subduction zone is responsible for the Earth's really huge earthquakes. The subducting slab is carried into the mantle, where it partially melts. The melted rocks then rise buoyantly upward through the crust to the surface, erupt, and form volcanoes. The Pacific Plate is subducting northwestward beneath Alaska, for example, resulting in large earthquakes there and in volcanism in the Aleutian Islands and Alaskan Peninsula. The line of volcanoes above the subduction zone is a magmatic arc.

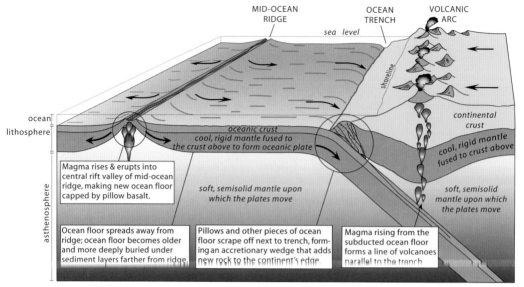

MID-OCEAN
RIDGE

OCEAN
TRENCH

VOLCANIC
ARC

sea level

shoreline

ocean
lithosphere

continental
crust

oceanic crust
cool, rigid mantle fused to
the crust above to form oceanic plate

cool, rigid mantle
fused to crust above

asthenosphere

Magma rises & erupts into
central rift valley of mid-ocean
ridge, making new ocean floor
capped by pillow basalt.

soft, semisolid mantle upon
which the plates move

soft, semisolid
mantle upon which
the plates move

Ocean floor spreads away from
ridge; ocean floor becomes older
and more deeply buried under
sediment layers farther from ridge.

Pillows and other pieces of ocean
floor scrape off next to trench, forming an accretionary wedge that adds
new rock to the continent's edge.

Magma rising from the
subducted ocean floor
forms a line of volcanoes
parallel to the trench.

In Mesozoic time, the Farallon oceanic plate spread eastward from a mid-ocean ridge and subducted beneath the North American continental plate. —Image courtesy of Keith Meldahl, from *Rough-Hewn Land: A Geologic Journey from California to the Rocky Mountains,* page 7, UC Press, 2011

TRANSFORM PLATE BOUNDARIES. A transform fault is a plate boundary where two tectonic plates slide past each other. The San Andreas fault system is probably the world's most studied and well-known transform plate boundary, because of its great earthquakes in the historic past and the hazard its future earthquakes pose to heavily populated areas of California. Along this boundary between the Pacific and North American Plates, Los Angeles on the Pacific Plate slips about 2 inches per year northwestward toward San Francisco on the North American Plate. That rate of strike-slip along the San Andreas fault system has been relatively constant over recent geologic time, resulting in about 130 miles of displacement in just the last 4 million years.

Faults, Faulting, and Earthquakes

The shifting of the plates causes the Earth's crust to flex and stretch. The surface rocks are brittle, so they break when the flexing and stretching exceed their strength. The breaks, fractures in the Earth's crust, are called faults when the block on one side of the fracture moves relative to the block on the other side. Southern California has many faults, so some terminology is needed here.

Faults are classified according to how one block is displaced relative to the other. Faults with side-to-side displacement are strike-slip faults. If you stand on one block and the one on the other side of the fault slips to the right, it is a right-lateral strike-slip fault, or right-slip fault for short. Similarly, a left-lateral strike-slip fault is a left-slip fault. Most strike-slip faults are vertical or nearly so, meaning the plane of the fault extends straight down into the crust. The San Andreas, San Jacinto, and Elsinore are the principal right-slip faults in southern California; the Garlock and Santa Ynez are its main left-slip faults.

Dip-slip faults are named according to the inclination of the fault and how the hanging wall block slips relative to the footwall. The hanging wall block "hangs" on the footwall, and if the hanging wall slips down the fault relative to the footwall, it is a normal fault. Such faults typically form in areas of crustal stretching.

If the hanging wall slips up the footwall on a fault inclined steeper than 45 degrees, then it is a reverse fault. If the fault inclination is less than 45 degrees, it is a thrust fault. Both reverse and thrust faults form in areas of crustal squeezing.

Faults with both horizontal and vertical components of displacement are called oblique-slip faults. Displacement can be such that a fault may be a right oblique normal slip fault, or perhaps a left oblique reverse slip fault. Few strike-slip faults exhibit pure horizontal displacement. Most of them have from ten to one hundred parts of horizontal displacement to one part of vertical. For example, along one stretch of the Elsinore fault in southern California, the vertical component of slip is 3,000 feet, whereas the strike-slip is 6 miles.

Faults are rarely visible in the field. The geologist maps them where there are abrupt discontinuities in rock structure or in rock types. In many instances it is difficult or impossible to determine the direction and amount of displacement along a given fault. It is necessary to see how some sort of preexisting feature, such as railroad tracks, a creek, the ground surface, or a line of trees have been displaced by faulting

Great crustal forces may be concentrated along a fault, which will rupture when those forces exceed the strength of rocks along the fault. That stored

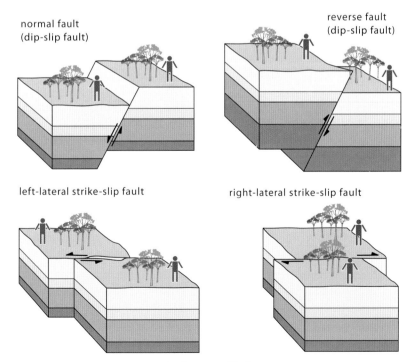

Main types of faults.

energy is suddenly released the way you would snap a bending stick. The energy radiates away from the fault as shaking—an earthquake—just as waves radiate from a splash on the surface of a pond. Typically, the longer a given fault, the greater the earthquake it may generate. In some cases a rupture along one fault may trigger displacement and an earthquake on a neighboring fault or a fault extension, so instead of a relatively short fault causing a moderate earthquake, several faults may be triggered almost instantly and combine into a large earthquake. Such fault triggering and linkage occurred in southern California's magnitude 7.2 Landers earthquake on June 28, 1992.

Geologic Processes in Desert Environments

A desert is a region of scant precipitation and high summer temperatures and evaporation, and some would add the criterion that a desert is incapable of supporting any considerable population. Nevertheless, most of southern California in the broad sense is regarded as the most heavily populated desert in the world, with 20 million of California's 10 million inhabitants.

The Mojave and Colorado Deserts of southern California are rain-shadow deserts, lying in the lee of the Sierra Nevada, Transverse Ranges, and Peninsular Ranges. Both may have formed as early as Oligocene time, but certainly by late Miocene time after those mountain ranges were high enough to block onshore winds from bringing precipitation from the Pacific Ocean. The little rainfall these deserts receive usually runs off quickly, commonly as flash floods, because vegetation is too scanty to retard precipitation runoff.

ALLUVIAL FANS. An alluvial fan, a characteristic depositional form in desert environments, is a fan-shaped, heterogeneous accumulation of boulders, gravel, and sand of all sizes at a mountain front. The sediment is transported and deposited there by a stream issuing from a narrow mountain canyon. Deposition occurs on the fan because the stream abruptly widens at the mountain front, where its velocity drops and it loses its power to transport sediment. Deposition also occurs on the fan because the stream water sinks into the porous, sandy alluvium.

Sediment is transported onto an alluvial fan by stream flows and as debris flows. Deposits by regular stream flows commonly grade into debris-flow deposits. Stream-flow deposits are typically bedded; their clasts (pebbles and cobbles) usually grade upward from large at the base of a bed to small at the top; and the clasts commonly touch one another. Debris-flow deposits usually lack bedding; their clasts may be randomly distributed and oriented within a bed; and the clasts are separated from one another by sand or mud. Alluvial fan deposits are called fanglomerate when they are cemented into firm rock.

PLAYAS. Low areas in the desert may accumulate runoff from streams laden with a suspended load of silt and clay and a dissolved load of salt. When the water evaporates, it leaves a flat floor of fine-grained sediment and salt called a playa. The surface layer may shrink as it dries, forming mud cracks, which typically are polygon-shaped. Later, strong winds pick up the dried sediment and carry it to sand dunes or even farther as great dust clouds.

Aerial view of an alluvial fan emerging from a deep, narrow mountain canyon.
—Marli B. Miller photo

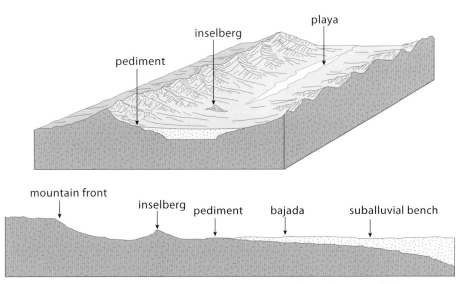

Pediments develop almost exclusively on granite in deserts because of the way granitic rocks undergo subsurface weathering in an arid climate. —Adapted from Putnam, *Geology*, 1964; used by permission form Oxford University Press

PEDIMENTS. Pediments are nearly flat, bare rock erosion surfaces on granite covered by a thin veneer of sand and gravel derived from the granite. They form by subsurface chemical weathering of the granite. Knobs of granite protruding above the veneer are called inselbergs. An area of thicker alluvium sloping toward the valley bottom is called a bajada.

BOULDER-STREWN MOUNTAINS. Many mountains in the Mojave Desert and the Peninsular Ranges are strewn with rounded granitic boulders, some of which are gigantic and certainly weren't carried there by a mere trout stream or even a flash flood. Instead, they formed in place, below the surface by chemical weathering of granite. Organic acid–bearing groundwater infiltrates rock fractures, typically along three sets of mutually perpendicular fractures that form during cooling of the granite at depth and its subsequent uplift. Just as an ice

Formation of Core-Stones and Boulder Pile Topography

Jointed granite (CA 18 roadcut in the San Bernardino Mountains, 33°15.770N, 117°09.395W)

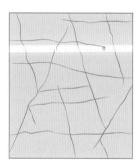

Weathering along joints to form rounded core-stones (Jacumba Mountains roadcut, 32°50.41N, 116°26.35W)
—Bill Elliott photo

Erosion of the weathered rock and uplift (Granite Mountains, Mojave Desert, 34°48.6N, 115°37.2W)

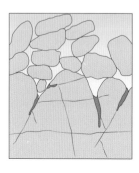

cube melts in your mouth first at its corners and edges, the acids slowly attack the corners and edges of the fractured rock cube, altering feldspars to clay. When the granite is uplifted to the surface, water and wind erosion removes the clay and decomposed rock, leaving behind the hard, rounded rock cores, called core-stones.

DESERT PAVEMENT AND DESERT VARNISH. Desert pavement is a natural residual concentration of wind-polished, closely packed pebbles, gravel, and other rock fragments, which mantle a usually flat desert surface and protect dust and fine sand beneath from wind and rain runoff unless the pavement is disturbed by human impact.

Desert varnish is a natural, dark brown stain of clay and various metallic oxides, including manganese, iron, and trace elements, just a fraction of a millimeter thick on rock surfaces. It is particularly common on granitic and metasedimentary rocks and on alluvial detritus atop desert flats. If the varnish is rich in manganese oxide, then the stain will be almost black. Iron-rich varnishes are chocolate brown. In some places, the varnish so effectively covers rocks that it is impossible to tell what they are without breaking off a piece to reveal a fresh surface.

Desert varnish is thought to form when and where windborne dust settles on rock surfaces, and then microorganisms (bacteria) extract elements from the dust and transform them into iron or manganese oxide. The small amount of elemental transfer may occur in solution or possibly by ionic diffusion through moisture films, such as dew and or infrequent rain. Oxides bind clay flakes together.

Off-road vehicles have disrupted this desert pavement surface of dark brown, desert-varnished pebbles to reveal light-colored, unvarnished sand and pebbles. Near Vidal Junction in the eastern Mojave Desert. (34°07.2N, 114°28.8W)

Desert varnish forms best on fine-grained rocks, where weathering, spalling, or heavy and frequent precipitation are minimal. Desert varnish doesn't form in humid climates, because rain washes the ions away too fast, and it doesn't form on the undersides of rocks.

Rates of varnish formation vary widely with local conditions. Thousands of years may be required to form a dark coating of varnish, whereas one study found that a good varnish coating formed on the surface stones of an alluvial deposit in the Mojave Desert in just twenty-five years.

GEOLOGIC EVOLUTION OF SOUTHERN CALIFORNIA

PROTEROZOIC EON
2,500 TO 541 MILLION YEARS AGO

Gneissic Basement Rocks

The oldest rocks in southern California are Proterozoic gneisses that are more than 1,600 million years old and perhaps nearly 2,500 million years old. The San Gabriel Gneiss makes up large parts of the central Transverse Ranges. The Pinto Gneiss crops out over large areas of Joshua Tree National Park. These rocks include well-foliated, locally folded and brecciated hornblende gneiss, biotite-hornblende gneiss, quartz-feldspar gneiss, and amphibolite. It is difficult to tell what they were before they were so thoroughly metamorphosed or where they formed. They may have been part of the original nucleus of the North American craton, or perhaps they were a small microcontinent added to the edge of the old craton.

Strongly folded and brecciated San Gabriel Gneiss of Proterozoic age is one of the oldest rocks in southern California. The breccia fragments are bound together by white granite veinlets. This outcrop is along the East Fork of the San Gabriel River. Sunglasses for scale. (34°17.01N, 117°44.81W)

PALEOZOIC ERA
541 TO 252 MILLION YEARS AGO

The Continental Shelf
In Paleozoic time, the western shoreline of the North American continent lay far to the east. Offshore to the west stretched a continental shelf resembling the flat and relatively shallow shelf off the East Coast of the United States today. Extensive layers of limestone, shale, and sandstone were deposited in the shallow ocean and along its shores. These Paleozoic rocks are well exposed on the Colorado Plateau and form many of the layered rock units in the Grand Canyon. Exposures of tilted, unmetamorphosed Paleozoic strata in the eastern Mojave Desert are part of these same widespread units. Schist, quartzite, and marble, thought to be late Paleozoic in age, exist in the Peninsular Ranges and are probably the metamorphic equivalents of the Mojave's Paleozoic rocks.

MESOZOIC ERA
252 TO 66 MILLION YEARS AGO

Subduction and Batholith Formation
The relative passivity of geologic events along the western margin of North America in Paleozoic time was interrupted by the convergence of the North American Plate with the Farallon Plate, named for the Farallon Islands about 30 miles offshore of San Francisco. About 180 million years ago, the denser ocean crust of the Farallon Plate began subducting beneath the lighter continental crust of the North American Plate, and the collision uplifted the North American Plate from Sacramento to Omaha, Nebraska. In northern and central

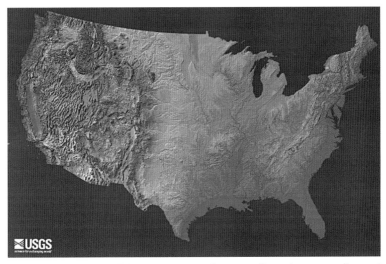

The high topography of the western United States reflects the extent of crustal uplift and damage to the North American Plate when the Farallon Plate collided with it and subducted beneath it in Mesozoic time. —From US Geological Survey

California, the Sierra Nevada represents the magmatic arc, the Great Valley represents the fore-arc basin, and the Coast Ranges are what's left of the accretionary wedge. In southern California, however, the San Andreas fault system has disrupted and displaced these older subduction structures.

Compressive forces associated with the Farallon Plate subduction folded much of the Paleozoic sedimentary rock layers throughout western North America. Slabs of Proterozoic and Paleozoic rocks were thrust over Mesozoic rocks along low-angle faults. The subduction also produced great volumes of melted rocks that rose from depths of 20 to 60 miles to intrude the crust and form not only the great Sierra Nevada Batholith in central California but also the equally great Peninsular Ranges Batholith in southern California and Baja California. These plutonic rocks intruded along the magmatic arc between 180 and 60 million years ago.

Intrusion of the batholiths was accompanied by the eruption of great volumes of volcanic rocks, now mostly eroded, but present in places as metamorphosed flows and plugs in southern California. The Sidewinder Volcanics of Late Jurassic age in the Mojave Desert and the Santiago Peak Volcanics of Late Jurassic and Early Cretaceous age in the Peninsular Ranges cooled from these volcanic eruptions.

A fore-arc basin formed between the magmatic arc and the down-going slab of the Farallon Plate as the crust subsided there. Sediments eroded from the continental interior and the magmatic arc accumulated in the basin as layers of sand, silt, and mud. These marine deposits exist now as Jurassic and Cretaceous sedimentary rocks in the western Transverse Ranges and along the southwestern edge of the Peninsular Ranges.

The top of the down-going Farallon Plate consisted of basaltic ocean floor with a veneer of water-saturated sediment, basaltic ash and sand, and radiolarian chert. Much of that sediment subducted beneath the North American Plate to great depths, where it was metamorphosed about 75 million years ago under moderate temperature and pressure to produce mafic schist and metabasalt. These distinctive rocks have been exhumed and are exposed at several places in southern California and western Arizona, where parts of the overlying North American Plate have been removed by erosion. Geologists call these eroded places tectonic windows.

The schist bodies include the Rand Schist in the western Mojave Desert, the Pelona Schist in the central Transverse Ranges, the Orocopia Schist in the Colorado Desert, and the Catalina Schist on Catalina Island. Geologists were uncertain how to relate one schist body to another until the concepts of plate tectonics gave clues. Now we realize that the schist exposures represent remnants scraped off the top of the Farallon Plate when it was subducted beneath the North American Plate. These schist bodies, all of low metamorphic grade, are thought to be separated from the overlying Proterozoic gneiss of the North American Plate by a low-angle, mylonitic thrust fault known as the Vincent–Orocopia–Chocolate Mountains thrust.

The schist varies in composition as well as name from province to province. Typically, it consists of quartz- and feldspar-rich schist, greenschist, epidote

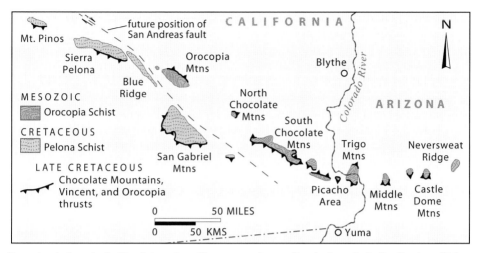

Tectonic windows in the North American Plate expose the pre–San Andreas fault distribution of Pelona and Orocopia Schists in the Transverse Ranges and the Chocolate Mountains in California and several places in western Arizona where erosion has reached the top of the subducted Farallon Plate.

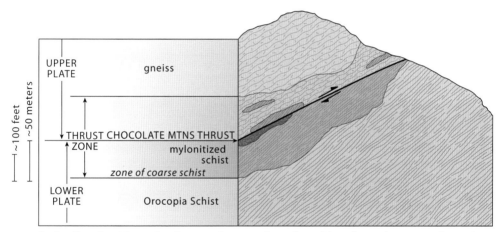

In the Chocolate Mountains, Proterozoic-age gneiss and granitic rocks are thrust upon Orocopia Schist of Late Cretaceous age. The thrust is thought to be the relict subduction zone between the ancient Farallon Plate and the North American Plate during Mesozoic time. —Modified from Dillon and others, 1990

amphibolite, and minor metachert and marble—rocks that are typical of the greenschist facies of metamorphism. The Pelona Schist has an aggregate thickness of between 1 and 2 miles beneath Mt. Baden Powell; its base is nowhere exposed. Radiometric age determinations give a metamorphic age around 75 million years, so it's likely the schist's parent rocks were deposited in Triassic and Jurassic time and then were subducted and metamorphosed in Cretaceous time.

CENOZOIC ERA

66 MILLION YEARS AGO TO PRESENT

Crustal Breakup, Rift Volcanism, and Basin Sedimentation

Erosion must have been intense at the close of the Mesozoic Era to remove the rocks covering the Sierra Nevada and Peninsular Ranges Batholiths, and uplift must have kept pace so that rocks initially emplaced at depths of 1 to 5 miles below the surface were at the surface at the beginning of Cenozoic time. In Late Cretaceous through Eocene time, great rivers issuing out of the continental interior eroded large areas of the southern Peninsular Ranges into almost flat plains with deep canyons.

During Oligocene and early Miocene time, much of the southern California region was above sea level. A major river issued from what is now the Mojave Desert and northern Mexico. It deposited extensive layers of gravel and sand, which were oxidized by the atmosphere to a distinctive red-brown color and are now widely exposed as the Sespe and Vasquez Formations in the western Transverse Ranges, and the Diligencia Formation in the Salton Trough.

A major river system deposited the Sespe Formation, one of several widespread Oligocene-age stream deposits in southern California. This exposure is along Old San Marcos Pass Road in the Santa Ynez Mountains. (34°26.68N, 119°47.79W)

Alluvial sediments accumulated in inland basins, while along the western North American coast, marine basins accumulated great thicknesses of sediments. Several basins subsided as fast as sediment filled them. In the Ventura Basin, 16,000 feet of marine sand, silt, and shale accumulated during the last 2.6 million years.

Much of the marine component of sediment in southern California basins was organic diatomaceous ooze, deposited in Miocene time. Upon heating at depth, the organic sediments became a source of extensive petroleum deposits in the Los Angeles and Ventura Basins. The Salton Trough had a brief marine incursion from late Miocene to early Pliocene time.

Once the subduction of the Farallon Plate was nearly complete in early Miocene time, the North American and Pacific Plates became juxtaposed. While the Pacific Plate moved northwestward and the North American Plate moved relatively westward, the upper mantle and lower crust beneath the western edge of the North America Plate flowed plastically northwestward with the Pacific Plate. As a consequence, the upper crust of the North American Plate stretched and fractured, creating the Basin and Range throughout most of Nevada and parts of Utah, Arizona, northern Mexico, and eastern and southern California. Elongated blocks of faulted crust foundered, forming basins, and rift volcanism occurred. The Salton Trough and the Gulf of California opened during Miocene and early Pliocene time as the Pacific Plate captured and dragged Baja California away from the Mexican mainland. Geologic evidence indicates that the early Salton Trough in the vicinity of Palm Springs was bounded by high-angle normal faults, exactly like those bounding crustal blocks in the Basin and Range province today.

Andesitic and dacitic volcanism was also widespread in middle Miocene time, voluminous in places, and accompanied by significant gold and silver mineralization, especially in the Mojave Desert. Rifting associated with crustal spreading allowed melted rock from the mantle to escape up basin-bounding faults not only in the Mojave, but also along the east and northeast edges of the Los Angeles Basin—the Glendora and El Modeno Volcanics—when it opened during rotation and translocation of the western Transverse Ranges. Basaltic andesite of the Vasquez Formation leaked up along faults in the Soledad Basin. Associated with the formation of the Ventura Basin are extensive tracts of andesite and basaltic andesite of the Conejo Volcanics in the Santa Monica Mountains and their offshore extensions on the northern Channel Islands.

At the same time as the crust stretched and southern California basins formed, great slabs of crust detached from basement rocks and slipped along low-angle faults into adjacent basins. These detachment faults, as they are called, were an enigma for many years because young rocks were placed upon older rocks, just the opposite as happens in standard low-angle faulting when the crust is compressed and shortened. The exhumed basement rocks were called metamorphic core complexes, and for many years their happy hunting ground was in the eastern Mojave Desert along the Colorado River. When geologists learned to recognize those disguised by subsequent deformation, metamorphic core complexes were also found in the Peninsular Ranges.

Development of the San Andreas Fault

Until about 24 million years ago, the Farallon Plate lay between the North American and Pacific Plates. As parts of the Farallon Plate became completely subducted beneath North America, the Pacific and North American Plates became juxtaposed along a transform plate boundary—the San Andreas fault system. Some fragments of the Farallon Plate were not completely consumed

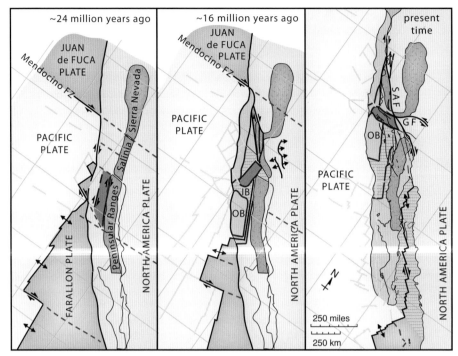

Tectonic model for Pacific and North America Plate interactions since 24 million years ago and formation of the western Transverse Ranges (green patch). The Los Angeles Basin is the triangular space at the north end of the Inner Borderland (IB) that opened as the western Transverse Ranges rotated clockwise and translated northward. OB is Outer Borderland; SAF is San Andreas fault; GF is Garlock faut; the ruled pattern depicts regions where the North American Plate underwent rifting, thus exposing underplated rocks from the top of the subducted Farallon Plate. —After Nicholson and others, 1994

but broke into microplates that were captured by the Pacific Plate. Subduction of other Farallon Plate fragments both north and south of the North American and Pacific Plate juncture continued, and the San Andreas fault system lengthened as more and more North American microplates were captured by the Pacific Plate.

By about 6 million years ago the Pacific Plate captured all of the land now lying west of the present San Andreas fault between San Francisco and La Paz, Mexico. South of the Transverse Ranges, the plate boundary jumped eastward into the Salton Trough and Gulf of California. There, it found already thinned, rifted crust and took over some major, high-angle Basin and Range faults east of a tough crustal slab of Mesozoic batholithic rocks—the future Peninsular Ranges. The new plate boundary in the Gulf of California consists of a series of spreading ridges and transform faults that connects the East Pacific Rise at the mouth of the gulf to the San Andreas transform fault.

The currently active trace of this transform fault is the San Andreas fault, and displacement of one plate relative to the other along the fault proceeds

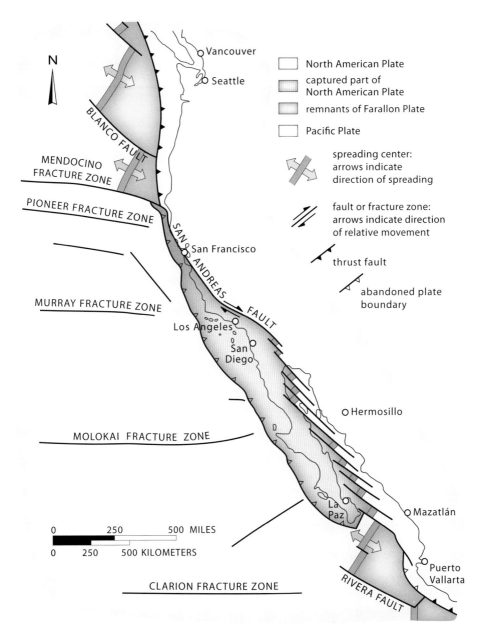

N

North American Plate
captured part of
North American Plate
remnants of Farallon Plate
Pacific Plate

spreading center:
arrows indicate
direction of spreading

fault or fracture zone:
arrows indicate direction
of relative movement

thrust fault

abandoned plate
boundary

Vancouver
Seattle

BLANCO FAULT

MENDOCINO
FRACTURE ZONE

PIONEER FRACTURE ZONE

SAN ANDREAS FAULT

San Francisco

MURRAY FRACTURE ZONE

Los Angeles
San
Diego

Hermosillo

MOLOKAI FRACTURE ZONE

La
Paz

Mazatlán

0   250   500 MILES
0   250   500 KILOMETERS

RIVERA FAULT

Puerto
Vallarta

CLARION FRACTURE ZONE

Western margin of North America showing the land captured from the North American Plate by the Pacific Plate. The rifted, captured slab then slid right-laterally along several transform faults in the Gulf of California and along the San Andreas fault. The western boundary of the land kidnapped by the Pacific Plate is an older, inactive, convergent plate boundary (open sawteeth) left there from earlier Farallon Plate subduction.

—After Irwin, 1990

at an average rate of about 2 inches per year. The shearing between the North American and Pacific Plates occurs across a 300-mile-wide zone, from the California coast to central Nevada, with about 70 percent of that displacement occurring along the San Andreas fault.

Rotation of the Western Transverse Ranges

The western Transverse Ranges block was caught up in the transform shearing along the San Andreas fault between the North American and Pacific Plates. The block rotated about 110 degrees clockwise during the last 18 million years or so as it also slipped northwestward to its present position. Geologic, geophysical, and paleomagnetic data for separation and rotation of the western Transverse Ranges is found by matching respective rocks and structures, such as those of the Poway Conglomerate of Eocene age. Its distinctive rocks were eroded from the continental interior and carried and deposited along an Eocene river course from northern Mexico to La Jolla, near San Diego. They are distributed across the Peninsular Ranges along that ancient river course, especially in the San Diego region, but nowhere else in southern California—except on parts of the northern Channel Islands, which are part of the rotated western Transverse Ranges.

Discovery of the San Andreas Fault

The San Andreas fault was discovered in 1906 when a 296-mile-long surface rupture occurred along the northern third of the fault in association with the San Francisco earthquake. Prior to the earthquake, bits and pieces of the fault had been mapped here and there in California, but no one realized how they joined together. Then in 1906–1907 H.W. Fairbanks walked the fault continuously from the northern end of the San Francisco rupture 400 hundred miles south and southeast to the Salton Sea and proved that it was one long continuous fault. Even then the significance of the maximum 20 feet of right-slip on the fault during the 1906 earthquake, extrapolated through geologic time, was not realized until Mason Hill and Tom Dibblee published a landmark paper in 1953. In it, they linked several formations across the fault and showed how rock units had been displaced as much as 300 miles over about 24 million years. At the time, however, few geologists had the regional view of California's geology that Hill and Dibblee possessed, and so their work was not fully accepted by several prominent California geologists.

In 1973 and 1976, Vince Matthews found that the unique 23.5-million-year-old Neenach Volcanics, a rock formation in the western half of Pinnacles National Park, on the Pacific Plate side of the San Andreas fault, perfectly match rocks in the western Mojave Desert, on the North American Plate side of the San Andreas fault 190 miles to the southeast. This news caused the doubters' heads and opinions to turn. Nowadays, we take the fault's great strike-slip for granted and can point to over thirty separate and compelling correlations across the fault, which clearly prove large fault displacement over geologic time.

The Present

Most of the landscape in southern California is certainly less than 10 million years old, and much of it is less than 1 million years old. As Pacific Plate motion became more localized in the Gulf of California, the San Andreas fault took on its present lazy S–shaped geometry, known as the Big Bend, which extends from southeast of the San Bernardino Mountains to the southern San Joaquin Valley. Part of what was once the upper crust of the North American Plate is being jammed into the Big Bend area, where considerable crustal squeezing and thickening have occurred. Extremely recent uplift, folding of rocks as young as Pleistocene age, and active thrust faulting occur across the Transverse Ranges. Hans Stille, a famous German geologist with a knowledge of worldwide tectonics, designated this very young phase of mountain building as the Pasadenan orogeny.

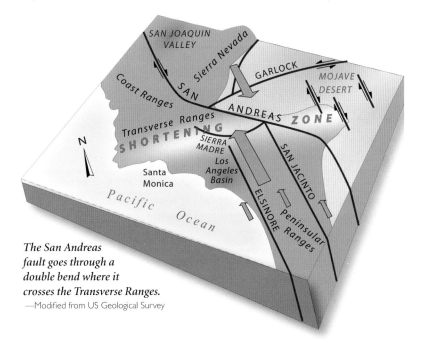

The San Andreas fault goes through a double bend where it crosses the Transverse Ranges.
—Modified from US Geological Survey

Frequent earthquakes are the most evident manifestation of this tectonic activity and make California one of the most seismically active areas in the world. These earthquakes have been associated with uplift of the mountains, stretching and squeezing of the crust, and slippage of Los Angeles ever closer to San Francisco. Of particular interest is the uplift of the Transverse Ranges. They are still rising along the Sierra Madre and Cucamonga fault zones, located at the base of the steep, 1-mile-high fault scarp along the southern front of the range. The destructive 1971 San Fernando and 1994 Northridge earthquakes caught seismologists off guard, because they did not yet understand and appreciate the tectonic setup of the Transverse Ranges and the role of the Pacific Plate grinding against the North American Plate. The mountains above the San Fernando Valley rose 8 feet at the time of the 1971 San Fernando earthquake.

The East Pacific Rise continues to crack into the North American continent in the Salton Trough, accounting for the rifting there and the sinking of most of the basin below sea level. Were it not for the Colorado River's delta deposits forming a dam between the Salton Trough and the head of the Gulf of California, the sea would inundate much of the basin, to a depth of 300 feet in places. In Pliocene time, before the delta existed, marine sediments of the Imperial Formation were deposited almost as far north as Palm Springs.

The rifting stretches and thins the crust so that the upper mantle is near the surface and is responsible for rhyolite volcanic domes at the southern end of the Salton Sea that are less than 3,000 years old. Geothermal power plants at

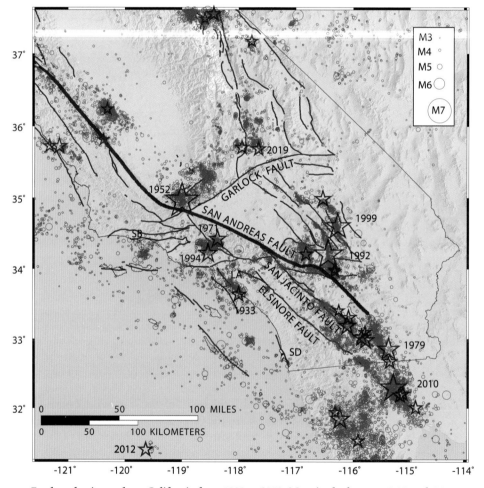

Earthquakes in southern California from 1932 to 2019. Magnitudes between 3.25 and 6.0 are gray circles, and magnitudes greater than or equal to 6.0 are red stars. —Seismicity recorded by the Caltech/USGS Southern California Seismic Network; map courtesy of E. Hauksson at Caltech

thc south end of the basin exploit the heat supplied there by the nearness of the upper mantle. Some volcanoes in the Mojave Desert are less than 20,000 years old and look as though they erupted yesterday. They are merely dormant and may erupt again tomorrow.

Evidence of ice age glaciation in southern California is found only on San Gorgonio Mountain in the eastern Transverse Ranges, but copious precipitation at the time fed ancient lakes and river systems, especially in the Mojave Desert.

Rock layers in the Monterey Formation are folded into an anticline at Zaca Lake, with layers dipping down to the right and the left. The rocks were folded during north-south crustal squeezing in the western Transverse Ranges about 4 million years ago. (34°47.0N, 120°02.5W)

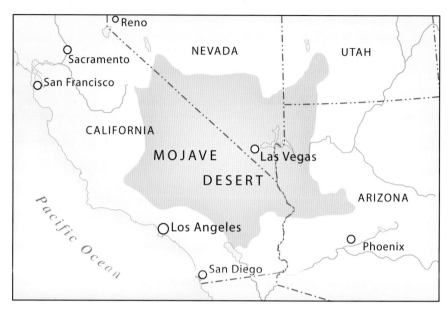

The Mojave Desert occupies 25,000 square miles in southeast California and stretches well into Nevada, Utah, and Arizona.

Aerial view southeast across the Mojave River toward the Bristol Mountains and Bristol Basin. Some geologists characterize the Mojave Desert as a region of highly eroded mountains drowning in their own debris.

MOJAVE DESERT

We simply need to see . . . wild country available to us, even if we never do more than drive to the edge and look in. It can be a means of reassuring ourselves of our sanity as creatures, a part of a geography of hope. —Wallace Stegner, *The Wilderness Letter*

The Mojave Desert is a vast, arid expanse of barren mountain ranges, broad flatlands, parched riverbeds and washes, extensive mesas, lofty sand dunes, dry lakes, colorful cinder cones, and black lava flows. Indeed, as John Steinbeck's Tom Joad said of the Mojave Desert, "This here's the bones of a country." You will find these bones, as exemplified by the geology, wonderfully exposed throughout the Mojave.

The Mojave is commonly referred to as high desert, because its elevations are mostly above 2,000 feet, in contrast to the Colorado Desert to the south, which drops below sea level in places. With the exception of the Colorado River on the California-Arizona border, most Mojave Desert streams flow into basins without external drainage. Water ponds in the lowest areas, usually flat, dry lakebeds called playas, until it evaporates in the summer heat.

Antelope Valley, the wedge-shaped western part of the Mojave, is bounded by the left-slip Garlock fault on the north and by the right-slip San Andreas fault on the southwest. The two fault zones converge near Lebec, at the west end of the wedge. The eastern part of the Mojave Desert, which includes the Mojave National Preserve between I-40 and I-15, blends indistinctly into the Basin and Range region to the north and east and the Colorado Desert region to the south.

Mojave Desert valleys are proportionally wider and the mountains are correspondingly more widely spaced than those in the Basin and Range of eastern California and Nevada. Typically, the mountains lack foothills, rising abruptly along faults from either alluvium or an eroded bedrock pediment. The Mojave mountain ranges are also less consistently oriented than those in the Basin and Range. The mountains in the north and east parts of the Mojave are oriented roughly north-south, whereas those in the southeastern Mojave lack any discernibly consistent trends.

The distributions and relationships among Mojave Desert rocks are complex. They range in age from Proterozoic gneiss to not-yet-solidified alluvial fan deposits and young cinder cones. In between are sections of Paleozoic-age stratified rocks, metamorphosed to various degrees; scattered sedimentary, metasedimentary, and metavolcanic rocks of Mesozoic age; a considerable abundance of Mesozoic-age plutonic igneous rocks; and volcanic and sedimentary rocks deposited in basins in Cenozoic time.

Major thrust faults cut Mojave Desert rocks in Middle Jurassic to Late Cretaceous time. In late Cenozoic time, the rocks were deformed into north- to northwest-trending folds and cut by steeply dipping faults and low-angle thrust faults. Many high-angle faults strike northwest with evidence of recent displacement, such as fault scarps in young alluvium. Most are northwest-striking, right-slip faults, although a domain of east-striking, left-slip faults prevails in the central part of the Mojave west of Baker.

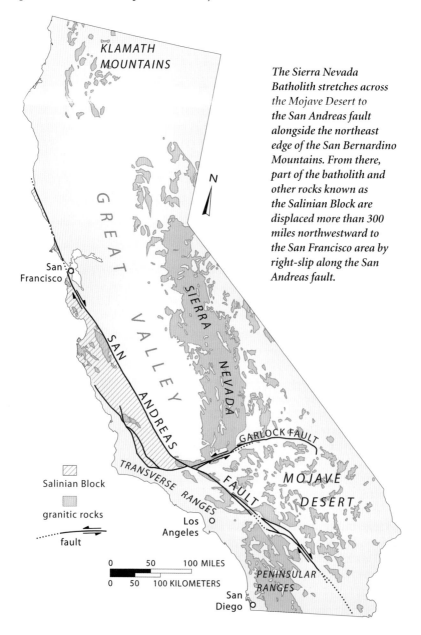

The Sierra Nevada Batholith stretches across the Mojave Desert to the San Andreas fault alongside the northeast edge of the San Bernardino Mountains. From there, part of the batholith and other rocks known as the Salinian Block are displaced more than 300 miles northwestward to the San Francisco area by right-slip along the San Andreas fault.

Abundant granitic rocks in the Mojave region are part of the great system of batholiths that formed along the Mesozoic-age subduction zone on the west edge of North America. They run the gamut of compositions from gabbro to true granite. The great bulk of the granitic rocks are quartz monzonite and granodiorite of Jurassic and Cretaceous age.

Volcanic rocks are abundant throughout the Mojave Desert. Although referred to as simply Tertiary volcanics on many geologic maps, two main age categories have been discerned. Widespread volcanic rocks southeast of Barstow are 24 to 20 million years old, whereas those in the latitude of Barstow and north to the Garlock fault are mainly 20 to 14 million years old. Late Miocene and younger mafic volcanic rocks, primarily basaltic andesite, are scattered throughout the Mojave. The distribution and age of the various volcanic assemblages reflect a major transition from intermediate and silicic volcanism to fundamentally different basaltic volcanism. The former began approximately 33 million years ago and ended 25 to 22 million years ago, probably related to cessation of Farallon Plate subduction in early Cenozoic time. A

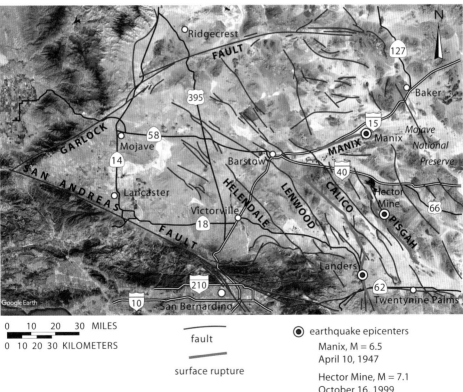

0 10 20 30 MILES

0 10 20 30 KILOMETERS

fault

surface rupture

◉ earthquake epicenters

Manix, M = 6.5
April 10, 1947

Hector Mine, M = 7.1
October 16, 1999

Landers, M = 7.3
June 28, 1992

Nearly all Mojave Desert faults are regarded as active, even though only a few are credited with earthquakes in historic time. Paramount among those are the 1992 Landers (magnitude 7.3) and 1999 Hector Mine (magnitude 7.1) earthquakes.

southeastward transition to basaltic volcanism from 19 to 13 million years ago overlaps the inception of Basin and Range faulting.

DETACHMENT FAULTS

Detachment faults are an integral structure in several eastern Mojave mountain ranges. Detachment faulting involves regional, low-angle normal faulting of an upper plate of younger rocks slipping off and away from a lower plate of older rocks called a metamorphic core complex. In contrast to thrust faults, which place older rocks over younger rocks and cause duplication of crustal sections, detachment faults cause their omission. The amount of crustal omission caused when the two plates are brought into juxtaposition is mind-boggling. In the Whipple Mountains, for example, detachment faults juxtapose an upper plate of Miocene-age sedimentary and volcanic rocks, deposited at the Earth's surface around 20 to 18 million years ago, with lower plate Proterozoic-age metamorphic crystalline rocks that underwent ductile deformation at crustal depths greater than 6 miles and temperatures in excess of 440°C. Subsequent exhumation and erosion of the upper plate allowed those lower plate metamorphic rocks to rise isostatically to the surface. The rapidity of that uplift from such deep crustal depths is one of the remarkable aspects of the metamorphic core complexes in this region.

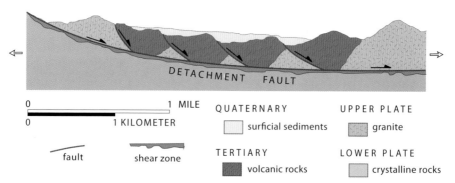

Diagrammatic cross section of a detachment fault complex in the Mojave Desert. Rotational normal faults along the detachment surface place younger rocks upon older and allow the crust to break away and stretch apart.

JOSHUA TREE NATIONAL PARK

Joshua Tree National Park covers a land area of 1,235 square miles—an area slightly larger than Rhode Island—and nearly 914 square miles are designated wilderness. The park is located in the Little San Bernardino Mountains, part of the eastern Transverse Ranges between the Salton Trough of the Colorado Desert and the Mojave Desert. Geologically, the park's rocks and structures belong to the Mojave Desert.

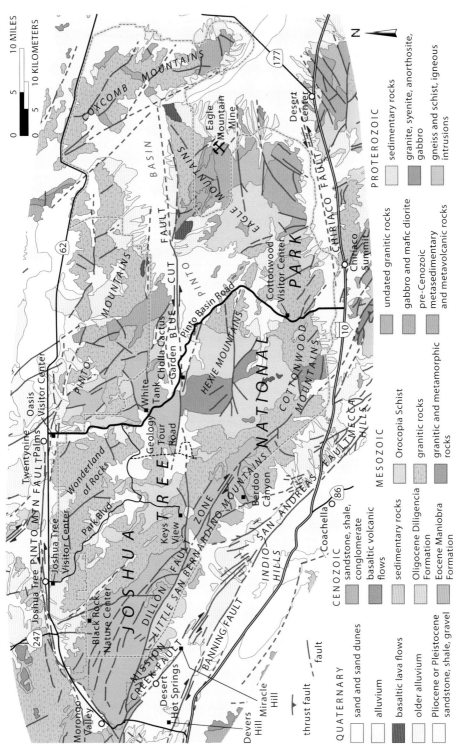

Geology of Joshua Tree National Park.

QUATERNARY

sand and sand dunes

alluvium

basaltic lava flows

older alluvium

Pliocene or Pleistocene
sandstone, shale, gravel

CENOZOIC

sandstone, shale,
conglomerate

basaltic volcanic
flows

sedimentary rocks

Oligocene Diligencia
Formation

Eocene Maniobra
Formation

MESOZOIC

Orocopia Schist

granitic rocks

granitic and metamorphic
rocks

undated granitic rocks

gabbro and mafic diorite

pre-Cenozoic
metasedimentary
and metavolcanic rocks

PROTEROZOIC

sedimentary rocks

granite, syenite, anorthosite,
gabbro

gneiss and schist, igneous
intrusions

thrust fault

fault

N

The wide-open spaces of Joshua Tree National Park are ideal for the teddy bear cholla cactus, a beautiful plant that you will regret getting too close to. (33°55.50N, 115°55.77W) —Ivar Midtkandalen photo

You can drive into the park either from the south entrance from I-10 (exit 168) or from the west or north entrances from CA 62 in Yucca Valley. Pick up the Park Service brochure at an entrance station to guide you to places mentioned in this geologic overview. For much more geologic detail, pick up splendid detailed geologic guidebooks by Dee Trent and Rick Hazlett (2002) or by Barbara and Robert Decker (2006).

The Cottonwood Springs/Pinto Basin Road cuts across the center of the park from the CA 62 entrances to the I-10 entrance. Unpaved side roads and hiking trails give access to various scenic locations. Keys View Road, which is paved but narrow and slow, leads to windy Keys View at an elevation of 5,185 feet. On clear days, you can see all the way across the Salton Sea into Mexico. You can also see a lot of fascinating geology from the Geology Tour Road, but it requires four-wheel drive.

Much of the north half of the park consists of granite, part of the huge intrusion of magma that formed the batholiths of the Sierra Nevada and Peninsular Ranges when the Farallon Plate subducted beneath the North American Plate in Mesozoic time. Proterozoic granite and metamorphic rocks, intruded by the granite, are also exposed in the park. Metasedimentary rocks, metamorphosed before Cretaceous time, crop out in some less accessible areas. The best place to see Proterozoic rocks is in a few roadcuts

Pinto Gneiss is a heterogeneous metamorphic rock consisting of black metabasalt and intricately folded layers of biotite-quartz-feldspar gneiss. Baseball cap for scale. (33°43.05N, 115°48.60W)

between I-10 and the Cottonwood Springs entrance station, where Pinto Gneiss is exposed.

Granite is exposed and accessible in the Wonderland of Rocks, especially in the Jumbo Rocks and White Tank areas. Rock climbers love this 12-square-mile maze of jumbled granite boulders and rock piles, rounded knobs and towers, gentle domes, and smooth cliffs. Look for Arch Rock in White Tank Campground, the Old Woman and Cyclops Rock in Hidden Valley Campground, the Trojan and the Ox along the Hidden Valley Nature Trail, Bread Loaf Rock near Belle Campground, and Skull Rock near Jumbo Rocks Campground.

If you climb some gentle outcrops of granite, you'll notice large, blocky crystals of white or gray potassium feldspar set among minerals grains that are all about the same size. Based on the kind and abundance of minerals, geologists give separate and daunting names to granitic rocks, such as syeno-granite, monzogranite, granodiorite, tonalite, and monzonite. Some of them take the name of the place where they are exposed, such as Twentynine Palms quartz monzonite and White Tank monzodiorite. The distinctions among them may be subtle and difficult without careful analysis, especially when cruising at the park's designated speed limits.

If you walk on and around the granitic rocks and through some of the ravines, you'll notice white veins slicing across the granite here and there. These

Rounded exposures of White Tank monzodiorite. (33°59.12N, 116°00.94W)

Fine-grained aplite dikes of quartz and feldspar intruded this granite and are more resistant to erosion than the granite. (33°59.12N, 116°00.94W)
—Tyson McKinney photo

light-colored, fine-grained veins of quartz and feldspar are called aplite dikes, whereas those with large crystals of quartz, feldspar, and mica are pegmatite dikes. They intruded along cracks and joints in the granite when it was cool enough to fracture but still contained some melted rock that could fill and crystallize in those fractures.

Several major faults bound Joshua Tree National Park and are considered active. Strands of the San Andreas fault lie along the southwest edge of the park in Coachella Valley. The Blue Cut fault slices east-west through the center of the park, and the Pinto Mountain fault comes out of Morongo Valley along the north edge of the park. You won't see much of these two faults, because they lie beneath valley fill, but some faults are nicely exposed along the Geology Tour Road and in canyons along the northeast edge of Coachella Valley.

A normal fault, slanting down to the left, separates sedimentary breccia (left) from granitic basement rocks (right) in Berdoo Canyon. (33°49.36N, 116°10.19W)

Joshua Trees

One of the most distinctive sights in much of the Mojave Desert is the Joshua tree, so named by Mormon settlers who saw it as the prophet Joshua with upraised arms leading his people into the promised land. The Joshua tree is a yucca (*Yucca brevifolia*) belonging to the lily family of plant. It occurs at elevations between 1,300 and 5,900 feet and ranges mostly within the geographical reach of the Mojave Desert, where it is considered one of the major indicator species for the desert.

Native Joshua trees and junipers once grew in profusion throughout the Mojave, especially in Antelope Valley before so much of it was cleared for farming and housing. Today, only remnant parcels of this majestic woodland community remain in the valley. You may visit an impressive stand of Joshua trees and other plants of the high desert at Arthur B. Ripley Desert Woodland State Park. It is located approximately 7 miles west of the Antelope Valley California Poppy Reserve on Lancaster Road (an extension of West Avenue I), 4 miles south of CA 138 via 245th Street West.

Road Guides for the Mojave Desert

INTERSTATE 10
INDIO—BLYTHE
96 miles

I-10 crosses the San Andreas fault onto the North American Plate about 4 miles east of Indio between PM 61 and PM 62 near Dillon Road (exit 146) and the Coachella Valley aqueduct. A prominent line of vegetation marks the fault location along the break in slope.

The highway then ascends a long grade along the south front of the Cottonwood Mountains, which lie in the south part of Joshua Tree National Park. The Cottonwood Mountains consist of light-colored Mesozoic granite that intruded darker Proterozoic metamorphic rocks. Outcrops in washes adjacent to the highway are sand and gravel beds shed southward from the Cottonwood Mountains in Pleistocene time and then tilted by deformation associated with the nearby San Andreas fault.

East of the Cactus City rest stop (exit 159), I-10 follows Shavers Valley, which contains the buried trace of the Chiriaco fault and separates the Cottonwood Mountains north of the highway from the Mecca Hills and Orocopia Mountains to the south.

About 6 miles east of the rest stop and 1 mile south of the highway (in the vicinity of PM 78) is a low, rather unremarkable brown hill, Buried Mountain, which consists of coarse sandstone deposited along an ocean shore in Eocene time. Boulders in the sandstone contain fragmented *Turritella* fossil snails with tightly coiled shells (see photo on page 294 in the road log CA 1: Santa Monica—Oxnard). The hill is completely surrounded by alluvium, and

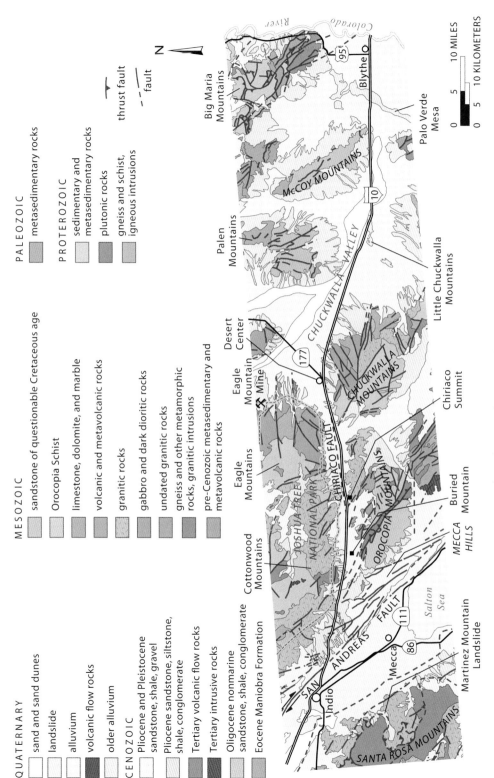

QUATERNARY

sand and sand dunes

landslide

alluvium

volcanic flow rocks

older alluvium

CENOZOIC

Pliocene and Pleistocene
sandstone, shale, gravel

Pliocene sandstone, siltstone,
shale, conglomerate

Tertiary volcanic flow rocks

Tertiary intrusive rocks

Oligocene nonmarine
sandstone, shale, conglomerate

Eocene Maniobra Formation

MESOZOIC

sandstone of questionable Cretaceous age

Orocopia Schist

limestone, dolomite, and marble

volcanic and metavolcanic rocks

granitic rocks

gabbro and dark dioritic rocks

undated granitic rocks

gneiss and other metamorphic
rocks, granitic intrusions

pre-Cenozoic metasedimentary and
metavolcanic rocks

PALEOZOIC

metasedimentary rocks

PROTEROZOIC

sedimentary and
metasedimentary rocks

plutonic rocks

gneiss and schist,
igneous intrusions

◂▾ thrust fault

—— fault

N

Geology along I-10 between Indio and Blythe.

surrounding hills are Mesozoic granite and Pliocene nonmarine sedimentary rock, so Buried Mountain is a geologic orphan out in the middle of the valley. It is probably bounded at depth by faults, but its relation to the surrounding mountains is enigmatic.

At exit 168, you may go north into Joshua Tree National Park (see the introduction to this chapter), or south along Box Canyon Road through the scenic and geologically interesting Mecca Hills (see the Salton Trough chapter).

Patton's Desert Training Center and the Orocopia Mountains

The 54-mile-long stretch of uninhabited desert along I-10 between exit 168 and exit 222 was exactly what General George S. Patton needed for desert warfare training during World War II before shipping troops off to North Africa to do battle with Axis forces. The Desert Training Center, which covered 18,000 square miles in southeastern California and western Arizona, commenced operations in 1942 and trained over one million men. It was the largest military training ground ever to exist. The desert floor is still scored by tracks made by tanks and other vehicles during those exercises. A museum at Chiriaco Summit (exit 173) honors General Patton.

The mountains on either side of I-10 between Indio and Blythe are so desolate and inaccessible, aside from some wells and peaks, that few landmarks in and around the mountains have been named. When UCLA professor John Crowell and his students discovered Eocene-age marine rocks in a big wash in the Orocopia Mountains south of Chiriaco Summit in the 1950s, they needed a name to give to the formation. Crowell named the wash Maniobra, which is Spanish for "maneuvers," because the wash was one of the central locations where General Patton held his wartime maneuvers. The Maniobra Formation shale and sandstone are so similar to oil-producing formations in Cuyama Valley on the north edge of the western Transverse Ranges that Crowell correctly postulated they have been displaced 240 miles from one another along the San Andreas fault. A brief, intense, but ultimately unsuccessful oil exploration boom ensued in the Orocopia Mountains in the hope that oil would be found there, too.

Half of the Orocopia Mountains consists of a lower plate of Orocopia Schist, the exhumed metamorphosed ocean crust of the Farallon Plate, and an upper plate of Proterozoic gneiss and Mesozoic granite separated by the Vincent–Orocopia–Chocolate Mountains thrust fault, which geologists think represents the zone of subduction between the Farallon and North American Plates. Eocene marine rocks and Oligocene sedimentary and volcanic rocks underlie much of the east half of the range. Rock exposures nearest the highway are Mesozoic granite. You'll need an off-road vehicle to see other rock formations in the Orocopia Mountains.

The particular combination of rocks and structures in the Orocopia Mountains is exceedingly significant for the geologic history of southern California, because the same combination of rocks is also found along the north flank of the San Gabriel Mountains, on the other side of the San Andreas fault, 140 miles to the northwest. Anorthosite, a relatively rare Proterozoic-age plutonic rock composed of more than 90 percent plagioclase feldspar, is especially significant, because in the western United States, it is found only in the Orocopia Mountains, in the central San Gabriel Mountains, and around Laramie, Wyoming.

Eagle Mountain Iron Mine

Eagle Mountain Mine is a gigantic, 1.5-mile-long by 0.5-mile-wide, abandoned open pit that can be seen from the Moon but not from I-10. These were the largest iron mines in the western United States until their closure in 1982. Both the town and mine of Eagle Mountain, 12 miles north of Desert Center, are behind locked gates in spite of several innovative revival efforts. The enormous open pits also have been under consideration for disposal of solid waste delivered by special trains from Los Angeles. From 1942 to 1980, the railroad crossed by I-10 at PM 95 hauled high-grade iron ore from the Eagle Mountains to the Ferrum siding on the Southern Pacific transcontinental railroad that paralleled CA 111 in the Salton Trough. The ore was then shipped to smelters in Fontana, 100 miles to the west, to produce steel for Liberty ships during World War II and ships and automobiles afterward.

The mine exposes a complex anticline with a core of Proterozoic basement rocks unconformably overlain by two metasedimentary rock units: a lower unit of dolomitic carbonate and quartzite, and a conglomeratic upper unit. A branching network of granitic sills, tens to hundreds of feet thick, intruded both units in Jurassic time and provided the heat and silica necessary to form an ore deposit known as skarn. The iron ore, contained in the minerals magnetite and pyrite, replaced carbonate-bearing rock, forming globular bodies of ore ranging from 30 to 300 feet thick in a zone nearly 6 miles long.

Chuckwalla Valley

From Desert Center, I-10 curves around the north side of the Chuckwalla Mountains and eastward through Chuckwalla Valley for 50 miles to the Palo Verde Valley, the Colorado River, and the city of Blythe. Like so many mountain ranges farther east in the eastern Mojave, the Chuckwalla Mountains are a wild, fairly inaccessible range of Mesozoic-age granite that intrudes and is in fault contact with Proterozoic-age granite. Much of Chuckwalla Valley is blanketed by relatively thin but extensive sand picked up from alluvial fans and funneled by prevailing northwest winds down the valley. The sand wraps around the south ends of the Palen and McCoy Mountains north of the highway, forming dunes in places.

McCoy and Palen Mountains

Mesozoic-age sedimentary rocks are rare in the Mojave Desert, but they are extensively exposed in the McCoy and Palen Mountains west of Blythe. There, sections of sandstone and conglomerate—5 miles thick in the McCoy Mountains and assigned to the McCoy Mountains Formation—lie upon Jurassic volcanic rocks. Poorly preserved fragments of fossil wood and dates on detrital

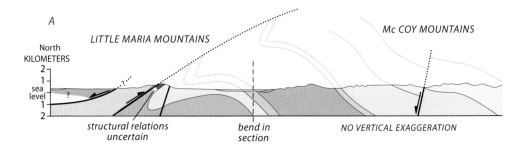

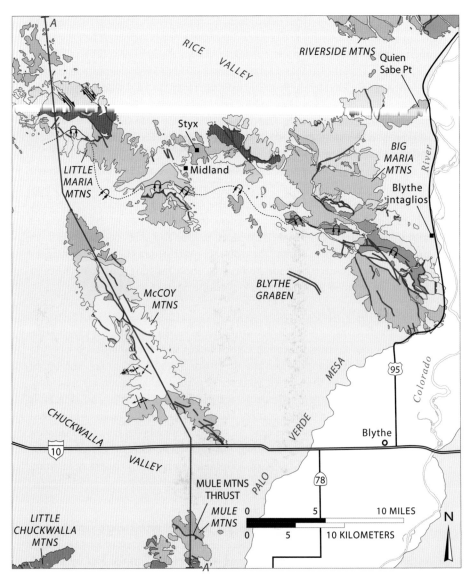

Geologic map of the McCoy, Little Maria, and Big Maria Mountains and structure section (A-A′) of the McCoy Mountains. —Modified from Stone, 2006

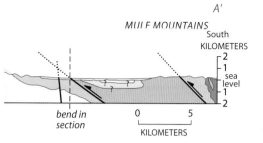

A'

MULE MOUNTAINS
South
KILOMETERS

bend in section

0   5
KILOMETERS

Sedimentary rocks in the McCoy Mountains are intensely deformed by thrust and strike-slip faults and by tight folds as shown in this structure section down the length of the mountain range. —Modified from Stone and Kelly, 1989

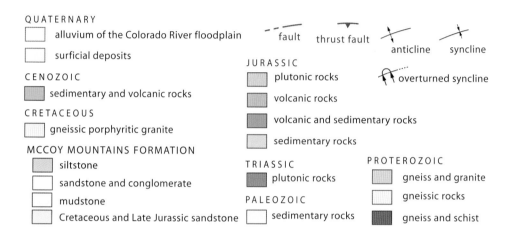

QUATERNARY
- alluvium of the Colorado River floodplain
- surficial deposits

CENOZOIC
- sedimentary and volcanic rocks

CRETACEOUS
- gneissic porphyritic granite

MCCOY MOUNTAINS FORMATION
- siltstone
- sandstone and conglomerate
- mudstone
- Cretaceous and Late Jurassic sandstone

fault   thrust fault

anticline   syncline

JURASSIC
- plutonic rocks
- volcanic rocks
- volcanic and sedimentary rocks
- sedimentary rocks

overturned syncline

TRIASSIC
- plutonic rocks

PALEOZOIC
- sedimentary rocks

PROTEROZOIC
- gneiss and granite
- gneissic rocks
- gneiss and schist

zircon grains indicate the strata are Late Jurassic and Cretaceous in age. The sedimentary layers were deposited by rivers in a narrow, west-northwest-trending basin or series of basins and then metamorphosed and deformed during southward thrusting of the Paleozoic and Mesozoic rocks in Late Cretaceous time.

INTERSTATE 15
Includes parts of Route 66
CAJON SUMMIT—BARSTOW
50 miles

I-15 enters the Mojave Desert at Cajon Summit and takes a straight shot across the desert to Barstow. An alternative, more scenic, and less traveled route to Barstow follows old US 66 (Route 66) from Victorville along the Mojave River. Cajon Summit, at 4,320 feet above sea level and 3,280 feet higher than San Bernardino, underscores the fact that the Mojave is high desert.

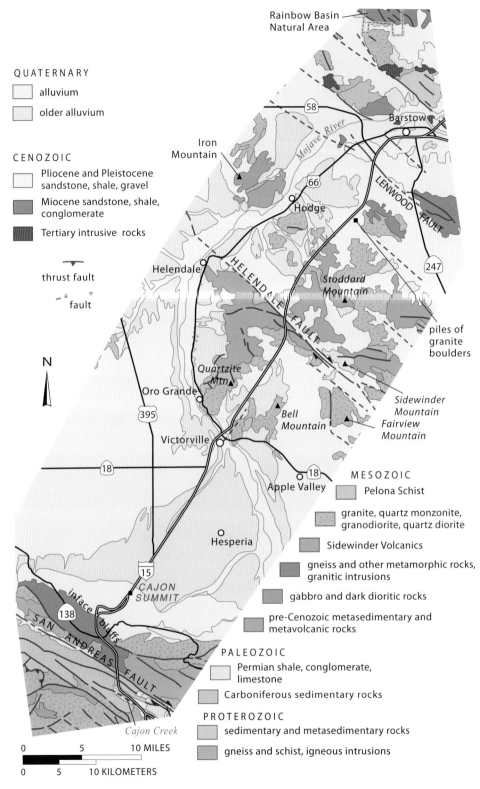

QUATERNARY

☐ alluvium

☐ older alluvium

CENOZOIC

☐ Pliocene and Pleistocene sandstone, shale, gravel

☐ Miocene sandstone, shale, conglomerate

☐ Tertiary intrusive rocks

⊥ thrust fault

⌐ fault

N

Rainbow Basin Natural Area

58

Barstow

Iron Mountain

Mojave River

LENWOOD FAULT

66

Hodge

247

HELENDALE FAULT

Helendale

Stoddard Mountain

piles of granite boulders

Quartzite Mtn

Sidewinder Mountain

Oro Grande

Bell Mountain

Fairview Mountain

395

Victorville

18

18

Apple Valley

Hesperia

MESOZOIC

☐ Pelona Schist

☐ granite, quartz monzonite, granodiorite, quartz diorite

☐ Sidewinder Volcanics

☐ gneiss and other metamorphic rocks, granitic intrusions

☐ gabbro and dark dioritic rocks

☐ pre-Cenozoic metasedimentary and metavolcanic rocks

PALEOZOIC

☐ Permian shale, conglomerate, limestone

☐ Carboniferous sedimentary rocks

PROTEROZOIC

☐ sedimentary and metasedimentary rocks

☐ gneiss and schist, igneous intrusions

15

CAJON SUMMIT

138

inface bluffs

SAN ANDREAS FAULT

Cajon Creek

0   5   10 MILES

0   5   10 KILOMETERS

Geology along I-15 and Route 66 between Cajon Summit and Barstow.

From Cajon Summit, I-15 descends about 20 miles northward toward Victorville down the gentle surface of ancient alluvial fans. All this alluvium was once shed from the north slopes of the San Gabriel Mountains across the San Andreas fault directly into the Mojave Desert. During Pleistocene time, the fans were displaced several miles right-laterally along the fault, so that they no longer receive sediment from the mountains (see discussion in the I-15 road guide in the Transverse Ranges chapter).

Mojave River

The Mojave River, one of the largest rivers with interior drainage in California, flows north out of the San Bernardino Mountains and east side of the San Gabriel Mountains for 150 miles into the Mojave Desert to its penultimate sink in the Soda Lake playa near Baker. In Pleistocene glacial time, the river continued north and joined the Amargosa River flowing into Death Valley. Even today, the river occasionally overflows into the Cronise Valley and Silurian Lake playas, flooding the community of Baker. Except during floods, the Mojave River flows mostly underground through unconsolidated alluvium. Near-surface bedrock forces it to flow aboveground at Victorville, Barstow, and Afton Canyon.

In Victorville, the Mojave River has cut a water gap through a resistant granite ridge formerly buried beneath alluvium. The river could have avoided the hard rock by flowing a short distance around it, but its course was already established in the alluvial cover, so it slowly cut down through the ridge. Route 66 follows the gentle downstream gradient of the Mojave River and railroad northward out of Victorville to Barstow.

Aerial view to the south of the Victorville water gap. The Mojave River flows toward the observer from the San Bernardino Mountains on the skyline and within the granite ridge behind CA 18, the highway in the foreground. (34°32.0N, 117°18.0W)

Victorville Cement Quarries

North of Victorville and the Mojave River, I-15 follows Bell Mountain Wash between low granitic hills that look like they have a dusting of snow, but the white patina is actually a coating of hardened calcareous dust emitted years ago by old cement plants. A modernized plant at Oro Grande, about 4 miles north of I-15, does not release dust. Well over 50 million tons of limestone for making cement, as well as several million tons of quartzite and many millions of tons of miscellaneous calcareous rocks including marble, have been quarried from these hills and processed in plants along the Mojave River since 1909. The high-quality cement is combined with rock, sand, and gravel to make concrete for highways, canals, airport runways, and bridge and building foundations. Alluvial fans and river channels are the main sources of rock, sand, and gravel for concrete aggregate and are also mined in the Victorville–Barstow–Lucerne Valley region. Oro Grande took its name from a large gold strike in 1868. Silver was also discovered a few years later but played out as quickly as the gold.

West of Oro Grande is the Southern California Logistics Airport, a warehousing and distribution center, which boasts the second longest public use runway in the United States (15,050 feet), surpassed only by that of Denver International Airport (16,000 feet). The airport is the main transportation hub for the seventy thousand troops traveling annually to and from the Army National Training Center at Fort Irwin, northeast of Barstow. It also serves as a boneyard for retired aircraft, and as an urban warfare training center for the US Armed Forces.

Sidewinder Volcanics and Granite between Victorville and Barstow

The large, symmetric hill on the west side of I-15 between the Mojave River and Stoddard Wells Road (exit 157) is a big landfill. Much of the nearly flat terrain north of it, but still west of the highway, is the Victorville pediment, an erosion surface of granite covered by a thin veneer of sand and gravel derived from the granite. Quartzite Mountain (elevation 4,532 feet) stands prominently a couple miles northwest of exit 157. It consists of quartzite interbedded with other metasedimentary rocks, including marble quarried extensively on the west side of the mountain for cement. These rocks layers were complexly folded, faulted, and metamorphosed at the end of Paleozoic time before intrusion of any of the granitic rocks in the area.

Most of the low hills north of Quartzite Mountain are made of Late Jurassic Sidewinder Volcanics. These light-colored, feldspar-rich rocks typically contain visible crystals within a fine-grained matrix. Debris from these rocks is unusually hard and durable during transport by rivers, so that rounded clasts of Sidewinder Volcanics have been found in Miocene and Pliocene conglomeratic rocks in the Los Angeles Basin, many miles from their source. In some places, the clasts have been recycled twice when, like tough ball bearings, they eroded from one sedimentary formation, were transported again, and then redeposited in a still younger formation. On the east side of I-15 east of the Stoddard Wells

A hard, resistant cap of dark Sidewinder Volcanics protects older granite beneath from erosion, giving rise to the bell shape of Bell Mountain. (34°35.0N, 117°13.0W)

Road, Bell Mountain looks like a volcano but instead is an erosional remnant of an ancient landscape when volcanic rocks covered the region.

I-15 crosses the Helendale fault (PM 55), at the base of the grade a mile or so south of Wild Wash Road (exit 165) in Turtle Valley. With a mapped length of 60 miles, it is one of the longer faults in the Mojave Desert and is named for the hamlet of Helendale on Route 66. It has an unknown amount of strike-slip displacement; the land southwest of the fault has moved up several hundred feet, as indicated by fault scarps along its surface trace. The main fault has a short southern strand that cuts through a big roadcut at the top of the grade (PM 54). Rocks in the roadcut are Sidewinder Volcanics, sliced by numerous minor faults. Turtle Mountain, also mostly Sidewinder Volcanics, extends several miles to the southeast.

More Jurassic granitic rocks crop out on the north side of the grade at Wild Wash Road (exit 165). From there I-15 continues north across alluvial fans around the base of Stoddard Mountain east of exit 165. Sidewinder Volcanics form most of Stoddard Mountain.

Between Hodge Road (exit 169) and Sidewinder Road (exit 175) are two small, isolated and anomalous, light gray bouldery outcrops, one on each side of I-15 at PM 63.5. Surrounded by a vast expanse of alluvial flats, they look like two orphans wanting to hitch a ride. They are light gray because they are frequent targets of graffiti vandals, so the highway maintenance people must paint them just as often. Beneath the gray paint is granite, a rock of the kind and type that underlies the Sidewinder Volcanics and Bell Mountain.

It is possible this granite outcrop along I-15 near the Lenwood exit was once deeply buried by volcanic rocks that have since eroded away. (34°47.2N, 117°07.5W)

Lenwood Fault

One mile north of Lenwood Road (exit 178), near the CA 58 interchange (exit 179), I-15 crosses the Lenwood fault, another major northwest-striking, strike-slip fault in the Mojave Desert. It is about 50 miles long but is very difficult to discern at this highway location. The fault, named for Lenwood on Route 66, is involved with the uplift of the Barstow anticline, the big, rounded hill south of Barstow. Geologists have found evidence that the hill is presently rising, probably because of movement on the Lenwood fault, although the fault has not been associated with any measureable earthquake activity or slip in historic time.

INTERSTATE 15
BARSTOW—BAKER
62 miles

Although situated in the middle of a formidable desert, Barstow has always been an important transportation hub because the north-flowing Mojave River rises to the surface here, providing the water so important for a desert crossroads. I-15 follows the Mojave River valley eastward from Barstow to Manix Lake playa and beyond to Soda Lake playa. The river flows underground through the alluvium along most of this route.

Barstow was a busy supply center for miners and prospectors who headed to Death Valley and the nearby mountains, where silver was discovered in 1881. It became even more important when the Atchison, Topeka & Santa Fe Railroad

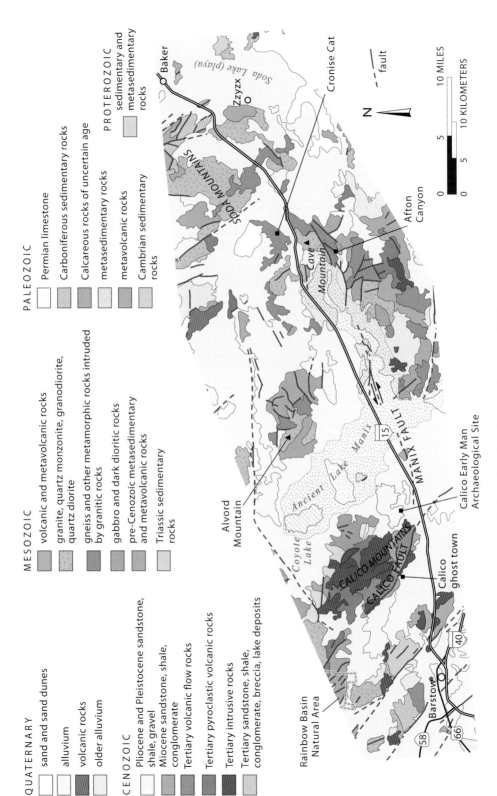

QUATERNARY

sand and sand dunes
alluvium
volcanic rocks
older alluvium

CENOZOIC

Pliocene and Pleistocene sandstone, shale, gravel
Miocene sandstone, shale, conglomerate
Tertiary volcanic flow rocks
Tertiary pyroclastic volcanic rocks
Tertiary intrusive rocks
Tertiary sandstone, shale, conglomerate, breccia, lake deposits

MESOZOIC

volcanic and metavolcanic rocks
granite, quartz monzonite, granodiorite, quartz diorite
gneiss and other metamorphic rocks intruded by granitic rocks
gabbro and dark dioritic rocks
pre-Cenozoic metasedimentary and metavolcanic rocks
Triassic sedimentary rocks

PALEOZOIC

Permian limestone
Carboniferous sedimentary rocks
Calcareous rocks of uncertain age
metasedimentary rocks
metavolcanic rocks
Cambrian sedimentary rocks

PROTEROZOIC

sedimentary and metasedimentary rocks

fault

Baker
Zzyzx
Soda Lake (playa)
SODA MOUNTAINS
Cronise Cat
Afton Canyon
Cave Mountain
Alvord Mountain
Ancient Lake Manix
Coyote Lake
15
MANIX FAULT
Calico Early Man Archaeological Site
CALICO MOUNTAINS
CALICO FAULT
Calico ghost town
Rainbow Basin Natural Area
Barstow
58
66
40

N

0   5   10 MILES
0   5   10 KILOMETERS

Geology along I-15 between Barstow and Baker.

From 17.1 to 16.8 million years ago dacite plugs like Buzzard Peak intruded sedimentary and volcanic rocks of the Pickhandle Formation, which is extensively exposed in the Calico Mountains northeast of Barstow. In the foreground below the bridge is the Mojave River channel, dry at the time of this photo. (34°54.4N, 117°01.33W)

established a depot here in 1885, a convenience that eventually led to Barstow becoming a favorite Route 66 weekend hideaway for early Hollywood movie stars until Palm Springs became more fashionable.

One of the prettiest rocks in the Mojave Desert is in and around Barstow. It is very fine-grained, light gray to pink to brick-colored dacite, a volcanic rock with tiny but visible crystals of plagioclase, quartz, and biotite. It erupted in Miocene time from volcanic conduits whose eroded remnants are called plugs. They form squat, flat-topped hills and mesas, such as Buzzard Peak, on the north edge of town near the Amtrak station and the Harvey House on North First Street. Buzzard Peak has a rugged, blocky appearance due to the columnar joints that formed in the lava when it cooled. To see it up close, from I-15 take Barstow Road (exit 183, CA 247) north to East Main Street, turn left, proceed about two blocks to North First Avenue, turn right, proceed to and cross the bridge to the outcrop. Notice that each of the blocks has a polygonal cross section, typical of columnar jointed lavas.

Calico Mountains

The Calico Mountains are a historically colorful mountain range north of Daggett and northeast of Barstow. Rich silver ore was discovered in these mountains in 1881, giving rise to a town that reached a population of four thousand in 1896. Between 1880 and 1896, $15 to $20 million worth of silver ore was recovered from this range before the price of silver plummeted and the town was abandoned in 1905. It has been restored to a contrived authentic appearance and is open to tourists via Ghost Town Road (exit 191).

The mountains and hills are made up of several rock types, with Waterman Gneiss of Proterozoic age on the west being separated by the Calico fault from Cenozoic-age river and lake deposits, volcanic rocks, and intrusive rocks to the east. The multicolored hill bearing the sign "Calico" in big white letters is mainly volcanic rock. Pastel brown, red-brown, orange, and pale yellow colors reflect hydrothermal alteration of the volcanic rocks by hot water during silver mineralization. Shallow volcanic rocks intruded the Pickhandle Formation of Miocene age, which consists of volcanic breccia and ash-rich sandstone dated at 19.4 to 19.0 million years. These rock layers have been deformed into remarkable folds. They formed in association with displacement along the northwest-striking Calico fault, which slices along the southwest edge of the mountains and gives rise to the abrupt mountain front there. Such folds are widespread in the southern Calico Mountains.

Silver was produced in the central part of the Calico Mountains along a northwest-trending zone about 5 miles long and a 0.5 to 2 miles wide. The richest silver mines were confined to an area extending from about 1 mile northwest of the Calico town site to about 2 miles east of it. The mines were developed in and along veins, fissures, and irregular ore bodies associated with

The intricate folds of laminated siltstone in the Pickhandle Formation in the Calico Ghost Town parking lot. (34°56.9N, 116°52.0W)

shallow intrusions of andesite and dacite. Silver mineralization was extensive in some intrusive bodies and the adjacent country rock. Veins of enriched secondary deposits in Wall Street Canyon were mined when the district first opened.

In 1963 exploration geologists found that the unremarkable, road-ringed hill 1 mile west of Calico is full of silver. It has not been mined because the costs of extraction, hauling, and refining would be more than the prevailing price of the silver. This may change if silver prices go up or costs go down.

Calico Early Man Site

The Calico Early Man Site, reached from Minneola Road (exit 198) about 15 miles east of Barstow, allegedly has some of the oldest archaeological artifacts in the Americas. The site is in a slightly folded alluvial fan that was dissected by streams prior to the development of lake shorelines around its eroded edge 20,000 or 30,000 years ago. Discovered by an amateur archaeologist in 1942 and excavated more extensively after 1964 by noted paleoanthropologist Louis Leakey, the site has yielded more than twelve thousand relics allegedly as old as 200,000 years before present, but probably more nearly 10,000 to 12,000 years before present.

I-15 crosses the Calico fault or one of its buried strands at Minneola Road (exit 198). One of its fault scarps dammed the Mojave River upstream from this point more than 12,800 years ago. Gray silt and clay beds, deposited in a lake impounded by the scarp, are well exposed in the riverbank southwest of the fault. Geologic studies of the fault indicate that four major earthquakes have occurred along it in the past 9,000 years.

Pleistocene Lake Manix

If you had driven the stretch of I-15 from Harvard Road (exit 206) to Afton Road (exit 221) around 45,000 to 19,000 years ago, you would have seen flamingos, pelicans, ducks, gulls, storks, cranes, and loons swimming and wading in a great freshwater lake teeming with fish. Overhead you would have seen eagles, great owls, and large predatory birds. Around the lake would have lived fascinating animals such as dire wolves, mammoths, ground sloths, horses, saber-toothed cats, deer, tapirs, horses, camels, llamas, bison, pumas, bears, coyotes, bighorn sheep, jackrabbits, and turtles. Many of these Pleistocene-age creatures are displayed at the George C. Page Museum next to the La Brea Tar Pits in Los Angeles. Juniper, sagebrush, and creosote brush covered the surrounding alluvial slopes, a woodland of pinyon, juniper, and live oak would have been at slightly higher elevations, and the nearby mountains would have supported dense white fir forests. All that remains of that world today, however, are rather unremarkable soft lake sediments of ancient Lake Manix, which covered about 200 square miles of the present-day Mojave Desert. The highway is built upon coalescing alluvial fans shed in much wetter times from mountains and hills north of the highway, which today slope gently toward the Mojave River south of the highway.

During Pleistocene time when the climate was wetter, the Mojave River filled Lake Manix to its maximum capacity. The lake had three long arms, and

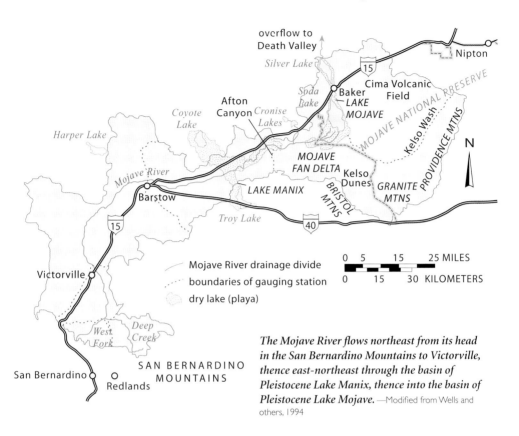

The Mojave River flows northeast from its head in the San Bernardino Mountains to Victorville, thence east-northeast through the basin of Pleistocene Lake Manix, thence into the basin of Pleistocene Lake Mojave. —Modified from Wells and others, 1994

eventually over a period of about 6,000 years, the lake waters rose enough to cut a channel through Afton Canyon at the end of its east arm, connecting the Mojave River to Soda Lake playa. Occasionally water spilled into Silver and Silurian Lake playas, and ultimately into the Amargosa River, which flowed into Death Valley. Under present conditions, however, flood runoff from the mountains is usually lost to alluvial aquifers along the river's length before it reaches its terminal basins. Sediments transported by the Mojave River are the source of windblown sand in the Devils Playground and Kelso Dunes in the western part of Mojave National Preserve southeast of Baker.

The hills north and south of the highway along this stretch were islands in the lake. Harvard Hill (elevation 2,038 feet), 2 miles southwest of the Harvard Road interchange (exit 206), is light gray to white Tertiary limestone and a bit of Tertiary andesite breccia, separated from Tertiary and Quaternary fanglomerate by a probable extension of the Manix fault. Three miles farther west, a long, low hill of north-dipping fanglomerate of late Miocene and Quaternary age has a fault along its south front that may be an extension of the Manix fault. The fault is also exposed in an I-15 roadcut (PM 91.5) on the north side of the highway.

Light gray, hydrothermally altered rocks mark the Manix fault zone between tan sedimentary layers of Miocene age on the east (right) against gently dipping, brown gravel beds of Pleistocene age on the west (left) at Call Box SB 15 917. (34°55.78N, 116°43.24W)
—Elizabeth O'Black Gans photo

North of the rest stop (exit 217), the squat, steep hill is pre-Mesozoic gneissic quartz diorite with northwest-dipping foliation. It is intruded by Jurassic granitic rocks. The intrusions are parts of a regional suite of Jurassic plutonic rocks making up much of the vast Fort Irwin National Training Center and the jagged Tiefort Mountains along the north skyline.

The dark gray hills south of the highway between Harvard and Afton Roads are the north end of the Cady Mountains, consisting of andesite breccia overlying Jurassic metavolcanic rocks that resemble the Sidewinder Volcanics.

Afton Canyon

One of the few places where the Mojave River flows on the surface year-round is in scenic Afton Canyon, called by some the Grand Canyon of the Mojave. As at Barstow and the Mojave Narrows in Victorville, impermeable bedrock is close to the surface so that the water is forced to flow aboveground, instead of percolating through porous sand and gravel below the surface.

At Afton Road (exit 221), 33 miles east of Barstow, a good gravel road heads south about 3 miles to the Mojave River and the scenic trestles that carry the railroad over it. The first half mile of the gravel road lies directly upon a beach bar built along the east shore of Pleistocene Lake Manix, 18,000 to 10,000 years ago. To get a good idea of the great extent and depth of the ancient lake, notice how high the beach bar is relative to the lake basin to the west. The lake level stayed high long enough for this beach bar to be built.

Two miles farther southeast along the gravel road is the first of three railroad trestles and the entrance to colorful Afton Canyon. Hydrothermal alteration of the volcanic rocks causes the variegated coloring. The spectacularly rugged cliffs of Pleistocene gravel layers are characteristic of badlands topography.

The Manix fault lies along the north side of 8-mile-long Afton Canyon, with left-slip displacement estimated to be as much as 5 miles. The zone of faulting is about 16 miles long and at least one-half mile wide. It produced a magnitude 6.5 earthquake in 1947. Up until 1992, that was the largest earthquake recorded

These rounded pebbles indicate that they achieved their flat shape when they sloshed back and forth on a Lake Manix beach. (35°04.15N, 116°24.65W)

The Manix fault separates gray sedimentary rocks (at left) from brown and reddish-brown alluvial deposits (at right) about a half mile downstream from Afton Canyon Campground. (35°02.3N, 116°22.5W)

in the Mojave Desert and the first to produce a surface rupture, even though the 2-inch-maximum, left-slip displacement was not especially noteworthy.

Cave Mountain

Cave Mountain (elevation 3,624 feet) is the brown, pyramidal peak on the south side of I-15, about 4 miles east of the Afton Canyon exit. The rocks in the Cave Mountain area are gneiss, biotite schist, marble, and Jurassic metavolcanic rocks, all intruded by Cretaceous granite. The different rock types cannot be easily distinguished because of a brown patina of desert varnish that completely coats the rocks. The highway follows the northwest front of Cave Mountain, where geologists have mapped a fault. Another fault is north of the highway along the steep, southeast front of Cronise Mountains.

Cronise Valley and the Cronise Cat

North of Rasor Road (exit 233), the Cronise Mountains consist of brown, desert-varnished Mesozoic granite. On their southeast flank, a small canyon is filled with a uniquely shaped sand dune having the profile of a cat sitting on its haunches, its tail hanging down and its ears perked up. Prevailing westerly winds, with occasional velocities close to 100 miles per hour, drive sand eastward to the top of the Cronise Mountains, forming climbing dunes on the mountains' northwest side. Wind carries sand over the ridge into Cronise Valley, but some of the sand is caught in a gulch on the southeast slope of the ridge and accumulates as the Cat, a falling dune. The Cat is best viewed westbound on the downgrade between Rasor Road and Basin Road (exit 230).

The source of the sand for both the climbing and falling dunes is Cronise Lake playa, west of Cronise Mountains. The sand accumulated in beaches there during high-water stands in Pleistocene time. The sand consists mostly of frosted quartz grains, with lesser amounts of feldspar and broken freshwater

Cave Mountain, which is covered with brown desert varnish, can be seen for many miles in all directions. (35°04.2N, 116°19.4W)

The Cronise Cat, a sand dune on the southeast side of the Cronise Mountains, formed when westerly winds carried sand east over the ridge crest. (35°07.2N, 116°18.0W)

clam and gastropod shells. Climbing dunes consist of medium-sized grains that are less coarse upslope, whereas falling dunes are composed of smaller grains that remain constant in size throughout their downslope extent.

Zzyzx and Soda Lake

In the 1940s, "Doc" Curtis Howe Springer developed a pond and operated a health resort around a spring on the west side of Soda Lake, which is usually a dry playa. He named it Zzyzx so it would be the last word in the English language. Now the oasis is home to the Desert Studies Center, a field station of the California State University operated under an agreement with the Bureau of Land Management. From exit 239 on I-15, Zzyzx Road goes south for about 5 miles over short, steep alluvial fans that interfinger with salty evaporite deposits of Soda Lake playa right along the road's edge. The black rocks along the road are dark gray-green metamorphosed volcanic breccia of Mesozoic age.

East of the Zzyzx Road exit, I-15 begins a 5-mile-long downgrade on late Pleistocene and Holocene alluvial fans to the settlement of Baker. Off to the southeast is a fine view across Soda Lake playa to the light brown sand of Devils Playground and beyond it to the Providence and Granite Mountains on the skyline. Soda Lake playa was the lakebed of Lake Mojave, which existed approximately 22,000 to 8,500 years ago. The Mojave River and its tributaries bring clastic and chemical sediment from the San Bernardino Mountains and the western Mojave Desert to the lakebed. In some wet years, the lake is entirely flooded, and when it dries up, white salt veneers the floor of the playa.

Prevailing northwest winds pick up the fine-grained sand and blow it into the Devils Playground and beyond. See the road guide for Kelbaker Road in this chapter to learn about geologic sights and sites south of Baker.

Permian Fossils at Baker

Most of the rocks between Cave Mountain and Baker are Mesozoic granitic rocks and Jurassic metavolcanic rocks pretty well obscured by desert varnish. The first undoubted Paleozoic sedimentary rocks, which are probably westward extensions of rocks in the Grand Canyon, are pervasively faulted, gray limestone outcrops in Nickel Mountain (previously called Baker Hill), adjacent to the frontage road 1 mile west of Baker. The hill resembles a honeycomb because of the numerous cavities formed by dissolution of the limestone. Search the limestone carefully to find fossil corals that are evidence of the Permian age and marine origin of the rocks.

INTERSTATE 15
BAKER—PRIMM, NEVADA
51 miles

A 2-mile-long basalt lava flow of Pleistocene age borders the north side of the long uphill grade east of Baker between Halloran Springs (exit 259) and Halloran Summit (exit 265). Its source is a cone-shaped volcanic plug at the east end of the flow about 2 miles west of Halloran Summit. Although basalt talus covers most of the slope, near and beneath the west end of the flow you can see that the lava flowed upon thin-bedded, tan sandstone and siltstone. Here at Halloran Springs, resistant lava flows and cinder cones protected the

View east across I-15 of the Halloran Springs basalt lava flow that erupted from the conelike volcanic neck above the vehicles near the right edge of the image. (35°23.9N, 115°55.6W)

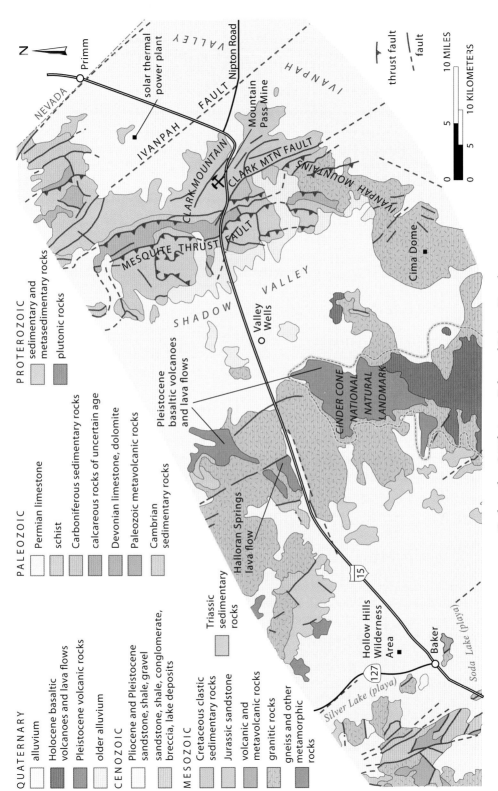

QUATERNARY

alluvium

Holocene basaltic
volcanoes and lava flows

Pleistocene volcanic rocks

older alluvium

CENOZOIC

Pliocene and Pleistocene
sandstone, shale, gravel

sandstone, shale, conglomerate,
breccia, lake deposits

MESOZOIC

Cretaceous clastic
sedimentary rocks

Jurassic sandstone

volcanic and
metavolcanic rocks

granitic rocks

gneiss and other
metamorphic
rocks

Triassic
sedimentary
rocks

PALEOZOIC

Permian limestone

schist

Carboniferous sedimentary rocks

calcareous rocks of uncertain age

Devonian limestone, dolomite

Paleozoic metavolcanic rocks

Cambrian
sedimentary
rocks

Pleistocene basaltic
volcanoes and lava flows

PROTEROZOIC

sedimentary and
metasedimentary rocks

plutonic rocks

thrust fault

fault

0   5   10 MILES

0   5   10 KILOMETERS

Geology along I-15 between Baker and Primm, Nevada.

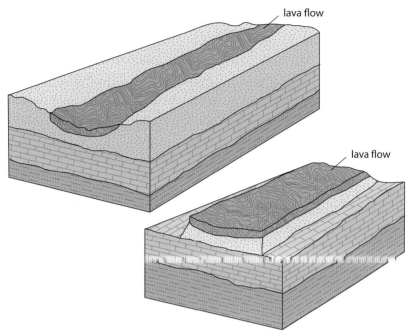

Lava flowed down a stream channel and hardened into rock that resists erosion and protects the softer rocks beneath it. As rocks adjacent to the lava flow erode away, a ridge or mesa of lava is left perched upon soft rocks of the former channel, a process called topographic inversion.

softer, underlying rocks and old soils from erosion, leaving behind lava-capped mesas and volcanic hills perched atop granite and alluvium. The Halloran Springs lava flow is an example of topographic inversion, where lava that once filled a valley now forms a ridge. Erosion in the last 5 million years or so has lowered the land surface in this part of the Mojave Desert a few hundred feet.

Cima Dome

Cima Dome is a low, 72-square-mile, gently sloping, almost perfectly symmetrical dome of alluvium and granite visible from the rest stop in Shadow Valley and reached by driving about 10 miles south of I-15 on Cima Road (exit 272). One of the largest and most symmetrical domal features in the United States, it rises 1,500 feet above the surface and has a small peak on it: Teutonia Peak (elevation 5,755 feet). The dome is made of granite of the Teutonia Batholith, one of the larger Jurassic to Cretaceous granitic complexes in the eastern Mojave Desert. It crops out over 1,200 square miles and consists of seven separate plutons.

Erosional forces of sun, wind, rain, and chemical decomposition have worked away for eons at this solid, homogeneous granite mountain, stripping away its cover rocks and reducing the old pluton to its present dome shape. Because the coarse granitic rock disintegrates rapidly and uniformly to gravel, or grus, in desert conditions, the perfection of the dome reflects the homogeneity of the underlying bedrock.

View south of Cima Dome, the slight rise on the horizon. Teutonia Peak is on its northeast (left) flank. (35°17.2N, 115°34.8W)

Mountain Pass Rare Earth Element Mine

From Shadow Valley, I-15 climbs a long grade through gray Paleozoic limestone and a forest of Joshua trees up to Mountain Pass (elevation 4,638 feet) at the south end of Clark Mountain. It is the highest point on I-15 between Barstow and Las Vegas, Nevada. There, Molybdenum Corporation of America has a large open-pit quarry in one of the largest known rare earth deposits in the world.

Most of the rare earth mineralization is restricted to carbonate-rich intrusions known as carbonatites within a northwest-trending, fault-bounded block of strongly foliated Proterozoic schist, gneiss, and migmatite. These rocks are

Aerial view of open-pit mining operations at Mountain Pass. The main rare earth ore body, discovered in 1949, is about 2,300 feet long and 200 feet thick, dipping about 50 degrees within the gneissic host rocks. (35°28.7N, 115°31.9W)

splendidly exposed in highway roadcuts between the pass summit and eastward to the point where the highway broadly curves northward and down into Ivanpah Valley. Ages of the metamorphic rocks exceed 1,730 million years. The younger intrusive rocks include granite, carbonatite, syenite (an orthoclase feldspar–rich rock), and shonkinite (a dark-colored, feldspar-rich rock with olivine, hornblende, and biotite), all about 1,400 million years old.

The ore body consists of 60 percent carbonate, 20 percent sulfates, 10 percent rare earth minerals, and 10 percent of other minerals. Bastnaesite, the principal rare earth mineral at Mountain Pass, contains varying amounts of the fifteen chemical elements known as rare earth or lanthanide elements. The main rare earth elements in the Mountain Pass bastnaesite are cerium, lanthanum, neodymium, praseodymium, samarium, gadolinium, and europium, all of which are used in color TV tubes, catalysts, computer components, petroleum refining, camera lenses, and magnets, and for the production of specialized glasses. In all, about forty different minerals have been cataloged in the Mountain Pass rocks.

Ivanpah Valley and Solar Energy

From Mountain Pass, I-15 descends east and then north down a steep grade into Ivanpah Valley, with its long playa. A couple miles west of the highway, shimmering like a desert mirage, is the Ivanpah Solar Electric Generating System. Reflected sunlight from 347,000 computer-controlled mirrors, each about the size of a garage door, focuses solar energy to enormous boilers atop three centralized towers. Water in the boilers is heated to 1,000°F to create high-temperature steam, which is then piped to a conventional turbine to generate electricity.

The low hills west and north of the solar power facility are gently folded limestone beds of late Paleozoic age. The Nevada border is located unmistakably at Primm.

Aerial view of Ivanpah Solar Electric Generating System, the largest of its kind in the world. The plant has a capacity of 377 megawatts, enough to provide the electrical needs of 140,000 homes. (35°32.1N, 115°37.1W)

INTERSTATE 40
Barstow—Needles
148 miles

The eastern Mojave Desert is a vast area of relatively uninhabited desert mountain ranges that rise in places over 1 mile above broad, extensive valleys. On hazy days, the distant mountains look like fog-shrouded warships plowing through a smoky sea. The military made extensive use of this region in World War II, not for naval exercises, but for preparation for desert warfare in North Africa. The scars of tank tracks are still visible in places, and some areas are contaminated with military waste. Over 2,350 square miles of the Mojave Desert are still claimed and used for military activities.

Nearly all of the mountains in the eastern Mojave Desert have a core of Proterozoic metamorphic rocks capped by or associated with Neogene volcanic rocks. Paleozoic marine sedimentary rocks, in places metamorphosed by Mesozoic granitic plutons, prevail in the Providence Mountains north of I-40 and the Marble Mountains south of I-40. Several young basaltic volcanoes also lie in the low area along Route 66 from Ludlow to Amboy, suggesting they may have erupted along a fault zone.

Route 66 and I-40 diverge at Ludlow, with a maintained stretch of US 66 following lowlands and springs across a stretch of desert mountains and valleys, whereas I-40 plows straight east, cutting only about 9 miles from the older Route 66.

Daggett Area

Daggett was a railroad camp and busy depot for the Calico mines in the late nineteenth century. Early motorists described Daggett as the worst place between New York and Mojave. From 1982 to 1986 it was home to an experimental solar thermal energy plant, still marked by two tall towers. A modern plant is now in operation adjacent to the old plant and is visible from the highway. A large US Marine Corps supply depot is also located at Daggett.

Elephant Mountain (elevation 2,674 feet) is a long, low, brown mesa a half mile north of Daggett and north of I-40. It consists of the same kind of Miocene-age dacite as is found in the several volcanic plugs in and around Barstow. Isolated dark patches of volcanic boulders, cobbles, and sand of Neogene age south of I-40 are surrounded by younger Quaternary alluvium between Daggett and Newberry Springs.

Newberry Springs and Newberry Mountains

The hamlet of Newberry Springs is located at the north end of the Newberry Mountains and on the west edge of Troy Lake playa. The springs are prolific and supply a large groundwater basin that augments the subsurface Mojave River. Wells tap the basin and provide water for over three hundred man-made lakes nearby. Several of the lakes are public recreation resorts, some are private, and others are catfish farms. In the old days, a train with twenty tank cars carried water from here to desert settlements between Newberry Springs and Needles.

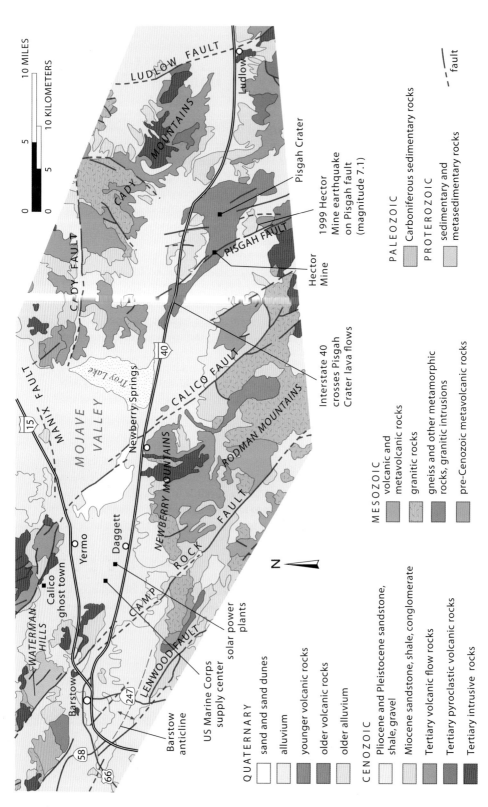

QUATERNARY

sand and sand dunes

alluvium

younger volcanic rocks

older volcanic rocks

older alluvium

CENOZOIC

Pliocene and Pleistocene sandstone, shale, gravel

Miocene sandstone, shale, conglomerate

Tertiary volcanic flow rocks

Tertiary pyroclastic volcanic rocks

Tertiary intrusive rocks

MESOZOIC

volcanic and metavolcanic rocks

granitic rocks

gneiss and other metamorphic rocks, granitic intrusions

pre-Cenozoic metavolcanic rocks

PALEOZOIC

Carboniferous sedimentary rocks

PROTEROZOIC

sedimentary and metasedimentary rocks

fault

Geology along I-40 between Barstow and Ludlow. See the map on page 65 for the section between Ludlow and Fenner.

The Newberry Mountains contain a thick, southwest-dipping, layered pile of andesite, tuff breccia, basalt, and fanglomerate of Miocene age. These rocks are faulted against a biotite granite pluton of Jurassic age that was quarried for gold at the Azucar Mine.

The Calico fault lies along the northeast base of the Newberry Mountains and strikes northwest across Troy Lake playa to the Calico Mountains. The highway crosses its surface trace about 1 mile east of the town site. Several little, isolated basaltic outcrops, including Black Butte (elevation 1,978 feet), about 2 miles north-northwest of Newberry Springs, cooled from magma that erupted along the fault.

Pisgah Crater

One of the youngest volcanoes in the Mojave Desert is Pisgah Crater, a Holocene-age cinder cone with a crater in its center. It is one of the several basaltic cinder cones and associated lava flows between Barstow and Amboy in the Lavic Lake Volcanic Field. At the rest stop 10 miles east of Newberry Springs, I-40 crosses Pisgah Crater's longest lava flow, which erupted and flowed 10 miles westward from the main cone. Except for some windblown sand upon it here and there, the flow looks as though it erupted yesterday.

You may drive into the lava field and near the edge of the cone by exiting I-40 at Hector Road (exit 33) and driving east about 5 miles on the National Trails

Viewed from I-40, Pisgah Crater is not especially remarkable because its red and black cinders have been extensively quarried for many years, thereby lowering and shrinking the cone. Cinders are used for road metal, railroad ballast, lawn substitutes, lightweight concrete aggregate, and barbeque bottom liners. (34°44.7N, 116°22.5W)

Highway (Route 66) to an unmaintained paved road, marked by a large black boulder, and then south about 1.5 miles to a locked gate. A hike farther south to the cone and east into the lava field will reveal many of the classic forms of lava, including aa with its rough and clinkery surfaces, and the smoother, ropy lava called pahoehoe. Lava tubes, long caves within flows that formed as magma exited the interior of the flows, are abundant; some are large enough to drive a freight train through. You'll also see lava vents with hardened spatter, hornitos, and tumuli, unique features that cool from erupted magma. Use caution on the hike: be aware that lava surfaces are uneven, rough, and jagged, especially the aa flows; mind the heat, particularly in the summer; and carry water.

A quarrying operation has obliterated half of the crater in the center of the cinder cone, but the central vent in the crater can be explored, and the northeast wall of the crater is still intact. Close inspection reveals that lava flows issued from the central vent, from beneath the cinder cone, and from many smaller vents east of the main cone. The size, type, and abundance of mineral crystals visible in the lava reveal three episodes of eruption. Assuming magma erupted periodically from a single magma chamber, then lava with the smallest crystals represents the oldest eruption, and that with the largest crystals resided the longest in the magma chamber before the last eruption, about 20,000 years ago.

The high, rugged, varicolored mountains north and northeast of Pisgah Crater are the Cady Mountains, the southeast lobe of which is Sleeping Beauty (elevation 3,979 feet). This desolate mountain range is a heterogeneous assemblage of andesitic and dacitic flows and flow breccia, volcaniclastic sedimentary rocks, and shallow intrusions, all intruded into and deposited upon weathered Mesozoic granite. The volcanic rocks erupted about 20 million years ago during the switch from subduction to transform fault tectonics along the California coast.

South of Pisgah Crater and Ludlow are the Lava Bed and Bullion Mountains, home to the very large and quite inaccessible Twentynine Palms Marine Corps Air Ground Combat Center, one of several regionally extensive military training areas in the Mojave and Colorado Deserts.

Hectorite at the Hector Mine

An open-pit quarry 3 miles west of Pisgah Crater is the only known economic deposit in the world of hectorite, a lithium-bearing, gel-forming type of bentonitic clay with a consistency almost like candle wax. In any application where bentonite is used, hectorite generally performs the same function with better efficiency. Refined hectorite is especially well suited for cosmetic and pharmaceutical applications and the brewing of beer.

At Hector the mineral occurs in volcanic ash beds interbedded with playa lake sediments and travertine chert, all deposited in an elongate fault zone trough in late Neogene time. The ash beds are overlain by Holocene-age basaltic lava flows from nearby Pisgah Crater. Deposition of the ash was contemporaneous with extensive hot spring activity that provided the heat and lithium-rich solutions to alter the ash to glassy tuff. The mine and the road to it are closed to the public.

1999 Hector Mine Earthquake

A magnitude 7.1 earthquake rumbled through the Hector area in the early morning hours of October 16, 1999. It's called the Hector Mine earthquake because the mine is the only named geographic feature near the surface rupture in this part of the Mojave Desert. The earthquake triggered minor landslides and caused cracking and displacements on the Pisgah Crater cinder cone. The surface rupture extended south-southeast from Pisgah Crater into the Twentynine Palms Marine Corps training center. A small group of geologists, coordinated by the US Geological Survey with permission from and accompanied by the marines, documented a 26-mile-long surface rupture with a maximum of 17 feet of right-slip along the Lavic Lake fault and the central part of the Bullion fault. Damage was minimal, other than a derailed Amtrak train because, as you can see, there are no structures to damage here.

The principal lessons learned from the earthquake are not only that many faults in the Mojave Desert must be considered as potentially active, capable of producing moderate to major earthquakes at any time, but also that the transform plate motion between the Pacific and North American Plates is not concentrated solely on the San Andreas fault but extends across a broad zone well into the Mojave Desert (see the map of faults on page 27).

Ludlow

Ludlow was, and still is, a gas station and restaurant stop for I-40 and Route 66 motorists. It was the terminus for the Tonopah & Tidewater Railroad, which brought mineral wealth, mainly borax, from Death Valley and nearby mining districts in eastern California. From its junction with the Atchison, Topeka & Santa Fe Railroad at Ludlow, the T&T went north past Zzyzx, across Soda Lake playa, through Baker, past Silver Lake playa, up Silurian Valley to the Amargosa River, and on to Beatty and Rhyolite, Nevada, near Death Valley, before completing its 200-mile odyssey to Goldfield and Tonopah, Nevada. It was abandoned in 1940 and torn up for scrap in 1942. Such is the sad history of many mining railroads in the Mojave.

Ludlow is situated on the Ludlow fault, another northwest-striking, right-slip fault in the Mojave. Broken-up rock along the fault probably forms a subsurface barrier to groundwater flow and accounts for the presence of springs at the town site. Rocks in the mountains north and south of Ludlow are Miocene dacite that may be related to the volcanic plugs in Barstow and at Elephant Butte near Daggett.

About 32 miles east of Ludlow, Kelbaker Road heads north from I-40 and passes many interesting geologic sights. See the guide for Kelbaker Road in this chapter.

Sacramento Mountains

East of Fenner, I-40 cuts across the north end of the Sacramento Mountains and skirts the south end of the Dead Mountains, both of which expose dark Proterozoic gneiss. Alluvial fans dissected by streams flank the east sides of the mountains. A detachment fault in the central Sacramento Mountains separates a lower plate of mylonitized crystalline gneiss and plutonic rocks of Proterozoic to Mesozoic age from an upper plate of Neogene-age sedimentary and volcanic rocks. The rock types and structural relationships are similar to those in the Whipple and Chemehuevi Mountains to the south, discussed in the road guide for US 95 in this chapter.

The Bigelow Cholla Garden Wilderness Area contains the densest concentration of Bigelow cholla cactus in California's Mojave Desert. It covers nearly 24 square miles in the northern Sacramento Mountains 19 miles west of Needles. This distinctive spiny cactus, known as teddy bear or jumping cholla, has a golden-spined cluster of jointed stems perched atop a tall stalk covered with old black spines. The spines are numerous, sharp, and painfully hard to extract, so keep your distance! You won't see much of the wilderness from I-40, so take the western US 95 exit (exit 133) and follow the dirt road south for about 200 feet. Turn right to access the Four Corners Pipeline and travel south along the west boundary of the wilderness.

Upon entering the town of Needles, look south across the Colorado River to the Mohave Mountains in Arizona to see a group of pointed Neogene volcanic rocks that give Needles its name.

US ROUTE 66
LUDLOW—FENNER
58 miles

If you are simply out for a historic and leisurely outing rather than a mad dash across the Mojave on one of the interstates, then "travel my way, take the highway that's the best. Get your kicks on Route Sixty-Six." Bobby Troup wrote those lyrics in 1946 about the "Main Street of America" and the "Mother Road" used by Midwesterners fleeing the Dust Bowl in the 1930s. Called the National Trails Highway today, Route 66 followed the Atchison, Topeka, & Santa Fe Railroad from Chicago to Santa Monica in southern California. Parts of the highway are obscure, realigned, or simply obliterated, especially through many towns and cities. Some of its best-preserved parts are in the Mojave Desert, although even there much of the original route was realigned in the early 1930s. The route through the Mojave followed a string of springs where steam locomotives obtained water. Tourist services sprang up at those water stops when the highway was put through, but the introduction of diesel locomotives and construction of I-40 from Ludlow to Fenner caused the settlements along that segment of Route 66 to become ghost towns or conglomerations of vandalized garages and gas stations, dilapidated shacks, rusted shells of automobiles, and assorted rubbish. They were never really towns but merely shady spots on the desert route.

The best place to pick up Route 66 when traveling east is at the California Route 66 Museum in Old Town Victorville, at the corner of Sixth and D Streets. There you will be able to procure all sorts of guidebooks, memorabilia, and trinkets. For geologic information between Victorville and Barstow, see the road guide in this chapter for I-15. For information between Barstow and Ludlow, see the guide for I-40.

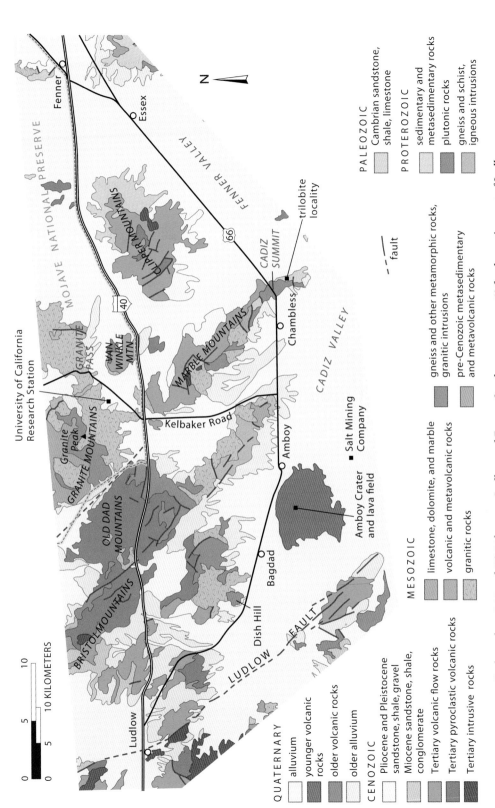

Geology along I-40 and US 66 between Ludlow and Fenner. See the map on page 60 for the section west of Ludlow.

QUATERNARY
- alluvium
- younger volcanic rocks
- older volcanic rocks
- older alluvium

CENOZOIC
- Pliocene and Pleistocene sandstone, shale, gravel
- Miocene sandstone, shale, conglomerate
- Tertiary volcanic flow rocks
- Tertiary pyroclastic volcanic rocks
- Tertiary intrusive rocks

MESOZOIC
- limestone, dolomite, and marble
- volcanic and metavolcanic rocks
- granitic rocks

gneiss and other metamorphic rocks, granitic intrusions

pre-Cenozoic metasedimentary and metavolcanic rocks

PALEOZOIC
- Cambrian sandstone, shale, limestone

PROTEROZOIC
- sedimentary and metasedimentary rocks
- plutonic rocks
- gneiss and schist, igneous intrusions

- - - fault

■ trilobite locality

N

MOJAVE NATIONAL PRESERVE

Fenner

Essex

CLIPPER MOUNTAINS

FENNER VALLEY

66

40

GRANITE PASS

VAN WINKLE MTN

University of California Research Station

Granite Peak

GRANITE MOUNTAINS

MARBLE MOUNTAINS

CADIZ SUMMIT

Chambless

CADIZ VALLEY

Kelbaker Road

Amboy

Salt Mining Company

OLD DAD MOUNTAINS

Amboy Crater and lava field

BRISTOL MOUNTAINS

Bagdad

Dish Hill

LUDLOW FAULT

Ludlow

0 5 10 KILOMETERS
0 5 10

Dish Hill

Dish Hill, also known as Siberia Crater, is a large brown cinder cone 16.5 miles east of Ludlow on the north side of Route 66. Although not as classic in shape or as prominent in the landscape as Amboy or Pisgah Crater, Dish Hill is famous for its volcanic bombs that contain granite from the upper crust and olivine-rich rocks from the Earth's upper mantle. The basaltic magma picked up these rocks on its way to the surface. When the volcano erupted, the magma congealed around the bombs as they flew through the air. You may find shiny, jet-black crystal fragments and flakes of the mineral kaersutite, a calcium titanium–bearing amphibole from the upper mantle and deep crust. It and the olivine-rich rocks are scattered on the alluvium on the south side of the volcano. A short gravel road leads northward from the highway to a parking area adjacent to a wash crossed by a railroad bridge. Walk under the bridge to gain access to the alluvial fan and the volcano.

Amboy Crater

Amboy Crater is a nearly circular basaltic volcano and prominent landmark on Bristol Lake playa, 25 miles east of Ludlow. It is such a prototypical volcanic cinder cone that when some pranksters ignited automobile tires in the crater one day, passing motorists and locals at Amboy saw the black smoke and were sure Amboy was erupting. No geologist would be surprised if it did erupt again at any time, and if it did, just imagine the chaos caused by the convergence of news media, off-road vehicle enthusiasts, and scientists!

The 250-foot-high cone and lava field are easily reached by a 1.5-mile-long trail that starts at a parking lot where some information plaques give conflicting information. The bronze BLM plaque says the volcano had six eruptive episodes, the last one being 500 years ago, but that is a misprint; it should say 5,000 years. The stainless steel plaque, on the other hand, says only four eruptive episodes occurred and the most recent was about 10,000 years ago, also not correct.

View to the north of Dish Hill, a young, horseshoe-shaped volcano, opening to the northwest. (34°36.7N, 115°56.7W)

Both aa and pahoehoe lava flows cover about 28 square miles around Amboy Crater. Amboy Crater's lava flows issued from the base of the cone and rafted away part of its west side. Some of the lava flows reach the highway, where you'll see that the basalt contains small crystals of olivine and plagioclase that make up about 5 percent of the rock. You may need a hand lens to see the 1- to 2-millimeter-diameter, pale-greenish olivine crystals and the glassy white, 2- to 3-millimeter-long crystals of plagioclase, both set in black glass. The volcano has four nested cinder cones in the main crater, with evidence of having erupted as much as 80,000 years ago.

Amboy is another one of the former water stops for the railroad and motorists. Gasoline, food, and lodging may or may not be available when you pass through the settlement. North of Amboy is the south end of the Bristol

Aerial view of Amboy Crater. It has the classic form of a volcanic cinder cone, and it has escaped the ravages of quarrying that occurred at Pisgah Crater. (34°32.7N, 115°47.4W)

Mountains, a faulted complex of Proterozoic metamorphic rocks intruded by Mesozoic granitic rocks and overlain by Neogene volcanic rocks.

Amboy Road leads south from Amboy across Bristol Lake playa, through Sheep Hole Pass to Dale Lake, and eventually to CA 62 at Twentynine Palms. Salt is harvested at Bristol Lake. Tepee-like piles of mud dot its surface along several long, water-filled salt evaporation ponds. Brine solutions are pumped from wells on the lakebed into the ponds, where the water evaporates, leaving behind the salt. Some 60 million tons of salt are still in reserve at this location.

Cambrian Trilobites in the Marble Mountains

Chambless, about 10 miles east of Amboy, is another former Route 66 watering stop that was pretty well deserted when cut off by I-40. The Marble Mountains, a few miles east of Chambless, are part of the federally protected Trilobite Wilderness. Fossiliferous sedimentary rocks of early Cambrian age were deposited in a shallow sea on an eroded surface of Proterozoic granite. Some of the Cambrian shale beds contain fossils of trilobites, which were small, hard-shelled crustaceans that resembled today's horseshoe crabs. Twelve species of trilobites have been found in the Latham Shale.

Route 66 crosses the Marble Mountains 3 miles east of Chambless, at Cadiz Summit, where roadcuts expose Proterozoic granite near the ruins of the Beacon Motel. A few miles southeast of the Marble Mountains, the Ship Mountains consist largely of Mesozoic granite.

Cambrian sedimentary rocks on the west side of the Marble Mountains. The oldest Cambrian sedimentary unit, the dark brown Prospect Mountain Quartzite, is overlain by reddish-gray, green, and gray Latham Shale. Overlying the shale is the gray, striped Chambless Limestone, the layer with eroded holes about halfway up the mountain. (34°35.2N, 115°31.5W)

Heads of trilobites, such as Mesonacis, *are common in the early Cambrian Latham Shale in the Marble Mountains; complete specimens as long as 8 inches have been collected here but are exceedingly rare. This is a complete, 3-inch-long specimen.* —Richie Kurkewicz photo

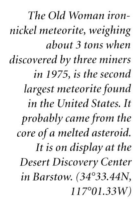

The Old Woman iron-nickel meteorite, weighing about 3 tons when discovered by three miners in 1975, is the second largest meteorite found in the United States. It probably came from the core of a melted asteroid. It is on display at the Desert Discovery Center in Barstow. (34°33.44N, 117°01.33W)

Fenner Valley

From Cadiz Summit to Fenner, Route 66 follows the Fenner Valley, one of the loneliest and driest parts of the Mojave Desert, interrupted only by a water stop at Essex. Founded by a fellow after his car broke down here, Essex lies almost at the geographic center of General George Patton's immense World War II Desert Training Center. The Fenner Valley is bounded on the northwest by the Clipper Mountains, which contain mostly Neogene volcanic rocks overlying Proterozoic rocks, and on the southeast by the north end of the Old Woman Mountains, so named because from some vantage points the profile of a peak resembles that of an old woman. Like so many other ranges in this part of the eastern Mojave Desert, the Old Woman Mountains consist of complex Proterozoic rocks intruded by Mesozoic granite.

The Piute Mountains, east of Essex, are a wild mountain range of mostly Proterozoic rocks that Route 66 crosses at Mountain Springs Summit (elevation 2,756 feet). You may join I-40 here or continue northeast along Route 66 to Goffs, another railroad water stop and siding. Notice the inselbergs, or granite knobs, protruding above the alluvium north of Goffs, all part of a large tract of Mesozoic granite in the Fenner Hills and other hills to the north.

Dead Mountains

Route 66 intersects US 95 at Arrowhead Junction, 15 miles east of Goffs. Dead ahead are the Dead Mountains, with their core of Proterozoic metamorphic rocks flanked on the west by Neogene red beds. These sedimentary rocks, mostly sandstone and siltstone well exposed along the highway southeast of Arrowhead Junction, are colored red by oxidation of iron-bearing minerals. A detachment fault, a low-angle normal fault caused by stretching of the Earth's crust, encircles the Dead Mountains at just about the break in slope, separating the Proterozoic rocks of the mountain core from the Neogene red beds on its flanks.

US 95
Blythe—Needles
97 miles

The California segment of US 95 between Blythe and Needles and beyond to Boulder City near Hoover Dam lies within a region called the Colorado River Extensional Corridor, which stretches over an area of 11,600 square miles, straddling the Colorado River in adjacent parts of Nevada, Arizona, and California. Many mountain ranges in this region contain geologic structures that formed during widespread crustal stretching in Miocene time. The stretching was so severe that rocks in the middle to lower crust were transported to surface levels along nearly flat-lying normal faults called detachment faults. Several mountain ranges, including the Whipple and Chemehuevi Mountains along US 95, are classic for their displays of detachment fault tectonics.

Blythe Intaglios

A pilot flying east of the Big Maria Mountains between Blythe and Las Vegas in 1931 noticed a group of gigantic figures outlined on the surface of two low mesas about 15 miles north of downtown Blythe and about 1 mile west of US 95 (PM 15.4). Since then, more than two hundred images, called intaglios or geoglyphs, have been discovered along the Colorado River from Nevada to the Gulf of California, and more than six hundred are known in the southwestern United States and nearby parts of Mexico. Their purpose and age are not known. They could range from 450 to 10,000 years old. Many have withstood the test of wind, rain, and time; others have fallen recent victim to motorcycles, SUVs, highway construction, and General Patton's tank-training exercises during World War II. The Blythe intaglios are protected today by a rather rough gravel road between two lines of fences and are open to the public at all times.

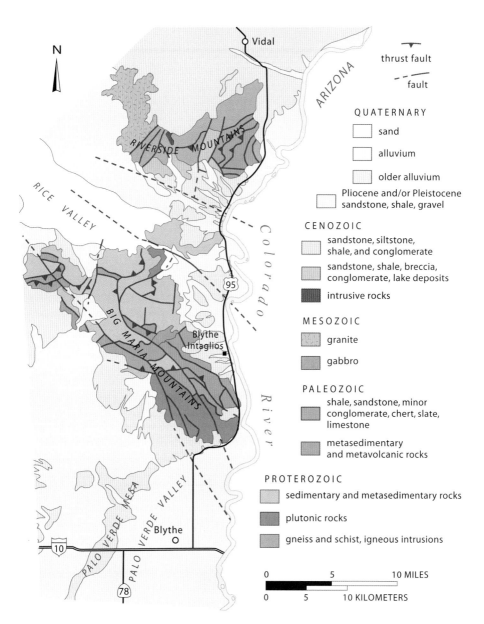

N

Vidal

ARIZONA

thrust fault

fault

QUATERNARY

sand

alluvium

older alluvium

Pliocene and/or Pleistocene
sandstone, shale, gravel

CENOZOIC

sandstone, siltstone,
shale, and conglomerate

sandstone, shale, breccia,
conglomerate, lake deposits

intrusive rocks

MESOZOIC

granite

gabbro

PALEOZOIC

shale, sandstone, minor
conglomerate, chert, slate,
limestone

metasedimentary
and metavolcanic rocks

PROTEROZOIC

sedimentary and metasedimentary rocks

plutonic rocks

gneiss and schist, igneous intrusions

RIVERSIDE MOUNTAINS

RICE VALLEY

Colorado

95

Blythe
Intaglios

BIG MARIA MOUNTAINS

River

PALO VERDE MESA

PALO VERDE VALLEY

Blythe

10

78

| 0 | | 5 | | 10 MILES |

| 0 | 5 | 10 KILOMETERS |

*Geology along US 95 between Blythe and Vidal. See map
on page 75 for route north of Vidal.*

Aerial image of one of the largest Blythe intaglios, a 171-foot-long human male. To create the intaglios, people scraped away the dark brown layer of desert pavement to reveal the tan, sandy soil beneath. Tire tracks indicate scale. (33°48.0N, 114°31.9W)

Big Maria and Riverside Mountains

Two of the most geologically complicated ranges in the Mojave Desert are the Big Maria and Riverside Mountains, both of which lie west of US 95 and the Colorado River between Blythe and Vidal. The Big Maria Mountains are mostly wilderness terrain that varies from gently sloping alluvial fans to many rough, craggy peaks bounded by steep, rugged canyons. The toes of the alluvial fans are truncated where they meet the Colorado River, such as near PM 21.4. The river flows south through Parker Valley and erodes Proterozoic bedrock of the Big Maria Mountains in places, such as near PM 24. Dune sand is piled up on the north end of the range.

The Big Maria Mountains consist of folded Paleozoic-age marble and dolomite in complex thrust relationships with Proterozoic gneiss and granite. Rocks in limbs of some of the folds were thinned by ductile flow to within 10 percent of their original thicknesses during their metamorphism about 75 million years ago at a peak temperature of 1,000°F deep in the Earth's crust. The folds trend east-west and reflect north-south crustal squeezing of the North American craton. Most crustal squeezing elsewhere in western North America was east-west, however, caused by Farallon Plate subduction beneath the North American Plate in Mesozoic time. In the Big Maria Mountains two large synclines verge south-southeast and are cross-folded by many tight recumbent folds. Late Neogene strike-slip faults are common throughout the range.

The sedimentary rocks in the Big Maria and Riverside Mountains, although metamorphosed, correlate with Paleozoic and Mesozoic sedimentary rock layers in the Grand Canyon, which were deposited along the edge of the North American craton. Classic formations, such as the Hermit Shale, Coconino Sandstone, and Kaibab Limestone, occur here in their metamorphosed forms. Triassic and Jurassic metasedimentary and metavolcanic strata, also intruded by Middle or Late Jurassic granitic rocks, are widespread in the Big Maria Mountains. You may collect nice hand samples of white marble, tan quartzite, black amphibolite, gray granite, white quartz, and green epidote in several of the big washes that flow east out of the Big Maria Mountains to US 95 between PM 17 and PM 22, about 18 miles north of Blythe.

Aerial view east along the axis of the syncline in the rugged Big Maria Mountains with the Colorado River valley in the background. The colorful stratigraphic section near the left edge of the image contains highly metamorphosed and deformed rocks correlated with the classic section of Paleozoic strata in the Grand Canyon. Light brown, early Paleozoic dolomite (P) is overlain by a thin white layer of Redwall Limestone (Mississippian). Supai Group (Early Pennsylvanian to Early Permian) forms the dark brown cliff (S). Recessive greenish-gray, quartz-rich schist and quartzite (HC) are probably equivalent to the Hermit Shale and Coconino Sandstone. The prominent buff-colored bed (K) is the marble equivalent to the Kaibab Limestone (Permian). Gray quartzite (NA) in the core of the syncline presumably correlates with the Navajo and Aztec Sandstones of Triassic age. The entire Paleozoic section in the left limb of the syncline dips beneath the foreground valley and comes back up in the right limb, upside down, in a much thinner complete section that continues to thin off into the distance along the ridge. Dark gray and black metavolcanic rocks of Jurassic age cap the crest of the range. (33°50.3N, 114°39.0W) —Warren Hamilton photo

The geology of the Riverside Mountains, while similar to that of the Big Maria Mountains, is further complicated by a detachment fault that separates the older metamorphosed rocks from overlying Neogene-age rocks. The western part of the Riverside Mountains consists of rocks in the upper plate of the flat-lying fault, mainly steeply dipping Neogene red beds, breccia, and some mafic and silicic volcanic rocks. The high, eastern part of the range lies structurally beneath the undulating detachment fault. The metamorphosed lower plate rocks are the same Proterozoic gneisses and Paleozoic and Mesozoic sedimentary rocks as those in the Big Maria Mountains and in so many of the nearby ranges to the north and east.

Whipple and Chemehuevi Mountains

Vidal Junction, at the intersection of US 95 and CA 62, lies in the middle of the broad Vidal Valley, which is filled with a thick blanket of alluvium shed from the surrounding mountains in Quaternary time. US 95 continues north from Vidal Junction through the broad, nearly featureless Chemehuevi Valley between the Whipple, Chemehuevi, and Turtle Mountains to its intersection with I-40. The mountains are so far from the highway, however, that it is difficult to see much of their rocks and structure.

The relatively high relief of and deep canyons in the Whipple and Chemehuevi Mountains offer some of the most spectacular exposures of detachment fault tectonics in western North America. The detachment faults formed during extreme stretching of the Earth's crust in the Colorado River Extensional Corridor during Oligocene to Miocene time.

Most of the upper plate has been eroded from the Whipple Mountains, but red-brown Neogene volcanic rocks and red beds lie above the detachment fault in the eastern and southern part of the range. On or near the crest of the range is a large, isolated remnant of the upper plate—Miocene sedimentary and volcanic strata. The detachment fault has a highly disturbed, 2- to 3-foot-thick ledge of fault breccia, a zone of small rock fragments pulverized by movement along the fault. The breccia, which is impregnated with the mineral chlorite, extends tens to hundreds of feet into the lower plate.

About a dozen miles south of Needles, the horseshoe-shaped Chemehuevi Mountains open to the east and expose a lower plate of layered gneiss and amphibolite of Proterozoic age with a Cretaceous-age granitic pluton that intruded the south and central part of the lower-plate rocks. The pluton is a crudely, concentrically zoned complex of five intrusions ranging from hornblende quartz diorite to garnet-bearing granite.

The upper plate, as is typical in ranges elsewhere in the Colorado River Extensional Corridor, consists of Neogene sedimentary and volcanic rocks, separated from the lower plate of Proterozoic rocks by a low-angle detachment fault. The volcanic rocks are flows of basalt, andesite and dacite, welded tuff, and breccia, all overlain by a sequence of welded tuff, basalt, and thick interlayered conglomerate, sandstone, and landslide breccia.

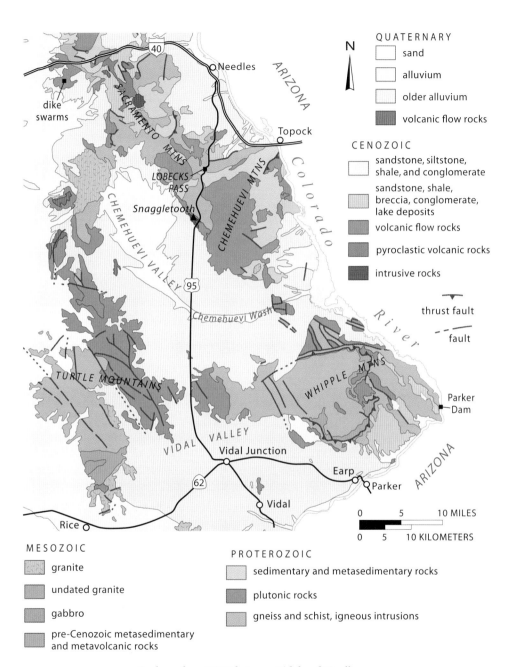

QUATERNARY
- [ ] sand
- [ ] alluvium
- [ ] older alluvium
- [ ] volcanic flow rocks

CENOZOIC
- [ ] sandstone, siltstone, shale, and conglomerate
- [ ] sandstone, shale, breccia, conglomerate, lake deposits
- [ ] volcanic flow rocks
- [ ] pyroclastic volcanic rocks
- [ ] intrusive rocks

thrust fault

fault

MESOZOIC
- [ ] granite
- [ ] undated granite
- [ ] gabbro
- [ ] pre-Cenozoic metasedimentary and metavolcanic rocks

PROTEROZOIC
- [ ] sedimentary and metasedimentary rocks
- [ ] plutonic rocks
- [ ] gneiss and schist, igneous intrusions

Geology along US 95 between Vidal and Needles.

Aerial view looking east upon the Whipple Mountains detachment fault, which lies above a lower plate of light gray to greenish Proterozoic-age crystalline basement (much of it covered with alluvium in washes). The upper plate rocks (jagged ridges) are the reddish and reddish-brown Neogene volcanic and sedimentary rock layers that dip to the right in the photo. (34°18.5N, 114°18.0W) —John C. Crowell photo

Dark brown, craggy Neogene volcanic rocks of the upper plate are separated by a detachment fault from light-gray, crystalline Proterozoic metamorphic rocks of the lower plate. US 95 passes this outcrop at Lobecks Pass near Snaggletooth in the Sawtooth Range on the west flank of the Chemehuevi Mountains. (34°40.5N, 114°37.2W)

CA 14
PALMDALE—MOJAVE—RED ROCK CANYON
61 miles

CA 14 crosses the San Andreas fault and enters the Mojave Desert at Palmdale, heading straight north across Antelope Valley through Lancaster to Mojave. Lancaster lies at the center of a large area of ground subsidence caused by withdrawal of groundwater for irrigation. Maximum recorded subsidence reached 2 feet between 1955 and 1967. At that time alfalfa ranches proliferated in the area while their landowners were hoping to be bought out for an international airport. The airport idea was abandoned and so were most of the ranches, especially when the water table was drawn down so deeply that ranchers had to install expensive pumps on deeper wells. Land subsidence is a common problem in desert basins throughout the western United States because the pumped water accumulated during wetter Pleistocene times and is not being replaced at the rate it's being withdrawn today. Subsidence presents serious engineering problems, especially for canals and waterways.

CA 14 crosses the high shoreline of Pleistocene Lake Thompson, now obscured by farming and urban development, in Lancaster at Avenue I. In Pleistocene time the lake extended 4 miles east and west of CA 14 and north to the Rosamond Hills. At its maximum, the lake covered as much as 370 square miles and was several tens of feet deep. A test well drilled near the south edge of the lake found 5,576 feet of alluvial sediments in the basin. The lake dried up during Holocene time and is now represented by the Rogers, Rosamond, and Buckhorn Lake playas, which may flood up to 75 square miles during unusually wet phases. Many archaeological sites have been found along former beaches.

Antelope Valley California Poppy Reserve
Take time out from geology to visit the headquarters for the Antelope Valley California Poppy Reserve about 4 miles south of PM 24 on CA 138. It is the epicenter of what can be an overwhelmingly beautiful show of spring wildflowers. In fact, if enough rain comes at the right time of year, the hills north and south of CA 138, especially around Gorman, resemble an artist's palette, colored with bright orange poppies, purple lupine, yellow desert dandelions, and many other desert flowers. In some years, growth of orange poppies may be so profuse that hillsides look as though lava flows are coming down them. To reach the reserve headquarters from CA 14, take CA 138 west to 170th Street W, drive south 5 miles to Lancaster Road, turn right, and go 5 miles.

Mining in the Rosamond Hills and Soledad Mountain
About halfway between Lancaster and Mojave, the highway cuts through the Rosamond Hills, which have hydrothermally altered, rhyolitic volcanic rocks in various shades of gray, red-brown, and pale green. These colorful rocks, part of the Tropico Group of Miocene age, include greenish-tan tuff containing fragments of previously formed rock, ash-rich sandstone, tuff breccia, conglomerate, and thin basalt flows. All are quarried for ornamental

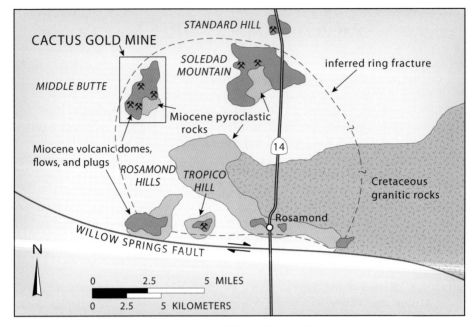

Miocene-age intrusions in the Rosamond Hills and Soledad Mountain are parts of a large, imperfect ring of volcanic outcrops that geologists postulate represents the remnants of a caldera about 10 miles in diameter. —Modified from Burnett and Brady, 1990

and roofing purposes. The abrupt south face of the hills is a degraded scarp along the Willow Springs fault.

Tropico Hill, with its pods and dikes of pink, fine-grained volcanic rock, is a famous mining area about 2 miles west and north of the CA 14 and Rosamond Boulevard intersection (exit 55). Gold, silver, and radioactive minerals were mined here prior to World War II. Colorful, thin veins of chalcedony gave the name Gem Hill Formation to part of the Tropico Group of rocks here and attracted many rock hounds. Nodules and geodes of agate, chalcedony, and opal are in found in glassy rhyolite in the Rosamond Hills 1 mile northwest of Rosamond.

About 5 miles south of Mojave at Backus Road (exit 61), look west about 6 miles toward the Cactus Mine dumps at Middle Butte. Discovered in 1933, this was one of the premier gold mines in the Mojave area. The tailings are the remnants of open-pit mining operations in several of the Neogene volcanic intrusions. Several mines discovered in the 1890s on Soledad Mountain produced about $23 million worth of gold before World War II. Gold was discovered at the Silver Queen and Dawn Mines in the 1930s, and as recently as 2020, an open pit and leach operation were in full swing at the Golden Queen Mine on Soledad Mountain.

Soledad Mountain (elevation 4,140 feet) is a rhyolite dome. It has been extensively quarried for hydrothermal deposits of gold and silver since 1894. (34°58.9N, 118°11.3W)

Garlock Fault at Mojave

The windblown town of Mojave grew from a wide spot in the road into a major rail collection and shipping point for mineral commodities for many miles around, especially borate ores that came by twenty-mule teams from Death Valley and by truck (now by rail) from Searles Valley. Limestone and marble from the Tehachapi area were carried to and shipped from Mojave.

At the north end of Mojave, CA 14 turns northeast, parallel to the front of the Tehachapi Mountains. The sharp, straight base of the mountains is the locus of the surface trace of the Garlock fault for about 20 miles to Jawbone Canyon. At 160 miles, the Garlock is one of the longest faults in southern California, and in contrast to most southern California faults, the Garlock is a left-slip fault with 30 to 40 miles of cumulative displacement over the last 10 million years. Look closely and see how some of the drainages come down out of the hills, then turn abruptly right for a short distance along the fault trace, then bend sharply to the left out onto the desert floor.

Jawbone Canyon

When you reach Jawbone Canyon, look west and up the canyon to see two big pipes coming down the hill. They are part of the largest siphon of the Los Angeles Aqueduct, which brings water 200 miles from the eastern Sierra Nevada to Los Angeles solely by gravity. Gold was discovered in the canyon, and several mines produced nearly $1 million each before ceasing operations in 1942. The railroad near the highway carries a wide range of industrial mineral salts mined from Searles Lake playa, at Trona, to Mojave.

Aerial view to the west from a point almost directly over US 395. The Garlock fault, the linear feature running from top to bottom in photo center, has displaced a stream drainage left-laterally (bottom of photo). (35°26.0N, 117°43.1W)

Red Rock Canyon State Park

Red Rock Canyon is a water gap carved in resistant, highly fractured basement rocks exposed in roadcuts at the south end of the canyon. Overlying Miocene rock layers dip uniformly northwestward. The creek is one of several streams that eroded deep canyons in the El Paso Mountains as they were being tilted and uplifted along the El Paso fault, a normal fault at the mouth of the canyon.

Colorful rock formations in Red Rock Canyon served as landmarks for twenty-mule-team freight wagons that stopped for water during the early 1870s. (35°21.8N, 117°58.7W)

The spectacular red, pink, white, gray, and black cliffs at Red Rock Canyon State Park consist of eighteen interlayered sedimentary beds and lava flows assigned to the Dove Spring Formation, which ranges in age from 12 to 8 million years old. Prominent red layers are sandstone beds deposited in ancient stream and river channels, white layers are ash-rich sandstone, and grayish layers are sandstone beds. In about the middle of the succession is a massive pink layer of ash-flow tuff, a mixture of volcanic ash and bits and pieces of other older rocks. When the tuff settled, hot ash and rock fragments welded together and formed a relatively resistant rock layer. Two prominent black lava flows of olivine basalt on the ridge crests are interbedded with the higher part of the sedimentary sequence.

More than eighty-eight species of late Miocene fossil plants and animals have been found in the Dove Spring Formation, including turtles, lizards, antelopes, ground squirrels, camels, rhinos, horses, snakes, bats, mice, foxes, skunks, and various birds. Fossil collecting is prohibited within the boundaries of Red Rock Canyon State Park—except by special research permit from the California State Parks authorities.

Due to its unique scenic features and proximity to Hollywood, Red Rock Canyon has frequently been used as a filming location for many TV series, advertisements, rock videos, and Western motion pictures, including such classics as *The Mummy, Radar Men from the Moon,* and *Jurassic Park.* Destiny's Child's 2005 music video "Cater 2 U" was also filmed at this location.

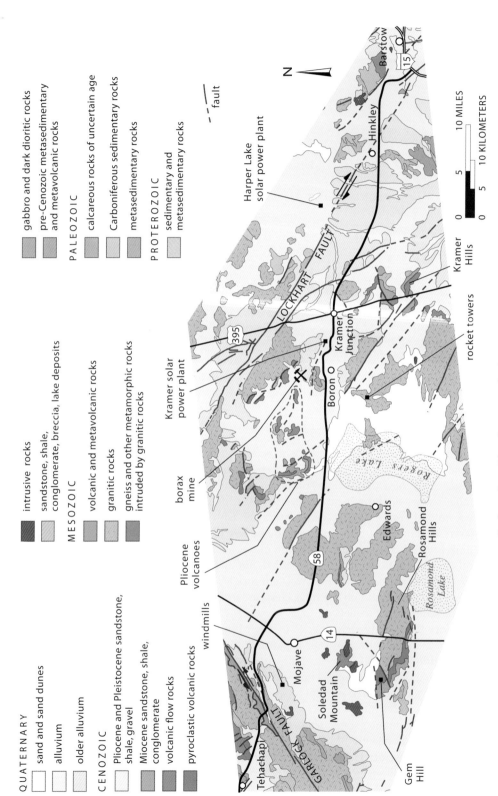

QUATERNARY

- ☐ sand and sand dunes
- alluvium
- older alluvium

CENOZOIC

- Pliocene and Pleistocene sandstone, shale, gravel
- Miocene sandstone, shale, conglomerate
- volcanic flow rocks
- pyroclastic volcanic rocks

MESOZOIC

- intrusive rocks
- sandstone, shale, conglomerate, breccia, lake deposits
- volcanic and metavolcanic rocks
- granitic rocks
- gneiss and other metamorphic rocks intruded by granitic rocks

PALEOZOIC

- calcareous rocks of uncertain age
- Carboniferous sedimentary rocks
- metasedimentary rocks

PROTEROZOIC

- sedimentary and metasedimentary rocks

--- fault

Geology along CA 58 between Tehachapi and Barstow.

CA 58
TEHACHAPI—BARSTOW
85 miles

Tehachapi lies on a plateau cut upon granitic rocks of the Sierra Nevada Batholith and veneered by river-deposited gravel and sand derived from weathering and erosion of that granite. Parts of the country rock that the batholith intruded include Paleozoic limestone and dolomite marble. Limestone was mined initially from a quarry south of Tehachapi, east of Antelope Canyon, and carried by tram down the mountain to a 5-mile-long narrow-gauge railroad that brought the rock to a cement plant at Monolith, east of Tehachapi. The City of Los Angeles constructed the Monolith plant in 1909 to produce cement for construction of the Los Angeles Aqueduct. After land title conflicts were resolved, limestone quarry operations moved to the big hill 2 miles northwest of the plant and 2 miles northeast of town. In its fifty-one years, Monolith Portland Cement produced more than 110 million barrels of cement—enough to build a two-lane highway around the world.

Tehachapi Pass and Wind Farms

East of Tehachapi through Tehachapi Pass and almost all the way to Mojave, CA 58 passes by and through the second largest wind power resource site in California. About five thousand wind turbines are spread across almost 50 square miles. The modern turbines generate about 3 megawatts each; collectively they generate about 800 megawatts, enough to meet the residential needs of 350,000 people annually. Ultimate design generation capacity is 1,500 megawatts when the field is fully developed. Statewide, wind power accounts for about 1 percent of California's energy demands.

Development of wind energy began in the Tehachapi Pass area in 1980. Newer, more efficient models have replaced most early turbines, each with its own electronic brain. They turn on when wind conditions are right and turn off when the wind is too strong or when a problem arises, and they may change directions as the wind changes. Wind speed here averages 14 to 20 miles per hour, ideal for wind power generation.

CA 58 intersects the Garlock fault at Cameron Road (exit 159), from which point the fault can be followed about 120 miles eastward to where it merges with the Death Valley fault zone, and about 40 miles westward to its intersection with the San Andreas fault.

Mojave

The town of Mojave is one of the windiest places in California. It lies at the junction of CA 58 and CA 14, a major desert intersection and raw materials transfer depot for much of historic time. Twenty-mule teams brought borate ores from the Death Valley region to the railroad transfer point at Mojave. Today, borax, boric acid, soda ash, salt cake, and salt are shipped by rail from Trona to Mojave for shipment elsewhere. Mojave is also an aeronautical center for flight-testing of experimental aircraft, and the dry climate is ideal for storage of all the surplus aircraft you see parked on the tarmac north of town.

Edwards Air Force Base and Rogers Lake Playa

Much of the flat desert east of Mojave is an eroded surface of granite covered by a variable thickness of alluvium, consisting mostly of granitic sand and gravel. You may see deeply weathered granite in low roadcuts between the end of the freeway part of CA 58 (PM 172) and exit 186 to Edwards Air Force Base. Rising above the desert floor are several granite knobs called inselbergs. You can also see small Miocene volcanic peaks, such as Brown Butte about 10 miles southeast of Mojave, and Castle Butte about 7 miles north of exit 186. The latter is one of a number of nearby basaltic buttes, plugs, and remnant lava flows surrounded by tuff, tuff breccia, and sandstone.

You cannot see much of Edwards Air Force Base from the highway. The largest features of the 470-square-mile base are two dry lake playas, Rogers (44 square miles) and Rosamond (21 square miles), which have served as emergency and scheduled landing sites for many aerospace projects, including the Bell X-1, Lockheed U-2, SR-71 Blackbird, and Space Shuttle.

Both dry lakebeds, vestiges of Pleistocene Lake Thompson, are some of the lowest and flattest parts of Antelope Valley and may collect large amounts of seasonal precipitation. Desert winds whip this water around on the lakebeds, polishing them and yielding a new, extremely flat surface in the process. The surface of Rosamond Lake playa differs in height by about 18 inches over its entire 30,000-foot length.

Aerial view southeast across Rogers Lake playa, once an occasional landing strip for the Space Shuttle. (34°55.0N, 117°50.0W)

Exit 194 (Gephart Road/Rocket Site Road) leads south to Leuhman Ridge, in the remote northeast corner of Edwards Air Force Base. Several rocket engine test stands stick out prominently along the top of the granite ridge. One of the largest rocket test sites in the United States, it was established in the late 1950s for static testing of Air Force missile engines, including the Atlas, Thor, and Minuteman missiles.

US Borax Open-Pit Mine

You probably know the soap product Boraxo and, from *Death Valley Days* on TV, the twenty-mule teams that carried ore out of Death Valley, but otherwise borate minerals are not especially familiar. Buried deep in the Mojave Desert, however, is one of the biggest and richest deposits of borax on the planet. Borax is the principal ore mineral, but eighty other borate minerals here include ulexite, kernite, and kurnakovite.

From the highway you can see only the waste dumps of the enormous open-pit mine northeast of the highway between Gephart Road (exit 194) and Borax Road (exit 196), but a short detour up Borax Road will take you to a visitor center right on the lip of the gigantic pit. The Kramer deposit was discovered in 1913 when a rancher drilled a water well. Just a few feet below the alluvial surface, which covers much of the western Mojave Desert, he found the top of a borate deposit that filled an isolated ancient lake basin. The extent of this world-class deposit became known in 1925, and production began in 1927. Depth to the ore body ranges from 140 feet in the north to about 1,100 feet in the south.

The Kramer deposit lies near the edge of a large, east-trending lake basin of late Miocene age. A 320-foot-thick, layered lens of borate-bearing evaporite beds is underlain and overlain by Pliocene basalt flows known as the Saddleback Basalt. The nearly pure sodium borate beds, with some thin layers of clay and siltstone, were probably deposited by thermal springs and surface streams. At least eight important west- and northwest-striking faults and folds cut the

The borax open-pit mine north of exit 196 is 1.5 miles long and hundreds of feet deep (35°02.5N, 117°40.9W) —Photo courtesy Rio Tinto Minerals

borate beds, which were uplifted, folded, faulted, and partly beveled by erosion during uplift of the Mojave block in middle Pliocene time. Following Quaternary uplift and erosion, alluvium was deposited on and covered the borate beds until the rancher drilled into them in 1913.

Solar Energy at Kramer Junction

One of the world's largest solar power production facilities, and one of three separate sites within 40 miles of one another, is 6 miles east of Boron, east of the county line at Kramer Junction in San Bernardino County. At peak output these three facilities can generate about 354 megawatts of electricity, enough to meet the electrical needs of about 200,000 homes. These solar facilities are referred to as advantageous peak facilities, because they operate at their peak when it is sunniest, which is also when local power requirements are greatest due to increased air-conditioning demand. Kramer Junction is an ideal solar power generation site because the sun shines there an average of 340 days per year. All three facilities are closed to the public, but a good view of the Kramer Junction facility may be had from the water tank hill, located northwest of the Kramer Junction intersection and accessible via a dirt road off US 395, 1 mile north of the intersection of US 395 and CA 58.

At the facility, the sun shines onto glass mirrors, shaped like half-pipes, which are 94 percent reflective, unlike a typical mirror, which is only 70 percent reflective. The mirrors automatically track the sun throughout the day. The sunlight reflects off the mirrors and is directed to a central tube filled with synthetic oil that heats to over 750°F. The reflected light focused at the central tube is seventy-one to eighty times more intense than ordinary sunlight. The synthetic oil transfers its heat to water, which boils and drives a Rankine cycle steam turbine to generate electricity. Synthetic oil, instead of water, carries the heat to keep the pressure within manageable parameters.

From Kramer Junction almost all the way to Barstow the highway lies upon Quaternary alluvium derived from the surrounding hills of Mesozoic granite. South of CA 58 and east of US 395 are the Kramer Hills, made of Mesozoic metavolcanic rocks intruded by Late Jurassic granitic rocks. The hills are a favorite rockhounding site for agate, jasper, green autunite, opalite, and gem-quality peridot. You can also find petrified palm tree wood.

Randsburg, Johannesburg, and Atolia Mines

About 20 miles north of CA 58 are the Rand Mountains, where placer gold was initially discovered in 1893. By 1897 Randsburg was the big boomtown of the West, with a population of 2,500 and three hundred buildings. Two miles to the northeast, its rival town, Johannesburg, was nearly as large and boasted not only a railroad station for the northern terminus of the Randsburg Railway but even a golf course in 1900. The main mining boom in the district was in the 1930s, and most activity ceased in World War II. Some placer deposits were active later, but water shortage limited most placering to dry washing, a tedious process using bellows to blow away the lighter particles, leaving the heavier, more valuable minerals behind. Most of the gold was in the Rand Schist and Atolia granodiorite (79 million years old) and was associated with intrusion of the Randsburg granodiorite (20 to 19 million years old). Ore was deposited in hydrothermally mineralized quartz veins that formed in fractures in fault breccia. The maximum depth of gold development was about 600 feet. Open-pit and heap leaching of low-grade deposits began in 1987. Increasing production costs, however, shut down these operations in 2003.

The Kelley Mine, discovered in 1919, was the largest single source of silver in California, producing about $16 million. Large-scale silver mining commenced in the 1930s just when gold production began to decline. Its unusually high-grade ores were concentrated in relatively small bodies and veins in the Rand Schist. The maximum depth of silver development was about 1,000 feet.

In 1904, placer miners discovered tungsten in the Atolia area, which became the main source of tungsten in California until 1938. The tungsten was used during World War I for steel manufacturing. Scheelite, the tungsten-containing ore mineral, formed in limestone of pre-Cretaceous age metamorphosed by quartz diorite. Hot, mineral-laden fluids entered steeply dipping, open fractures in the limestone and chemically combined with it to form veins of scheelite in a mineralized zone about 2 miles long and 500 feet wide. Most of the veins pinched out at depths of 170 to 260 feet. Placer deposits were also important where sand- to cobble-size masses were dug up like potatoes, although the richest placer deposits were mined underground from well-defined alluvial channels. Some masses of pure scheelite weighed several hundred pounds.

You can reach the mining district by following US 395 north from CA 58 across about 24 miles of monotonous Quaternary and Pleistocene alluvium and low granitic outcrops. California mining reclamation law requires removal of all buildings, back-filling of pits, detoxification, and revegetation, all of which were completed in 2005 in the Randsburg area, so little remains to be seen of the once extensive mining activity.

Hinkley Area

The low hills north and east of Hinkley contain a 10,000-foot-thick assemblage of severely deformed and chloritized quartz diorite gneiss, calcite and dolomite marble, and quartzite. The metasedimentary rocks were probably deposited on the same continental shelf as similar strata of late Proterozoic to early Paleozoic age elsewhere in the southern Great Basin.

Wastewater in a power company's cooling towers near Hinkley contained dissolved hexavalent chromium (Cr^{+6}). Contaminated water discharged into unlined ponds, from which it leaked into the groundwater over an area about 2 miles long and 1 mile wide near the company's plant. Erin Brockovich was able to link an unusually high incidence of lung cancer among Hinkley residents to hexavalent chromium in the groundwater and successfully brought a lawsuit against the power company, as documented in the movie *Erin Brockovich.*

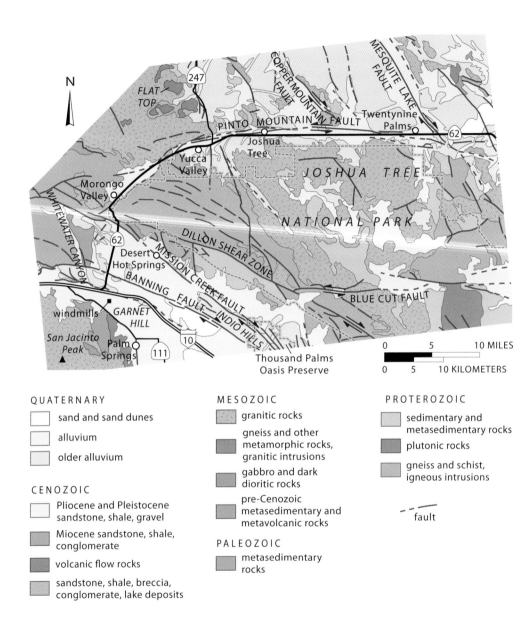

N

MESOZOIC
QUATERNARY

247
FLAT
TOP
PINTO MOUNTAIN FAULT
Twentynine
Palms
Joshua
Tree
62
Yucca
Valley
JOSHUA TREE
Morongo
Valley
NATIONAL PARK
WHITEWATER CANYON
62
DILLON SHEAR ZONE
Desert
Hot Springs
MISSION CREEK FAULT
BANNING FAULT
BLUE CUT FAULT
windmills
GARNET
HILL
INDIO HILLS
San Jacinto
Peak
Palm
Springs
10
111
Thousand Palms
Oasis Preserve

COPPER MOUNTAIN FAULT
MESQUITE LAKE FAULT

0   5   10 MILES

0   5   10 KILOMETERS

QUATERNARY

☐ sand and sand dunes

▨ alluvium

▨ older alluvium

CENOZOIC

☐ Pliocene and Pleistocene
sandstone, shale, gravel

▨ Miocene sandstone, shale,
conglomerate

▨ volcanic flow rocks

▨ sandstone, shale, breccia,
conglomerate, lake deposits

MESOZOIC

▨ granitic rocks

▨ gneiss and other
metamorphic rocks,
granitic intrusions

▨ gabbro and dark
dioritic rocks

▨ pre-Cenozoic
metasedimentary and
metavolcanic rocks

PALEOZOIC

▨ metasedimentary
rocks

PROTEROZOIC

▨ sedimentary and
metasedimentary rocks

▨ plutonic rocks

▨ gneiss and schist,
igneous intrusions

– – – fault

Geology along CA 62 between North Palm Springs and Twentynine Palms.
Also see maps on pages 29 and 75.

CA 62
North Palm Springs—Arizona Border
157 miles

CA 62 commences at I-10 in North Palm Springs. It crosses the Banning fault at PM 1.6 and the Mission Creek fault at PM 6.6, about 200 yards north of North Indian Canyon Drive. Both faults are active strands of the San Andreas fault. Devers Hill, which lies between the two faults a mile or so east of the highway, is an erosional remnant of older alluvium surrounded by more recent alluvial sand and gravel.

The surface trace of the Mission Creek fault is easily seen on aerial images where it slices southeastward through the community of Desert Hot Springs to Miracle Hill. The fault forms a subsurface barrier to groundwater flow in that stretch, so that the water table reaches the surface north of the fault where vegetation flourishes. Several hot springs along the fault stem from hydrothermal activity at depth.

Pinto Gneiss in Morongo Valley
Between PM 6.6 and PM 9, CA 62 ascends a deep canyon carved in the Pinto Gneiss, the oldest rock in the high desert region of Joshua Tree National Park. Gneiss is a metamorphic rock that forms when preexisting rocks undergo solid-state changes in mineral composition, grain size, and texture due to high temperature, pressure, and chemical activity deep in the Earth's crust. The Proterozoic age and composition of the Pinto Gneiss are similar to gneiss in Death Valley and in the San Gabriel Mountains. Radiometric analyses yield two ages of metamorphism, 1,650 million years and 1,400 million years.

Former sedimentary and igneous rocks were metamorphosed into the Pinto Gneiss. (33°43.1N, 115°48.6W)

Much of the Pinto Gneiss is dark gray with a prominent layered texture called foliation, but some is much lighter, even nearly white and only faintly foliated. Some of the gneiss is composed of light and dark granitic rock. The biotite-rich Pinto Gneiss is very dark and formed from the metamorphism of preexisting sedimentary and volcanic rocks.

A safe and scenic place to inspect the gneiss is on the grounds of the Big Morongo Canyon Preserve, 1 mile northeast of the town of Morongo Valley. A branch of the Morongo Valley fault lies at the base of the hills at the preserve where groundwater rises along the fault and replenishes ponds.

Pinto Mountain Fault

Morongo Valley is a triangular-shaped fault block bounded by the left-slip Pinto Mountain and Morongo Valley faults on its north and south edges, respectively, and by the right-slip Mission Creek fault on its west edge. Three major creeks drain across Morongo Valley instead of down its length, indicating that uplift of the mountains is so recent that the creeks drain out of the mountains and across the valley as if it weren't there.

The highway proceeds northeast through Morongo Valley along the buried trace of the Morongo Valley fault and then up a long grade to the community of Yucca Valley. The fault merges with the largely concealed trace of the Pinto Mountain fault, which extends 54 miles eastward from the San Bernardino Mountains to the Pinto Mountains in Joshua Tree National Park. It is the northernmost of three east-west striking, left-slip faults east of the San Andreas fault in the ranges east and southeast of Joshua Tree National Park; the other two are the Blue Cut and Chiriaco faults.

The Pinto Mountain fault is poorly expressed along its length, but here and there, especially a mile or so north of the highway in the vicinity of the community of Joshua Tree, fault scarps and sag ponds in late Holocene alluvium attest to its presence and suggest that the fault has been active in recent geologic time. The Pinto Mountain fault has accumulated a maximum of 10 miles of left-slip displacement, based on realignment of some of the Proterozoic and Mesozoic basement rocks. Of this, 6 miles occurred since Pleistocene time, based on the displacement of unique Pleistocene fanglomerate units. The fault has not recorded a significant earthquake in historic time.

A visitor center for Joshua Tree National Park is in Joshua Tree. See the introduction to this chapter for a discussion of the park's geology.

Twentynine Palms to Earp at the California State Line

Twentynine Palms is the principal service center for the sprawling Twentynine Palms Marine Corps base lying mostly north of CA 62. East of Twentynine Palms, CA 62 passes into the wide-open spaces of the Mojave Desert and becomes one of the loneliest and quietest highways in southern California. In fact, you'll see scant evidence along much of the route that anyone has ever made a mark on the land.

The Sheep Hole Mountains are 3 to 4 miles northeast of Dale Lake playa. Their southwest edge is bounded by a northwest-striking fault. The straight range front and the truncated, triangular-shaped ends of ridges indicate that the fault displacement is geologically recent. The southeast half of the Sheep Hole Mountains consists of the light-colored Mesozoic-age granite and granodiorite that is so ubiquitous throughout the Mojave.

A few miles east of Dale Lake, CA 62 passes granitic rocks south of the highway along the north boundary of Joshua Tree National Park and then proceeds 23 miles around the north end of the rugged and aptly named Coxcomb Mountains. The Coxcombs consist of 60 square miles of Cretaceous granite laced by mostly northwest-striking faults. The granite intruded Cretaceous sedimentary rocks assigned to the McCoy Mountains Formation and contains remnants of older rock it intruded—Jurassic-age igneous rocks metamorphosed to greenschist facies.

You expect to see sand in the desert, and the Mojave won't disappoint you. An incredible amount of loose, windblown sand and numerous sand dunes have accumulated on some of the valley floors and on the west flanks of the hills and mountains. CA 62 crosses an especially extensive accumulation of sand east of Dale Lake to Clarks Pass (PM 60 to PM 63). It also blankets much of Cadiz Valley between the Calumet Mountains on the west side of the valley and the Kilbeck Hills and Iron Mountains on the east side. Sand surrounds the Cadiz Lake playa in the center of the valley and has poured over the Kilbeck Hills into Ward Valley east of the Iron Mountains. Prevailing northwest winds carry the sand downwind from alluvial fans shed from several granitic mountains.

Much sand blankets the edges of Cadiz Valley and its granite knobs, known as inselbergs. The Iron Mountains are in the background. (34°05.3N, 115°18.6W)

Granite Pass (elevation 1,430 feet, PM 87), one of several so-named passes in the Mojave Desert, is the divide between granite at the south end of the Iron Mountains and at the north end of the Granite Mountains. An extensive blanket of sand lies between the pass and the abandoned settlement of Rice. Several large, isolated dune fields are south of Rice in Rice Valley.

The Arica Mountains are little mountain range about 5 miles southwest of Rice. They are a metamorphosed sequence of sedimentary rocks that were deposited on the continental shelf of the North American craton in late Paleozoic time. These rocks can be correlated with the classic Paleozoic formations in the Grand Canyon in northern Arizona: the Redwall Limestone, Supai Group Hermit Shale, Coconino Sandstone, and Kaibab Limestone. These rock units have been recrystallized to marble, phyllite, and quartzite in the Arica Mountains, but their metamorphism was less severe than in the Big and Little Maria Mountains and the Riverside Mountains southeast of here, as is discussed in the US 95 road guide in this chapter. A low-angle fault separates this Paleozoic sequence from an underlying Proterozoic basement of quartz-feldspar-biotite gneiss. The Paleozoic rocks were intensely folded and cut by small thrust faults related to the larger folds. Neogene-age normal faulting and doming are related to a detachment fault that is not exposed in the Aricas but probably underlies them. The entire range is surrounded by alluvium and windblown sand.

From Rice, CA 62 proceeds eastward across the flat, alluvium-blanketed Vidal Valley to Earp and the Colorado River. Although the town site of Earp is named after Wyatt Earp, he lived Vidal, about 15 miles west of Earp, while he prospected extensively and mostly unsuccessfully for gold and copper in the Whipple Mountains. The mountains are described in the road guide for US 95, which CA 62 intersects at Vidal Junction.

KELBAKER ROAD
INTERSTATE 40—BAKER
55 miles

Kelbaker Road extends 55 miles northward from I-40 (exit 78) across the central Mojave Desert, through some spectacular and diverse desert geology and scenery, to I-15 at Baker. Although it is paved, road services are lacking, aside from water at Kelso. Within the stretch of road between I-40 and Granite Pass, Kelbaker Road crosses an old granite pediment now covered with a thin veneer of alluvium of Holocene and Pleistocene age. Isolated granite inselbergs poke up through the alluvium.

Kelbaker Road passes over Granite Pass, between the Granite Mountains on the west and the Horse Hills on the east. The Granite Mountains, one of several such named mountains in California, are made of granitic pinnacles and boulder piles that formed by subsurface chemical weathering and were subsequently uplifted.

The Granite Mountains are the site of the 3.5-square-mile Sweeney Granite Mountains Desert Research Center, one of the University of California's

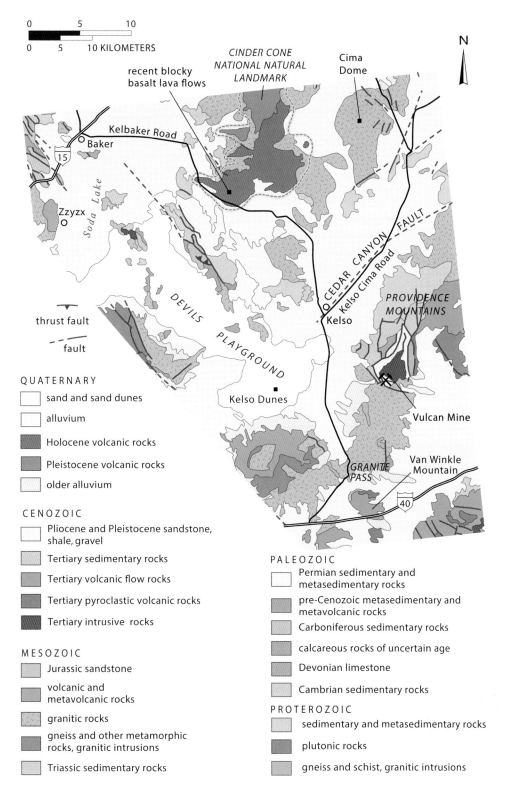

Legend:

QUATERNARY
- sand and sand dunes
- alluvium
- Holocene volcanic rocks
- Pleistocene volcanic rocks
- older alluvium

CENOZOIC
- Pliocene and Pleistocene sandstone, shale, gravel
- Tertiary sedimentary rocks
- Tertiary volcanic flow rocks
- Tertiary pyroclastic volcanic rocks
- Tertiary intrusive rocks

MESOZOIC
- Jurassic sandstone
- volcanic and metavolcanic rocks
- granitic rocks
- gneiss and other metamorphic rocks, granitic intrusions
- Triassic sedimentary rocks

PALEOZOIC
- Permian sedimentary and metasedimentary rocks
- pre-Cenozoic metasedimentary and metavolcanic rocks
- Carboniferous sedimentary rocks
- calcareous rocks of uncertain age
- Devonian limestone
- Cambrian sedimentary rocks

PROTEROZOIC
- sedimentary and metasedimentary rocks
- plutonic rocks
- gneiss and schist, granitic intrusions

Geology along Kelbaker Road between I-40 and Baker.

forty-three protected natural areas, totaling 1,172 square miles. It is the largest and most diverse university owned and operated system of its scope in the world. The system was created in 1965 in response to the increasing loss and disruption of available field sites for educational and research purposes. The Granite Mountains site hosts a broad range of natural history, botany, biology, and geology classes, as well as architecture classes specializing in passive solar design.

Kelso Dunes

Kelso Dunes are the highest and most prominent dunes in the vast, generally featureless, sandy Devils Playground. The active dunes cover an area of about 15 square miles and are surrounded by a larger area of lower elevation, vegetation-stabilized dunes. The total volume of sand is about one-fourth cubic mile. Three large, east-northeast-trending ridges, about 525 feet high and about 6,000 feet apart, make up the core of the dune field. Access to the dunes is gained from the end of a 3-mile-long gravel road, which branches west from Kelbaker Road about 6 miles north of Granite Pass and 8 miles south of Kelso.

The Mojave River carries sand through Afton Canyon and onto Soda Lake playa, from whence it blows into the Devils Playground. Prevailing northwest winds blow most of the sand to Kelso Dunes at the south end of Devils Playground. Less frequent north, south, and east winds balance the strong westerlies and cause the sand to accumulate at Kelso Dunes. Luminescence dating of the

A gang of students sets out to climb the highest part of Kelso Dunes, the third highest dunes in North America. (34°54.2N, 115°43.1W)

dunes indicates that most of the dune field accumulated around 24,000 to 9,000 years ago, with later additions around 1,500 to 400 years ago. The dunes lie upon early to late Pleistocene alluvial fans.

Kelso is one of twenty-seven dune fields in various parts of the world that emit sound when their surface is disturbed and sand slides down one of the dune's steep slopes. Sounds produced by desert dunes have been variously described as roaring, squeaking, singing, musical, the deep note of an organ, a distant airplane, or even a distant locomotive whistle. The production of singing sound in desert dunes is not as common as the squeaking of beach sands, but try it. Walk on the steep, lee sides of the dunes and cause the sand to avalanche. Shearing between adjacent layers of moving sand and compaction of the loose grains apparently produces the sounds, but the cause is by no means settled.

Kelso Dunes are also unusual for their appreciable content of dark, heavy minerals, chiefly magnetite, probably derived from the iron ores of Cave Mountain and Afton Canyon or from magnetite-rich granite in the area. Minor amounts of zircon, ilmenite, monazite, rutile, garnet, and cassiterite are also present. The wind concentrates these minerals in streaks and patches to such an extent that attempts to mine them for their magnetite content have been made but without evident economic success.

Vulcan Mine

About 4 miles south of Kelso, an unmaintained paved road forks southeastward to the Vulcan Mine, formerly the site of a major open-pit iron ore mine in the southern Providence Mountains. The iron was extracted from faulted magnetite-bearing, magnesium-silicate rocks, or skarn, at the contact between intrusive granitic rocks to the south and carbonate rocks to the north. The deposit formed where iron minerals replaced Paleozoic limestone during intrusion of the Jurassic-age granite. The Vulcan Mine supplied iron ore for steel plate needed to manufacture Liberty ships at the Kaiser Steel plant in Fontana, California, from 1942 to 1947. It was abandoned when the sulfur content of the ores increased at depth to a point where they were unsuitable for the blast furnace. The larger of the two ore bodies is 700 feet long and about 325 feet wide. Someday, when other, cheaper sources have been exhausted, Vulcan Mine may resume production. In the meantime, stay away from the pit and do your mineral collecting on the mine dumps, where you may find magnetite, hematite, pyrite, chalcopyrite, calcite, dolomite, serpentine, limonite, and epidote.

As you drive down the long grade from the Vulcan Mine Road toward Kelso, passing the Providence Mountains to the east, look for the silhouettes of volcanoes on the northern skyline ahead of you. They are but a few of the young volcanoes in the Cinder Cone National Natural Landmark.

East of Kelbaker Road between Kelso Dunes and the railroad station at Kelso, the west side of the Providence Mountains exposes gray marine clastic and carbonate sedimentary rocks dipping down to the south. They were originally deposited upon a continental shelf in Paleozoic and Mesozoic time and then were intruded by Jurassic and Cretaceous granitic plutons.

All that remains of the Vulcan Mine today, besides huge waste dumps and low-grade sulfurous ore, is an enormous open pit several hundred feet deep whose steep sides expose the ore body (dark gray) and the Cambrian limestone country rock (dipping white layers). Quaternary gravel and sand unconformably overlie the white carbonate rock at the end of the pit. (34°55.4N, 115°34.0W)

Kelso

Kelso was a Union Pacific Railroad water stop for its steam locomotives during the late nineteenth and early twentieth centuries. A splendid, pseudo-Spanish-style depot and Harvey House dining facility were built here and for many years provided overnight accommodations for train crews and longer stays for railroad personnel brought to the area by emergencies such as flash-flood washouts or derailments. The advent of diesel locomotives obviated the principal need for the depot, the imposing structure fell into disrepair until it was renovated to house the Kelso Depot Visitor Center, which provides information, exhibits, and an art gallery and bookstore, as well as restrooms and a picnic area.

Cinder Cone National Natural Landmark

You enter Cinder Cone National Natural Landmark about 5 miles north of Kelso, where Kelbaker Road passes through Neogene fanglomerate in the low pass between the Kelso Mountains on the east and the Marl Mountains on the west. The landmark features thirty-two basaltic cinder cones and accompanying lava flows in an area of 41 square miles. The cinder cones are among the youngest in the Mojave Desert, ranging from 7.6 million years old to 13,000 years old. No volcanologist would be surprised to see basalt lava erupt out here at any time.

Some of the lava flows contain pieces of ultramafic and mafic rock as well as granitic rocks that were plucked off the walls of the volcanoes' magma chambers and conduits and partially melted by the hot lava during transit. The ultramafic rocks contain the minerals clinopyroxene, orthopyroxene, olivine, and spinel, suggesting an upper mantle origin at temperatures exceeding 2,400°F.

Kelbaker Road passes near a black lava flow, then it descends a long grade before bending west toward Baker. It crosses a few miles of Holocene and Pleistocene alluvial fan deposits shed from drainages in the Cima Volcanic Field, 15 miles to the east. About a half mile east of Baker at the East Mojave Scenic Area sign, Kelbaker Road crosses gravel of a subdued beach ridge containing 12,200-year-old fossil shells, left by creatures that lived in Pleistocene Lake Mojave.

Violent eruptions lasting from a few hours to several weeks built these cinder cones on top of older lava flows, scattering molten debris that hardened into volcanic bombs, cinders, and ash. Some of the cinder cones are quarried for their black and colorful, red-brown cinders. (35°11.2N, 115°47.1W)

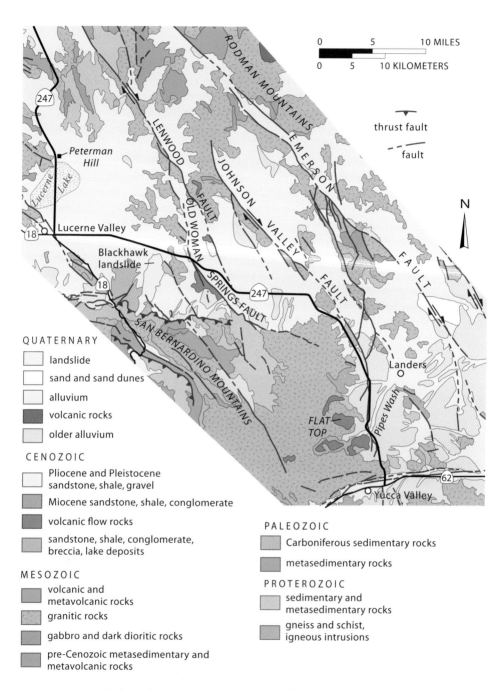

QUATERNARY

☐ landslide

☐ sand and sand dunes

☐ alluvium

■ volcanic rocks

☐ older alluvium

CENOZOIC

☐ Pliocene and Pleistocene sandstone, shale, gravel

▨ Miocene sandstone, shale, conglomerate

▨ volcanic flow rocks

▨ sandstone, shale, conglomerate, breccia, lake deposits

MESOZOIC

▨ volcanic and metavolcanic rocks

▨ granitic rocks

▨ gabbro and dark dioritic rocks

▨ pre-Cenozoic metasedimentary and metavolcanic rocks

PALEOZOIC

▨ Carboniferous sedimentary rocks

▨ metasedimentary rocks

PROTEROZOIC

☐ sedimentary and metasedimentary rocks

▨ gneiss and schist, igneous intrusions

0   5   10 MILES

0   5   10 KILOMETERS

◥ thrust fault

– – – fault

Geology along CA 247 between Yucca Valley and Lucerne Valley.

YUCCA VALLEY—BARSTOW
84 miles

CA 247 (Old Woman Springs Road) heads north along the north edge of Yucca Valley across the concealed trace of the Pinto Mountain fault, and then ascends a long upgrade through boulder piles of granite in the Western Hills Estates area. The road dips into and out of Pipes Wash (PM 5.3), whose former creek drained a large part of the eastern San Bernardino Mountains in Pleistocene time, incising a channel more than 100 feet deep for 15 miles across the desert floor. Although Pipes Wash is dry now, groundwater is forced close to the surface by granitic bedrock here, some of which is exposed west of the of the highway in Pipes Wash. CA 247 then climbs up onto an ancient erosion surface on granite near Pioneertown.

Flat Top (PM 6.6), a remnant of an olivine basalt lava flow perched atop a pillar of granite, was once continuous with other mesas west of CA 247, such as Black Lava Butte and Black Hill. The basalt ranges in age from 9.3 to 6.9 million years. Because lava flows down gulches and toward low areas, not along the crests of ridges, the layer of basalt capping Flat Top gives an indication of the amount of erosion in this area since extrusion of the lava flow. Given the age of the lava flow and the average thickness of granite that has been eroded from around the mesas, Doug Yule and Jim Spotila (2010) calculated an erosion

Similar to Flat Top, this little mesa just east of Flat Top features a basalt flow (dark) overlying an ancient erosion surface carved into granite (light rock below). The hard lava flow protected the deeply weathered granite beneath it from further erosion even as the surrounding granite was eroded down to the present land surface. (34°12.6N, 116°26.7W)

rate of about 0.02 to 0.06 millimeters per year. That doesn't seem very rapid in human terms, but multiply that by 7 to 9 *million* years and you can appreciate that a lot of erosion has happened here.

1992 Landers Earthquake

The town site of Landers in Homestead Valley, about 8 miles north of Yucca Valley and 2 miles east of CA 247, was the epicenter of the June 28, 1992, Landers earthquake (magnitude 7.3), one of the strongest to strike southern California in the twentieth century. Prior to the earthquake, seismologists believed that such a major earthquake was impossible in the Mojave Desert because no fault had been mapped in the Mojave sufficiently long to generate that large an earthquake. The Landers quake broke segments of five separate faults having an aggregate rupture length of about 53 miles, plenty long enough to make a magnitude 7 earthquake. There isn't much for an earthquake to damage in this part of California, so the Landers area was a pretty good place to have a magnitude 7.3 event.

The earthquake was felt all over the western United States, as far north as Boise and Seattle, east to Denver, and south to Cabo San Lucas in Baja California, Mexico. The magnitude, amount of slip, large region it was felt in, and comparatively low damage were not the only surprises. Low-level seismic activity was triggered almost instantaneously beneath the restless but dormant volcanoes

Galway Lake Road was displaced 18 feet right-laterally during the 1992 Landers earthquake. (34°33.551N, 116°34.048W)

of Mt. Lassen, Mt. Shasta, and the Long Valley Caldera near Mammoth, California. More than five thousand aftershocks occurred during the first two weeks following the earthquake. Even more surprising, Landers was the first earthquake that conclusively triggered earthquakes on other distant faults. One was a magnitude 6.4 earthquake three hours later at Big Bear in the San Bernardino Mountains. Another was a magnitude 5.7 earthquake a day later at Little Skull Mountain, about 50 miles northeast of Las Vegas.

Ruby Mountain (elevation 4,357 feet), about 3 miles north of the turnoff to Landers, exposes dark-colored, mafic intrusive rocks of Mesozoic age intruded by light-colored granitic rocks. CA 247 skirts the east end of the San Bernardino Mountains between Landers and Boone Road.

Johnson Valley

CA 247 crosses the south end of the northwest-striking Lenwood fault about a half mile west of the intersection with the road that goes south to Two Hole Spring. Two Hole is one of several major springs aligned along the Old Woman Springs fault at the northeast edge of the San Bernardino Mountains. The fault cuts all but the most recent alluvial channels, indicating its youthfulness. The springs issue from fractured Pliocene basalt that is in fault contact with Pleistocene alluvium. CA 247 crosses the Old Woman Springs fault 0.3 mile west of Bessemer Mine Road.

The north side of the San Bernardino Mountains supported short-lived gold and silver mines in the late nineteenth century. Several of the mines reopened in the late twentieth century with the rising price of gold. The Santa Fe gold mine, located near the head of the Blackhawk Landslide, was one of the richer mines, producing gold from a thick, white limestone unit that crops out along the north face of the mountains.

Blackhawk Landslide

Ten billion cubic feet—700 million tons—of thoroughly shattered marble and breccia fell 0.75 mile almost vertically from Blackhawk Mountain in the San Bernardino Mountains and then flowed 5.6 miles out onto the Mojave Desert. It traveled 7.5 times farther than it fell, so somehow friction had to be reduced to allow it to flow so far. Geologists postulate it traveled upon a cushion of air at a minimum of 75 miles per hour. Extreme air movement has been witnessed during a major landslide. Following the 1959 magnitude 7.3 Hebgen Lake earthquake near Yellowstone National Park, the side of a mountain in Madison Canyon tore loose. Survivors in a nearby campground related how they had to hang onto trees for dear life as wind issuing from beneath the slide tore off their clothes.

CA 247 passes north of the Blackhawk landslide between Green Rock Mine Road and Camp Rock Road. Little can be seen of the slide from the highway except for its gullied, scarplike front. Its shattered, broken rock is exposed in a quarry near the toe of the slide. Carbon-14 ages of freshwater snail shells in pond deposits in the slide and radiocarbon age determinations on desert varnish indicate the slide is more than 17,400 years old.

Aerial view of the Blackhawk landslide, the long, hummocky lobe stretching from the right edge of the image almost all the way to the left edge. The lobe is 30 to 100 feet thick, 1.5 miles wide, and 4 miles long. (34°24.8N, 116°47.1W)

Broken marble clasts are exposed in a vertical quarry face cut into the toe of the Blackhawk landslide near Lucerne Valley. Other nearby landslides indicate this area has a long history of large-scale bedrock avalanching. Sandal for scale. (34°25.30N, 116°47.22W)

If you have a four-wheel drive vehicle, take the road up the south side of Blackhawk Canyon to obtain a good overall viewpoint of the slide. On your way, you will also encounter a spectacular thrust fault that places Baldwin Gneiss of Proterozoic age upon Old Woman Sandstone of Miocene age.

Lucerne Valley

The flat-floored Lucerne Valley lies on the north edge of the San Bernardino Mountains, with the Granite, Ord, and Fry Mountains on the northwest, north, and northeast sides, respectively. As much as 800 feet of alluvium and clay have been shed into the valley by coalescing alluvial fans from the surrounding mountains. The Fry Mountains, on the north side of CA 247 at the end of the Green Rock Mine, are capped with black basalt.

Major northwest-striking faults related to the Helendale right-slip fault subdivide the valley into at least three groundwater basins. Overdrafting of groundwater caused water table levels to decline as much as 50 feet in the 1950s, and many domestic wells went dry. The falling water table also caused giant desiccation cracks to form on the surface of Lucerne Lake playa.

The highway crosses some old sand dunes on the north shore of the Lucerne Lake playa. Peterman Hill (elevation 3,208 feet), a small promontory on the north edge of Lucerne Lake, exposes Paleozoic metasedimentary rocks intruded by hornblende diorite and gabbro. These older country rocks are enclosed within the younger granite of the region. A quarry in the hill is developed in high-calcium and high-magnesium marbles. There you can find

Faulted, white marble is intruded by greenish-black, hydrothermally altered diorite and gabbro in a quarry face on Peterman Hill in the Lucerne Valley. Trenching shovel for scale. (34°32.49N, 116°56.48W)

Fine-grained, red-brown andradite garnet and green epidote.

massive red-brown andradite garnet and massive green epidote produced by the reaction of intrusive gabbro and diorite with marble. One mile west of Peterman Hill and west of CA 247 is a small remnant of carbonate rock that was once mined in vain by the sandpaper industry for its garnets. Now it is a favorite collecting site for rock hounds.

Daggett Ridge

A long, straight stretch of CA 247 crosses Stoddard Valley, a popular off-road vehicle area in this part of the Mojave Desert, and it then climbs a long, north-west-trending ridge with a landfill operation at its crest. Roadcuts expose river-deposited sand and gravel of the same kind and type that underlie Stoddard Valley. Here on Daggett Ridge, however, sand and gravel beds have been uplifted high above their surroundings and folded into a gentle anticline between the Lenwood and Hinkley faults. Because of the magnitude of recent uplift of the alluvial deposits, geologists consider the Lenwood fault to be a major seismic hazard.

SALTON TROUGH

*A man that cometh to a cross-roads must turn
his back upon the one way to follow the other.*
—Edna St. Vincent Millay, *The King's Henchman*

The Salton Trough, the deep basin that hosts the Salton Sea and extends south to the Gulf of California, is part of the Colorado Desert, a subarea of the large Sonoran Desert of Arizona and Mexico. The Colorado Desert is lower in elevation, and thus warmer, than the Mojave Desert to the north. Before a canal breach caused the Colorado River to flow uncontrolled into the region in 1905 and 1906, forming the Salton Sea, the lowest part of the trough was known as the Salton Sink. Most of it was a desolate place, especially in hot, dry summers. Large farms, golf courses, and small towns dot the region now, and it is still very hot and humid. On some summer days, towns in the basin may record the highest temperatures in the nation, even hotter and certainly more humid than Death Valley.

The Salton Sea divides the Salton Trough into Coachella Valley to the north and Imperial Valley to the south. At the north end of the basin are the two highest mountain peaks in southern California: San Jacinto Peak (elevation 10,834 feet) and San Gorgonio Mountain (elevation 11,499 feet). The Whitewater River drains a large part of the San Bernardino Mountains and enters the north end of the Salton Trough in San Gorgonio Pass (aka Banning Pass) near Palm Springs. The Alamo River flows northward from Mexico to the south end of the Salton Sea. The New River, an arroyo eroded in 1905 when the entire Colorado River flowed into the Salton Trough, is not a natural stream, but it does collect irrigation runoff that flows north from Mexico.

The Salton Trough is one of the most geologically youthful tectonic features in North America, even though it is forming within some of California's oldest rocks. The boundary between the North American and Pacific Plates changes here from the San Andreas fault, a transform plate boundary, to the East Pacific Rise, a divergent plate boundary that cleaves the Baja California peninsula away from mainland Mexico, forming the Gulf of California. As the East Pacific Rise extends northward into the continent, it forms the Salton Trough, a fault-bounded, lozenge-shaped rift basin between the eastern Transverse Ranges to the east on the North American Plate and the Peninsular Ranges to the west on the Pacific Plate. The trough continues to stretch apart and sink today. Coachella Valley, north of the Salton Sea, is 3 to 5 miles wide, about the same dimensions as the Dead Sea rift opening between the African and Arabian Plates.

The San Andreas fault enters the northeast side of the Salton Trough as the Mission Creek and Coachella Valley–Banning faults. They merge at the southeast end of the Indio Hills to become the southern San Andreas fault, which continues southeastward through the Mecca Hills and Durmid Hill. It ends at Bombay Beach, where it connects with the Brawley Seismic Zone, an onshore

Nearly all faults in the Salton Trough are thought to be active, with several significant earthquakes in historic time. The largest historic shock on the US side of the border was the 1940 El Centro earthquake (magnitude 7.1) on the Imperial fault.

spreading center made up of a diffuse array of short, en echelon fault segments beneath the south end of the Salton Sea. Faults in the seismic zone produce swarms of small earthquakes. A swarm may have as many as three hundred shocks within a day or two, sometimes with one or two as great as magnitude 5.8. Damage may include a few cracks in Brawley's older buildings and some hay bales tumbling from stacks in the fields.

The highly irregular southwest margin of the Salton Trough is outlined by the Elsinore and San Jacinto faults and other related faults that strike northwest. The San Jacinto fault commences in the east end of the San Gabriel Mountains, passes southeastward along the west side of the city of San Bernardino, and thence into the northeast edge of the Peninsular Ranges. It then it slices into the southwest side of the Salton Trough as a zone of overstepping, en echelon fault segments. It connects with the Imperial fault at El Centro and continues into Baja California to join the East Pacific Rise. Together the San Jacinto and Imperial faults have a combined length of 160 miles.

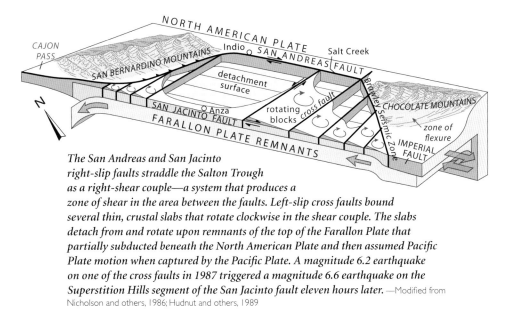

The San Andreas and San Jacinto right-slip faults straddle the Salton Trough as a right-shear couple—a system that produces a zone of shear in the area between the faults. Left-slip cross faults bound several thin, crustal slabs that rotate clockwise in the shear couple. The slabs detach from and rotate upon remnants of the top of the Farallon Plate that partially subducted beneath the North American Plate and then assumed Pacific Plate motion when captured by the Pacific Plate. A magnitude 6.2 earthquake on one of the cross faults in 1987 triggered a magnitude 6.6 earthquake on the Superstition Hills segment of the San Jacinto fault eleven hours later. —Modified from Nicholson and others, 1986; Hudnut and others, 1989

Analysis of seismic refraction data, obtained by producing shock waves at the ground surface and measuring how they are refracted at depth, allows geologists to determine the shape of the basin below its thick accumulation of sediment. The Salton Trough is an asymmetric basin with especially deep places in its southwest corner near El Centro and along its northeast margin beneath the town of Mecca. The depth to basement varies greatly, from 7,000 feet in northern Coachella Valley to more than 20,000 feet near the United States–Mexico border. One of the subsidence basins in the Brawley Seismic Zone is 3 miles long, 3 miles wide, and 3 miles deep! It lacks surface expression because it is buried by sediment.

The Salton Trough is filled with fine- to very coarse-grained, dominantly nonmarine sediments of late Miocene to Holocene age. These stratified sediments lie upon pre-Cenozoic igneous and metamorphic rocks in places and are in fault contact with them elsewhere. Most of the sediments were deposited as alluvial fans and lakebeds, but the sequence also contains late Miocene and early Pliocene marine beds that accumulated in a shallow, northward-extending arm of the Gulf of California from 6.3 to 5.6 million years ago. These sedimentary layers contain reworked fossils of Cretaceous-age forams derived from the Mancos Shale in Utah and Colorado, indicating that the bulk of the sediment was transported intermittently to the basin by the Colorado River since mid-Pliocene time. As the Colorado River shifted back and forth across the Imperial Valley, mud, sand, and lake deposits of the delta became interlayered laterally with coarse-grained sandstone and conglomerate of alluvial fans along the bedrock margin of the basin.

Salton Trough Earthquakes

Many of the faults in the Salton Trough cut and displace rocks that are as young as Holocene in age. Abundant features, including faulted landslide deposits, faulted alluvial fans and terraces, deflected drainages, scarps, aligned valleys, and linear barriers to groundwater flow, attest to the high level of late Pleistocene and Holocene activity of the faults in the Salton Trough.

The largest historic earthquake in the US part of the basin was the 1940 El Centro earthquake (magnitude 7.1) on the Imperial fault. That earthquake displaced the United States–Mexico border 15 feet right-laterally. A magnitude 6.6 earthquake occurred on the same fault in 1979, but all of the displacement was on the US side of the border, and the maximum right-lateral displacement was 3 feet. Other notable earthquakes in the Salton Trough have occurred on the Banning strand of the San Andreas fault (1948, magnitude 6.4), the southern San Jacinto fault (1968, magnitude 6.8), the North Palm Springs fault (1986, magnitude 6.2), and the Superstition Hills fault (1987, magnitude 6.6).

The May 1940 earthquake on the Imperial fault displaced this roadside ditch 10 feet 3 inches right-laterally. —T. C. Clark photo

The segment of the San Andreas fault zone from Indio to Durmid Hill is one of the most seismically inactive stretches along its entire 800-mile length. Major earthquakes have not been documented along that segment in more than 350 years, although the geomorphic evidence clearly indicates that the fault has been very active in the past 10,000 years. With so much historic activity at each end of this segment of the San Andreas fault, as well as along much of its remaining length in California, seismologists are understandably concerned that the probability of a major earthquake is quite high here—perhaps as high as 50 percent in the next thirty years.

Lake Cahuilla and the Salton Sea

Over the last 3 million years, the Colorado River formed a large fan delta, a gently sloping alluvial deposit, in the lowland between the Salton Trough and the Gulf of California. The crest of the fan is about 40 feet above sea level, high enough to impound lakes, even much larger than the present Salton Sea, whenever the Colorado River migrates from one side of the fan to the other.

During Quaternary time, ancient lakes repeatedly filled the Salton Trough to a high-stand level about 35 to 50 feet above mean sea level. Collectively, all these lakes are referred to as Lake Cahuilla. The highest shoreline, estimated to be 37,000 years old, is preserved around the basin like a bathtub ring. The lake is known to have filled six times in the interval between AD 680 and AD 1712, judging from radiocarbon dating of charcoal and fish bones in its shore deposits. The most recent high stand was in AD 1663 plus or minus 22 years. Around the margin of the basin today, lakebed sediments interfinger with

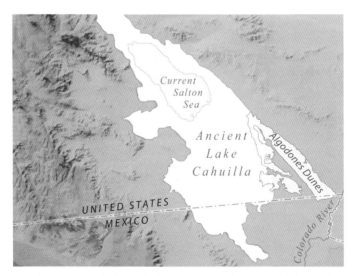

At its maximum extent, Lake Cahuilla was a huge, freshwater body covering over 2,000 square miles to a depth of more than 300 feet. It was almost 100 miles long by 35 miles across at its widest point, extending from the Colorado River delta in Mexico north to the vicinity of Indio, six times the size of the present Salton Sea.

alluvial fan, river, braided stream, fan delta, landslide, and windblown deposits derived from the bounding mountains. Despite the suitable heat, adequate reservoir rocks, and good structural traps, economic hydrocarbons have not been found in the Salton Trough, owing primarily to the lack of carbon-bearing source rocks to generate oil.

The present lake accidently formed in 1905 when engineers attempted to increase water flow into the area for farming. They dug irrigation canals from the Colorado River, where it flows through Mexico, to the Imperial Valley. Fearing a silt buildup, however, they cut into a bank of the river to increase the water flow. The resulting outflow washed out the engineered canal, and the river flowed uncontrolled into the Salton Sink for two years. Now various dams on the Colorado help reduce the likelihood of the river ever flooding and flowing into the sink again. More likely, and without human interference, the lake basin will dry up sooner than later.

The Salton Sea is currently California's largest lake, but it is also the most recent yet smallest of all the lakes that once occupied the Salton Trough. Because it has no outlet to the sea, water is removed only by evaporation, and the lake's dimensions wax and wane according to agricultural runoff and rainfall. The average length of the lake is about 35 miles; it varies in width from 9 to 15 miles and has a maximum depth of 44 feet. The present water surface lies about 230 feet below sea level, and its floor, at -280 feet, is the second lowest spot in North America behind Death Valley, at -284 feet.

ALGODONES DUNES

The Algodones Dunes, a remarkably huge and long, northwest-trending pile of sand, are the largest tract of desert dunes in North America. They occupy a 45-mile-long, 5-mile-wide stretch of the southeast part of the Salton Trough. The dunes are flanked by alluvial fans from the Chocolate and Cargo Muchacho Mountains 10 miles away on the east, whereas cultivated fields bound them abruptly on the west. Some of the dunes are as much as 300 feet high. Hugh T. Osborne Lookout Park, accessed from CA 78, sits at the top of a large dune and gives a good view of the dunes' setting. Hordes of dune-riding enthusiasts descend on the Algodones Dunes on winter weekends and may hinder your view of untrammeled dunes. Vehicles are not permitted in the dunes north of the highway.

Many types of sand dunes make up the Algodones, including barchan, crescent, star, and linear dunes up to 60 feet high with sinuous crests. Large, simple crescent dunes are north of CA 78, whereas those around the lookout parking area have highly variable crest orientations, simple frontal faces, and crescent dunes superposed on their back slopes.

Shoreline deposits of Pleistocene- to Holocene-age Lake Cahuilla northwest of the dune field are considered to be the source of the sand. Modern alluvial fans east of the Algodones make little contribution. The wind varies in direction and strength during the year, but most of the sand in the dunes is transported an average of 6 to 12 inches per year by winds that blow southsoutheast during passage of storm fronts in winter and spring.

View to the north of Algodones Dunes across CA 78 from Hugh T. Osborne Lookout Park. (32°59.01N, 115°7.96W)

WORLD-CLASS GEOLOGIC SITES

Two world-class geologic sites exist in the Salton Trough, often visited by geologists and students from around the world. The Mecca Hills feature folds and faults in the San Andreas fault zone and metamorphic rocks that once were sediments on the seafloor of the Farallon Plate. Split Mountain Gorge features several huge landslides, with automobile-size blocks that slid off the neighboring mountains into soft sediments on the floor of the sea occupying the Salton Trough about 5 million years ago. Both sites have helped geologists understand the evolution of the Salton Trough.

MECCA HILLS: BOX CANYON AND PAINTED CANYON

The Mecca Hills, one of three large uplifts along the San Andreas fault in the Salton Trough, is the best studied of the three because its rocks are almost 100 percent exposed. It is also one of the few places along the entire length of the San Andreas fault where basement rocks are clearly involved in deformation associated with the faulting.

The Mecca Hills feature a block of highly folded and faulted Pliocene and Pleistocene sedimentary rocks squeezed between two major faults. The Painted Canyon fault separates the folded rocks from less-deformed rock on the northeast, which consists of Pinto Gneiss and Orocopia Schist overlain by a thin veneer of sedimentary rocks that are similar to folded rock of the Mecca Hills. The San Andreas fault separates the folded rocks from the basin fill on the southwest, much of which is Pleistocene and younger sediments that are about 13,000 feet thick beneath Mecca.

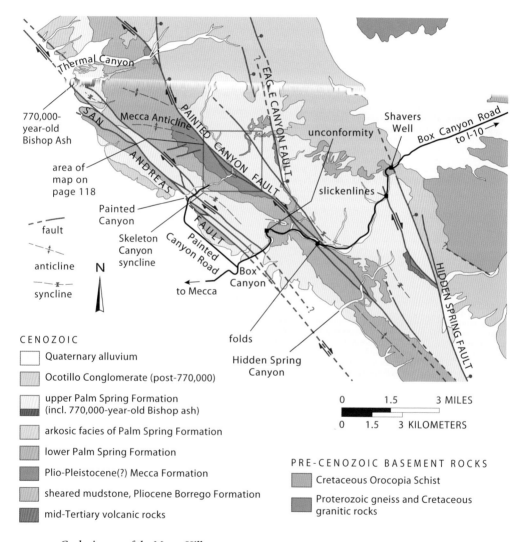

CENOZOIC

☐ Quaternary alluvium

▨ Ocotillo Conglomerate (post-770,000)

▨ upper Palm Spring Formation
(incl. 770,000-year-old Bishop ash)

▨ arkosic facies of Palm Spring Formation

▨ lower Palm Spring Formation

▨ Plio-Pleistocene(?) Mecca Formation

▨ sheared mudstone, Pliocene Borrego Formation

▨ mid-Tertiary volcanic rocks

PRE-CENOZOIC BASEMENT ROCKS

▨ Cretaceous Orocopia Schist

▨ Proterozoic gneiss and Cretaceous granitic rocks

Geologic map of the Mecca Hills. —Modified from Fattaruso and others, 2014; Sylvester and Smith, 1976

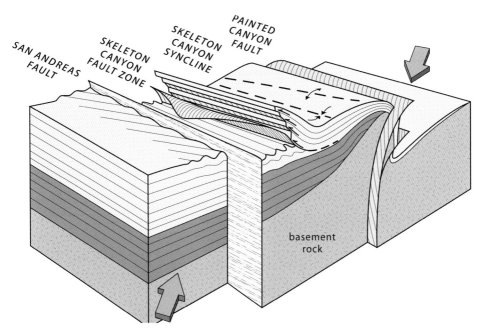

Sedimentary rocks caught between the San Andreas and Painted Canyon right-slip faults are squeezed and deformed into folds, whereas the basement rocks are crushed and deformed by fracturing between granules.

To tour the Mecca Hills, follow Box Canyon Road (66th Avenue) east through the community of Mecca and past 3 miles of grapefruit groves and vineyards. The vineyards grow grapes for raisins because the hot climate tends to promote a high sugar content that isn't especially desirable in wine. The road rises up to sea level about 100 feet before it crosses the Coachella Canal, which brings irrigation water into Coachella Valley from the Colorado River.

Box Canyon

Box Canyon Road commonly floods during the August monsoon season and sometimes is partly washed away. You cross the San Andreas fault about one-fourth mile east of the first rock outcrops beyond the canal, but you won't see a fault scarp or a laterally displaced road stripe on the highway to mark its location. The fault, covered by the highway and modern stream deposits, lies between the cliff of indurated stream gravel and sand at the mouth of Box Canyon and a gently folded sequence of tan sandstone interbedded with light gray-green siltstone of upper Palm Spring Formation. These sediments were deposited as lakebeds in the Mecca Basin, a Pliocene-age part of the Salton Trough. The sediments were derived largely from granitic and gneissic basement rocks similar to those in the Little San Bernardino Mountains in Joshua Tree National Park about 10 miles north of the Mecca Hills.

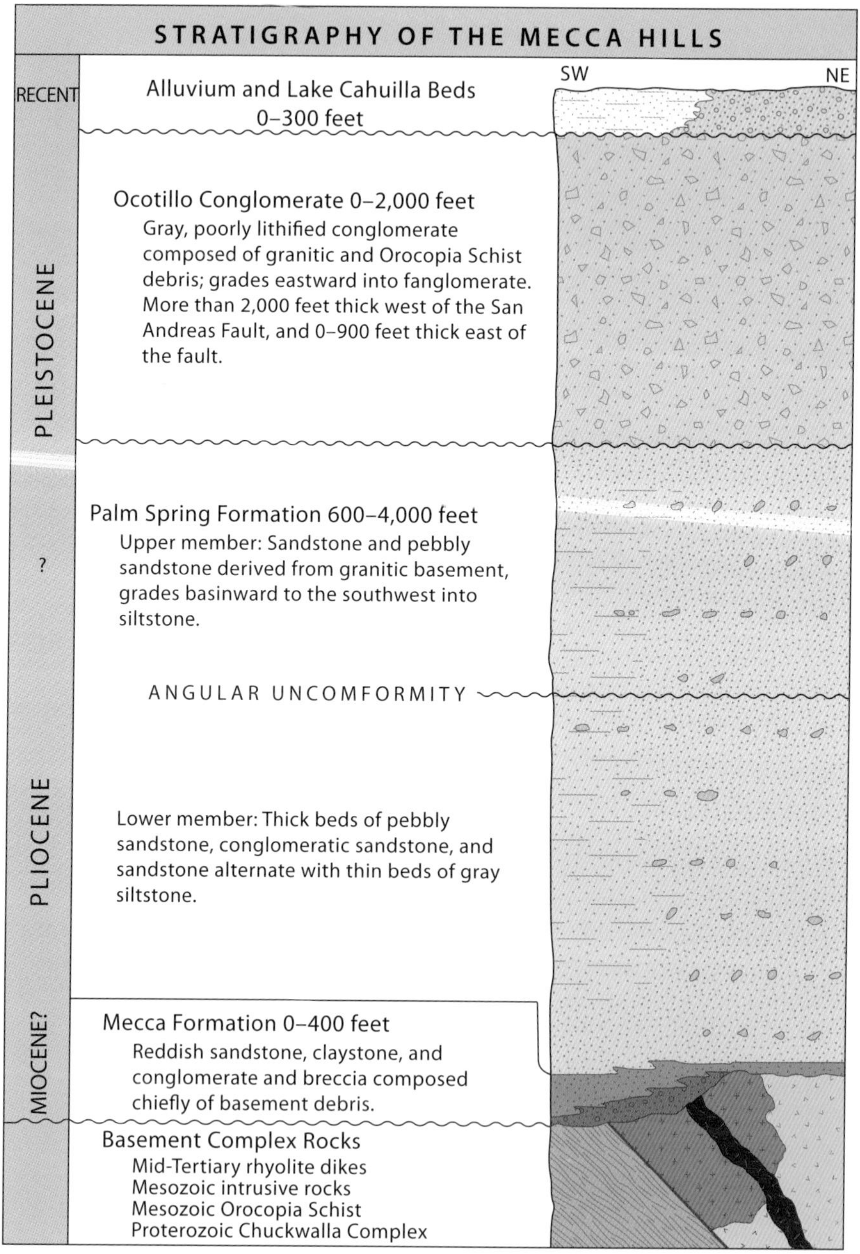

STRATIGRAPHY OF THE MECCA HILLS

SW   NE

RECENT	**Alluvium and Lake Cahuilla Beds** 0–300 feet

PLEISTOCENE

Ocotillo Conglomerate 0–2,000 feet
Gray, poorly lithified conglomerate composed of granitic and Orocopia Schist debris; grades eastward into fanglomerate. More than 2,000 feet thick west of the San Andreas Fault, and 0–900 feet thick east of the fault.

?

Palm Spring Formation 600–4,000 feet
Upper member: Sandstone and pebbly sandstone derived from granitic basement, grades basinward to the southwest into siltstone.

ANGULAR UNCOMFORMITY

PLIOCENE

Lower member: Thick beds of pebbly sandstone, conglomeratic sandstone, and sandstone alternate with thin beds of gray siltstone.

MIOCENE?

Mecca Formation 0–400 feet
Reddish sandstone, claystone, and conglomerate and breccia composed chiefly of basement debris.

Basement Complex Rocks
Mid-Tertiary rhyolite dikes
Mesozoic intrusive rocks
Mesozoic Orocopia Schist
Proterozoic Chuckwalla Complex

Look closely as you drive around the first of two major bends in the highway and see a gentle angular unconformity in the northwest canyon wall between thick-bedded, light gray sandstone below and tan sandstone above. The beds above the unconformity were deposited after the lower rocks had been uplifted, tilted, and eroded, evidence of the ongoing uplift and erosion here.

Angular unconformity (between arrows) between light gray, lower Palm Spring Formation sandstone and gray siltstone beds, and tan pebbly sandstone of the upper Palm Spring Formation in Box Canyon. Note vehicle for scale. (33°35.6N, 115°58.9W)

About 1 mile farther up the canyon, beds of the same stratigraphic sequence steepen considerably as they become increasingly involved in folding. Once around the first major curves in the highway, the road trends east-southeast, parallel to the strike of the beds and to the trend of some tight synclines and broad anticlines.

The highway crosses the Painted Canyon fault where the tilted gray beds pass abruptly into a nearly flat-lying, thinly interbedded sequence of reddish-brown sediments deposited by a river in a delta. The latter beds are fine-grained sandstone and siltstone here, but as you continue up the canyon, notice how they coarsen toward their source in the mountains to the north, passing gradually into coarse-grained stream deposits and then into alluvial fan deposits.

About 2 miles up the canyon from the Painted Canyon fault, a spectacular array of gently plunging scratches called slickenlines adorns a vertical slab of rock on the Hidden Spring fault. In some instances, it is possible to determine the sense of slip along a fault by feeling which direction feels rough or smooth when you carefully slide your hand on the polished surface parallel to the slickenlines. Try it. You should conclude the surface feels smoothest when you slide your hand to the left, indicating that the wall beneath your hand slipped to the right. Geologists have matched rocks on each side of the fault and have concluded that the right displacement has been approximately 2 miles along the Hidden Spring fault since the rocks were deposited in Pliocene and Pleistocene time.

An anticline in the lower Palm Spring Formation of Pliocene to Pleistocene age in Box Canyon, Mecca Hills. (33°35.4N, 116°03.6W)

A tight syncline in the lower Palm Spring Formation in Box Canyon, Mecca Hills. (33°35.1N, 115°56.9W)

The Orocopia Schist, a gray rock typical of the several bodies of schist elsewhere in southern California and southwest Arizona, is exposed in roadcuts at Shavers Well near the head of Box Canyon. Tightly folded outcrops of greenschist with the minerals albite, epidote, and chlorite may be closely inspected about one-quarter mile up the canyon from Shavers Well. Before metamorphism, the schist was probably graywacke, mudstone, and volcanic rocks deposited on the Farallon Plate seafloor in latest Mesozoic to early Cenozoic time. These sediments were subducted and metamorphosed beneath the North American Plate, then uplifted along with parts of the overlying Proterozoic

The surface of the Hidden Spring fault has an array of slickenlines at the edge of Box Canyon Road a half mile south of Shavers Well. (33°36.4N, 115°55.1W)

Roadside outcrop of Orocopia Schist at Shavers Well at the head of Box Canyon on the east side of the Mecca Hills. (33°37.13N, 115°55.04W)

gneiss of the North American Plate. The fault contact between the gneissic upper plate and the schist lower plate—the Vincent–Orocopia–Chocolate Mountains thrust fault—is not exposed in Box Canyon.

Painted Canyon

More Mecca Hills geology may be seen in Painted Canyon along a well-maintained dirt and gravel, 5-mile-long public corridor into the Mecca Hills Wilderness Area. Driving more than 50 feet off the road in Painted Canyon is not permitted, and you run the risk of getting stuck in sand if you do.

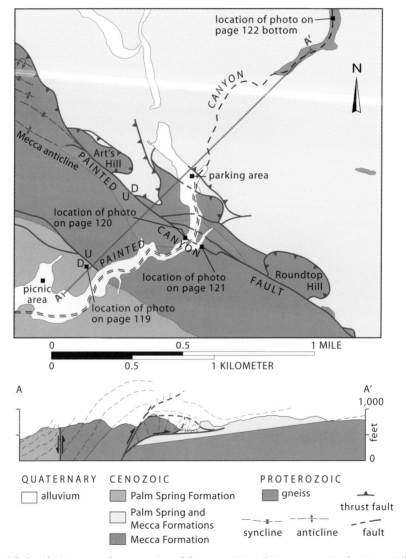

Simplified geologic map and cross section of the upper Painted Canyon area in the Mecca Hills.

From Box Canyon Road, the route proceeds 2 miles northwest, parallel to the San Andreas fault, whose gouge zone is the red-brown ridge in the hills on the right (northeast) side of the road. The road makes a broad, nearly 90-degree right bend across the desert floor toward Painted Canyon. You cross the San Andreas fault at the mouth of Painted Canyon. A short walk up Skeleton Canyon, the big canyon to the right of the road, will take you to where you can see how the red-brown clay gouge zone has been squeezed up like toothpaste along the fault. The gouge zone is about 100 feet wide and readily distinguished by disk-shaped chunks of siltstone and sandstone derived from the walls of the fault and incorporated in the gouge. In places along Skeleton Canyon, chunks of clay gouge have fallen onto the floor of the wash, were picked up by flood-water, and acquired a coating of pebbles as they tumbled along. Most of these armored mud balls range from the size of a golf ball to that of a grapefruit.

The first part of Painted Canyon exposes soft siltstone beds that merge grad-ually into fine-grained sandstone of the upper Palm Spring Formation. The rock layers are gently folded here in the core of the Skeleton Canyon syncline, as seen on the left (northwest) side of the road. After continuing up canyon a quarter mile or so, however, indurated beds of upper Palm Spring sandstone and pebbly sandstone abruptly sweep up on the southwest flank of the Mecca anticline, the main fold in the northwest part of the hills, and dip about 60 degrees down canyon. The road passes through these rock layers into steeply dipping, interbedded tan sandstone and greenish-gray siltstone beds of the

Fold pair in the lower Palm Spring Formation in Painted Canyon. (33°36.8N, 116°00.4W)

lower Palm Spring Formation. About 200 feet before encountering dark red-brown Mecca Formation, you'll see an anticline and syncline pair developed at the base of the lower Palm Spring Formation.

The Mecca Formation, which underlies the Palm Spring Formation, is made up of coarse red-brown sandstone, conglomerate, and breccia derived primarily from the Orocopia Schist and Pinto Gneiss. The Mecca Formation was deposited on an eroded surface of the older rocks, but in places it is also in fault contact with them. It is considered to be late Miocene in age, but neither the Mecca nor the Palm Spring Formation contains age-diagnostic fossils, so their depositional ages are tenuously reckoned from geologic relations observed in the Fish Creek Mountains, about 50 miles away in the southwest corner of the Salton Trough. The dark red-brown color of the Mecca Formation in Painted Canyon is due to iron oxides produced by weathering of iron-rich biotite and chlorite in the gneiss and schist.

The veritable artist's palette of multicolored basement rocks is made of shattered, dark gray Pinto Gneiss, Proterozoic gray granite, intrusions of Mesozoic gray granite, and intrusions of light orange rhyolite dikes of early Miocene age. The Mecca Formation lies unconformably upon the basement rock on the northwest side of the canyon and is in fault contact with it on the southeast side of the canyon. The steep, southwest-dipping Painted Canyon fault slices through the basement here in the canyon, shattering the rocks and juxtaposing dissimilar types of basement rocks.

The Painted Canyon fault cuts through the colorful basement rocks in the northwest wall of Painted Canyon. (33°36.96N, 116°00.00W)

The Painted Canyon fault separates crushed black and white gneissic basement at the left from reddish-brown Mecca Formation conglomeratic sandstone at the right in the southeast wall of Painted Canyon. (33°36.89N, 115°59.84W)

Park at the end of the road and view the folds in the Mecca and Palm Spring Formations in the canyon walls around you. Basement rocks may be explored by walking about a half mile up the deep canyon of grayish-brown sandstone on the right. At first Palm Spring Formation sandstone beds dip up canyon. After 100 yards or so, the rocks pass through the axis of a gentle syncline so that they dip gently down canyon, and from there as you walk up the canyon, you walk stratigraphically down section. After a quarter mile or so, dark gray, foliated gneiss comes to the surface in the floor of the canyon. The gneiss is overlain by a veneer of Mecca Formation, from 1 to 6 feet thick, with angular fragments of gneiss and schist in coarse sand. Impressive outcrops of gneiss rise higher and higher on the canyon walls as you continue up the canyon.

Eventually you'll come to a steep, slippery, dry fall in the gneiss. It is a risky climb to proceed farther, although about 100 feet upstream from the fall are outcrops of a light-colored diorite cut by dark gray diabase dikes. Geologist John Crowell realized that these rocks are identical to those associated with anorthosite in the western San Gabriel Mountains, on the other side of the San Andreas fault, 160 miles away. They provide another tie for determining San Andreas fault displacement. Orocopia Schist, still overlain by a thin veneer of Palm Spring and Mecca Formations, crops out near the head of Painted Canyon.

Pinto Gneiss in Painted Canyon. If you drilled a deep hole into the gneiss here, you would pass through the Vincent–Orocopia–Chocolate Mountains thrust fault into Orocopia Schist. (33°37.5N, 115°59.5W)

Two geologists admire the unconformity (arrows) in upper Painted Canyon, where the flat-lying Mecca Formation was deposited on an eroded surface of Pinto Gneiss. (33°37.59N, 115°59.41W)

SPLIT MOUNTAIN GORGE

Split Mountain Gorge, south of CA 78 in the southwest corner of the Salton Trough, ranks high on the list of southern California geologic sites. The nearly vertical walls of the gorge expose a spectacular sequence of late Cenozoic marine turbidites, nonmarine alluvial fans, and landslide deposits. These sediments were deposited in the Salton Trough during the initial tectonic subsidence of the basin before and during the origin of the early Gulf of California. The turbidite deposits, which settled out from submarine debris flows, were deposited during the only incursion of marine water into the Salton Trough.

The route into the gorge involves about 3 miles of off-road driving, some of which may be in soft sand. From CA 86, take CA 78 west 16.5 miles to Ocotillo Wells. From its junction with CA 86 and San Felipe Creek, the first 5 miles of CA 78 westward are on a roller coaster of broad humps and swales. They are a damaging artifact of the underlying expansive, clay-rich (smectite) lake sediments of Lake Cahuilla, which expand when wet and contract when dry.

Aerial view southwestward of Split Mountain Gorge, which once contained a perennial stream—Fish Creek—before a flash flood inundated the canyon in the 1920s with sediment, forcing the stream to percolate underground through the sediment. Warning: Do not be in the canyon if it looks like heavy rain off to the southwest! (33°00.9N, 116°06.7W) —John C. Crowell photo

The lush green area a few miles southwest of the CA 86 and CA 78 junction is San Sebastian Marsh, an Area of Critical Environmental Concern that is below sea level and was a large bay in ancient Lake Cahuilla. The marsh collects all the major creeks and washes draining the Peninsular Ranges to the west. These protected riparian habitats and marshes are critical to the survival of many rare, threatened, or endangered desert plant and animal species recognized by state and federal governments. Off-road vehicles and other mechanized equipment are not permitted in the area.

Turn south at Ocotillo Wells and follow the paved road 8.5 miles to Fish Creek Wash. The main road continues straight ahead to a gypsum mine, but you turn right and follow the tracks up the sandy wash into the canyon.

Fish Creek, which flowed here before the rocks were uplifted, cut a deep gorge perpendicular to the axis of a broad anticline. The oldest rocks in the core of the anticline are the sandy, red-brown sedimentary rocks low in the cliff at the mouth of the canyon. These rocks, the lower sandstone member of the Elephant Trees Formation, were deposited by a braided stream, beginning

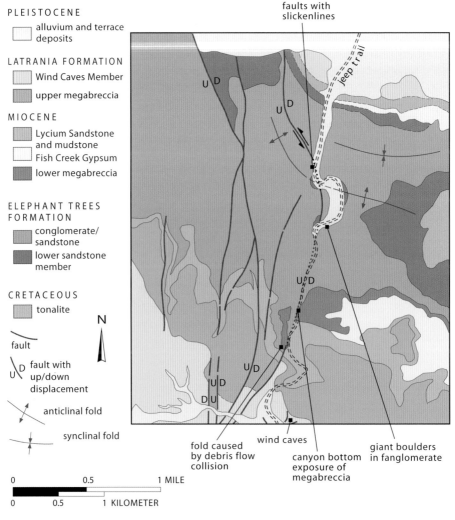

Geologic map of Split Mountain Gorge and the lower Fish Creek area.
—Map courtesy of Rebecca Dorsey, with modifications

This cliff in Split Mountain Gorge exposes braided stream deposits in the lower one-fourth of the cliff, and faulted alluvial fan deposits in the upper three-quarters. (33°00.9N, 116°06.8W)

about 8 million years ago. Notice the nearly horizontal scratches or slickenlines on the surfaces of the fractures in the rocks. Slickenlines form when one block of rock slides past another along a fault.

Continue around a lazy S–curve into a long straight section of the canyon that is eroded along a fault. Proceed south along the canyon into progressively younger rock layers in the south flank of the anticline. Overlying the lower sandstone member of the Elephant Trees Formation is a thick succession of very coarse alluvial fan deposits containing large, angular granite boulders, the upper member of the Elephant Trees Formation.

Overlying the alluvial fan deposits is a massive gray breccia that consists solely of granite detritus ranging in size from dust to large angular blocks the size of automobiles. The breccia is a huge landslide deposit, 100 feet thick and extending 2 miles both east and west of the gorge. It shook loose from the steep face of the Fish Creek Mountains about 6.4 million years ago, shattered on impact, and then flowed 7 miles west and south at high speed toward the Vallecito Mountains. Notice its flat base and how it sliced the tops off some boulders in the underlying deposit. Such a slide mass is called a *sturzstrom*, a German word for a catastrophic rockfall or rock slide.

A thick deposit of Fish Creek Gypsum overlies the sturzstrom in the heights above the east side of the canyon. The sturzstrom probably formed a dam

Alluvial fan deposits in a canyon wall of Split Mountain Gorge. The beds containing large boulders are debris-flow deposits. The more uniform sandy layers were deposited by braided streams. (33°00.4N, 116°06.8W)

Exposures of brecciated granitic rock in Split Mountain Gorge are just a small part of an enormous 300-million-cubic-yard rock-debris avalanche. (33°00.1N, 116°06.9W)

behind which water ponded and evaporated so that gypsum precipitated. Well-bedded, yellow-brown turbidite beds overlie the gypsum on the east side of the canyon. They were deposited during the only marine incursion into the Salton Trough, 6.3 million years ago. A second, stratigraphically higher sturzstrom slid into and overlies the thick sequence of well-bedded, brown turbidite sandstone, which in turn overlies the gypsum and older slide.

At a place in the canyon about 2 miles from its mouth, the turbidite beds were complexly folded by the second sturzstrom when it plowed into the still-soft turbidite beds. The sandstone layers had to be fairly pliable to bend as coherently as they did. Notice that the fold is exposed on only one side of the canyon. In fact, nowhere along the canyon do the exposures directly match each other across the canyon walls, because the steep fault along the length of the canyon separates formation contacts and rock units about one-quarter mile left-laterally.

After a couple more curves, the canyon opens into a wide badlands with many miles of passable canyons cut into fine-grained marine clay and sandstone beds. These sediments, deposited in a shallow sea and along beaches, belong to the Imperial Formation of late Miocene and early Pliocene age. They were deposited during the only marine incursion into the Salton Trough.

A magnificent anticline in Split Mountain Gorge formed when the upper sturzstrom (visible on right), plowed into turbidite beds (center and left), buckling and pushing them upward. The entire folding event probably took only a few minutes or hours. (32°59.8N, 116°06.9W)

The roads in the badlands area are sandier than that in the gorge and lead to canyons with such intriguing names as Mollusk Wash, Oyster Shell Wash, Camels Head Wash, Syncline Wash, and No Return Canyon. Heed the name of the latter canyon and explore this area only with a 4WD vehicle, plenty of water, and splendid guidebooks by Remeika and Lindsay (1992) and by Lindsay and Lindsay (2006).

Road Guides for the Salton Trough

INTERSTATE 8 AND CA 98
OCOTILLO—YUMA, ARIZONA
84 miles

CA 98 parallels I-8 from Ocotillo almost to Yuma, Arizona, and provides a more leisurely and interesting drive over the rather featureless Yuha Desert and flat agricultural land. This guide covers both roads.

The hamlet of Ocotillo takes its name from the indigenous plant *Fouquieria splendens*, which is widespread throughout the deserts of the southwestern United States and Mexico. Its slender, spiny stalks are up to 15 feet high and, with abundant rainfall, they become lush and green and sport bright red flowers like little pennants at the top of each stalk.

Plaster City, 10 miles east of Ocotillo on I-8, is the aptly named site of a US Gypsum plant. US Gypsum is the largest processor and distributor of wallboard in the United States and the largest North American manufacturer of a myriad of gypsum products that include plaster of paris, joint filler, and acoustical ceiling panels. A 3-foot-wide, narrow-gauge railroad—the last active industrial narrow-gauge railway in the United States—hauls gypsum ore to the Plaster City plant from a large quarry 20.5 miles north of here at the mouth of Split Mountain Gorge. The quarry is estimated to contain 25 million tons of gypsum. According to quarry officials, Native Americans mined alabaster—fine-grained gypsum—here long ago to make utensils for cooking and eating. Sculptors today may call the quarry to obtain alabaster that the quarry cannot use. The gypsum precipitated when water ponded and evaporated behind one of the sturzstroms from the adjacent Vallecito Mountains.

Yuha Desert, El Centinela, and Crucifixion Thorn Natural Area
The Yuha Desert is a mostly desolate area of windblown sand and dry washes in the southwest corner of the Salton Trough west of the El Centro and Calexico agricultural area and between I-8 and the Mexican border. It is part of the much larger Sonoran Desert of Arizona and Mexico. The Crucifixion Thorn Natural Area in the Yuha Desert is a splendid place to view the unique vegetation of the Sonoran Desert, including crucifixion thorn, ironwood, palo verde, ocotillo, mesquite, and creosote. Spring is usually the best time of year to visit the area, because wildflowers and blooms will abound from various desert plants after

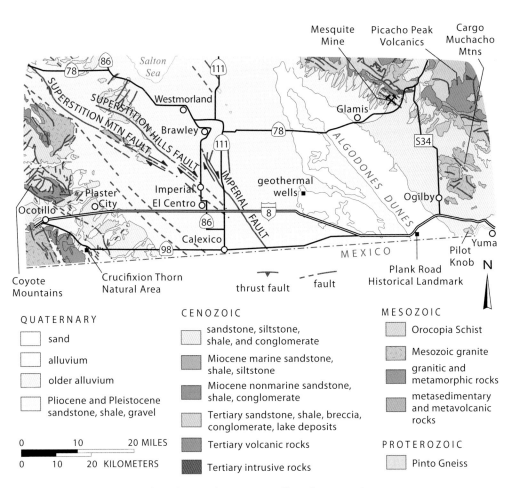

Geology along I-8 between Ocotillo and Yuma, Arizona.

Map labels:

Salton Sea

Mesquite Mine · Picacho Peak Volcanics · Cargo Muchacho Mtns

86 · 78 · 111

Westmorland

SUPERSTITION MTN FAULT

SUPERSTITION HILLS FAULT

Glamis

Brawley

78

111

ALGODONES DUNES

S34

Plaster City

Imperial

geothermal wells

Ocotillo

El Centro

IMPERIAL FAULT

8

Ogilby

86

Calexico

98

MEXICO

Yuma

Pilot Knob

Plank Road Historical Landmark

Coyote Mountains

Crucifixion Thorn Natural Area

thrust fault · fault

N

Legend:

QUATERNARY

sand
alluvium
older alluvium
Pliocene and Pleistocene sandstone, shale, gravel

CENOZOIC

sandstone, siltstone, shale, and conglomerate
Miocene marine sandstone, shale, siltstone
Miocene nonmarine sandstone, shale, conglomerate
Tertiary sandstone, shale, breccia, conglomerate, lake deposits
Tertiary volcanic rocks
Tertiary intrusive rocks

MESOZOIC

Orocopia Schist
Mesozoic granite
granitic and metamorphic rocks
metasedimentary and metavolcanic rocks

PROTEROZOIC

Pinto Gneiss

0   10   20 MILES
0   10   20 KILOMETERS

On a clear winter morning, El Centinela in Mexico appears to be just across the street from CA 98, making it an especially prominent and helpful landmark used by pioneers and Native Americans to guide them through the Yuha Desert. The Cocopah people also know it as Wi'Shspa. (32°37.2N, 115°42.6W)

sufficient winter rains. To reach it from Ocotillo, take CA 98 southeast for 8 miles. The natural area is located at the corner of CA 98 and Coyote 2 Road (32°40.179N, 115°53.314W).

The Yuha Basin is a fairly topographically flat region in the Yuha Desert, consisting of Pliocene and Pleistocene sedimentary formations of the kind that are better exposed and studied in the Coyote Mountains. El Centinela (elevation 2,262 feet), a fault-bounded ridge of granitic rocks, appears to be in the United States but is located about 2 miles on the Mexican side of the border.

Power and Water in the Imperial Valley

North of El Centinela and on CA 98 between Brockman Road (County Road S30) and the New River are the Mount Signal and Calexico solar farm projects, a very large area of concentrated photovoltaic solar panels projected to produce 100 megawatts of power for San Diego. The New River, which is just a wide, deep ditch today, came into existence in 1905 when the Colorado River breached a canal. I-8 crosses it at PM 29.5 and CA 98 crosses it almost in the center of Calexico.

The Alamo River, a natural and perennial source of water for the Salton Sea, carries water northward from Mexico. CA 98 crosses the Alamo River 0.4 mile east of the junction with CA 7, and I-8 crosses it about 2 miles east of CA 7.

CA 98 parallels the 80-mile-long All American Canal eastward from Calexico until it joins I-8 at exit 143. I-8 then parallels the canal to Pilot Knob at the Colorado River. Built in the 1930s, the canal was the largest irrigation aqueduct in the world at the time, carrying a maximum of 26,155 cubic feet per second. The aqueduct conveys water from the Colorado River into the Imperial Valley and is the valley's only agricultural water source. Six distribution canals irrigate up to 630,000 acres of cropland.

Six geothermal power plants with a mean capacity of 110 megawatts operate in the 23-square-mile East Mesa Geothermal Field, located north of I-8 about 18 miles east of El Centro. The hot water resource is between 6,000 and 7,500 feet below the surface and has an average temperature between 300°F and 360°F. Discovered in 1972, commercial production commenced fourteen years later and peaked in 1989. Most of the water is reinjected.

Land subsidence associated with withdrawal of water for geothermal production is an ongoing problem with costly effects on the design and operation of canals everywhere in California. When water no longer occupies pore spaces in the unconsolidated sediments, they compact further and the land subsides. Ground subsidence has been detected over 40 square miles around the production area at East Mesa, well within the reach of the East Highline Canal and almost to the All American Canal. Maximum subsidence in the geothermal field was 3 inches in the ten years after production began, with a maximum rate of subsidence of about 0.75 inch per year.

Old Plank Road Historical Landmark

The Algodones Dunes (see the section on the dunes in the introduction to this chapter), about 35 miles east of El Centro, were a formidable barrier for early

A single-lane plank road, 8 feet wide, carried traffic across the Algodones Dunes a century ago. It was rough and exposed to sandstorms, and required frequent maintenance. (32°42.6N, 114°55.3W)

cross-country motorists. The first road across the dunes was a 6.5-mile-long plank road built in 1915. It effectively connected the extreme lower section of southern California to Arizona and provided the last link in a commercial route between San Diego and Yuma. Four-inch-thick planks were spiked together and bound with steel in 8-by-10-foot sections. When shifting sand covered parts of the road, the sections could be moved with a team of horses. Only about 1,500 feet of the road are preserved today, at a site 3 miles west of Grays Well Road (exit 156). A historic marker is about 150 feet east of the tamarisk trees at the site of the former Grays Well.

Pilot Knob

Pilot Knob (elevation 876 feet), about 50 miles east of El Centro and 8 miles southeast of Ogilby, is an erosional remnant of igneous rocks, gneiss, and schist of Proterozoic age. It was a landmark for riverboat traffic on the Colorado River in the nineteenth century before construction of the Laguna Diversion Dam across the river in 1903–1905, part of that ill-fated project to divert some river water into the Salton Sink.

Cargo Muchacho Mountains

The Cargo Muchacho Mountains, an extensive gold mining district about 7 miles north of I-8, are the southeastern appendage of the southeast- to east-trending Chocolate Mountains. Maintained and unmaintained side roads east of Ogilby Road (County Road S34) give vehicular access to the core of the mountains and their mines. The name Cargo Muchacho, meaning "loaded boy," derived from a story that two boys were out chasing horses one day and wandered back into the family camp that evening with their shirts loaded with gold.

The main rocks are highly deformed gneisses with minor mafic schist of Proterozoic, Paleozoic, and Mesozoic age. These crystalline rocks are inferred to be part of the upper plate of the Vincent–Orocopia–Chocolate Mountains thrust fault. Deformed quartzite, white marble, and marble containing the calcium silicate mineral wollastonite crop out on the east side of the range. Andesitic and dioritic dikes are present in places. Native gold and gold-bearing sulfides, such as pyrite, are concentrated on the west side of the range in both metamorphic and granitic rocks and are found with the nonvaluable minerals quartz, calcite, sericite, and chlorite. The gold mineralization is in nearly horizontal vein networks along east-west faults, possibly thrust faults. The deposits are up to 8 feet thick and have been mined to depths of as much as 1,000 feet. Appreciable amounts of silver and copper also have been recovered in the district.

Kyanite, an aluminum silicate mineral that forms during high-pressure regional metamorphism, was mined from three neighboring deposits along the southwest flank of the Cargo Muchacho Mountains 3 miles north of Ogilby. Stubby pale greenish-blue crystals occur in quartz-muscovite schist with black

Pale blue kyanite crystals in quartz, quartzite, and quartz-muscovite schist from the Vitrefax Mine (32°51.5N, 114°47.6W) in the Cargo Muchacho Mountains.

tourmaline and may be collected on some of the mine dumps. The ore varied from about 15 to 35 percent kyanite. It is an acid resistant material used in the ceramics and porcelain industry to make products, such as spark plugs and kilnbricks, that need to withstand high temperatures.

The Cargo Muchacho mines are some of the most hazardous in the desert southwest. Only a few dilapidated buildings and some mine shafts that drop 1,000 feet or more remain of former mining operations. Vitrefax Hill, with its many cuts and loading chutes, may appear very attractive for exploring, but loose soil above deep cuts and various other perils make the area extremely dangerous.

Picacho Peak Volcanics

An extensive area of Cenozoic volcanic rocks, mostly rhyolite and called the Picacho Peak Volcanics, is 15 miles north and east of the Cargo Muchacho Mountains and extends to the Colorado River. Their age is between 25 and 23 million years. Bits and patches of these rocks have been mapped throughout the Chocolate Mountains and as far northwest as the Mecca Hills, 85 miles northwest of the Cargo Muchachos, where they have been displaced along the San Andreas fault. Picacho State Recreation Area, along the Colorado River north of Yuma, is a beautiful yet very out-of-the-way place to see these rocks.

INTERSTATE 10

BEAUMONT—INDIO

50 miles

San Gorgonio Pass

A high wall of mountains rims the north and east sides of the Los Angeles region except where breached by passes. Three of the passes—Tejon, Cajon, and San Gorgonio—are carved along the San Andreas fault. Of the three, San Gorgonio Pass, the narrow, east-trending valley between the San Jacinto and San Bernardino Mountains, is the lowest in elevation and has the gentlest gradient. Its highest point is near Beaumont (elevation 2,580 feet), east of which the pass slopes gently 7 miles to Cabazon (elevation 1,800 feet). In another 7 miles, I-10 crosses the Whitewater River (elevation 1,350 feet) into Coachella Valley. Indio, 30 miles southeast of Cabazon, is 10 feet below sea level. Note that the floor of the east-west pass slopes to the south, particularly in the vicinity of Cabazon, where the pass is about 2 miles wide. This south slope of about 8 percent is far greater than the 1.5 percent gradient of I-10 through the pass.

Eastern San Gorgonio Pass is one of the most highly developed areas for wind energy in California due to its unique combination of atmospheric and geographic features. When air over the desert heats up, it rises and creates a pocket of lower pressure near the surface. This pocket, acting like a vacuum, pulls in cooler ocean air from the west. When the cooler air funnels through the narrow pass, it is compressed and accelerated to average speeds of 14 to 21 miles per hour. Most of the turbines in the pass operate when the winds are between 15 and 50 miles per hour. Collectively, they produce over 683 megawatts of power each year, sufficient for the annual electrical consumption of all the residences in Coachella Valley. When you drive by, you may notice some turbines are out of service, perhaps for routine maintenance, modifications, or replacement.

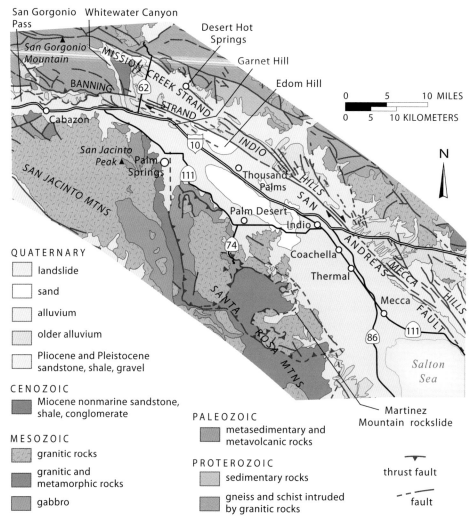

Geologic map of the Coachella Valley.

San Gorgonio Pass lies between two of the loftiest peaks in southern California: San Jacinto Peak (elevation 10,834 feet) on the south (in this image) and San Gorgonio Mountain (elevation 11,499 feet) in the San Bernardino Mountains north of the pass. More than 2,100 power-generating windmills dot the floor of the pass. (33°53.0N, 116°34.0W)

Because the pass is fairly wide and straight and because the San Jacinto Mountains rise abruptly from the floor of the pass as if fault controlled, some geologists have postulated that the pass is a block of Earth's crust bounded by reverse faults. As additional evidence for a fault along the south side of the pass, they cite the absence of large alluvial fans around the base of the mountains and the fresh-looking nature of the granitic rocks that suggest little exposure to weathering. The so-called South Pass fault, however, has no other geophysical, geologic, or geomorphic expression.

A complex system of low-angle thrust faults and through-going, high-angle to moderately dipping strike-slip faults is on the north side of San Gorgonio Pass. These faults combine to accommodate uplift of the San Bernardino Mountains, as well as strike-slip along the San Andreas fault zone. One of these strike-slip faults, the San Gabriel–Banning fault, lies about 2 miles north of I-10 and separates Proterozoic-age metamorphic rocks on the north from smooth-sloped Pliocene-age fanglomerate on the south. The distribution of various rocks in the area suggests that right-lateral displacement occurred between 7.5 and 4 million years ago, when the fault was the active strand of the San Andreas fault zone.

Cabezón means "large head" in Spanish; here in San Gorgonio Pass it refers to the large, dome-shaped hill about 1 mile north of I-10 and 1 mile west of the Whitewater River. The hill, identified by a line of wind machines along its ridge crest, is uplifted along the Garnet Hill fault and exposes river deposits of the Cabezon Formation of Pleistocene age. A deep reddish-brown soil capping the hill indicates it has been exposed for more than 100,000 years.

Whitewater River Fan, Garnet Hill, and Sandblasting

The Whitewater River drains a large part of the San Bernardino Mountains and then discharges into the east end of San Gorgonio Pass, building a constricted alluvial fan into the northwest end of Coachella Valley. Huge, white granite boulders and coarse debris on the fan surface attest to the power of this river to do geologic work.

Powerful winds blow frequently through the pass across the Whitewater River fan and down I-10 into the valley. As they do, they pick up fine sand and dust, causing intense sand and dust storms that have sandblasted paint from countless cars and frosted innumerable windshields. An extensive field of low sand dunes covers the area between I-10 and CA 111 almost all the way from Whitewater to Thousand Palms. Notice the 4-foot-long metal sheaths on the upwind side of some wooden utility poles, installed to prevent them being worn away by sandblasting.

The thick line of tamarisk trees along the railroad is a windbreak that helps to prevent sand from burying the tracks. The trees were imported from north Africa but now have spread all over the southwestern United States and are a major pest along many waterways, especially along the Colorado River.

That the prevailing winds have been unchanged for centuries is clearly shown by a spectacular array of sand-blasted boulders that litter the northwest end of Garnet Hill, the 1-mile-long, low hill south of I-10 and north of the tracks at Indian Canyon Drive (exit 120). The boulders—polished, pitted, fluted, and deeply grooved by the wind—consist of granitic gneiss, schist, and marble

Sand-blasted boulder on Garnet Hill. Small red pocketknife for scale. (33°54.0N, 116°32.4W)

from the San Jacinto Mountains, which loom above Palm Springs southwest of Garnet Hill. The blasting sand comes from the broad Whitewater River alluvial fan. This degree of sandblasting requires adequate, but not too abundant, abrasive material, such as windblown ice or quartz sand; sparse vegetation; strong, nearly constant wind; and topography that allows wind to act on the surface. Such a combination of conditions is quite rare on Earth.

Garnet Hill is an anticline of friable sandstone and gray, silty claystone of the marine Imperial Formation, deposited in Pliocene time, overlain unconformably by the Cabezon fanglomerate of Pleistocene age. Both rock units have been folded and upwarped geologically recently along the north side of the Garnet Hill fault.

Palm Springs and the Aerial Tramway

Palm Springs lies at the foot of one of the sheerest mountain faces in North America. San Jacinto Peak, towering 10,834 feet above the city, is only 5.5 miles as the crow flies from downtown Palm Springs (elevation 475 feet). Several large springs discharge from the mountain base and provide abundant water for the city's landscaping and many golf courses. A hike up into the Indian Canyons area will take you to these springs and streams and the lush growth of native palm trees they support. Drive south on Indian Canyon Drive to South Palm Canyon Drive and proceed to the tollgate. Posted signs will help you find your way.

From Chino Canyon at the north edge of Palm Springs, you can take an aerial tramway to near the top of San Jacinto Peak. The rotating tram car whisks you up the sheer cliffs of Chino Canyon from its warm base at 2,645 feet above sea level to a cool point at 8,516 feet and gives you a remarkable view of the north end of the Salton Trough. On a clear day you may look across Joshua Tree National Park and see Mt. Charleston west-northwest of Las Vegas, Nevada, 200 miles away.

The tramway also provides a splendid view of the rocks and intrusive relationships in the Santa Rosa and San Jacinto Mountains National Monument, established in 2000 to preserve this unique landscape. Metamorphic rocks are beautifully exposed in the lower and middle parts of Chino Canyon between the two tramway stations. They include folded recrystallized limestone, schist with calcium silicate minerals, quartz-mica schist, and gneiss with cool-looking streaks of minerals.

The San Jacinto pluton, which is exposed over 250 square miles and can be seen at the top of the tramway, intruded the metamorphic rocks. Granodiorite is the most widespread rock type in the pluton. Tonalite, diorite, and a small amount of gabbro are exposed in the outer parts of the pluton. A small stock of olivine norite, a rock similar to gabbro, crops out near the second tramway tower from the bottom, and hornblende diorite is the oldest and most common mafic rock in the Chino Canyon area. Most striking in this traverse across the pluton is the great variety and number of dikes, ranging from pegmatite and fine-grained diorite and tonalite to coarse-grained granodiorite dikes. It may be difficult to recognize each kind of rock and dike during the quick trip up the tramway, but you may study them more closely by walking back down the service road toward CA 111 from the first tram station.

Completed in 1963, the Palm Springs aerial tramway rises 1 mile vertically over a 2-mile distance. Five towers, ranging in height from 50 feet to 200 feet, stand in between the end points. Helicopters made twenty thousand round trips up and down the canyon to assemble and emplace the towers and their foundations. (33°551.5N, 116°33.5W)

Edom Hill

Edom Hill, a mile or so northeast of the I-10 and Date Palm Drive intersection (exit 126), looks like a giant sand dune, but instead it's rock folded within the San Andreas fault zone and now blanketed with windblown sand. You can identify the hill not only by its hulking prominence on the valley floor and the communication towers at its crest, but also by the off-road vehicle tracks all over it. The main trace of the San Andreas fault lies along its northeast side.

Out here in the middle of Coachella Valley, the sedimentary fill is more than 7,000 feet thick, judging from detailed gravity interpretations and from the Texas Company's Edom Stone 1 well drilled to a depth of 7,468 feet in

Edom Hill in 1947. The thickness of the sedimentary fill increases southeast-ward down the axis of the Salton Trough to 13,000 feet at Mecca and more than 20,000 feet at the Mexico border. The Edom well penetrated 1,600 feet of the marine Imperial Formation of late Miocene to early Pliocene age, the thickest section of that formation anywhere in the Salton Trough. The bottom of the well is in red-brown conglomeratic sandstone 2,070 feet beneath the base of the Imperial Formation. Seven other oil wildcats have been drilled in the Salton Trough, six before 1927. All were dry, known in the petroleum industry as "dusters."

Indio Hills and Palm Tree Oases

The Indio Hills, covered by windblown sand on the northwest end, were uplifted along faults in the San Andreas fault zone. The folded and faulted strata, well-exposed in highly dissected badlands, belong to the Imperial and Palm Spring Formations of Pliocene to Pleistocene age. The San Gabriel–Banning fault lies on the southwest side of the hills and the Mission Creek strand is on the north-east side. The two faults merge at depth, converge at the southeast end of the hills, and continue southeastward into the Salton Trough as the southern San Andreas fault.

As you drive southeast on I-10 between Ramon Road (exit 130) and Washington Street (exit 137), look northeast about 5 miles and notice a dull greenish-gray line of palm tree oases along the south base of the Indio Hills.

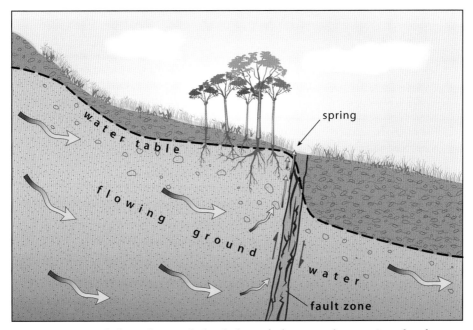

Oases commonly form where crushed rock along a fault acts as a dam, causing subsurface groundwater to rise to the surface along the fault. —Modified from Decker and Decker, 2006

Willis Palms, a fine growth of California's only native palm tree (Washingtonia filifera), is on the San Gabriel–Banning fault where it forms a subsurface barrier to groundwater flow, causing water to emerge as springs along the fault trace. (33°49.5N, 116°19.6W)

They grow along the uphill side of the southern San Andreas fault, whose gouge forms a subsurface barrier to the flow of groundwater.

Thousand Palms Canyon Road crosses the trace of the San Gabriel–Banning fault at Willis Palms. You may view a prominent, southwest-facing fault scarp with abundant palm trees at its base by taking Ramon Road (exit 130) east about 6 miles off I-10 and then traveling north on Thousand Palms Canyon Road for about 1 mile. Continue northeast through the canyon to Thousand Palms Oasis, situated on the trace of the Mission Creek strand, to see the largest palm tree oasis in the Salton Trough.

CA 86
COACHELLA—BRAWLEY
68 miles
See maps on pages 134 and 145.

Big, ragged, dark brown outcrops and hills west of Coachella consist of late Paleozoic gneissic rocks. Geologists have determined that these huge blocks slid off the high Santa Rosa Mountains on low-angle detachment faults into the Salton Trough. Geophysical studies have revealed the presence of additional enormous blocks now completely buried beneath Coachella Valley's thick alluvium blanket.

Groves of date palm trees abound in Coachella Valley between Indio and Mecca. The palm trees are not native to North America. Instead, cuttings were imported from the Middle East during the 1920s and cultured in Coachella Valley to produce some of the finest dates in the world. Date palms thrive in this climate, where summer temperatures on any given day are often the highest in the nation. The date farms rely on groundwater for irrigation. You may see citrus trees flourishing beneath palms in some of the groves. Stop by one of the shops where you can taste and purchase dates. We highly recommend date shakes!

Santa Rosa Mountains and the Martinez Mountain Rockslide

The Santa Rosa Mountains, reaching an elevation of 8,716 feet at Toro Peak, are one of the many ranges in the Peninsular Ranges. They are not especially well studied geologically because the steep slopes and wilderness status favor bighorn sheep more than geologists. Late Paleozoic metamorphic rocks here include dolomitic marble, biotite schist, and quartzite, all intruded by Mesozoic granitic rocks. In places, the rocks are intensely sheared in the Santa Rosa mylonite zone, which is part of a 60-mile-long belt of Late Cretaceous or early Eocene deformation along the eastern face of the northern Santa Rosa Mountains. There, a stacked sequence of five low-angle faults cuts complexly deformed mylonitic plutonic and metasedimentary rocks. Two strands of the San Jacinto fault right-laterally displace the zone.

Spectacular alluvial fans line both sides of the Salton Trough. Those on the west side start at about 3,000 feet in elevation and extend down to sea level in the basin. The fans are relatively steep and consist of granitic and metamorphic debris that ranges from sand up to boulders, all eroded from the mountains. Larger, lower-relief, and finer-grained alluvial fans enter the Salton Trough from the east and are better seen and studied along CA 111.

In the 6-mile stretch south of Coachella, look west to the base of the mountain range and see the steep, stubby scarp of the Martinez Mountain rockslide in the mouth of a big canyon. You may obtain a good view of its toe by taking a short drive west on 64th Avenue and walking up to the top of the flood control berm. The rockslide is the second largest in the United States and consists of 300 to 400 million cubic yards of granitic rock debris. Its head near the top of Martinez Mountain is at 6,562 feet elevation, and the toe is at 180 to 300 feet, so the total vertical fall was about 1.2 miles, over a distance of about 4.5 miles. Slides carrying granitic blocks up to the size of small automobiles rumbled down the east side of the mountain three separate times, judging from the superposition of successive lobes of debris.

The rocks were probably fresh when the landslide occurred, so the age of the slide can be determined by the condition of its surface. The clasts are highly fractured, desert-varnished, and spheroidally weathered. Many clasts have disintegrated into granules. An alluvial fan on the toe of the slide contains dark, desert-varnished clasts. Channels have developed on the slide, and closed depressions have filled with sediment. The landslide probably occurred between 20,000 and 16,000 years ago, when the climate was moister than today, resulting

Aerial view of the Martinez Mountain rockslide. The debris flowed from right to left, with the rounded hills at bottom left being the toe of the slide. (33°35.1N, 116°15.7W)
—Gary S. Rasmussen photo

in rapid erosion, oversteepening of slopes, and increased water pressure in rock joints. A large, nearby earthquake could have triggered the slide.

The Martinez Mountain rockslide lies upon the much larger Pinyon Flat landslide, which extends along the east side of the Santa Rosa and San Jacinto Mountains from Palm Springs to a point about 8 miles southeast of Valerie Jean. The head scarp of that landslide is near Alpine Village on CA 74 at an elevation of 3,950 feet.

Travertine Rock and Lake Cahuilla Shorelines

Waves eroded shoreline features around ancient Lake Cahuilla, including shoreline cliffs, beaches, sandbars, and long barrier beaches where the lake bottom had a gentle slope. Steep boulder beaches and cliffs as much as 35 feet high mark the southwest shoreline. Thick calcareous tufa was deposited by algae on shoreline rocks.

Tufa covers the granitic boulders at the base of Travertine Rock, which is just south of 86th Avenue. The rock connects to the mountain front by a sandbar, called a tombolo, and is now covered by a grape vineyard. The rock was a little island in the lake, so the bare, desert-varnished granitic rock at its top lacks tufa. Do keep a sharp eye out for rattlesnakes among the boulders if you decide to climb to the top of the point.

In the 10-mile stretch of CA 86 between Travertine Rock and Salton City, look along the base of the Santa Rosa Mountains to the west and observe the

Tufa on boulders on the lower part of Travertine Rock was created by algae that secreted calcium carbonate on submerged rocks in Lake Cahuilla where sunlight reached down into the lake water to a depth of several tens of feet. (33°25.40N, 116°03.53W)

Rocks below the highest shoreline of ancient Lake Cahuilla are covered with tan tufa, whereas bare, brown, desert-varnished bedrock is above the line. The shoreline deposits have been dated at about 37,000 years before present. (33°24.4N, 116°03.5W)

horizontal black-and-white line on the face of the mountain slopes. The line, from 45 to 75 feet above present sea level, is the highest water mark of Lake Cahuilla.

Elmore Ranch Fault

CA 86 lies upon a relatively flat desert floor that once was the bottom of ancient Lake Cahuilla, but here and there the highway ascends a long gentle slope to another, higher level of the desert floor. Each of these gentle slopes crosses the location of a northeast-striking, south-side-up, left-slip fault, known as a cross fault. The slope at Elmore Desert Ranch, about 4 miles south of the Border Patrol Station, crosses the Elmore Ranch fault. These northeast-striking cross faults in the Imperial Valley and the south end of the Salton Sea span the gap between the northwest-striking San Andreas and San Jacinto faults (see diagram on page 107).

The low hills a few miles west of Westmorland are the Superstition Hills, and behind them lies the higher Superstition Mountain. Both are squeezed-up basement rocks within the San Jacinto fault zone. Cross faults cut southwest-ward through the hills and terminate against the Superstition Hills fault, a strand of the San Jacinto fault. You may see jet fighter aircraft practicing aerial acrobatics over Superstition Mountain, which lies within a US Navy bombing and gunnery range.

New River

One mile west of Brawley, CA 86 dips into the New River arroyo, which is about 30 feet deep and 300 feet wide here. The river formed in 1905 when aqueduct water from the Colorado River flooded the valley on its way to the Salton Sink. At first the flood covered the valley floor as a sheet of water 50 miles wide, but as the Salton Sink gradually filled, the floodwaters coalesced and carved a channel—the New River—that fed a delta where the river ended in the Salton Sink. Headward erosion proceeded upstream through the soft sediments of the valley floor at the rate of 600 feet per day. Meandering river, levee, pond, and floodplain deposits are well-exposed in roadcuts along the arroyo. They probably formed during similar flooding of the Colorado River in prehistoric time.

CA III
Calexico—Mecca
85 miles

CA 111 begins at the Mexico border in Calexico and proceeds north across rich agricultural land in the Imperial Valley, where the principal crops are alfalfa, corn, melons, onions, tomatoes, and sugar beets. Despite its flat, stable appearance, this valley is one of the most seismically active areas in California. The 37-mile-long surface trace of the Imperial fault strikes southeastward from a few miles north of the city of Imperial across the border into Mexico. It was responsible for the magnitude 7.1 El Centro earthquake on May 18, 1940, which offset the border 15 feet right-laterally. A magnitude 6.5 earthquake occurred on the US segment of the fault on October 15, 1979, but with only 3 feet of right-slip. The 2010 El Mayor–Cucupah quake, with a magnitude of 7.2, occurred on the Laguna Salada fault, an extension of the Elsinore fault in Mexico. The quake damaged buildings in Calexico.

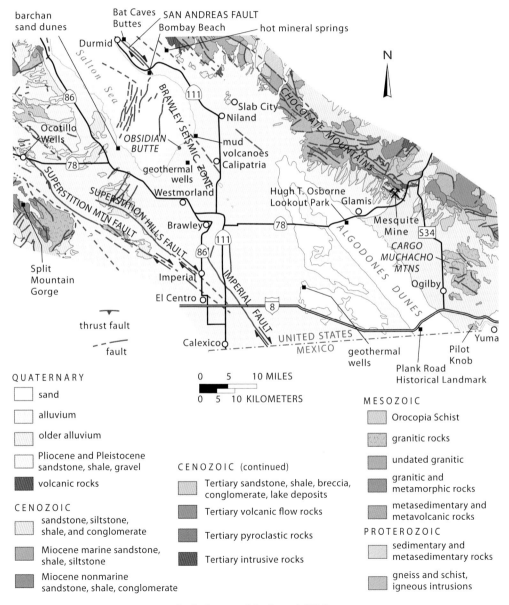

Geologic map of the Imperial Valley.

You are well below sea level in the Imperial Valley. At an elevation of -45 feet, El Centro is the largest city below sea level in the western hemisphere. To see just how low you are, head 1.5 miles west of CA 111 on Keystone Road to its intersection with CA 86 south of Brawley. About two-thirds up the side of a white tank of a sugar plant is a Sea Level sign.

CA 111 dips into the New River arroyo on the north side of Brawley, where the highway heads north from CA 78. Farther north at the intersection with S26, CA 111 crosses the New River again. Carved in 1905 and 1906 by an accidental, human-caused breaching of the Colorado River, this channel is very new, geologically speaking.

Mesquite Gold Mine in the Chocolate Mountains

On the horizon east of Brawley are the Chocolate Mountains, the north end of a large basement uplift that extends southeastward into southwestern Arizona. Finely disseminated gold is extracted from the Mesquite open-pit mine in those mountains about 5 miles northeast of Glamis. It is one of the largest gold mines in the country. The gold occurs as tiny particles concentrated along northwest-striking, high-angle faults in highly shattered biotite gneiss of Proterozoic age—the upper plate of the Vincent–Orocopia–Chocolate Mountains thrust fault. The rocks lack gold just 2 to 3 feet away from faults. The gold mineralization has been dated at about 32 million years. The source of the gold is not known, but it's noteworthy that the Mesquite Mine is part of a very large area of low-grade gold production, including Gold Basin, 10 miles to the north near Midway Well, the Picacho Peak Volcanics 20 miles to the east, and the Cargo Muchacho gold district 15 miles to the southeast.

The Mesquite Mine abuts the Chocolate Mountain Aerial Gunnery Range, which covers 720 square miles, and is also adjacent to the site where the County of Los Angeles, almost 200 miles away to the northwest, is preparing a huge landfill, southern California's first permitted to receive waste by railroad. The site is well suited to be a landfill because of its desert climate, distance from groundwater, distance from residential development, proximity to the railroad, and preexisting use for mining. It will use the mine's rock and soil stockpiles as well as the mine's water and power supply systems. Its approved footprint is about 3.5 square miles, providing capacity for approximately 600 million tons of residual nonhazardous waste over an estimated one hundred years of disposal operations.

Rhyolite Domes, Geothermal Power, and Mud Volcanoes

The upper mantle is only 5 miles or so below the surface of the Imperial Valley because of the way the East Pacific Rise spreads the basin and thins the crust. Heat from the mantle reaches the surface at the south end of the Salton Sea, creating rhyolite domes and mud volcanoes and providing geothermal energy. The heat causes calcareous sediments and carbonate fossils in the thick pile of sediments to release carbon dioxide gas. The carbonate grains and microfossils were brought here by the Colorado River from the Mancos Shale in Utah and Colorado. Colorless gas bubbles rise up through the ground over the entire

*The Mesquite Mine, an abandoned gold mine, has five open pits that are
so enormous they can be seen from the Moon. (33°23.4N, 116°53.5W)*

south part of the Salton Trough. You may see bubbles in the water in irrigation
drainage ditches.

The dark gray domes at the south end of the lake are the latest of a series
of volcanic eruptions from the top of the mantle. The rock is a frothy form of
rhyolite called pumice that is so porous and light it floats on water. When the
domes erupted about 3,000 years ago, clumps of pumice floated on the lake that
existed then and were washed up along its shoreline. You can see the clumps
interlayered within some older lakebeds exposed in gulches on the east shore
near Durmid.

The Sonny Bono Salton Sea National Wildlife Refuge complex, which
extends along the south shore of the Salton Sea, provides viewing platforms to
see not only migrating birds, but also the volcanic domes. North of Calipatria,
turn west off CA 111 onto Sinclair Road and drive due west for about 5.5 miles
to reach the rhyolite domes and the main viewing area in the refuge.

These domes also contain the glassy, jet-black form of rhyolite called
obsidian, which encloses sparse pieces of basalt, sandstone, and granite that
were broken and incorporated by the magma as it rose from below.

Nine separate geothermal power plants exploit the heat at the southeast
end of the Salton Sea. Geothermal wells pump hot water in excess of 500°F to
power plants, where it flashes to steam and drives turbines that generate electric

power, supplying about 10 percent of San Diego's energy. Some of the large, 18-inch-diameter pipes along the roads carry hot water from the wells; others return water from the power plants to reinjection wells. Large, 15-foot-high, upside-down loops in the pipes absorb shaking during earthquakes.

Bubbling water, which is cool in winter and warm (about 100°F) in summer, has created a remarkable series of active mud volcanoes, called gryphons, about 2 miles south of Wister. Turn off CA 111 at Davis Road and proceed south past a series of shallow ponds separated from one another by low levees.

Two of the five rhyolite domes at the southeast end of the Salton Sea. Young lake sediments have buried even older domes, indicating that earlier episodes of volcanism have occurred. Frequent small earthquakes indicate tectonic activity is ongoing. (33°10N, 115°38W)

This obsidian extrusion oozed viscously from a crack in the Red Hill rhyolite dome at the south end of the Salton Sea. (33°11.83N, 115°36.65W)

Gryphons have classic forms resembling shield volcanoes, stratovolcanoes, calderas, and lava flows. (33°12.0N, 115°34.7W)

Private duck clubs and the State of California operate these ponds as duck and goose shooting sites during migration season. Davis Road passes some dilapidated concrete frame buildings, site of a dry-ice plant from 1934 to 1954. It condensed the carbon dioxide gas from fifty-four wells ranging in depth from 500 to 800 feet. Gas still bubbles up in the pools and puddles around the wells. The site was also the location of a mineral spa where folks would come to bathe in the warm water and mud.

At the south end of Davis Road at its intersection with Schrimpf Road, a flat field behind No Trespassing signs has as many as ninety pools of bubbling water and gryphons in various stages of activity and formation. Stay off the gryphons so that you don't wreck them for others to enjoy, and don't slip and fall into one of the pools. This small area of pools and gryphons releases about 8 tons of carbon dioxide into the atmosphere every day.

Bombay Beach and Hot Springs

From Wister to North Shore, CA 111 is on an extensive flat surface—the bottom of ancient Lake Cahuilla. Many gullies and washes have been eroded into the surface since the lake dried up about 400 years ago. The Salton Sea is also drying up, so that Bombay Beach is one of several desert settlements that

Aerial view to the southeast over the floor of ancient Lake Cahuilla. Bombay Beach is the square town site on the east edge of the Salton Sea. The vegetated stream channel crossed by CA 111 (upper left) flows from artesian springs to the east. (33°21.0N, 115°43.8W)

has come upon hard times because the lake continues to lower in level and become more saline.

Bombay Beach marks the south end of the San Andreas fault, which can be followed almost continuously from the nearby railroad tracks northwestward for 600 miles to Tomales Bay, north of San Francisco. South of the tracks the San Andreas fault has transformed to the multiple fault strands of the Brawley Seismic Zone beneath the Salton Sea and the Imperial Valley.

Construction workers, needing a water source to mix concrete for the Coachella Branch of the All American Canal, discovered hot springs at the north end of the Chocolate Mountains in 1938. The water was full of minerals and too hot to use, so the workers dug settling ponds to cool the water and remove excess minerals. The ponds were abandoned after the canal was completed, but another group of construction workers rediscovered them ten years later. They bathed in the ponds after work and recognized the therapeutic and healing effects of the artesian mineral water. Several spas, including the Fountain of Youth Spa accessed via Hot Mineral Spa Road, later grew up around other sources of hot water. Exploratory geothermal wells were drilled nearby as deep as 18,000 feet without finding a developable resource.

Durmid Hill and Salt Creek Wash

CA 111 proceeds northwestward along the northeast shore of the Salton Sea for about 9 miles from Bombay Beach to a long, low hill on the right. Known as Durmid Hill, this is the southernmost of three uplifts caused by squeezing of the crust along the San Andreas fault in the Salton Trough, the other two being the Mecca Hills and the Indio Hills. The fault lies almost along the southwest base of the small buttes on the skyline, called Bat Caves Buttes. They consist of tilted, river-deposited sandstone beds of Pliocene age that formed little islands above the high stand of Lake Cahuilla.

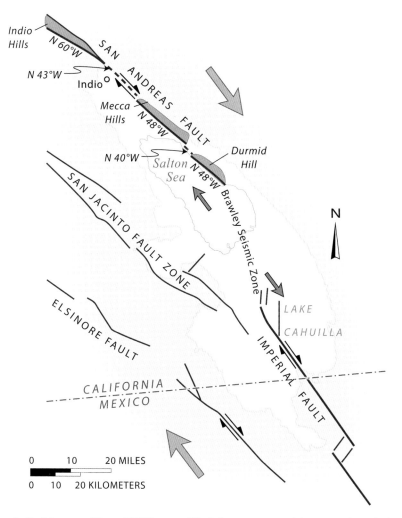

Indio, Mecca, and Durmid Hills are uplifted along segments of the San Andreas fault zone that strike at an angle more west of north than the prevailing plate motion.
—After Bilham and Williams, 1985

Salt Creek Wash cuts the north end of Durmid Hill. Stop and park to see an odd sight: The creek channel seems to terminate just a couple hundred feet upstream of the railroad bridges. There, the San Andreas fault has displaced the creek channel about 100 feet right laterally. Walk under the railroad bridge, proceed about 400 feet to the northeast, and you will find a dry arroyo carved along the San Andreas fault where you can stand with one foot on the North American Plate and the other on the Pacific Plate.

A couple miles northwest of Salt Creek is Ferrum, the abandoned junction of a railroad that went up Salt Creek Wash to iron mines in the Eagle Mountains. Henry Kaiser developed the mines during World War II to produce steel for the construction of Liberty ships on the west coast. The eroded necks of four little volcanoes are exposed in Salt Creek Wash between the Chocolate and Orocopia Mountains. The type and age of these volcanic rocks are identical to some volcanic breccias and lavas near Palmdale, 160 miles to the northwest, on the southwest side of the San Andreas fault. The little volcanoes in Salt Creek Wash shed lava and debris across the fault 35 to 23 million years ago, and since that time the Pacific Plate has slipped northwestward along the fault, bringing the rocks on the southwest side of the fault to Palmdale. The tie between the breccias and lavas is one of about thirty geologic correlations that can be made across the San Andreas fault to establish the timing and amount of right-slip along the fault.

Orocopia Mountains and Orocopia Schist

Between Ferrum and North Shore, a large gray mountain mass occupies the skyline to the east and northeast—the Orocopia Mountains. The virtually inaccessible mountain range consists almost entirely of gray and green schist with minor amounts of the green mineral actinolite and white vein quartz. This great body of schist, about 1 mile thick, is very similar to a body of schist at Sierra Pelona near Palmdale, 160 miles away, on the Pacific side of the San Andreas fault. Before metamorphism, the Orocopia Schist and other similar schist bodies in southern California and southwestern Arizona were probably graywacke, mudstone, and volcanic rocks deposited on the Farallon Plate seafloor in latest Mesozoic to early Cenozoic time. They were subducted and metamorphosed beneath Proterozoic gneiss in the North American Plate. The Vincent–Orocopia–Chocolate Mountains thrust fault is the contact between the gneiss in the upper plate and the schist in the lower plate and is exposed in the Orocopia and Chocolate Mountains.

Mecca Hills

East of Mecca lies the Mecca Hills, a true mecca for geologists. The hills expose rocks folded along the San Andreas fault, as well as rocks that were once seafloor sediments on the surface of the Farallon Plate that existed off the coast of California in Mesozoic time. The Mecca Hills are discussed in detail in the introduction to this chapter.

PENINSULAR RANGES

Except by the measure of wildness we shall
never really know the nature of a place.
—Paul Gruchow, *A Backyard Robin, Ho-Hum*

One of the principal geologic features of the west margin of North America is its chain of granitic batholiths, including the Sierra Nevada and Peninsular Ranges Batholiths. They formed in Jurassic and Cretaceous time when the Farallon Plate subducted beneath the North American Plate. As part of the subduction process, hundreds of molten bodies of magma, called plutons, were generated deep within the Earth's crust. They rose into the upper crust, where they intruded Paleozoic and Mesozoic sedimentary and volcanic rocks. The many plutons coalesced into a few batholiths, forming a magmatic arc, or chain, of intrusive granitic rocks and extrusive volcanic rocks above the subduction zone.

The Peninsular Ranges plutons metamorphosed the older sedimentary and volcanic rocks into marble, slate, schist, quartzite, gneiss, and metavolcanic rocks, creating a great diversity of unusual metamorphic minerals in the process. Other semiprecious minerals and gems crystallized in veins from magmatic fluids lingering in fractures of the cooling rocks.

In Cretaceous and Paleogene time, the Peninsular Ranges Batholith was uplifted and eroded into a broad, nearly flat plain—a peneplain. Big rivers transported sediments westward from the interior of the North American continent across the peneplain and deposited them on the seafloor of a long fore-arc basin west of the Peninsular Ranges magmatic arc.

The Pacific Plate came into contact with the North American Plate about 23 million years ago when most of the Farallon Plate had subducted beneath the North American Plate. As the Pacific Plate slid northwestward alongside the North American Plate, it captured a slice of the fore-arc basin along what is today the San Diego–San Clemente coastline. The slice was rafted and rotated away from the North American Plate the way you might use a cake knife to cut, slide, and rotate a slice of cake away from the cake. As that slice of fore-arc basin rocks rotated clockwise 110 degrees, the Pacific Plate carried it northwestward about 130 miles. On the way, the slice was uplifted and crumpled like a rug to form the western part of the east-west trending Transverse Ranges.

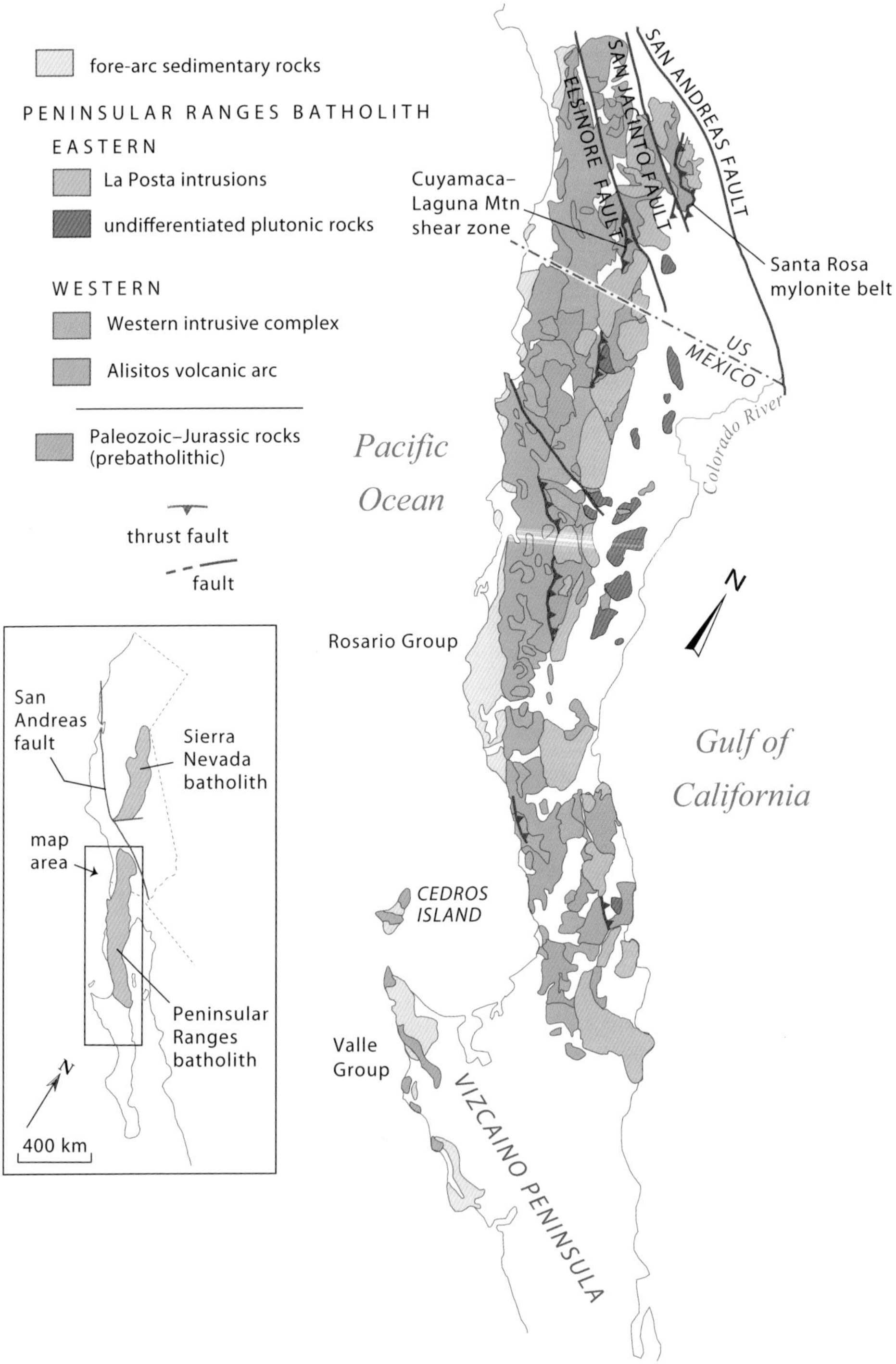
fore-arc sedimentary rocks
PENINSULAR RANGES BATHOLITH
EASTERN
La Posta intrusions
undifferentiated plutonic rocks
WESTERN
Western intrusive complex
Alisitos volcanic arc
Paleozoic–Jurassic rocks (prebatholithic)
thrust fault
fault
San Andreas fault
Sierra Nevada batholith
map area
Peninsular Ranges batholith
N
400 km
SAN ANDREAS FAULT
SAN JACINTO FAULT
ELSINORE FAULT
Cuyamaca–Laguna Mtn shear zone
Santa Rosa mylonite belt
US
MEXICO
Colorado River
Pacific Ocean
N
Rosario Group
Gulf of California
CEDROS ISLAND
Valle Group
VIZCAINO PENINSULA

Peninsular Ranges Batholith in southern California and northern Baja California.
—Map courtesy Kimbrough and others, 2001, and modified with permission

PENINSULAR RANGES BATHOLITH

The Peninsular Ranges Batholith stretches discontinuously 490 miles from Riverside at the south edge of the Transverse Ranges south to the 28th parallel on the Baja California peninsula in Mexico. The entire batholith has remained a rigid, stable block during the development of the San Andreas fault system and the rifting of the Gulf of California in Neogene time.

The Peninsular Ranges Batholith rivals its more widely known sister, the Sierra Nevada Batholith, in size and complexity. It is more accessible than the Sierra because many more roads traverse it, but less well-exposed because of soil and chaparral cover. The southern California portion of the Peninsular

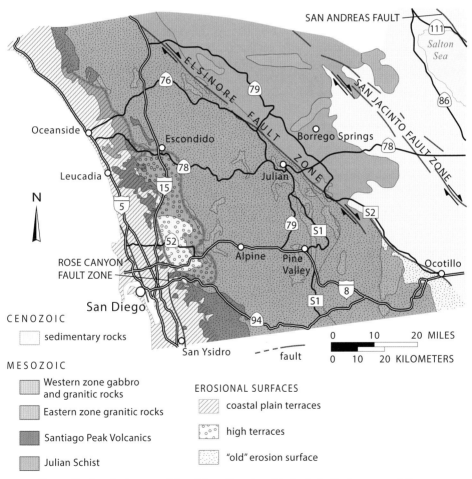

Generalized geologic map of San Diego County with the Late Cretaceous and Eocene erosion surface, high terraces, and coastal plain terraces of the Peninsular Ranges.

Ranges Batholith contains more than one hundred distinct plutons, ranging in composition from olivine-hypersthene gabbro to muscovite-biotite granite. Tonalite and granodiorite plutons are the most abundant. Each spatially and petrographically distinct pluton cooled as deep as 9 miles beneath the Earth's surface. The plutons developed during two distinct phases, one during Jurassic time (170 to 160 million years ago) and the other during Cretaceous time (126 to 75 million years ago). Their ages and intrusion depths decrease eastward across the batholith.

Geologists divide the southern California portion of the Peninsular Ranges Batholith into two parts, separated by wide transition zones, based on differences in both the batholithic rocks and rocks older than the batholith. The older, western zone plutons intruded Mesozoic oceanic crust and volcanic rocks, and consist of three main types of rocks: dark-colored gabbro (oldest), gray tonalite, and light-colored granodiorite (youngest).

The eastern zone tonalitic and granodioritic plutons, which are generally larger than those of the western zone, intruded Paleozoic and Mesozoic continental crust toward the end of subduction zone activity in Late Cretaceous time. Paleozoic marble is especially significant in the Riverside area, where large bodies of country rock completely encased by plutonic rocks have been extensively quarried by the cement industry.

The batholith intruded three main geologic units of Mesozoic age: the Middle Jurassic Bedford Canyon Formation; its presumed metamorphic equivalent, the Julian Schist; and the Early Cretaceous Santiago Peak Volcanics. The Bedford Canyon Formation consists of thousands of feet of quartz sandstone, shale, siltstone, and claystone, all deposited on the seafloor of the continental shelf and then metamorphosed to quartzite and quartz mica schist. The Julian Schist consists of several types of cordierite-, andalusite- and sillimanite-bearing schist, as well as gneiss and a sequence of carbonate-bearing quartzites derived from metamorphism of siltstone and shale. Both the Bedford Canyon Formation and the Julian Schist were deformed and metamorphosed during middle to late Mesozoic subduction and intrusion of the Peninsular Ranges Batholith.

The Santiago Peak Volcanics erupted 128 to 106 million years ago onto an eroded surface of the Bedford Canyon Formation. The rocks are composed of a thick, entirely land-deposited sequence of volcaniclastic breccia, welded tuff, lava flows with visible crystals, dikes, and small intrusions that range from basalt to rhyolite, although intermediate rocks, such as andesite, predominate.

During final stages of crystallization, some of the Peninsular Ranges plutons gave off hydrothermal solutions and hot gases, which intruded the surrounding country rocks in the north part of the batholith and crystallized as veins and coarsely crystalline pegmatite dikes. Many dikes can be traced continuously hundreds of feet; others are merely discontinuous pockets and granular masses containing quartz, albite, muscovite and lepidolite micas, and black tourmaline, also called schorl. Pegmatite dikes in the largest and best known areas, Pala and Mesa Grande, have yielded gem-quality crystals of quartz, spodumene, garnet, topaz, beryl, and world-renowned pink and green tourmaline. The pegmatites crystallized between 100 and 96 million years ago.

Gray and brown Julian Schist and quartzite in roadcut exposures in Box Canyon are intruded by light-colored pegmatite dikes associated with intrusion of the 94-million-year-old La Posta pluton of the Peninsular Ranges Batholith. (33°00.8N, 116°27.0W)

The quartz-rich plutons readily decompose into gravel and sand, which accumulate in the creeks and washes of the mountains and then are carried by streams to the coast to nourish the splendid beaches of the San Diego region.

ELSINORE, SAN JACINTO, AND ROSE CANYON FAULTS

The Peninsular Ranges, an uplifted, westward-tilted plateau between the Pacific Ocean and the Salton Trough, is broken into several large, elongate, subparallel blocks by major, northwest-striking faults, both dip-slip and strike-slip. The blocks have a northwest-trending topographic and structural grain that butts abruptly against the east-west grain of the Transverse Ranges on the north and extends south into Baja California.

The Elsinore fault is one of the several major strands of the San Andreas fault system in southern California. This right-slip fault extends 110 miles northwestward from the Mexican border to the north end of the Santa Ana Mountains, where it splits into the Whittier and Chino faults. The Whittier, also a right-slip fault, carries some of the Elsinore fault's displacement into the Los Angeles Basin. It produced a magnitude 5.9 earthquake in 1987 that was felt all over southern California and caused eight fatalities and $358 million in damage. The Laguna Salada fault is the probable continuation of the Elsinore fault into Baja California, where it produced a magnitude 7.2 earthquake on April 4, 2010. It was probably responsible for a magnitude 7 earthquake in the same area in 1892. The only historic earthquake on the Elsinore fault north of the border was a magnitude 6 earthquake on May 10, 1915.

The Elsinore fault is not a single planar break but an array of overstepping, right-slip faults in a zone as much as 2 miles wide between the northeast side of the Santa Ana Mountains and the southwest edge of the Perris Plain. It has about 6 miles of right-lateral displacement and about 1,200 feet of vertical displacement in the Lake Elsinore area.

The San Jacinto fault is the most seismically active fault system in southern California, having generated eight magnitude 6 or greater earthquakes since 1899. It extends southeastward from the eastern San Gabriel Mountains along the northeast side of the Perris Plain and the southwest side of the Salton Trough. South of Borrego Springs, the fault steps out into the Salton Trough and morphs into the Imperial fault near the town of Imperial. That fault continues across the border and connects to the series of spreading ridges and transform faults at the north end of the East Pacific Rise in the Gulf of California.

Several right-slip faults extend through the San Diego metropolitan area and have contributed to the creation of San Diego Bay. Various fault strands have strike-slip, normal, oblique, or reverse components of displacement. South of downtown San Diego, the Rose Canyon fault breaks into several subparallel splays that underlie much of the central and south parts of San Diego Bay. This fault zone cuts sediment younger than 10,000 years in Rose Canyon, 4 miles north of San Diego Bay. Other parts of the fault zone in the Mt. Soledad, La Jolla, Mission Bay, and downtown areas of San Diego are regarded as hazardous Holocene-age faults. Geologists postulate that the Rose Canyon fault is the south extension of the Newport-Inglewood fault zone that generated a destructive, magnitude 6.3 earthquake in Long Beach in 1933.

THE OLD EROSION SURFACE, PERRIS PLAIN, AND THE POWAY CONGLOMERATE

At the end of Cretaceous time and into Eocene time, big rivers eroded an extensive plateau on the upper surface of the batholith and cut deep canyons into it. The Perris Plain, a large, rectangular area of generally low relief, is a remnant of that erosion surface, known as a peneplain to geologists. Bounded by the Elsinore and San Jacinto faults, the Perris Plain is an internally unfaulted, structural block of eroded Cretaceous batholithic and older rocks. Various low bedrock hills within the Perris Plain rise like tepees to heights of several hundred feet above the surrounding flats. Intervening valleys are filled with Neogene nonmarine sediments and volcanic rocks. You may obtain a good impression of the plain's topographic character by driving I-215 from Murrieta through Sun City and Perris to Riverside.

One of those Eocene rivers was the Ballena River, predecessor of the San Diego River. It eroded 155-million-year-old (Jurassic) volcanic clasts from

Colorful, rounded Poway Conglomerate pebbles and cobbles in a sandy matrix at Lake Murray. Scale is 15 centimeters. (32°47.2N, 117°02.3W)

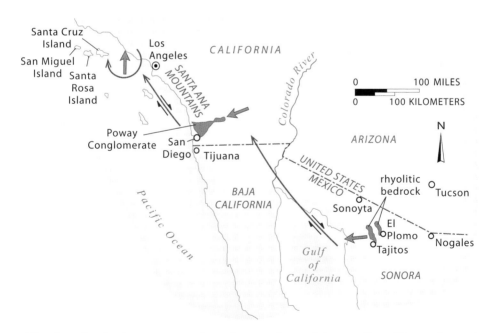

A Late Jurassic volcanic source terrane in northwestern Sonora fed a west-directed Eocene river and submarine fan system that was subsequently offset along right-slip faults during the opening of the Gulf of California. The distinctive conglomerate of the fan is also found in the northern Channel Islands, supporting the hypothesis that rocks in the Transverse Ranges were once an extension of rocks in the Peninsular Ranges but were rotated and displaced to the north. —Modified from Abbott, 1999

Sonora in northern Mexico, and carried them in a deep canyon across the old erosion surface to the coast and directly into the sea. There, it created a fan delta that supplied a submarine fan. The alluvial deposits, consisting of conglomerate, gravel, and sand, are collectively known as the Poway Group for exposures near the northern San Diego County town of Poway. The Poway Conglomerate and Stadium Conglomerate, named for exposures around the football stadium in Mission Valley, are the most distinctive units of the group. Eighty percent of the Jurassic-age cobbles are slightly metamorphosed rhyolitic to dacitic volcanic and volcaniclastic rocks. Quartzite comprises the remaining 20 percent. The well-rounded, moderately well-sorted cobbles vary in color from pale yellow and gray through reddish-purple to black. They are as durable as ball bearings and hard to break with a hammer, so that it is almost impossible to drill wells through conglomerate layers. The sandstone matrix contains calcareous nanoplankton that provide the Eocene age of the Poway Group.

In Neogene time, the Peninsular Ranges were uplifted and the Perris Plain down dropped along the Elsinore fault zone. The Peninsular Ranges tilted westward as a stable block, bounded on the east by the Perris Plain and on the west by the faulted, unstable continental shelf. Deformation has been minor within the stable block, so the old erosion plateau, now standing at elevations as high as 6,000 feet, is preserved.

Coastal terraces on the southeast tip of San Clemente Island, as viewed from Pyramid Head. *(32°48.5N, 118°25.6W)* —Phillip Colla photo/Oceanlight.com

Coastal Terraces

Along the west edge of the Peninsular Ranges, ocean waves eroded the bedrock at sea level, forming flat platforms subsequently uplifted into a series of steps, or terraces, covered with thin deposits of nonmarine sand, gravel, and boulders. The youngest terraces formed in late Quaternary time. Older, higher terraces are at elevations of 700 to 800 feet at the west edge of El Cajon Valley, uplifted this high after they formed during earlier Pleistocene sea levels.

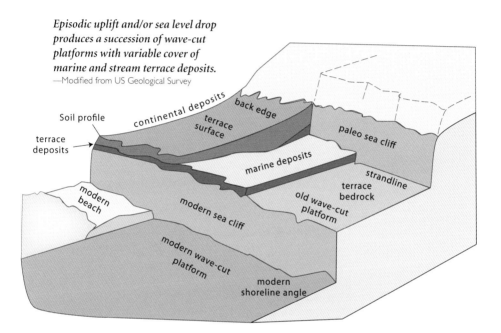

Episodic uplift and/or sea level drop produces a succession of wave-cut platforms with variable cover of marine and stream terrace deposits.
—Modified from US Geological Survey

ROAD GUIDES FOR THE PENINSULAR RANGES

INTERSTATE 5
SAN YSIDRO—SAN CLEMENTE
72 miles

Along this route, I-5 follows the coastal plain, from where it extends 15 miles inland at the border to only 1 mile wide at San Onofre. Seaside cliffs, accessible via short side trips from I-5, offer spectacular exposures of sedimentary rocks deposited in the fore-arc basin in Late Cretaceous to Paleogene time, as well as younger sediments deposited by rivers eroding the uplifted Peninsular Ranges in Neogene time.

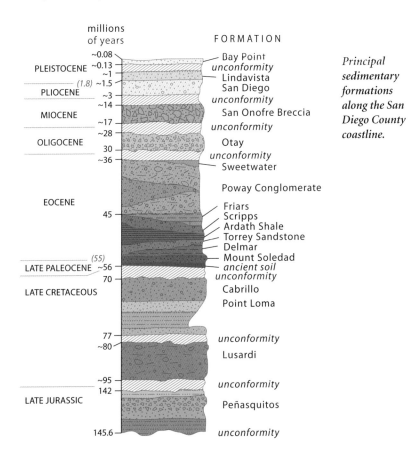

Principal sedimentary formations along the San Diego County coastline.

San Diego Bay and the Silver Strand

Three first-class natural harbors exist on the US west coast: San Diego Bay, San Francisco Bay, and Puget Sound in Washington. San Diego Bay owes its existence to the Tijuana River and how its sand is deposited along the coast.

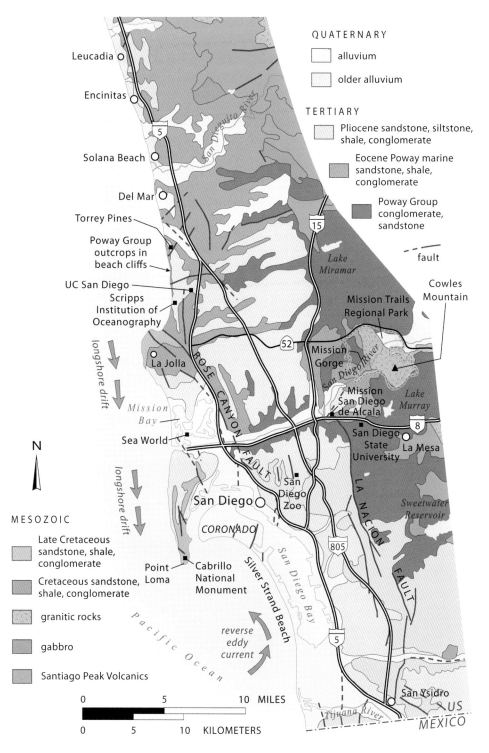

Geology along I-5 from the United States–Mexico border to Leucadia.

The river flows westward from Mexico and then empties into the Pacific Ocean a couple miles north of the border. Whereas net annual transport of beach sand along most of the southern California coast is from north to south, a counterclockwise eddy current in the San Diego bight carries Tijuana River sand northward to Coronado and North Island, forming a long, narrow beach bar that connects North Island to the mainland. This 6-mile-long, 0.3-mile-wide stretch of narrow, sandy beach, called the Silver Strand, forms the west boundary of San Diego Bay.

Like so much of the California coastline, however, the Silver Strand is fighting a losing battle to wave erosion. The sand lost to the sea is not being replaced naturally, because dams on the Tijuana River trap sand before it can reach the sea. Instead, sand is dredged periodically from the San Diego Harbor and deposited at the south end of North Island and along the length of the spit. That operation widens the spit sufficiently so that huge condominium apartments now dominate the length of the Silver Strand. Maybe some day the Tijuana River dams will fill with sediment and become useless for water storage and flood control, and then sand will be released to replenish the Silver Strand naturally. Don't hold your breath!

Point Loma

Point Loma is at the end of a long peninsula that rises from a syncline through Mission Bay at Ocean Beach to the peninsula's tip, where it attains a height

The colorful, east-dipping Point Loma Formation conglomerate and mudstone of Cretaceous age on the west side of Point Loma cliffs are among the few rock formations in California containing dinosaur fossils. (32°40.1N, 117°14.7W)

of about 400 feet. The fairly flat top of the peninsula is capped by Pleistocene sandstone and conglomerate deposits lying unconformably upon much older, gently dipping Late Cretaceous and Eocene fore-arc basin formations. The gap in the sedimentary record represents nearly 50 million years of no deposition, or if sediments were deposited, they were eroded away. The cliffs on the west side of the peninsula are sheer and undergoing constant wave erosion, whereas the gently inclined east side of the peninsula slopes gradually into San Diego Bay, so that many homes and developments are right along the water's edge. The slope is punctuated with large prehistoric and active landslides that endanger structures higher up the slope.

One of the best harbor views in the world is from Cabrillo National Monument, at the south tip of Point Loma. On clear winter days, the panorama stretches from Mexico to the San Gabriel and San Bernardino Mountains east of Los Angeles. On a really clear day, you may see the Coronado Islands to the southwest, off the northwest coast of Mexico, and San Clemente Island, one of the southern Channel Islands, to the west-northwest.

Mission Bay

I-5 passes along the east side of Mission Bay, an expansive recreation area of waterways, bays, and islands that includes Sea World. The bay occupies a coastal lowland and former delta of the San Diego River, which changed its course periodically during the nineteenth century as a result of major floods. Before 1821, the river usually entered San Diego Bay. The river was diverted permanently to Mission Bay in 1876 to prevent San Diego Bay, site of the US Navy's Pacific Fleet, from silting up. Sediment flow into Mission Bay was reduced significantly in 1935 by construction of El Capitan Dam 27 miles upstream. Today, the river is confined to a 1,000-foot-wide channel along the south side of Mission Bay. A trio of jetties shunts longshore drift seaward so that shallow sandbars do not block the San Diego River or the entrance to the Mission Bay yacht basin.

Mission Bay Park was created from 1946 to 1954 by dredging wetlands and making new land from the dredged material. With the current emphasis on preservation of coastal wetlands, it is doubtful a permit could be obtained today for such destruction and reclamation as created this 7-square-mile park.

Poway and Stadium Conglomerate

The apex of the Poway alluvial fan system in the San Diego region is exposed in gravel quarries near the town of Lakeside on CA 67, 18 miles northeast of San Diego. The main body of the fan is exposed along the shores of Lake Murray, located in the southern section of Mission Trails Regional Park, and in road-cuts along Friars Road on the north side of Mission Valley between I-805 and I-15. The submarine part of the alluvial system is exposed in the beach cliffs north of Scripps Pier in La Jolla, and on the northern Channel Islands of San Miguel, Santa Rosa, and Santa Cruz. Distribution of the Poway Conglomerate in San Diego County and on the northern Channel Islands constitutes some of the primary evidence supporting the hypothesis for the clockwise rotation and northwest translation of the western Transverse Ranges from the San Diego coast to their present position.

Poway boulders up to 3 feet in diameter are found in one of the many quarries at Lakeside, about 12 miles east of I-15, where the rocks discharged from a deep gorge onto the coastal plain in Eocene time. (32°54.6N, 116°56.5W)

The Poway Conglomerate in Scripps beach cliffs was deposited in a submarine fan above older black shale. The contact between the two units is an unconformity. (32°52.1N, 117°15.2W)

Torrey Pines State Reserve

The State of California set aside Torrey Pines State Reserve to preserve some unique trees that grow only here and on Santa Rosa Island, but four rock formations spectacularly exposed in the sea cliffs are equally interesting. The two lowermost formations, the Delmar Formation and the Torrey Sandstone, are both 48 million years old (middle Eocene). The overlying Lindavista Formation is a mere 1 million years old (middle Pleistocene) and the Bay Point Formation above it ranges from 400,000 to 120,000 years old (late Pleistocene). The unconformity between Eocene and Pleistocene formations indicates rocks layers of intermediate age were either eroded away or not deposited in the first place.

The Lindavista Formation, a widespread terrace deposit in the San Diego area, caps ridges and mesas from the Mexican border northward to Carlsbad. Because the overlying Bay Point Formation consists of weakly indurated sediments, the Lindavista Formation, which is not exposed in the Torrey Pines sea cliff, erodes into badlands topography with very steep slopes and cliffs less than 20 to 30 feet high.

Geologists have identified four wave-cut coastal terraces in the Torrey Pines State Reserve, but terrace steps are not obvious here because they are covered by younger sediment and have been eroded. A layer of cobbles overlain by younger sedimentary layers marks the top of the wave-eroded platform on each terrace.

Thin-bedded gray Delmar Formation (1) is exposed in the lower quarter of this 100-foot-high Torrey Pines cliff. Three massive beds of tan, pale-green and reddish Torrey Sandstone (2) are exposed in the middle of the sea cliff. The uppermost, rilled, brown cliffs are the late Pleistocene Bay Point Formation (3). (32°55.1N, 117°15.5W) —Photo courtesy J. R. Morgan

During winter months, the beach cliff is undercut at high tide when storm waves toss the hard beach pebbles and cobbles against the cliff. The cliff top slumps onto the beach when the undercut is too great, and the fallen debris is removed by the same storm waves.

Coastal Lagoons

I-5 proceeds northward along the coast like a roller coaster from the tops of high, vegetated and urbanized, wave-cut terraces down into and across wide valleys eroded into those terraces. Bridges carry I-5 across several flat, swampy lagoons in those valleys: San Dieguito at Del Mar, San Elijo near Solana Beach, Batiquitos near Leucadia, and Agua Hedionda and Buena Vista at Carlsbad. These lagoons were some 100 feet lower in elevation during the last glacial advance, about 17,000 years ago, when water was tied up in ice sheets that covered the northern parts of the continent. Sea level was about 300 feet lower,

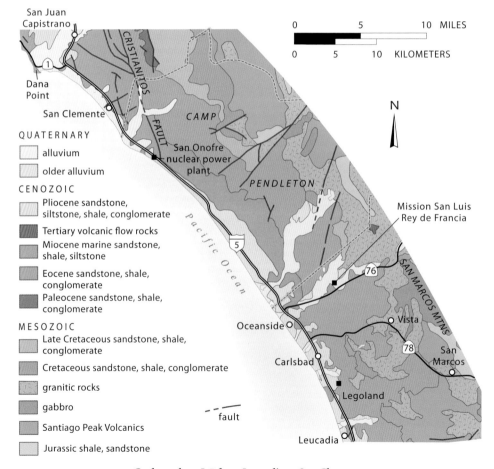

Geology along I-5 from Leucadia to San Clemente.

and deep canyons were eroded into the exposed continental slope. Sea level rose and flooded the canyons when the glaciers melted, and streams deposited muddy sediment to fill the canyons to their present levels. Houses and shopping malls have been deposited on the muddy canyon sediments.

The San Dieguito River is one of the largest rivers in the San Diego region. It flows across its floodplain and empties into the sea at Del Mar. Here conditions are similar to those at the mouth of almost every stream emptying into the sea along the southern California coast in that many of the rivers maintain a direct connection to the ocean only at the time of floods. Otherwise, longshore currents are strong enough to build a sandbar across the mouth of the stream, forming a lagoon or slough that may extend inland for a couple miles. The amount of water and extent of the lagoon depends upon how fast the water seeps through the bar and into the sea. Notice that the Del Mar racetrack lies on the San Dieguito River floodplain; exceptionally heavy rainfall has flooded it in past years.

Camp Pendleton Terrace

Established during World War II, the Camp Pendleton Marine Corps training center covers 187 square miles with a 17-mile-long coastline, the last major undeveloped part of the southern California coast south of Santa Barbara. A large part of the center lies upon a wide, elevated coastal terrace covered with

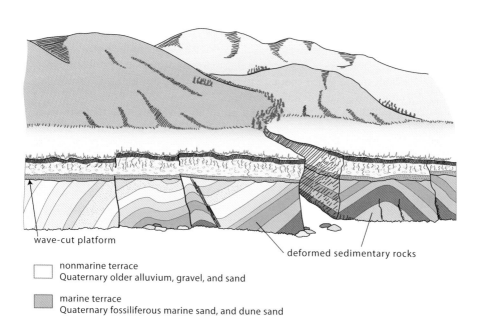

wave-cut platform

deformed sedimentary rocks

☐ nonmarine terrace
Quaternary older alluvium, gravel, and sand

▨ marine terrace
Quaternary fossiliferous marine sand, and dune sand

Breakers erode a flat surface, or wave-cut platform, into the bedrock below the surf, and beach and marine sands are deposited on the beveled bedrock. As the coast is uplifted, nonmarine sediments are deposited over the top of the flat surface, forming a coastal terrace.

unconsolidated sand and gravel dated at 125,000 years. I-5 is on the terrace almost continuously from Oceanside to San Onofre. Before it was elevated to its present height, this terrace was a little below sea level.

The Camp Pendleton terrace has been uplifted rather slowly, at a rate of about 3.6 inches per 1,000 years at San Onofre and 10 inches per 1,000 years at Dana Point. Uplift rates farther north in the Transverse Ranges part of the southern California coast are equal or greater: 6.4 to 8 inches per 1,000 years at Malibu, but more than 80 inches per 1,000 years at Ventura. The highest terrace remnant at Camp Pendleton, about 1,250 feet above sea level, is about 780,000 years old, for a rate of 20 inches per 1,000 years. These numbers are artifices of convenience, however, because the uplift is probably episodic, with several feet occurring at a time in association with local earthquakes.

Remnants of several terraces are well displayed at Camp Pendleton and may be the last undeveloped mainland sequences remaining on the southern California coast. Asphalt, houses, and concrete have generally covered and obliterated terraces elsewhere, such as those on the Palos Verdes Peninsula in the Los Angeles Basin.

Cristianitos Fault and San Onofre Nuclear Generating Station

You'll have to stroll along the beach to see the Cristianitos fault, but it is wonderfully exposed and well worth the short walk. Take Basilone Road (exit 71), named for Medal of Honor recipient John Basilone, turn left at the top of the offramp, cross I-5, and follow the frontage road past Trestles, a favorite local surfing beach, then south a couple of miles to San Onofre State Beach (entrance fee).

The park lies in an area of active landslides along coastal terrace bluffs between I-5 and the Pacific Ocean. Park at the head of Trail No. 1, about 200 yards past the entry kiosk, and hike a trail from the parking lot down to the beach through castellated coastal terrace deposits that ring a large, semicircular landslide amphitheater. Walk up the beach about a half mile toward the power plant to reach the fault. It is best to make this walk at low tide.

The Cristianitos fault is a right-oblique strike-slip fault that juxtaposes drab gray-brown, vegetation-draped Monterey Formation of late Miocene age, to the south, against yellow, marine sandstone of the San Mateo Formation of Miocene and Pliocene age, which crops out in a long, unbroken layer all the way to the nuclear power plant to the north. The sandstone, shale, and fault have been planed flat by a wave-cut platform and overlain by 3 feet of unfaulted alluvial deposit of boulders, cobbles, and red-brown alluvial sand and gravel determined to be 125,000 to 100,000 years old. The remainder of the cliff consists of about 40 feet of younger alluvium. Because the wave-cut platform and its overlying sediments are unfaulted, the fault is considered inactive by California State criteria, which define an active fault as one that has slipped in the last 35,000 years.

About one-half mile up the beach from the fault is the San Onofre Nuclear Generating Station. It was constructed securely upon the 20-foot-high, sea cliff foundation of San Mateo Formation sandstone and began operation in 1983. The station produced 2,254 megawatts of power per year, enough to serve the

The Cristianitos fault (arrows) juxtaposes the yellow San Mateo Formation sandstone (1) with the tan Monterey Formation (2). The dashed line indicates a wave-cut platform overlain by unfaulted boulders and cobbles and alluvial sand and gravel (3). A Quaternary-age landslide in the shale covers much of the fault contact, so scramble up a debris slope for a good view of the fault or use binoculars to see it from the beach. (33°21.79N, 117°32.73W)

needs of 2.75 million households per year, equivalent to 188 billion cubic feet of natural gas, until permanent shutdown of its units 2 and 3 in June 2013. Eighteen square miles of solar panels would be required to duplicate the power generated by the station.

A couple of miles north of San Clemente at San Juan Capistrano, I-5 goes from the Peninsular Ranges into the Los Angeles Basin via freeway corridors through Orange County suburbs.

INTERSTATE 8
OCEAN BEACH—OCOTILLO
90 miles

Along this route, I-8 transects several of the more than one hundred plutons of the Peninsular Ranges Batholith and also traverses its old erosion surface. The route commences in Ocean Beach, across the San Diego River from Sea World, and proceeds east along the floor of the San Diego River in Mission Valley for about 8 miles. Cliffs along each side of the valley expose the Stadium Conglomerate of the Poway Group, composed mostly of metamorphosed rhyolitic to dacitic volcanic

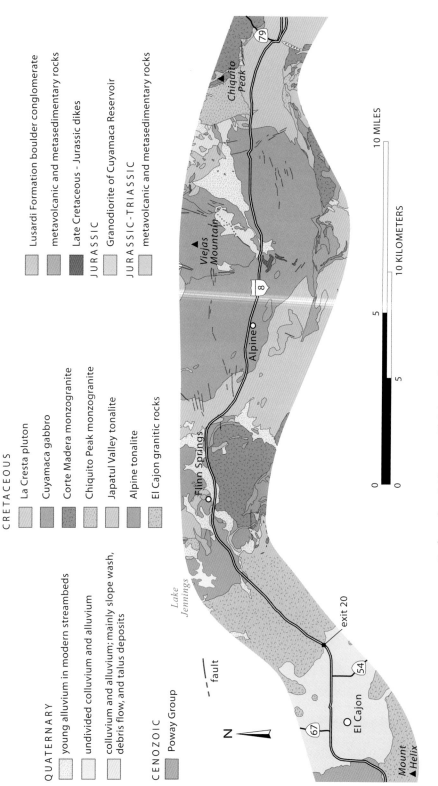

CRETACEOUS

Lusardi Formation boulder conglomerate

metavolcanic and metasedimentary rocks

Late Cretaceous - Jurassic dikes

JURASSIC

Granodiorite of Cuyamaca Reservoir

JURASSIC-TRIASSIC

metavolcanic and metasedimentary rocks

CRETACEOUS

La Cresta pluton

Cuyamaca gabbro

Corte Madera monzogranite

Chiquito Peak monzogranite

Japatul Valley tonalite

Alpine tonalite

El Cajon granitic rocks

QUATERNARY

young alluvium in modern streambeds

undivided colluvium and alluvium

colluvium and alluvium; mainly slope wash, debris flow, and talus deposits

CENOZOIC

Poway Group

- - - fault

N

Geology along I-8 between El Cajon and CA 79. —Modified from Todd, 2004

10 MILES

10 KILOMETERS

and volcaniclastic cobbles within a sandstone matrix. The conglomerate, which was deposited by a west-flowing river system during Eocene time, is up to 150 feet thick on the north side of the valley near Qualcomm Stadium.

From Fairmont Avenue (exit 8), I-8 climbs past San Diego State University and the town of La Mesa, over Grossmont Summit, and down into El Cajon Valley. Santiago Peak Volcanics are exposed on both sides of the College Avenue off-ramp (exit 10). Stadium Conglomerate is exposed in numerous roadcuts between College Avenue and Grossmont Summit.

East of Lake Murray Boulevard (exit 11), you'll see Cowles Mountain (elevation 1,591 feet) about 5 miles to the north, and east of CA 125 (exit 14B), Mt. Helix (elevation 1,373 feet) is about 3 miles to the southeast. Both Cowles and Helix are prominent exposures of Peninsular Ranges Batholith rocks. El Cajon Valley is bounded on its south and east sides by batholith rocks, and by Eocene clastic sedimentary rocks on the west and north sides, where landslides abound. On the valley floor, batholith rocks are overlain by a thin layer of Eocene-age Friars Formation and by an even thinner veneer of Holocene alluvium. The Friars Formation consists of fine-grained lagoonal and brackish water deposits of the Poway Group.

Plutons of the Peninsular Ranges Batholith

East of this one-time farming and ranching area in El Cajon Valley, I-8 begins a 65-mile-long climb from Greenfield Drive (exit 20) through granitic and metamorphic rocks over the range summit to the west edge of the Salton Trough. Along the way you'll pass through ten or so granitic plutons of the Peninsular Ranges Batholith, consisting mainly of tonalite, with its high proportion of dark iron and magnesium silicate minerals, to granite and granodiorite with abundant lighter-colored sodium, potassium, and aluminum silicate minerals. These rocks rose from great depths as molten rock about 120 to 102 million years ago and crystallized into large individual plutons. As you drive this stretch of highway, try to distinguish the rock types from the way they crop out and weather. Tonalite forms subdued topography with gray-weathering boulders poking up between thick coastal chaparral, gabbro is similar to tonalite but with darker outcrops and reddish-weathering soils, and granodiorite is light gray and erodes to boulder-pile topography. The plutons intruded dark, varicolored, foliated rock called the Julian Schist.

From Greenfield Road in El Cajon almost to Lake Jennings Park Road (exit 23), I-8 passes through the El Cajon biotite granite pluton. You'll see the granitic rock in roadcuts, as boulders on the hillsides, and making up all the nearby mountains.

Between Harbison Canyon Road (exit 27) and Tavern Road (exit 30), you drive through deeply weathered pyroxene-biotite tonalite of the La Cresta pluton, ranging in age from 110 to about 102 million years. Its relatively rapid rate of chemical weathering and erosion creates a low, rolling topography with grayish soils. Near Tavern Road, the La Cresta pluton has a gradational contact with enclave-rich, pyroxene-biotite tonalite of the Alpine pluton, which is about 108 million years old. It is not a good idea to stop along I-8 to study

Peninsular Ranges Batholith rocks, clockwise from upper left: gabbro, tonalite with fragment of mafic enclave, granodiorite, biotite granite.

these rocks in freeway roadcuts, but a fine place to do so is near the town of Alpine. Take Tavern Road (exit 30) to Alpine Boulevard, which parallels I-8 on its south side. Along the 2-mile stretch that heads west to Peutz Valley Road, deep roadcuts expose weathered La Cresta tonalite, along with unweathered core-stones—boulders of the tonalite that remain behind after the surrounding weathered tonalite has eroded away.

You can study the unweathered interior of the Alpine pluton in fresh outcrops at the intersection of East Victoria Drive and Victoria Place, north of Alpine Boulevard. (Drive east on Alpine Boulevard through Alpine to East Victoria Drive, then turn north.) This tonalite is less mafic than La Cresta tonalite.

About 7 miles east of Tavern Road, a vista at PM 35 (only for eastbound travelers) overlooks the Sweetwater River Canyon, one of several deep canyons that was cut into the batholith during Late Cretaceous and Eocene time. The Sweetwater River flows 55 miles west-southwestward across the mountains and empties into San Diego Bay about 7 miles southeast of San Diego. The river is thought to have emptied originally into El Cajon Valley and then into the Eocene-age Ballena River, providing additional erosive power to carve Mission Gorge.

A large, triangular-shaped roadcut north of the vista on the north side of I-8 exposes light gray granite cut by several mafic dikes. Tonalite, with its occasional dark gray outcrops, makes up most of the subdued hilly area south of the vista point.

Roadcut in weathered pyroxene-biotite tonalite of the La Cresta pluton. Boulders on the surface and within the granite are unweathered core-stones. (32°52.32N, 116°47.12W)

Ghostlike clots of dark rock, so common in the Alpine tonalite, have variable shapes, compositions, and textures and probably represent mafic dikes intruded into and disrupted by the tonalite when both were in a molten state. Blue pencil for scale. (32°50.7N, 116°45.0W)

Roadcut exposure of four black mafic dikes in gray granite. Dikes are common in the Peninsular Ranges Batholith. (32°50.3N, 116°30.6W)

The type locality for La Cresta tonalite is at the intersection of I-8 with CA 79, or Japatul Valley Road, at exit 40. A type locality is the first major place a rock is described and named. About 1.5 miles east of the interchange, the roadcut on the south shoulder of I-8 exposes a good example of this 109-million-year-old pyroxene-biotite tonalite. Look on the north side of the highway for a small roadcut in brick-red residual soil—an errant remainder of the Eocene-age erosion surface.

Roadcut exposures of chocolate-brown rock west of the Pine Valley exit (exit 45) are Julian Schist intruded by dikes from still another granitic pluton. Between the Sunrise Highway (exit 47) and Buckman Springs Road (exit 51), I-8 proceeds down Cottonwood Valley, which was eroded along an extremely deformed part of a shear zone in the Cuyamaca-Laguna Mountains. A prong of biotite-hornblende tonalite of the Granite Mountain pluton intruded northward into the shear zone and underlies the broad southern part of the valley. Quaternary landslides coalesce along the west side of the valley.

Much of the eastern zone of the Peninsular Ranges Batholith is made up of the Granite Mountain and La Posta plutons. A large roadcut in the Kitchen Creek on-ramp (exit 54) for I-8 eastbound exposes a sharp contact between La Posta tonalite and the older Morena tonalite. The latter has no sign of deformation that can be related to intrusion of the La Posta pluton, even though the La Posta is banded and strongly foliated parallel to the contact.

The La Posta tonalitic pluton is the largest of all the plutons in the batholith, covering over 540 square miles in eastern San Diego County from the community of Vallecitos south into Baja California. It extends about 35 miles along I-8 from approximately Kitchen Creek (exit 54) to the east edge of the In-Ko-Pah Mountains. It ranges in age from 104 to 94 million years. Geologists have determined that the pluton represents a single, enormous pulse of magma that slowly cooled inward, forming a series of concentric rock units. The magma intruded to a depth of about 6 miles, but east of Carrizo Gorge, the intrusion depth was about 11 miles. Between La Posta Creek (PM 57) and Crestwood Road (exit 61), La Posta tonalite weathers to a light tan color. Its mineral type and size vary, from rocks with small to large biotite crystals to those containing hornblende.

In the vicinity of Kitchen Creek Road, the topography changes from that of high mountains and deep, narrow valleys to an elevated mountain plateau with meadows and rounded granite ridges. The mountains maintain these features while gradually rising to the range summit at Crestwood (elevation 4,181 feet). Pull off on Crestwood Road and park in the casino parking lot for some good views across the Eocene erosion surface. The mountains are covered with brush, whereas live oaks are numerous in the valleys.

Jacumba Volcanics

I-8 descends from the crest of the Peninsular Ranges into Jacumba Valley via a steep-walled canyon with boulder-covered sides and ridges. The 93-million-year-old rock is a true granite a little younger than the La Posta pluton. *Jacumba*

View south from Crestwood Road area across low hills. The nearly flat surface in the background is a remnant of the erosion surface carved on the Peninsular Ranges batholithic rocks in Eocene time. (32°42N, 116°21W)

means "hot water" in the language of the Kumeyaay people, and sulfurous warm springs there are considered by many to be medicinal.

The highway crosses Carrizo Creek at the exit 73 for Jacumba. East of the creek on the south side of the highway, you'll see Round Mountain (elevation 3,367 feet), a large, symmetrical volcanic neck of Miocene age. I-8 passes through roadcuts in the volcano's lava flows, ridges in the lava where it buckled from the pressure of the building volcano, and pyroclastic lahar deposits—mudflows that rushed down the volcano during the eruptions. Resistant mesas northeast of Jacumba preserve nearly horizontal remnants of andesitic lava flows that step down to the east across faults to roadcut

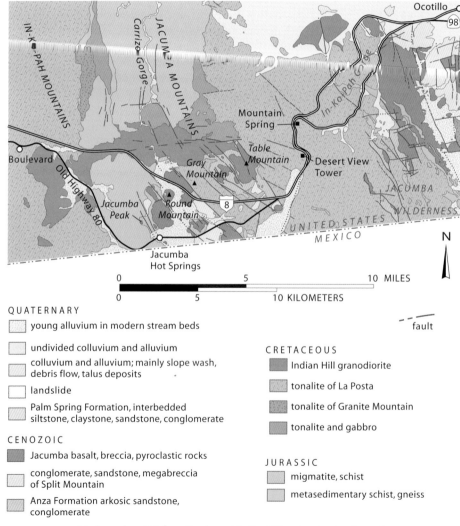

Geology along I-8 from Boulevard to Ocotillo. —Modified from Todd, 2004

exposures along County Road S2 in the Anza-Borrego Desert. Many of the flows have a lower, baked zone of brick-red rock that formed when the lavas flowed out across the gravel and conglomerate surface about 19 to 12 million years ago. An abandoned quarry near the base of Table Mountain exposes thick accumulations of pink and purple volcanic fragments and ash that were deposited as a cinder cone.

In-Ko-Pah Gorge

I-8 continues its abrupt descent of about 2,640 feet over 11.5 miles through In-Ko-Pah Gorge to the floor of the Salton Trough. La Posta granodiorite, between the summit at Crestwood Road (exit 61) and Mountain Springs Road (exit 80), contains bodies of dark mica schist cut by many dikes of very coarse, muscovite-bearing pegmatite. You may obtain an up-close view of the inner biotite-muscovite part of the pluton in granite boulders at Desert View Tower (exit 77). The tower is worth the small price of admission to obtain an appreciation of the great efforts required to put a highway through the gorge and for a spectacular view of the Salton Trough to the east and the Salton Sea to the northeast, 37 miles away.

Long before construction of I-8, the area around Mountain Springs was a stopping place on the several generations of trails and wagon roads that preceded primitive automobile roads. The bench in and around the Mountain Springs exit is thought to be the surface of a massive landslide off the east side of the Peninsular Ranges. Jumbled and brecciated granitic rocks on both sides

The natural color of tonalite is light gray on fresh surfaces in the In-Ko-Pah Mountains, but a patina of reddish-orange desert varnish covers weathered surfaces of the boulder-pile mountains. (32°40.4N, 116°05.6W)

of the highway at the base of the Mountain Springs grade are regarded as the toe of the slide.

Los Angeles—Beaumont
78 miles

I-10 starts in the Los Angeles Basin. We'll begin our tour of it east of the Los Angeles River. Most of the route lies in the San Gabriel and San Bernardino Valleys and across the north edge of the Peninsular Ranges.

Monterey Hills

East of the Los Angeles River, I-10 skirts the north edge of the Monterey Hills, a west-trending extension of the Puente Hills. A steep, south-dipping sequence of Pliocene siltstone, mudstone, and conglomerate forms the hills and is typical of the sedimentary fill in the northern Los Angeles Basin. Late Miocene shale and sandstone of the Puente Formation, also dipping moderately or steeply southward, form the Puente Hills south of the highway. Streams that existed before the Puente Hills were uplifted cut channels across the hills during their uplift. Now the streams have been diverted by the uplifted hills, so that the old channels are wind gaps carrying I-710 and various main north-south boulevards, including Monterey Pass Road and Atlantic Boulevard.

Five miles east of Atlantic Boulevard (exit 23A), I-10 enters the San Gabriel Valley, an intensely urbanized region lying upon an extensive apron of huge alluvial fans stretching eastward from Pasadena to San Bernardino. The sediment was shed southward from numerous deep canyons in the southern front of the San Gabriel Mountains.

The Whittier Narrows is a water gap about 2 miles south of I-10 between the Montebello Hills to the west and the Puente Hills to the east. Both the Rio Hondo and the San Gabriel Rivers flow from the San Gabriel Valley through the narrows to enter the Los Angeles Basin. I-10 crosses the Rio Hondo between exits 27 and 28. The October 1, 1987, Whittier Narrows earthquake, which measured 5.9 on the Richter scale, had its epicenter here. It caused eight fatalities, injured several hundred, and left property damage estimated at $358 million in the east Los Angeles area.

Kellogg Hill

The La Vida shale member of the Monterey Formation is exposed at Kellogg Hill, where I-10 goes over the north end of the San Jose Hills between West Covina and CA 71. The La Vida member is white, thin-bedded, platy, siliceous shale, clay shale, and siltstone.

East of the Kellogg interchange, I-10 skirts the south edge of brown hills of the 16-million-year-old Glendora Volcanics of middle Miocene age. Predominantly andesite and basalt, they lie unconformably on Mesozoic plutonic rocks exposed in grass-covered spurs along the north flank of the Chino Hills. Wells

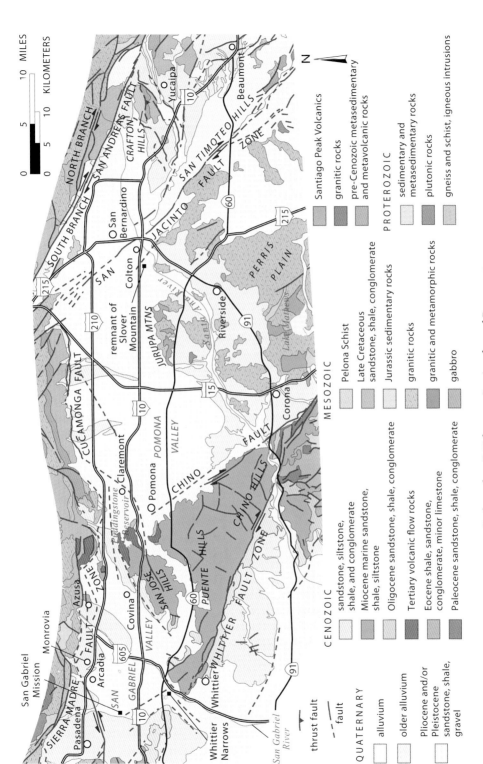

Geology along I-10 between Los Angeles and Beaumont.

QUATERNARY

CENOZOIC

- alluvium
- older alluvium
- Pliocene and/or Pleistocene sandstone, shale, gravel
- sandstone, siltstone, shale, and conglomerate
- Miocene marine sandstone, shale, siltstone
- Oligocene sandstone, shale, conglomerate
- Tertiary volcanic flow rocks
- Eocene shale, sandstone, conglomerate, minor limestone
- Paleocene sandstone, shale, conglomerate

MESOZOIC

- Pelona Schist
- Late Cretaceous sandstone, shale, conglomerate
- Jurassic sedimentary rocks
- granitic rocks
- granitic and metamorphic rocks
- gabbro

- Santiago Peak Volcanics
- granitic rocks
- pre-Cenozoic metasedimentary and metavolcanic rocks

PROTEROZOIC

- sedimentary and metasedimentary rocks
- plutonic rocks
- gneiss and schist, igneous intrusions

thrust fault

fault

have penetrated as much as 3,500 feet of the formation beneath the city of Covina. Extrusion of the Glendora Volcanics is thought to have coincided with the opening of the Los Angeles Basin when the Transverse Ranges rotated clockwise away from the Peninsular Ranges.

Colton, Riverside Cement Quarries, and Minerals

The northernmost exposures of the Peninsular Ranges are south of I-10 in the Jurupa Mountains. There, tonalite of the Peninsular Ranges Batholith intruded and metamorphosed Paleozoic rock, especially limestone, which has been quarried and mined extensively for concrete cement products. You'll see the forlorn remnant of the largest quarries near Colton, about one-half mile south of I-10 between Pepper and Rancho Avenues (exits 69 and 70A, respectively). Today, a shapeless mound is all that is left of Slover Mountain, once a 700-foot-high hill of marble.

Other large surface and underground quarries are located between Colton and Riverside. The most famous quarry is Crestmore, which has produced millions of tons of limestone for the manufacture of Portland concrete cement since it first opened in 1908. The many mine openings, quarry exposures, and tens of thousands of feet of diamond-drill cores make these hills a natural laboratory to study the compositions, ages, and spatial relations of some particularly complex rocks and minerals.

The tonalite intrusion at Crestmore metamorphosed a large, magnesium-rich limestone body to coarse marble. Subsequently, a relatively small, pipelike mass of fine-grained granite intruded part of the tonalite and metamorphic rocks. Siliceous fluids in the intrusion produced a 50-foot-thick zone of chemically altered rock in one of the main limestone bodies. Most of the inner part of the altered rock consists of brown grossularite garnet with lesser amounts of diopside, wollastonite, idocrase, and monticellite. Of particular interest to mineralogists, however, are the great variety and highly variable amounts of nearly one hundred unusual minerals produced by the alteration. Some of these minerals were first discovered and identified at Crestmore, including crestmoreite, riversideite, californite, ellestadite, and wilkeite.

Mt. Rubidoux (elevation 1,329 feet) is a granite ridge in the middle of Riverside and is its main landmark. A white cross surmounts the middle of the ridge's three peaks, which are replicated in freeway retaining walls as a pattern of three arches with a cross in the center arch. The Santa Ana River flows along the northwest base of the ridge, separating Riverside from Jurupa Valley, where granite hills are cut by pegmatite dikes containing minerals that give their names to local streets, including Pyrite, Feldspar, and Rutile Streets and Limonite Avenue.

Santa Ana River

I-10 crosses the Santa Ana River, the largest river in the Los Angeles metropolitan area, at the intersection of I-10 and I-215. With a length of 75 miles, it provides almost 70 percent of the total water recharge for the Santa Ana River basin. Its headwaters rise in crystalline igneous and metamorphic rocks of the San Gabriel, San Bernardino, San Jacinto, and Santa Ana Mountains.

Thick alluvial fan deposits of sand and gravel underlie parts of the river system upstream of San Bernardino. The river crosses sandstone and shale in the foot-hills, unconsolidated alluvial deposits in the valleys between San Bernardino and Corona, and stream deposits downstream of Santa Ana Canyon. It empties into the Pacific Ocean at Huntington Beach.

The river system has been greatly modified in the last one hundred years or so by diverting river discharge with dams and man-made channels, partly within old river floodplains and partly at the upper parts of the great alluvial fans shed from the surrounding mountains. The fans are ideal sites for the infiltration and lateral migration of water to replenish copious quantities of water withdrawn by thousands of wells in the inland valleys and the coastal plain of Orange County.

The Santa Ana River is notable in the seismic history of southern California. Gaspar de Portolá's land expedition was encamped on the bank of the river on July 28, 1769, when an earthquake occurred during the night. According to Juan Crespí, the expedition's recorder, the earthquake was so strong that it threw the river out of its banks. This was the first written record of an earth-quake in California. Its magnitude has been estimated as 6 on the Richter scale.

Crafton Hills and Yucaipa Plain

The Crafton Hills preserve an isolated fragment of the Vincent–Orocopia–Chocolate Mountains thrust, the major low-angle fault that represents the contact between the old North American continent and the subducted Farallon Plate. The southern one-fifth of the hills is made up of Proterozoic-age gneiss. The central two-fifths of the hills consist of gneiss, and both gneissic units are in thrust contact with Pelona Schist, which makes up the northern two-fifths of the hills. Roadside exposures along the north side of I-10 between Wabash Avenue (exit 82) and Yucaipa Boulevard (exit 83) were cut in highly frac-tured gneiss. The roadcuts are now mostly covered with retaining walls and restraining nets to inhibit loose rocks and slides from falling onto the highway.

West of the Crafton Hills to the head of San Gorgonio Pass at Beaumont, I-10 traverses an old, gently sloping surface of unconsolidated, coalescing allu-vial fans called the Yucaipa Plain. Wide, flat-floored arroyos have been eroded into the plain by the same intermittent streams that carried and deposited sand and gravel from the eastern San Bernardino Mountains a few miles to the north. Recent uplift has rejuvenated the streams, incising new gullies about 10 feet below the old arroyo floors.

INTERSTATE 15
SAN DIEGO—CORONA
97 miles

I-15 starts at its T intersection with I-5 next to Naval Base San Diego and along-side San Diego Bay about 3 miles southeast of downtown San Diego. Between the base, which is the US Navy's largest on the west coast, and Mission Valley, I-15 proceeds north through canyons cut into pebbly conglomerate and marine sand-stone and siltstone of the San Diego Formation, which was deposited in a large,

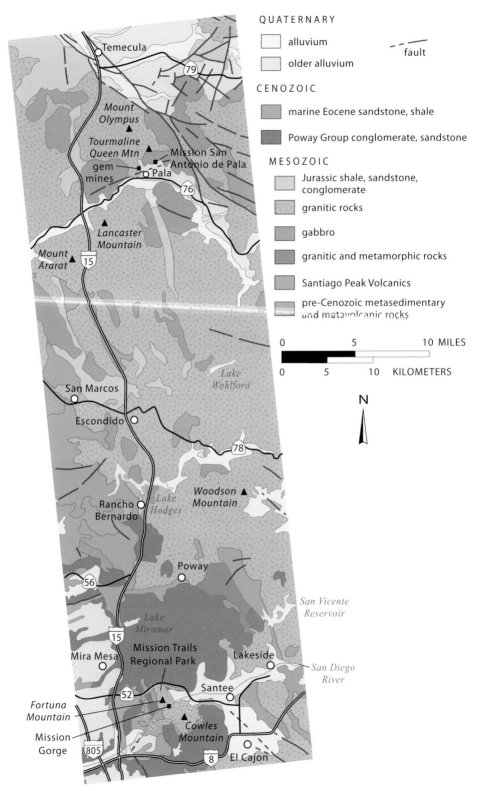

QUATERNARY

| | alluvium |
| | older alluvium |

- - - fault

CENOZOIC

| | marine Eocene sandstone, shale |
| | Poway Group conglomerate, sandstone |

MESOZOIC

	Jurassic shale, sandstone, conglomerate
	granitic rocks
	gabbro
	granitic and metamorphic rocks
	Santiago Peak Volcanics
	pre-Cenozoic metasedimentary and metavolcanic rocks

Temecula

79

Mount Olympus ▲

Tourmaline Queen Mtn ▲

gem mines ■

Mission San Antonio de Pala

Pala

76

Lancaster Mountain ▲

Mount Ararat ▲ 15

0   5   10 MILES

0   5   10 KILOMETERS

N

Lake Wohlford

San Marcos

Escondido

78

Woodson Mountain ▲

Rancho Bernardo

Lake Hodges

Poway

56

San Vicente Reservoir

Lake Miramar

15

Mira Mesa

Mission Trails Regional Park

Lakeside

San Diego River

52

Santee

Fortuna Mountain ■

Mission Gorge

Cowles Mountain ▲

805

8

El Cajon

Geology along I-15 from I-8 in San Diego to Temecula.

open, crescent-shaped bay in middle to late Pliocene time. Red-orange to brown, gravelly and sandy terrace deposits of Pleistocene age overlie the formation.

Mission Valley and Mission Gorge

Mission Valley (exit 6B) has existed for 50 million years, eroded by a river, called the Ballena, issuing out of northern Mexico in middle Eocene time. The river carved a deep canyon, Mission Gorge, at the site of Mission Trails Regional Park, about 5 miles northeast of the I-8 and I-15 intersection. For such a river to come out of Mexico and flow to the sea across what is now the Peninsular Ranges, the landscape had to look very different than today. Before the Gulf of California existed, the river and its tributaries eroded a flat, low-relief surface, which is now a subdued yet high-elevation flat across the Peninsular Ranges. The river course was eventually displaced right-laterally by the San Andreas fault system during the opening of the Gulf of California, and the mountains rose, cutting off the river's headwaters. The San Diego River occupies the valley, but less water comes down Mission Valley today than it did before about 20 million years ago.

Kearny Mesa

I-15 ascends through conglomeratic and sandy layers of the San Diego Formation and onto the broad, flat Kearny Mesa between exits 12 and 14. The mesa, on which Marine Corps Air Station Miramar is located, is one of many terraces along the San Diego coastal area. Known as the Lindavista terrace, it's about

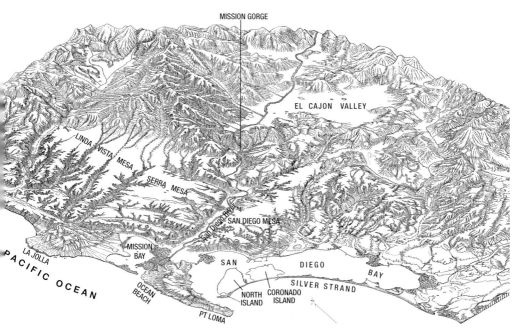

Coastal terraces and mesas of the San Diego region. —Drawn by E. Quayle in Hertlein and Grant, 1944

400 feet above sea level and part of a series of terraces formed by wave action over 1 million years ago, either when sea level was 400 feet higher than today, or more probably because the land has risen 400 feet over the last 1 million years. As you drive north past the air station runway on the west side of the highway, look east to see if you can pick out the much older, higher (elevation about 800 feet), and greatly dissected Poway terrace.

Santiago Peak Volcanics

Red-brown-weathering Santiago Peak Volcanics are exposed in roadcuts on the west side of the highway 1 mile north of Miramar Road (exit 14). Deep in the roadcut, they are dark, angular, and blocky rocks. In the surrounding area, they seem to poke up through the Eocene sedimentary rocks as if they intruded the layers, but they didn't. These Early Cretaceous volcanic rocks erupted as lava flows and were subsequently uplifted. Because of their extreme resistance to weathering and erosion, they formed ridges and peaks around which younger Eocene sediments were deposited. In fact, Santiago Peak Volcanics form many of San Diego County's highlands, including Black Mountain (elevation 4,051 feet), the Del Cerro highlands near Lake Murray, and San Miguel Mountain (elevation 2,565 feet) near Jamul.

From Carmel Mountain Road (exit 21) north about 3 miles to Rancho Bernardo Road (exit 24), deep roadcuts expose gray to greenish-gray mudstone and yellow-gray Eocene sandstone of the Mission Valley Formation, which is prone to ubiquitous, small landslides and has to be held up by large retaining walls. The clay-rich layers impede percolation of groundwater, so slip surfaces may form along the bedding planes.

Gabbro, Tonalite, and Granodiorite

Three distinctive rock units of the Peninsular Ranges Batholith are well exposed in roadcuts and hillslopes over the 35 miles of I-15 between Rancho Bernardo and the Elsinore fault zone at Temecula. San Marcos gabbro of Cretaceous age is one of the main components of the batholith. It forms the prominent, barren, and typically red-brown hillside of Bernardo Mountain (elevation 1,150 feet), 1 mile west of the bridge over Lake Hodges (between exits 26 and 27).

You may study outcrops of the batholith in fresh roadcuts along Old US 395 (Centre City Parkway), which is the frontage road for, and a more leisurely drive than, I-15. You can reach Centre City Parkway via exit 33 or 37. Fresh, black, coarsely crystalline gabbro is exposed on Old US 395 roadcuts about 1.25 miles south of Deer Springs/Mountain Meadow Road (exit 37).

Tonalite is more easily eroded than gabbro and granodiorite, so it forms gently rolling hills and subtle valleys in the Escondido region. The best and safest place to study tonalite is in a big roadcut on Old US 395 at Call Box 395 58 on the east flank of Mt. Ararat (elevation 891 feet).

Bedford Canyon Formation slate is exposed in the vicinity of Gopher Canyon Road (exit 41). Ridges east and west of the highway consist of grano-diorite, but Santiago Peak Volcanics are just about the only rocks exposed in the roadcuts because they are so resistant to weathering.

Granodiorite is the third major plutonic rock type in this part of the batholith. Fresh outcrops are tan, resistant, and blocky, as you will see along the Champagne Highway section of Old US 395 in the vicinity of Lawrence Welk Resort between I-15 exits 37 and 41. Hillslopes behind the resort are littered

Roadcut exposure of San Marcos gabbro on Old 395. (33°10.793N, 117°06.903W)

Roadcut exposure of tonalite with pieces of dark mafic rock enclosed within it. Pencil for scale. (33°14.883N, 117°09.108W)

with tan core-stones boulders, a typical boulder-pile outcrop style of granodiorite throughout the batholith.

From the graceful, single-span bridge carrying Lilac Road high over I-15 north of exit 43, the highway descends the south slope of the San Luis Rey River valley between Mt. Ararat to the west and Keys Canyon to the east. It crosses the San Luis Rey River at its junction with CA 76, where avocado orchards thrive on nutrient-rich, reddish gabbroic soil. The soil color indicates a high iron content, typical of mafic rocks, such as the San Marcos gabbro that prevails in this area. As the highway climbs the north slope of the valley, notice how reddish-brown gabbroic soils alternate with the light-colored, bouldery outcroppings of granodiorite.

Pala Gem-Bearing Pegmatite

The pegmatite dikes of San Diego and Riverside Counties are world famous for deposits of tourmaline (elbaite and schorl), beryl, spessartine, and spodumene. Spectacular pink and green elbaite crystals are found in pockets within the pegmatite dikes in private quarries in the Pala, Ramona, Rincon, and Mesa Grande mining districts. The Pala mine owners have small museums and will let you collect from the mine dumps for a fee. Take CA 76 east from I-15 (exit 46) for 5.6 miles to the community of Pala, then travel north a few miles on County Road S16 to the mines along Pala Creek.

Tourmaline Queen Mine near Pala has produced some extraordinarily beautiful specimens of elbaite, a member of the tourmaline group. This pair of 9-inch-tall, dark red crystals grows from a quartz crystal accompanied by smaller tourmaline crystals. This mineral specimen is unique and famously known to mineralogists worldwide as the Rabbit Ears. —Photo courtesy of John Veevaert, Trinity Mineral Company

About one hundred different minerals have been reported in the Pala pegmatites. The most abundant elements in the minerals are boron, phosphorous, beryllium, bismuth, cesium, lithium, niobium, tantalum, tin, rubidium, antimony, thorium, and vanadium. The abundance of tourmaline in pegmatites throughout the Peninsular Ranges Batholith indicates the high concentration of boron in the batholith's magmas.

Many pegmatite dikes are so well exposed that they stand out on smooth slopes as north- and northwest-trending, light-colored, riblike projections. Some dikes are uniformly tabular, others may branch or pinch or swell, and some are as much as 1 mile long. In places a single dike may branch into several subparallel dikes. Most gem-bearing pegmatites are in gabbro or tonalite plutons and pinch out or terminate against other rock types. The pegmatite dikes formed between 100 and 96 million years ago when residual magma crystallized as veins along well-developed fractures in the older gabbro plutons.

Elsinore Fault Zone and Temecula Valley

About 1.3 miles north of the San Diego–Riverside County line, I-15 passes the California Highway Patrol station in a canyon bounded by boulder-pile slopes of granodiorite. North of the station, I-15 crosses the Elsinore fault scarp and descends into Temecula Valley. The Elsinore fault, one of the major strands of the San Andreas fault system, controls much of the topography in this area, including the linear Temecula Valley and the steep front of the Elsinore Mountains. As you make the descent into the valley, you'll see on the northeastern skyline the highest peak in southern California: San Gorgonio Mountain (elevation 11,499 feet), in the San Bernardino Mountains.

I-15 crosses the Santa Margarita River, which flowed through here before the Elsinore and Santa Ana Mountains existed. It carved Temecula Canyon, which you can look down west of I-15 at PM 58, as the mountains were rapidly uplifted in late Neogene time. Several spectacular floods have roared down this impressive, steep-walled gorge in historic time.

Low-grade metamorphic rocks of the Jurassic and Triassic Bedford Canyon Formation make up the mountains west of Temecula Valley. Granitic plutons intruded and metamorphosed these rocks in Cretaceous time. The intrusive contact is on the south side of the Santa Margarita River. North of the river, the Santa Rosa Plateau consists of Bedford Canyon Formation overlain by 8-million-year-old basalt cones and lava flows of Mesa de Burro. The same basaltic rocks also underlie alluvium in Temecula Valley and cap hogbacks east of the Elsinore fault zone, indicating uplift along the fault of about 1,200 feet in the Temecula and Murrieta area.

The Elsinore fault zone strikes northwestward through the communities of Temecula, Murrieta, and Wildomar. Numerous fault blocks and slices complicate the faulted trough. The central part is filled with nearly 3,000 feet of poorly solidified, nonmarine sandstone of the Pauba Formation, eroded from the local batholithic rocks. Sparse horse and mastodon fossils give its depositional age as 3.7 to 3.2 million years. The 770,000-year-old Bishop Ash, which erupted near Mammoth Mountain in eastern California, has also been found in Temecula Valley.

Rapid urbanization of Temecula Valley in the mid-1980s increased groundwater pumping and irrigation, which in turn caused differential subsidence and hydrocompaction of valley sediments in 1987–88. Ground fractures formed above strands of the Elsinore fault in Temecula and Murrieta subdivisions,

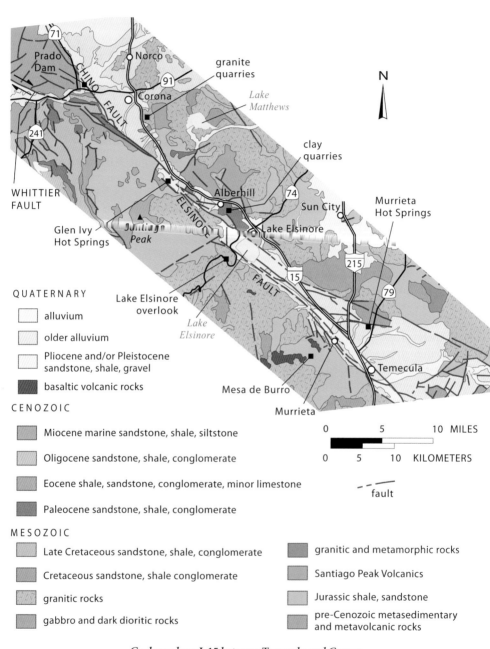

QUATERNARY

☐ alluvium

▨ older alluvium

☐ Pliocene and/or Pleistocene
   sandstone, shale, gravel

■ basaltic volcanic rocks

CENOZOIC

▨ Miocene marine sandstone, shale, siltstone

▨ Oligocene sandstone, shale, conglomerate

▨ Eocene shale, sandstone, conglomerate, minor limestone

▨ Paleocene sandstone, shale, conglomerate

MESOZOIC

▨ Late Cretaceous sandstone, shale, conglomerate

▨ Cretaceous sandstone, shale conglomerate

▨ granitic rocks

▨ gabbro and dark dioritic rocks

▨ granitic and metamorphic rocks

▨ Santiago Peak Volcanics

▨ Jurassic shale, sandstone

▨ pre-Cenozoic metasedimentary
   and metavolcanic rocks

0   5   10 MILES

0   5   10 KILOMETERS

– – – fault

Geology along I-15 between Temecula and Corona.

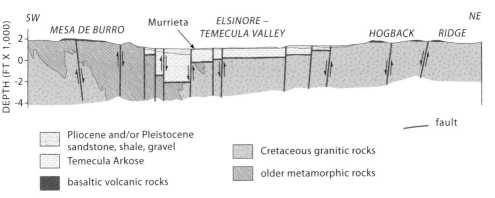

Simplified structure section across Temecula Valley.

forcing great expenditures of private and public funds in litigation and remediation.

Lake Elsinore Overlook

The right-slip Elsinore fault steps left from the southwest side of Temecula Valley to the northeast at Lake Elsinore, forming a rectangular basin that hosts the lake. You may have a splendid overview of the lake and the system of faults bounding it from a high point on CA 74, which climbs the main fault scarp southwest of the lake. At the junction of I-15 and CA 74 (exit 77), head southwest on CA 74 and proceed 4 miles across the valley floor and around the northwest end of Lake Elsinore. CA 74 then turns right and climbs 4 miles up a steep, winding route on the Elsinore fault scarp past high roadcuts in fresh, gray granite. From a roadhouse parking lot at PM 8, Lake Elsinore spreads out before you with the rectangular basin around it. Resistant buttes and hills poke up above the flat Perris Plain to the northeast beyond the lake. Farther northeast are San Jacinto Peak and San Gorgonio Mountain, about 60 miles and 75 miles away, respectively.

From the overlook the nearly rectangular arrangement of active faults bounding Lake Elsinore is easily distinguished by prominent scarps. Together, the faults constitute a pull-apart basin between two right-stepping, parallel strands of the Elsinore fault system, the Glen Ivy and Willard faults. The Lucerne fault at the northwest end of the lake, and the unnamed north-striking fault at the southeast end of the lake are normal faults, on which vertical displacement amounts to about 1,200 feet.

The size and shape of the alluvial depression suggests about 4 miles of horizontal displacement on the Elsinore fault. However, a Cretaceous pluton contact is right-laterally offset about 6 miles. This tells us that some displacement occurred before development of the Elsinore pull-apart basin. Displacement began about 1 million years ago.

Elsinore, named in 1884 for the Danish castle made famous in Shakespeare's *Hamlet*, was known for its mineralized hot springs that issued along the northeast side of the lake. In 1890, however, an irrigation canal disrupted the water table, so that now hot water is obtained only from thermal wells. The City of Elsinore utilized well water until around 1970 when 5 parts per million of fluoride was found in it, more than five times the recommended limit. Aqueduct water from the Colorado River and runoff from the San Jacinto River presently feed the lake.

Aerial view northwestward of Lake Elsinore, a pull-apart basin bounded by right-slip faults (dashed lines) in the Elsinore fault zone. The Santa Ana Mountains are on the left; the San Jacinto River has built a delta into the southeast corner of the lake. (33°39.7N, 117°21.0W)

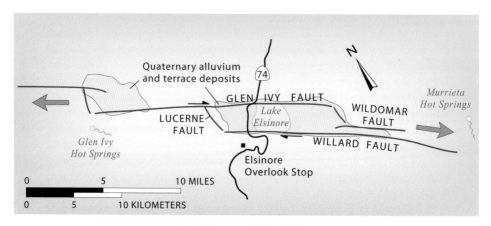

Fault diagram of Lake Elsinore.

Santa Ana Mountains

The Santa Ana Mountains are the main landform at the northwest end of the Peninsular Ranges. They extend about 23 miles in a northwest direction with two high peaks, Modjeska Peak (elevation 5,496 feet) and Santiago Peak (elevation 5,687 feet) forming Saddleback Ridge, which dominates the skyline. The range contains an east-dipping, mainly marine sedimentary rock sequence about 4,500 feet thick, ranging in age from Late Cretaceous to early Pliocene. These rocks unconformably overlie Cretaceous granitic rocks, Jurassic Santiago Peak Volcanics, and slightly metamorphosed, thin-bedded slate, graywacke, and quartzite of the Bedford Canyon Formation.

The Santa Ana Mountains are a natural barrier between fast-growing, residential San Bernardino Valley to the northeast and Orange County job centers to the southwest. A proposal to connect these two areas via a multibillion-dollar tunnel beneath the Santa Ana Mountains is still on the drawing boards.

Temescal Valley Quarries

I-15 continues along the northeast side of the Santa Ana Mountains northwest of its junction with CA 74. It follows an 18-mile-long, troughlike depression bounded on the southwest by the Elsinore fault scarp and drained to the northwest by Temescal Wash. Like Temecula Valley, Temescal Valley is floored with late Pleistocene and Holocene alluvial fan deposits. Cenozoic sedimentary rocks and older crystalline basement rocks are also exposed here and there on the valley floor, whereas the high ground on each side of the valley consists almost entirely of granite and Santiago Peak Volcanics.

Roofing granules, high-silica sand, clay, low-grade lignite coal, and even tin (in 1890–1892) have been quarried and mined from time to time in Temescal Valley. Of particular interest are the red-brown clay quarries on the valley floor at Alberhill. They yield high-quality fire clay, which is especially suited for uses that involve high temperatures, such as brick and ceramics.

Severe weathering of Cretaceous crystalline rocks yielded highly aluminous clay that was redeposited in Paleocene time as the Silverado Formation, whereas deeply weathered residuum of the Santiago Peak Volcanics yielded low alumina, iron-rich clays. These different clays could be blended to make many different ceramic products, such as fine pottery, clay sewer pipe, brick pavers, roofing tiles, clay pots, firebrick, lignite coal, and modeling clay. One famous pottery company on Catalina Island used Alberhill clay until the 1940s to produce pottery that is extremely collectible today. Many original buildings in Los Angeles used Alberhill bricks, including UCLA's iconic Royce Hall and Powell Library, both built in the 1920s. Silica sand, also recovered from the Silverado Formation, was used to manufacture glass bottles.

Roadcuts along I-15 in the Lake Elsinore area expose dark brown Bedford Canyon Formation and more massive, dark gray Santiago Peak Volcanics, both intruded by tan Cretaceous granite. The hills along the highway give way as you approach Corona. Between Cajalco Road (exit 91) and Ontario Avenue (exit 93) and 1 or 2 miles northeast of the highway is a long, tan granite ridge. Several large quarries have been cut in the ridge, yielding not only granite slabs for kitchen counters, but also much granite that is crushed to make aggregate for asphalt and cement for products such as concrete pipe.

Santa Ana Canyon and Puente Hills

The Elsinore fault, which I-15 has faithfully followed between Temecula and Corona, splits into the Whittier and Chino faults at Corona. They bound the Puente Hills, an uplifted tract of Pliocene sedimentary rocks that forms a choke point with hard crystalline basement rocks at the north end of the Santa Ana Mountains. During Quaternary time, the Santa Ana River was forced to swing around the north end of the Peninsular Ranges, cutting an easier route through softer sedimentary rocks of the eastern Puente Hills, while the Puente Hills and Santa Ana Mountains were intermittently uplifted. Wells drilled in the Chino Basin pass through lake sediments, indicating the uplift repeatedly caused temporary ponding of the river.

Prado Dam, at the upper end of Santa Ana Canyon, is a large flood-control and water conservation project constructed for Orange County and operated by the US Army Corps of Engineers. It controls 2,255 square miles of the river's 2,450-square-mile watershed and is designed to store 200,000 acre-feet of water.

The Puente Hills are made of the Puente Formation of late Miocene age, which consists of sandstone and siltstone deposited in deep seawater. The walls of Santa Ana Canyon expose Puente Formation turbidite deposits, consisting of interlayered, northwest-dipping beds with coarse sandstone at the base and grading upward into siltstone at the top. Ripped-up, bent, broken, and shattered lenses of siltstone are common.

The Puente Hills are uplifted by displacement along the Puente Hills thrust fault, a deep fault that isn't exposed at the surface but has been imaged by industry seismic reflection data. Some geologists maintain that the north end of the Santa Ana Mountains is being shoved under the Puente Hills, causing their uplift. The uplift rate is a relatively slow 0.1 inch per year, based on mapping and dating of Quaternary-age terraces in Santa Ana Canyon. Some of these flat surfaces, known as strath terraces, were former valley floors eroded in bedrock that have since been uplifted and dissected by streams.

CA 78
Carlsbad—Ocotillo Wells
97 miles

From the avocado groves of Escondido to the apple orchards in Julian, CA 78 is a winding, two-lane highway that climbs steadily upward over rolling hills of grass and oak woodland developed on granitic rocks of the Peninsular Ranges Batholith. You'll catch glimpses of the granite in and around Ramona, deeply weathered in most roadcuts and as boulder-pile topography in fields and canyons. Between Witch Creek and Wynola, granitic rocks intrude older rocks broadly lumped with the Julian Schist. Mica schist crops out in Julian and in roadcuts in the upper part of Banner Canyon.

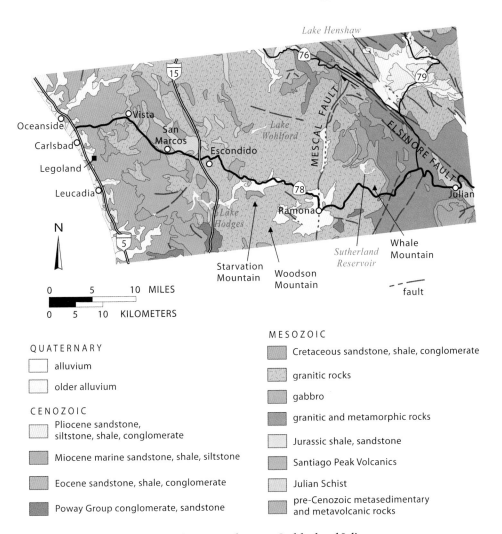

Geology along CA 78 between Carlsbad and Julian.

Julian

Julian became a tent city overnight when lode gold was discovered in February 1870. The gold belt in Julian Schist is about 12 miles long, from about 1 mile north of Julian south to Cuyamaca Rancho State Park. The gold deposits formed when small amounts of high-temperature, mineral-bearing rock were forced into tiny cracks under extreme pressure. Gold mining in the region never amounted to much, with the exception of the Stonewall Mine in Cuyamaca Rancho State Park, which produced the modern equivalent of about $60 million. Today, the economy of quaint little Julian centers around apples

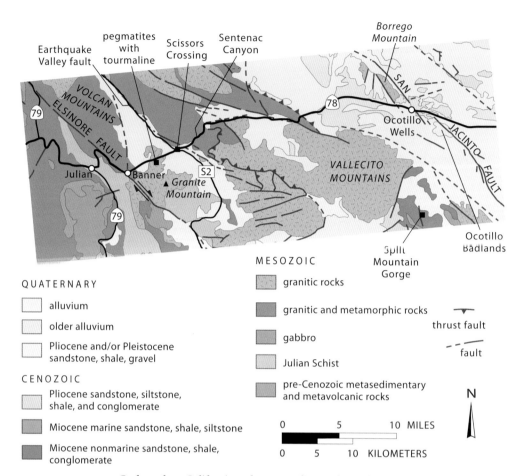

Geology along California 78 between Julian and Ocotillo Wells.

and tourism. A tourist experience well worth the small price of admission is a guided tour of the Eagle and High Peak gold mine, located about 1 mile east of downtown Julian at the east end of C Street.

Banner Canyon

The Elsinore fault lies along the length of Banner Canyon, over which looms Volcan Mountain, east of the fault (peak elevation 5,353 feet). The mountain's average surface elevation is 1,000 feet higher than the corresponding surface at Julian west of the fault. The linear, steep-walled Banner Canyon is cut in slightly altered granitic rocks along the fault. The fault zone narrows from about 200 feet in Rodriguez Canyon to about 10 feet in Banner Canyon, a width it maintains until it reaches Lake Henshaw. Short, discontinuous lines of green

View southeast down Banner Canyon and up Rodriguez Canyon along the trace of the Elsinore fault. The fault trace is part way up the northeast side of the canyon through the heavier vegetation. Granite Mountain (elevation 5,633 feet) is on the skyline. (33°04.5N, 116°33.3W)

vegetation on the northeast canyon wall are locations of springs along the trace of the fault. Benches and faceted ends of ridges also mark the fault trace. CA 78 crosses the fault at PM 65 near the Banner Store and follows the line of vegetation south of the highway and east of the store up Rodriguez Canyon. A significant earthquake has not occurred along this segment of the fault in historic time.

Tourmaline in Pegmatite Dikes

You may inspect some pegmatite dikes at close hand in roadcuts at the crest of the Cigarette Hills between PM 68.5 and 68.7. The white dikes intruded gray granite and consist mostly of quartz and feldspar, but look for crystals of black

Schorl crystals on granite.

This pegmatite dike, cutting granite in the Cigarette Hills, contains black tourmaline (schorl) crystals. (33°05.350N, 116°30.888W)

tourmaline, also called schorl. If you are lucky, you may find some as long as your finger with nice crystal faces. Park off the road in a wide area east of the roadcut and walk back to it.

Sentenac Canyon

From an elevation of 2,230 feet, CA 78 follows San Felipe Creek northeastward down Sentenac Canyon, a water gap between Grapevine Mountain (elevation 3,955 feet) on the north and Sentenac Mountain (elevation 3,068 feet) on the south. These mountains have been uplifted along the Earthquake Valley fault, so that water flow from San Felipe and Earthquake Valleys is partially dammed at the entrance to Sentenac Canyon (PM 70), thus forming Sentenac Cienega (marsh). The overflow of water continues through the canyon but goes below the surface 2.5 miles east of the marsh, a unique riparian area and one of the last undeveloped mountain wetlands in southern California. It was added to

Anza-Borrego Desert State Park in 1998 and is a prime site for botanists and bird-watchers. Roadcuts along the canyon expose complexly folded Julian Schist cut by granite and pegmatite dikes.

At the intersection of CA 78 and County Road S3 (PM 77) at Yaqui Well and the Tamarisk Grove Campground, the highway roadcuts are in landslide deposits of white granite whose fragments range from fine sand to large angular blocks up to several feet in size. These landslide deposits, shed from highly fractured areas of granite in the Vallecito Mountains, cover an extensive area to the south. The deposit is similar to many other megaslide deposits in the region, such as those in Split Mountain Gorge.

This section of CA 78 through Yaqui Well is a small part of the 1,210-mile-long Juan Bautista de Anza National Historic Trail, which extends from Nogales on the United States–Mexico border in Arizona through the California desert and coastal areas of southern and central California to San Francisco. Spanish commander de Anza established this land route in 1775–1776.

Ocotillo Wells

The physiographic boundary between the Peninsular Ranges and the Salton Trough roughly coincides with the San Jacinto fault, which lies along the southwest edge of the playa on the north side of the highway across from the settlement of Ocotillo Wells (PM 92.2). The Borrego Mountain earthquake in 1968 (magnitude 6.8) produced a surface rupture along the southwest edge of this playa. The rupture continued to the northwest end of the playa and split into a pair of left-stepping, en echelon faults. The granitic ridge of Borrego Mountain (elevation 1,196 feet) is squeezed up between the faults like a watermelon seed between your fingers.

Most of the area east of Ocotillo Wells and north of CA 78 is a state vehicle recreation area. Come out here on any long weekend except in summer and see enormous encampments of RVs, dune buggies, ATVs, and off-road motorcycles, all churning up the desert floor and raising a dust cloud that may hang over the desert for days after they leave.

Split Mountain Gorge, a world-class geologic site, is 11 miles south of Ocotillo Wells. For discussion of it, see the introduction to the Salton Trough chapter.

Aerial view south across Borrego Mountain, a squeezed up slice of granitic basement between overstepping strands of the San Jacinto fault. (33°10.2N, 116°10.1W)

LOS ANGELES BASIN

What dust of extinct lions sleeps peaceably under our feet everywhere! The soil of this world is made of the dust of Life, the geologists say. —Thomas Carlyle, 1795–1881

The Los Angeles Basin is both a modern geographic lowland and a geologic basin that has accumulated a great thickness of sediments, especially in the last 16 million years. The geographic Los Angeles Basin lies between the Pacific Ocean on the southwest, the Santa Monica Mountains and Puente Hills on the north, and the Santa Ana Mountains on the east. It is about 50 miles long in a northwest direction and about 20 miles wide, covering 4,083 square miles. Long before the Los Angeles metropolitan area became urbanized, early Spanish missionaries in 1769 described the region as a broad plain generously endowed with cottonwood and alder trees. That plain is now filled with eighty-eight incorporated cities, contained only by the mountains and sea.

A great number of roads crisscross the Los Angeles Basin, but the geology lies beneath urban development and behind highway landscaping and sound-proofing walls. Rather than follow roads in this chapter, we've focused on specific sites and topics. Depending on the atmospheric visibility, splendid views may be had across the Los Angeles Basin: southward from Mt. Wilson in the San Gabriel Mountains, northward from Signal Hill in Long Beach, westward from the San Jose Hills in La Puente, and southeastward from the terrace of the J. Paul Getty Museum in West Los Angeles.

FORMATION OF THE BASIN

The geologic Los Angeles Basin is a relative newcomer in southern California, having formed in the last 16 million years in response to complex interactions within the evolving San Andreas fault system. As presented and discussed in the introduction to this book, the western Transverse Ranges broke away from the Peninsular Ranges and rotated 110 degrees clockwise, leaving a triangular basin between the two ranges. At first, the incipient breaks were healed with volcanic extrusions, such as the Glendora and El Modeno Volcanics around 16 million years ago. As rotation increased, the basin opened farther, revealing Farallon and North American Plate basement rocks in the widening gap. Sediment from the surrounding highlands was deposited directly on this basement.

Simultaneous with their capture and rotation by the Pacific Plate, the western Transverse Ranges also translated northwestward about 40 to 55 miles along the right-slip San Gabriel fault, the geologic predecessor of the San Andreas fault. As the block of rock moved north, the Los Angeles Basin stretched and subsided. During late Miocene through Pliocene time (6 to 4 million years ago), however, right-slip along the San Andreas fault jumped farther into the North American Plate. This caused uplift of the Transverse Ranges, and the Los Angeles Basin rapidly filled with sediment. Microfossil studies indicate that the basin's seawater depth gradually decreased from more than 4,000 feet to about 750 feet in the interval between early and late Pliocene time.

Today, the urbanized part of the Los Angeles Basin lies on a flat-surfaced blanket of marine and nonmarine Pleistocene and Holocene deposits up to 3,000 feet thick. They overlie, in turn, older marine sedimentary rocks having a known thickness of at least 30,000 feet in the central part of the basin, where wells have not reached the basement rock. The deepest oil well, southwest of downtown Los Angeles, is 19,000 feet deep and still in late Miocene rock layers. El Toro Plain, at the southeast end of the Los Angeles Basin, overlies a synclinal depression that is quite shallow compared to the rest of the basin. Basement rocks there are only 4,000 to 6,000 feet below sea level.

The landscape vividly expresses the tectonic instability, rapid uplift, and squeezing of the basin in late Pliocene and Pleistocene time. Many of its hills are uplifted folds transected by rivers and streams that flowed across the locus of the future hills prior to their uplift. As many as thirteen sets of wave-cut terraces have been mapped along the coastal part of the basin and are evidence of recent uplift. The highest terrace is the flattened top of Palos Verdes Hills, at an elevation of 1,300 feet above sea level. This terrace was cut at sea level by waves about 1.5 million years ago and has since been elevated to its modern level.

Some of the elevated hills in the basin sit atop major oil fields associated with active faults, notably the right-slip Newport-Inglewood and Whittier fault zones. The Newport-Inglewood fault zone is about 1 mile wide and stretches 46 miles across the southwest part of the Los Angeles Basin from Newport Beach to West Los Angeles. The ground-up rock along the fault zone, called gouge, impedes groundwater flow and saltwater intrusion, separating the east and west groundwater basins of the Los Angeles coastal plain.

The west side of the fault zone has been downthrown about 2,000 feet at basement level, where it separates Mesozoic and Proterozoic igneous and metamorphic rocks on the northeast from the Mesozoic Catalina Schist on the southwest. Some geologists maintain that the fault zone at basement level is a vestige of the Mesozoic-age subduction zone, and that it was reactivated as a strike-slip fault in Cenozoic time. The destructive Long Beach earthquake (magnitude 6.3) occurred on the Newport-Inglewood fault zone in March 1933, causing 115 fatalities and $6 million in losses. Damage was particular severe to public school buildings, shocking the California State Legislature and leading to passage of the Field Act, one of the first pieces of legislation that mandated earthquake resistant construction for public schools.

Despite the fact that the Newport-Inglewood fault is active, other young faults have carried the Santa Monica Mountains southward over the north edge of the basin and over the northwest end of the Newport-Inglewood fault. We know this because the relatively small Sawtelle oil field, north of Wilshire Boulevard on I-405 (exit 55B or between PM 31.5 and 31.9), is located on the Newport-Inglewood fault zone but *beneath* the Hollywood–Santa Monica fault. Wells that reach the oil-producing rock layers have passed through the north-dipping Santa Monica fault.

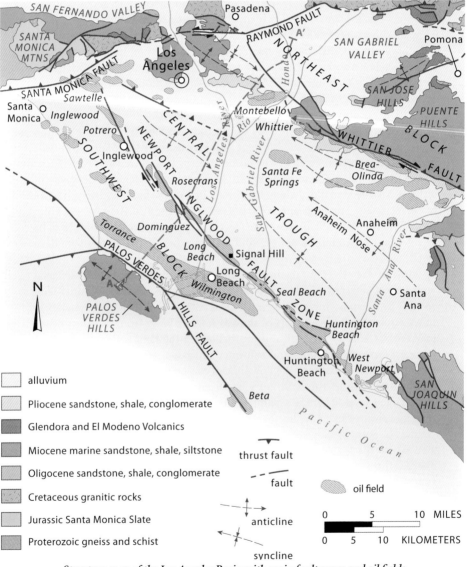

Structure map of the Los Angeles Basin with main fault zones and oil fields.
—Map compiled from Wright, 1991, and Yerkes and others, 1965

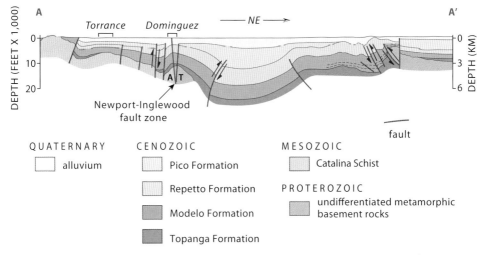

Structure section across the deep part of the Los Angeles Basin. Line of section A–A' is in the map on page 202. —Modified from Wright, 1991

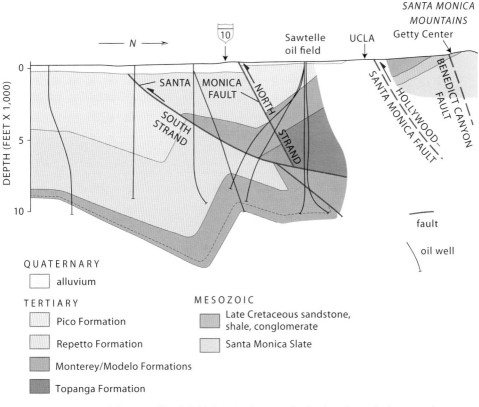

Cross section of the Sawtelle oil field showing how north-dipping thrust faults carry the Santa Monica Mountains southward upon the north edge of the Los Angeles Basin. Oil production is from beneath the thrust fault. The location of this cross section is shown on the map on page 288. —Modified from Tsutsumi and others, 2001

OIL FIELDS AND THE MONTEREY FORMATION

Besides hosting a staggering plethora of automobiles and trucks, multitudes of giant palm trees, and the glitz and glitter of nearby Hollywood, the Los Angeles Basin is one of the major petroleum-producing areas in the world, with sixty-two oil fields, from which over 8 billion barrels of oil and 8 million cubic feet of gas have been produced since 1880. If the average football stadium can hold 2 million barrels of crude oil, 4,000 stadiums would be needed to hold just what has been produced from the basin so far. Some analysts estimate that it still holds another 8 billion barrels.

Few areas in the world have produced so much oil from such a small area and from such a limited volume of sedimentary rocks. The Los Angeles Basin contains an estimated 2,250 cubic miles of sediment, of which 1,600 cubic miles are oil field areas. During 1923, production from the Signal Hill, Santa Fe Springs, and Huntington Beach oil fields accounted for 20 percent of the world's total production. Since 1932 twelve of the fields have produced between 100 million and 1 billion barrels of oil each. The Huntington Beach field and the giant Wilmington field have produced over 1 billion and 3 billion barrels, respectively, and are still major producers.

The oil formed from marine organic matter in late Miocene shale beds of the Repetto, Modelo, and Monterey Formations, and, where present, from the Topanga Formation. For the organic matter to convert to oil, the rock had to be buried below 8,000 to 10,000 feet at temperatures exceeding 327°F. Today, most of the oil is found in the pore spaces of turbidite sandstones, deposited on the seafloor in Miocene and Pliocene time. The oil migrated from shale beds into these sandstone reservoirs along vertical faults and fractures, although many of the thin, turbidite sand beds contain oil generated in adjacent shale interbeds. The total thickness of oil-bearing beds is as much as 6,500 feet in some parts of the basin.

Perhaps the most studied and storied rock formation in central and southern California is the Monterey Formation, or Monterey Shale, because organic parts of the formation are the source for about 99 percent of the petroleum in these regions. Named for distinctive white outcrops and cliffs in and around the city of Monterey in central California, it crops out widely in the western Transverse Ranges and underlies much of the Los Angeles Basin.

The Monterey Formation is a complex sedimentary unit consisting chiefly of soft diatomaceous shale and mudstone, in places converted to hard silica-cemented rocks, such as chert and porcellanite. Diatoms are microscopic, single-celled plants that grow in water, and when they die, their silica remains sink to the seafloor. Limestone and phosphatic shale also make up significant parts of the Monterey Formation. In western Santa Barbara County, compaction and pressure have converted the soft rocks into very hard rocks that are foliated like schistose metamorphic rocks with a distinct crenulation lineation, or wrinkling, of their thin layers.

The evolving climate of the Pacific Ocean changed the composition of the Monterey Formation over time, from predominantly calcareous to

This boulder of Monterey Formation on a Santa Barbara beach has alternating layers of white porcellanite and brown phosphatic shale. (34°24.28N, 119°45.12W)

predominantly siliceous. Initially, relatively warm climatic conditions favored calcareous deposition from blooms of calcareous nano floras. Increased cooling between 14 and 10 million years ago led to increased upwelling that favored siliceous phytoplankton (diatoms). Organic-rich phosphatic shale is common in the middle of the Monterey Formation, whereas the upper Monterey is distinctly siliceous.

Long Beach Oil Field and Signal Hill

If you are on I-405 and blink at just the wrong moment when approaching Cherry Avenue (exit 29A) in Long Beach, you'll miss seeing a couple of pump-jacks that are remnants of the Long Beach oil field, also known as the Signal Hill oil field. Total production of the entire field has been about 1 billion barrels. It holds the distinction of leading all fields in the recovery of oil per surface area, at about 500,000 barrels per acre. A few wells have produced over 2 million barrels each. Before the discovery of oil and before production was booming in the 1920s, Signal Hill consisted of several large undeveloped farms and small, underdeveloped subdivisions. These lands were converted to exclusive use by oil operations and industrial users when more and more oil was found and produced. Today, as production declines, residential construction is gradually replacing abandoned oil wells and facilities.

The Long Beach oil field occupies the crest of a narrow, elongate, northwest-trending, uplifted and arched block between the Cherry Hill and Northeast Flank faults, which are segments of the Newport-Inglewood fault zone. The fault zone has been active since Miocene time, but the uplift of Signal Hill occurred entirely in Pleistocene time. About 2,500 feet of right-slip displacement and 900 feet of vertical displacement have occurred along the fault zone at Signal Hill.

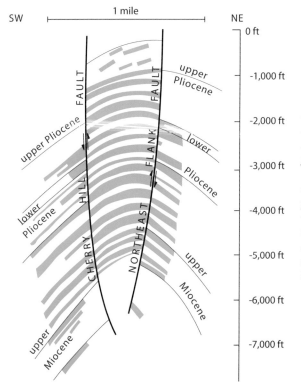

Schematic structure section across the Long Beach oil field at Signal Hill. The green pattern depicts petroleum-producing zones within a 6,000-foot-thick sequence of alternating sandstone and shale beds.

So many oil derricks covered Signal Hill in the 1920s and 1930s that passers-by termed it Porcupine Hill. (33°47.8N, 118°09.6W) —Los Angeles Water & Power Associates photo

Houses have proliferated around operating pumpjacks on Signal Hill, taking advantage of views of Los Angeles and the Pacific Coast. (33°47.8N, 118°09.5W)

If it's a clear day, detour to the top of Signal Hill (elevation 365 feet) for splendid views south over Long Beach Harbor and north over the Los Angeles Basin to the Santa Monica Mountains. To reach Hilltop Park from I-405, take exit 29A and go south on Cherry Avenue to Willow Street and then two more blocks to Skyline Drive. Turn left and proceed up to the park. If you follow Skyline Drive farther east to its intersection with East Hill Street, you will come to Discovery Well Park. The well here was Shell Oil Company's Alamitos No. 1, completed March 23, 1921, with an initial flow of 590 barrels per day.

On a clear day, you can see some artificial islands in San Pedro Bay from Hilltop Park. They were constructed as drilling platforms and now host colorful prismatic towers, which are camouflaged drilling rigs in the offshore part of the Wilmington oil field. Also look closely and see the *Queen Mary*, a retired ocean liner, located across from a white dome that once housed Howard Hughes's *Spruce Goose*. The giant Wilmington oil field, flanked on its west side by the Palos Verdes Hills, is the long hill about 5 miles west of Signal Hill. Catalina Island is 30 miles to the south.

Baldwin Hills and Inglewood Oil Field

The Baldwin Hills (elevation 513 feet) are the highest and most prominent of the hills along the Newport-Inglewood fault zone. The Inglewood oil field, discovered in 1924, occupies the central part of the Baldwin Hills and is typical of the fields discovered during the Los Angeles oil boom in the 1920s. The oil is trapped in a northwest-trending anticline with a large fault block at its crest.

Wells penetrated middle Miocene sedimentary beds at a depth of 8,760 feet. Late Miocene, Pliocene, and Pleistocene marine sediments overlie them, but only late Pliocene and Pleistocene sediments are exposed at the surface. The main production zones include both the highest and lowest stratigraphic horizons known to yield oil in the Los Angeles Basin. Around 1,000 wells produced between 2 and 3 million barrels of oil annually between 1990 and 2012, with a total close to 400 million barrels since 1924.

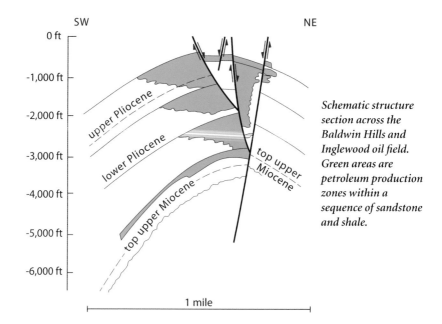

Schematic structure section across the Baldwin Hills and Inglewood oil field. Green areas are petroleum production zones within a sequence of sandstone and shale.

A water reservoir, once located at the top of the Baldwin Hills east of the main fault, ruptured on December 14, 1963, as a result of leakage and subsurface erosion along a fault beneath the main reservoir dam. The fault was recognized and mapped during excavations for the reservoir, which was built in 1951, long after oil production had been underway and well after subsidence of the ground surface had been noted. Property damage and loss of life led to litigation to hold the oil producer responsible. The producer settled out of court in spite of a strong case that tectonic movement along the fault, not subsidence as a result of oil withdrawal, was the cause of the rupture and reservoir failure.

To reach Baldwin Hills from I-405, take exit 47 (La Cienega) and proceed north about 3.5 miles to the entrance to Kenneth Hahn State Recreation Area. The route goes through the Inglewood oil field to a park at the top of the hill. Baldwin Hills was the site of the Olympic Village for the 1932 Olympic Games held in Los Angeles Memorial Coliseum.

Huntington Beach Oil Field

Discovered in 1920, the Huntington Beach oil field is the largest on the Newport-Inglewood trend and is one of several oil fields in southern California that has produced in excess of 1 billion barrels since discovery. The oil is produced from sands ranging in age from late Miocene to middle Pliocene in a complexly faulted, west-trending anticline. The folding and faulting occurred during Pliocene time, whereas the topography of the area today reflects only mild Pleistocene folding. Wells have been drilled to 9,000 feet at Huntington Beach without penetrating basement rock. Some wells have been completed by slant drilling to sites as far as 4,800 feet offshore. The oil field stretches for nearly 2 miles along CA 1 today, between PM 26 and PM 28, but it isn't the forest of wooden derricks today that it was during its 1930s heydays.

Timber oil derricks along the Pacific Coast Highway in Huntington Beach in the 1930s. (33°40N, 118°01W) —Photo courtesy Orange County Archives

Seal Beach Oil Field

The Seal Beach oil field, also on the Newport-Inglewood trend, underlies the estuary of the San Gabriel River. Discovered in 1924, it is projected to yield 225 million barrels. Oil was trapped in late Miocene and Pliocene sands in a doubly plunging anticline. As the anticlinal hill rose during folding, the San Gabriel River maintained its course across its center. Eventually, the river's great volume and low gradient caused it to meander back and forth and carve a channel across the anticline, leaving a wide valley between two low hills: Alamitos Heights to the northwest and Landing Hill to the southeast.

Wilmington Oil Field

The Wilmington oil field at Long Beach is not only a large field, at 22 square miles, but its oil production is also huge: 3 *billion* barrels, that is, nearly half of the total Los Angeles Basin production. Discovered in 1932, Wilmington produced 216,000 barrels of oil per day at its peak production in 1969. The oil field lies adjacent to Los Angeles Harbor on a well-developed, northwest-trending, anticlinal structure overlying a subsurface ridge of Catalina Schist.

Five northeast-striking normal faults divide the field into six structural blocks and prevent oil from migrating from one block to another. So much oil and water have been extracted over time that the field has subsided more than 20 feet to the point where much of it is below sea level. Subsidence reached a maximum of more than 2 feet per year in 1951 and 1952. From 1952 onward, the subsidence rate decreased until 1960, when water, separated from the oil, was reinjected into the reservoir. By 1966 stabilization was achieved, and the area partially rebounded. You may see walls and dikes built in and around the oil field to prevent the sea from flooding it.

LOS ANGELES RIVER

The Los Angeles River drains a large watershed that includes the Santa Susana Mountains, San Gabriel Mountains, and San Fernando Valley. Its periodic floods once provided rich sedimentary deposits across its floodplain, although today most of the river discharges to the sea through a concrete channel. Deliberate efforts are gradually restoring riparian ecosystems with native plant and animal species that once flourished along the meandering river.

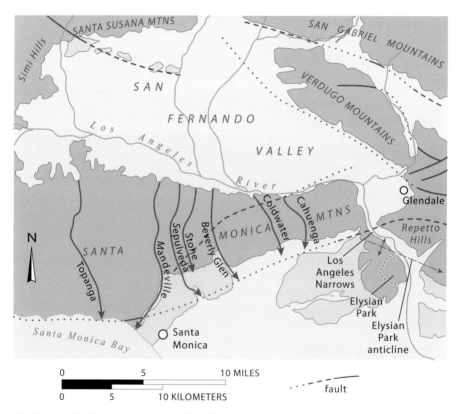

The Los Angeles River was progressively deflected eastward across and around the eastern Santa Monica Mountains during Pleistocene time, leaving deep wind gaps behind. I-405 follows Sepulveda Canyon; US 101 follows Cahuenga Pass; and I-5 follows the present course of the river at the east end of the range. Brown shading indicates pre-Pleistocene rock.

Aerial view north over the Santa Monica Mountains toward the San Fernando Valley with I-405 in Sepulveda Pass in 1962, when the air was usually clear and the traffic light. The great depths of the pass and adjacent Stone Canyon (denoted by arrow) were cut by the Los Angeles River prior to its eastward deflection by the rise of the Santa Monica Mountains. —Los Angeles Water & Power Associates photo

In prehistoric time, the river had a much different course from the San Gabriel Mountains to the sea. Geologists think the Los Angeles River once flowed straight south from the mountains across a gently rolling surface with only a few low hills, reaching the sea near Santa Monica. About 4 million years ago, however, the Santa Monica Mountains began to rise as a broad, eastward-propagating arch, much like a mouse burrowing under a rug. At first, river erosion kept pace with the uplift and carved the deep Mandeville Canyon, but continued uplift forced the river to shift eastward, where it cut Sepulveda Pass. The river subsequently cut and progressively abandoned additional deep and narrow canyons across the range until it reached its present channel through the Los Angeles Narrows around the east end of the mountains and thence across the Los Angeles Basin to the sea at Long Beach.

The Los Angeles River lies in a broad, shallow trench in the San Fernando Valley, meandering through a flat plain cut into sand and gravel. In the Los Angeles Narrows, however, it lies in a flat-bottomed, steep-walled canyon less than 1 mile wide. The canyon cuts across the sandstone core of the Elysian Park anticline, which developed in late Pliocene and Pleistocene time. Water flows in this part of the river year-round because sandstone bedrock is at the surface instead of gravel and sand. The original Los Angeles pueblo, founded in 1781, was established at this perennial water source. The sandstone beds that line the narrows are poorly consolidated, structurally weak, and prone to landslides visible in the steep cliffs west of I-5. Much of the river has been straightened and lined with concrete to mitigate flooding.

Ballona Creek, which enters the Pacific Ocean at Marina del Rey, follows part of the ancestral course of the Los Angeles River. The river flowed here when sea levels were much lower than today. At the time, Ballona Creek's channel was about 300 feet deep near the coast and more than 50 feet below present sea level 2 to 3 miles inland. The channel subsequently filled with alluvium so that during the postglacial rise in sea level in Holocene time, the river's course shifted eastward across the Los Angeles Basin and now drains into San Pedro Bay at Long Beach.

La Brea Tar Pits

The La Brea Tar Pits at Hancock Park and the adjacent George C. Page Museum of the Natural History Museum of Los Angeles feature a world-class collection and display of fossilized Pleistocene plants and animals. The park and museum are located at 5801 Wilshire Boulevard.

During the latest glacial period from about 40,000 to 8,000 years ago, oil oozed upward from sand layers a few thousand feet below the plain and collected on the surface of shallow, water-filled depressions. Volatile components of the oil vaporized, leaving a thick, tarlike residuum of asphalt covered by stagnant pools of rainwater and dust. Herbivorous animals walked across this treacherous quagmire only to be trapped and then firmly mired in the asphalt. Carnivorous predators sought the hopelessly trapped prey also becoming mired

Mammoths at tar pits, oil slicks on the water, and the George C. Page Museum. (34°03.8N, 118°21.3W)

in the grip of tar. Much more recently, the pits were a major source of roofing tar for Los Angeles.

The plant fossils indicate that Los Angeles was cooler and moister 30,000 to 15,000 years ago than at present. Many of the recovered fossils of mammals are similar to animals inhabiting southern California today, but the larger Pleistocene species are no longer found in North America. Ferocious saber-toothed tigers, lank dire wolves, colossal mammoths, and huge American lions are just a few of the animals that once patrolled most of the broad Los Angeles plain and ruled over such lesser Pleistocene animals as elephants, horses, camels, bisons, antelopes, sloths, birds, insects, and amphibians. You won't see these animals walking around Hancock Park, but an astonishing and nearly complete fossil record of these ice age animals is splendidly displayed at the adjoining George C. Page Museum.

SAN JUAN CAPISTRANO

Junipero Serra founded Mission San Juan Capistrano in 1776 in the lower part of the San Juan Valley. One of the earliest settlements in California, it is also one of the most beautiful and photographed of all missions in California. It has become a favorite tourist site for watching cliff swallows that return every March from their winter home in Argentina. Across the railroad tracks from the mission and depot is the Los Rios Street Historic District, often called the oldest neighborhood in California because some adobes date to the late eighteenth century.

Ruins of Mission San Juan Capistrano, circa 1900, after a major earthquake in 1812. The present mission structure is a reconstruction. —Harold Taylor photo, from Taylor and Elliott family collection

I-5 proceeds up Arroyo Trabuco through the San Joaquin Hills following the axis of a syncline consisting of brown, micaceous shale of the Capistrano Formation. The arroyo was eroded by a stream that maintained its course while the southeast end of the San Joaquin Hills rose.

COASTAL REGION OF THE BASIN

Most of the coastal geologic sites in this section can be accessed from CA 1, aka PCH or the Pacific Coast Highway, although little of the geology mentioned below is apparent from the highway because of urbanization. Look for information signs that indicate coastal access roads and paths. Be careful not to mistake several faux rock retaining walls for in situ geology in the commercial part of Laguna Beach.

This section of the southern California coastline is west of the Newport-Inglewood fault zone, so the basement rocks here are Catalina Schist and the San Onofre Breccia, a sedimentary rock consisting of rock fragments eroded from the schist. Both rock units are exposed along CA 1 in places, principally at Dana Point and the Palos Verdes Hills, where they are overlain mostly by the Monterey Formation.

Dana Point

The spectacular, resistant sea cliff at Dana Point consists of the San Onofre Breccia, an unsorted assemblage of blocks, boulders, and cobbles of mainly blue-gray glaucophane schist, but also greenschist, amphibolite, and gabbro, in a matrix of red and gray sandstone. The size of the clasts ranges from rounded and angular sand grains to refrigerator-size boulders. The breccia accumulated in early to middle Miocene time at the base of a steep escarpment geologists

The gray-blue boulders and cobbles consist of glaucophane schist in the San Onofre Breccia at Dana Point. (33°27.6N, 117°42.5W)

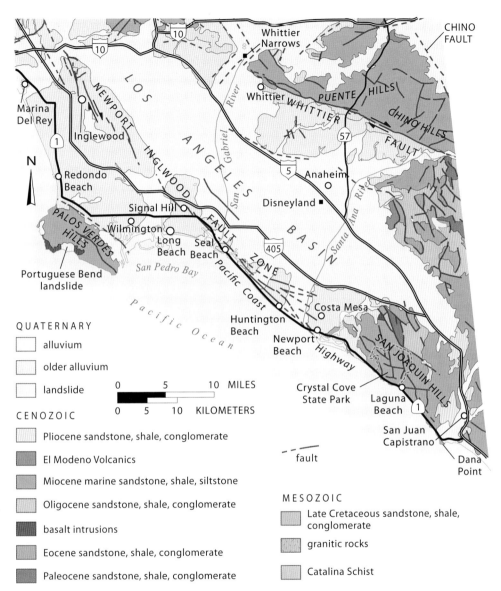

Geology along the coast from San Juan Capistrano to Marina del Rey.

interpret as a fault scarp. Because the schist clasts in the breccia contain the mineral glaucophane, we know the schist originally formed under the high pressure and low temperature conditions that typify the Catalina Schist rocks and their metamorphism in a subduction zone, geologic conditions that are completely unlike those prevailing in southern California today.

The fault scarp source of the breccia was west of today's coastline, from highlands exposed only when the western Transverse Ranges rotated off the top of oceanic rocks of the Farallon Plate. Such rocks are exposed today on Catalina Island and in the Palos Verdes Hills. They have also been reached by some deep drill holes southwest of the Newport-Inglewood fault zone.

The San Onofre Breccia is about 2,600 feet thick at Dana Point. It thins north and east from Laguna Beach and San Juan Capistrano to Mission Viejo and is exposed as far south along I-5 as Oceanside. It was deposited on an eroded surface of the Sespe, Vaqueros, and Topanga Formations. In places the breccia interfingers with the Topanga and Monterey Formations.

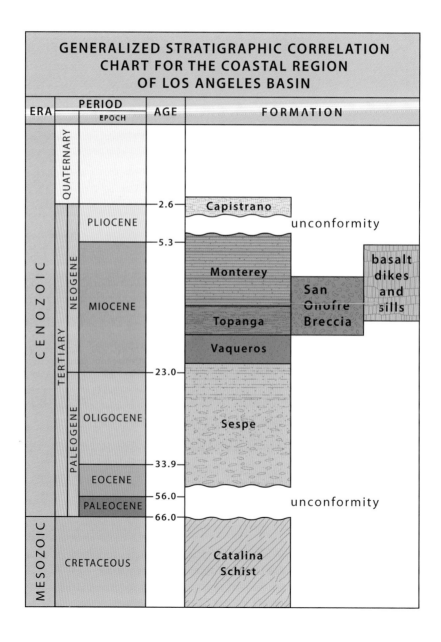

The Dana Cove fault juxtaposes the San Onofre Breccia and the less compe-tent and younger Capistrano Formation in the cliff overlooking Dana Point Harbor in Capistrano Bay. The bay formed here because the Capistrano Formation eroded faster than the more resistant breccia exposed at Dana Point. Details of three submarine canyon channels are beautifully exposed in these cliffs of the Capistrano Formation. Bottom currents leading southwestward from the shoreline of the Los Angeles Basin scoured the channels and depos-ited sandstone and pebbly clasts in 2,000- to 5,000-foot-deep seawater.

Dana Point is named for Richard Henry Dana, Jr., a Harvard-trained lawyer, seaman, and author of the classic sea journal *Two Years Before the Mast*. His writings describe his 1835–1836 voyage on the merchant ship *Pilgrim* from Boston around Cape Horn to California. According to Dana, Capistrano Bay was "the most romantic spot on the California coast." To see the cliff exposures at Dana Point, take exit 79 from I-5 and drive west on CA 1, then turn left on Dana Point Harbor Drive. Proceed to its end, park at the Ocean Institute, and take the beach access path between the cliff and museum building.

Pebbly sandstone with large siltstone clasts fills the lower part of a submarine canyon channel in the Capistrano Formation at Dana Point Harbor. The upper half of the cliff is a turbidite sequence of 3-foot-thick sandstone beds and lesser, thinner siltstone beds. (33°27.6N, 117°42.5W)

Laguna Beach

The 10 miles of coastline from Dana Point to Laguna Beach is a scalloped succession of headlands and coves consisting of outcrops of resistant San Onofre Breccia and less resistant Monterey Formation shale. Walk down to the south end of Laguna Beach to pools and blowholes on a beveled, wave-carved surface of San Onofre Breccia. At the north end of the beach, Vaqueros sandstone and conglomerate contain glaucophane grains derived from the schist in the breccia. Coastal terrace gravel was deposited on top of the eroded surface of the sandstone. A basalt dike with columnar jointing forms the promontory at the north end of the beach cove. Basalt dikes are also exposed in the three low, residence-covered promontories that overlook Laguna Beach. These dikes intruded the Topanga Formation sandstone.

Two miles north of Laguna Beach at Irvine Cove, the geology changes from the Monterey Formation to the Oligocene and early Miocene Temblor Formation. Headlands are fewer, and the sea cliffs are less sheer and rugged than those south of Laguna Beach.

Crystal Cove State Park

Some of the best and most easily accessible exposures of Monterey Formation along this coast may be viewed on a 1-mile hike along the beautiful beach at Crystal Cove State Park. Use the Los Trancos entrance (PM 13.4) to access the beach and then walk south of the cottages at low tide if possible.

The sea cliffs and eroded bedrock platform at their base are cut into hard, folded layers of the 12- to 6-million-year-old Monterey Formation. A prominent ledge of sand, cobbles, and fossil shells is high up on the side of the sea cliff,

This block of sandstone with cobbles and shells fell from a resistant ledge in the cliff. Notice how the shells in this Pleistocene-age rock look quite similar to modern shells that you might find along the beach today. (33°34.37N, 117°50.36W)

unconformably overlying the eroded upper surface of the Monterey Formation. The ledge rocks and fossils were deposited on a beach that existed 105,000 to 80,000 years ago. Thus the unconformity represents a period of lost geologic record when rocks younger than the Monterey Formation and older than the ledge eroded away or were never deposited—a time span of roughly 6 million years. Erosion has undermined the ledge, so that large blocks tumble down the cliff onto the beach south of the cottages.

The Monterey Formation here at Crystal Cove consists of thin-bedded siliceous shale, dolostone, porcellanite, and chert, all formed by the conversion of clay and diatomaceous ooze to rock. Embedded within these rock layers are hard, compact pillow-shaped rock masses from a few inches to more than 12 feet in diameter. Called concretions, these geologic oddities come in many shapes, but most are either spheres or disks. They are aggregates of inorganic matter, such as calcite or silica, which form around a nucleus like a bit of pyrite, a tiny fossil, or a bone fragment. Concretions usually have a concentric internal structure that forms as successive layers of mineral accrete to the surface, causing the radius and volume to grow with time.

Spectacularly folded and crenulated Monterey Formation beds are wonderfully exposed in a cliff beneath the vista point above Little Treasure Cove. Such isolated folds generally form when unconsolidated sediments slump downslope on the seafloor, perhaps because of shaking during an earthquake.

A cliff of middle Miocene basaltic lava flows crops out at the south end of Crystal Cove. The flows cooled quickly to form well-defined, prismatic columns.

Folded Monterey Formation above Little Treasure Cove. (33°34.78N, 117°51.11W)

Columnar-jointed basalt at the south end of Crystal Cove State Park. (33°33.38N, 117°49.19W)

The inland portion of Crystal Cove State Park is in the San Joaquin Hills, where numerous intrusive and extrusive andesitic and dacitic volcanic rocks interfinger with the Topanga and lower Monterey Formations. Eight discontinuous coastal terraces are exposed on the higher slopes of the hills. The oldest and highest is estimated to be about 1.3 million years old, eroded about the same time the hills were uplifted.

Newport Bay

CA 1 between Crystal Cove and Newport Bay is built upon 125,000- and 80,000-year-old coastal terraces that overlie the eroded top of uplifted Miocene and Pliocene rock layers, which surround the bay. Before residential and commercial urbanization modified this narrow stretch of coastline, Newport Bay was an undeveloped, shallow coastal bay and marsh at the mouth of the Santa Ana River, but it was enlarged and deepened by dredging in 1896. The spoils were dumped on mudflats to make Balboa, Lido, and Harbor Islands. A sandbar between the bay and the ocean was widened, creating Balboa Peninsula, now a long, splendid, sandy beach.

Prior to the 1941 construction of the Prado flood control dam near Corona, 25 miles upstream of Newport Bay, the Santa Ana River and its great load of sediment emptied directly into the bay during floods. At all other times, the river meandered through marshland behind a huge sandbar, eventually reaching the sea at Corona del Mar, southeast of Newport Bay. A man-made channel breached the sandbar in 1921, and two long jetties were constructed to prevent sand from naturally repairing the breach by means of longshore drift.

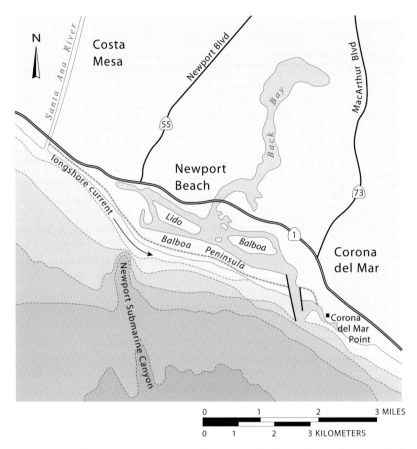

Newport Harbor is a lagoon behind Balboa Peninsula, formerly a sandbar supplied with sand by southward longshore drift and from Santa Ana River floods.

The jetties have been extended seaward beyond the edge of the narrow continental shelf, so that sand brought down along the coast today is deflected by the jetties and spreads out on the ocean floor, where the sea is too deep for breakers to form and pick up sand to return it the beach. The sand then funnels down Newport Submarine Canyon and so is forever lost to California beaches.

Marshes and Lagoons

From Newport Beach north to Long Beach, streams as wide as 2 to 3 miles meander through flat-bottomed, steep-walled valleys and through swamps and extensive marshlands, carrying sediment across wide, sandy beaches to the sea. Coastal longshore currents bring sand southeastward from the Los Angeles and San Gabriel Rivers and dam the mouths of streams, so that lagoons and marshes form behind beach bars. Because of the great emphasis on flood control and the consequent building of hundreds of debris basins in the mountains, less sand and gravel reach the coast today than in the past, and the beaches will gradually shrink to narrow masses of cobbles and boulders.

Bolsa Chica Lagoon lies directly north of the Huntington Beach oil field between PM 28 and PM 30 on CA 1. It is one of the largest remaining saltwater marshes in California and just one of several being restored in the Huntington Beach area. Its 2 square miles of wetlands and upland habitat have been restored to its pre-urbanization condition.

Palos Verdes Hills

The high, flat-topped Palos Verdes Hills were a peninsula, separated from the Los Angeles Basin by an arm of the sea, just before the ice age began. The hills are an elevated anticline with a core of Catalina Schist draped with Miocene, Pliocene, and Pleistocene marine sedimentary rocks. The predominately fine-grained, glaucophane-epidote schist is exposed only at the surface in one small canyon.

The Palos Verdes Hills are famous in the geologic literature for their thirteen steplike, wave-cut terraces, which encircle the hills like bathtub rings. Although residential development almost completely masks the terraces, concentrically arranged roads around the southwest seaward slopes generally outline them. The multiplicity of terraces indicates that the hills were uplifted episodically, with height differences from one terrace to the next ranging from 75 to 200 feet.

Terrace deposits are present on all sides of the hills, but they are best developed on the seaward side, where they were exposed to the strongest cutting force of the waves. The lower and intermediate terraces are generally better preserved than the highest ones, because they have not been exposed to erosion as long as the higher ones.

Aerial view of residential development on coastal terrace flats in the Palos Verdes Hills. (33°45.9N, 118°24.5W)

A terrace would form at sea level during a pause in uplift, and it would have a veneer of gray beach sand that was subsequently overlain by earthy, brown, nonmarine alluvium. Then the peninsula would rise again, followed by another standstill and terrace-cutting event, then another uplift, another pause, and so on, until the hills reached their present elevation. Fossils in the upper-most terrace indicate the hills have been uplifted nearly 1,300 feet in about 1.5 million years. The youngest terrace is already warped, telling us that the defor-mation is quite young.

The southwest flank of the Palos Verdes Hills is notched by several beau-tiful coves among intricately and deeply scalloped capes and headlands, whose resistant rocks withstand wave attack better than those in the coves. This side also contains several major landslides that slip imperceptibly and inexorably seaward. The two largest and most damaging slides are at Portuguese Bend and Abalone Cove, which you will pass over if you drive along Palos Verdes Drive. The road rises and falls over the slides like a roller coaster.

Redondo Submarine Canyon and Sand Dunes

Directly offshore from Redondo Beach is the second largest submarine canyon along the California coast, only slightly smaller than that in Monterey Bay. Starting at a point one-half mile offshore in water 258 feet deep, the canyon descends to a depth of 1,752 feet over a distance of 8 miles. Near the center of the canyon is a submarine oil seep, and on a calm day oil and gas bubble to the surface in Santa Monica Bay. The canyon was probably carved during glacial times when sea level was about 300 feet lower than it is today.

A 10-mile-long ridge of sand dunes, now mostly covered by housing devel-opments, stretches along the Santa Monica Bay shoreline from Redondo Beach to Playa del Rey. Most of the sand is brought to the shore by rivers and creeks from the inland mountains and valleys. Southeast-directed winds and the ocean currents move the sand along the shore down the coast to Redondo Canyon, where it leaves the nearshore waters and flows into deep, submarine troughs.

Marina del Rey Breakwater

At several places along the Santa Monica Bay coastline, as at Marina del Rey, breakwaters and jetties extend beyond the surf line into the sea for the conve-nience of boaters seeking safe harbor and for trapping sand to enhance beaches. Breakwater performance has been less than completely satisfactory, because the area of quiet harbor water draws in extremely fine sediment particles held in suspension, allowing mudflats to develop so that periodic dredging is required to keep the harbor and channels open.

TRANSVERSE RANGES

*Curious how a place unvisited can take such hold on the
mind so that the very name sets up a ringing.*
—John Steinbeck, 1962, *Travels with Charley: In Search of America*

Only six mountain ranges in North America have an east-west orientation: the
Brooks Range in Alaska, the Uinta Mountains in Utah, the Wichita and Ouachita
Mountains in Oklahoma and Arkansas, the south end of the Appalachians in
Alabama, and southern California's Transverse Ranges, so called because they
are transverse to the general northwest orientation of most mountain ranges in
the western United States.

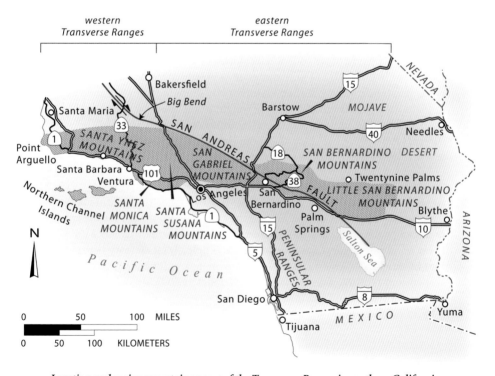

Location and major mountain ranges of the Transverse Ranges in southern California.

The eastern and western Transverse Ranges have completely different rocks types and origin, but they are related because of their geographic setting and recent uplift. The eastern part, comprising the San Gabriel and San Bernardino Mountains, and the Little San Bernardino Mountains in Joshua Tree National Park, contains some of the oldest and most unusual plutonic and metamorphic rocks in California. The western Transverse Ranges are characterized by a thick succession of Late Jurassic, Cretaceous, and Cenozoic sedimentary rocks.

Both the eastern and western Transverse Ranges have been deformed and uplifted in the last 5 million years because of convergence of the Pacific and North American Plates in the region of the Big Bend of the San Andreas fault, which is the transform boundary between the two plates. The massive Peninsular Ranges, carried northwestward by the Pacific Plate, ram against and beneath the southwest edge of the North American Plate, thereby uplifting the crystalline rocks of the eastern Transverse Ranges and the sedimentary rocks of the western Transverse Ranges, rumpling them like a rug.

Most of the major faults strike east-west in the western Transverse Range and have left-slip displacements, in contrast to the northwest-striking, right-slip faults of the San Andreas fault system that prevail throughout most of southern California.

WESTERN TRANSVERSE RANGES

The western Transverse Ranges include the Santa Ynez, Santa Susana, and Santa Monica Mountains, the northern Channel Islands, and the associated Ventura Basin. Their strongly folded sedimentary rock layers are strikingly similar to those in the Peninsular Ranges, with older formations recording a lengthy history of mostly marine sedimentation along the edge of the continent and younger deposits filling local basins that formed later. In fact, the western Transverse Ranges were once attached to the Peninsular Ranges, but right shear between the Pacific and North American Plates caused this terrane to be torn away from the Peninsular Ranges about 19 million years ago. It became attached to the Pacific Plate and rotated 110 degrees clockwise, even while it was carried northwestward by the Pacific Plate to its present position. Extensive reverse faults and numerous folds formed during the north-south crustal squeezing that created the western Transverse Ranges. Sedimentary deposits as young as Holocene age are folded, indicating the deformation continues to this day.

Ventura Basin

The Ventura Basin, a sediment-filled lowland occupied by the Santa Clara River, is a structurally complex, east-trending, elongate synclinal trough in the western Transverse Ranges. It formed during major tectonic episodes of rapid subsidence and filled with 40,000 feet of mostly clastic sedimentary rocks ranging in age from Cretaceous to Holocene, including one of the thickest sections of Pliocene and younger-aged sediments anywhere in the world. The Cenozoic geologic record is unusually complete, so that within a 3-mile radius

STRATIGRAPHY OF THE SANTA BARBARA-VENTURA AREA

ERA	AGE PERIOD		EPOCH		FORMATION	THICKNESS (feet)	DESCRIPTION
CENOZOIC	QUATERNARY		HOLOCENE		alluvium	0-250	gravel, sand, silt
			PLEISTOCENE		Casitas	0-3,000	gravel, pebbly sandstone
					Santa Barbara	0-2,200	fine sand, minor siltstone and claystone (unconformity)
		NEOCENE	PLIOCENE	Upper	Pico	0-2,200	siltstone, fine sandstone, basal conglomerate
				Lower	Sisquoc Shale	0-3,000	diatomaceous clay shale
			MIOCENE	Upper	Monterey	1,700–3,000	soft fissile to hard platy siliceous shale, organic and calcareous shale
				Middle	Rincon Shale	1,700	dark mudstone
				Lower	Vaqueros Sandstone	0–900	sandstone, pebble conglomerate
	TERTIARY		OLIGOCENE		Sespe / Alegria	2,500	sandstone, siltstone, conglomerate / sandstone
					Gaviota	0–1,000	buff sandstone
		PALEOGENE	EOCENE	Upper	Coldwater Sandstone	0–3,000	sandstone, thin beds of sandy siltstone
					Sacate	2,500–3,000	claystone, minor sandstone
					Cozy Dell Shale	1,800–4,000	claystone, minor sandstone
				Middle	Matilija Sandstone	1,000–2,000	feldspar-rich sandstone
					Anita	0–1,000	clay shale, sandstone
				Lower	Juncal	3,400–5,000	gray shale with brown sandstone interbeds
			PALEOCENE			UNCOMFORMITY	
MESOZOIC	CRETACEOUS		Late		Jalama	2,200	dark claystone, minor thin sandstone beds (fault contact)
			Early		Franciscan		graywacke, shale, chert, greenstone, serpentinite
	JURASSIC		Late				

of a single site in the basin near Santa Paula, you can study rocks representing at least a part of every geologic epoch since the beginning of Eocene time.

The Ventura Basin probably began to develop in Late Cretaceous time when subduction of the Farallon Plate beneath the North American Plate formed a large fore-arc basin west of what is now the Peninsular Ranges. Thick sections of marine sandstone and shale were deposited in the submerged basin in Cretaceous and Eocene time. During late Eocene and Oligocene time—from about 38 to 25 million years ago—part of the basin underwent a period of tectonic transition, still not completely understood, which brought the basin above sea level. We know this because sedimentation was dominated by river and lake deposits, such as the Sespe Formation. The basin subsided again in Miocene time, accumulating a great thickness of Monterey Formation organic shale that eventually became the principal source rock for petroleum in the region.

By the end of Miocene time, about 5 million years ago, the fore-arc basin rocks began to rise and form the mountains of the western Transverse Ranges, with several smaller basins in between, including the Ventura, Ridge, and Soledad Basins. Fossil evidence indicates that by about 4 million years ago the sea inundated the central part of the Ventura Basin to a depth of 5,000 feet. The basin continued to sink even until Holocene time, although at a reduced rate, with sediments eroded from the growing mountains filling the basin faster than the rate of subsidence. North-south squeezing uplifted the basin and formed such major structures as the Ventura anticlinorium and the San Cayetano, Oak Ridge, and Red Mountain faults. Localized uplift, anticlinal folding, and deep erosion around the basin margins began less than 1 million years ago.

Conejo and Santa Cruz Island Volcanics

Conejo Volcanics and Santa Cruz Island Volcanics are the names applied to very large areas of Miocene volcanic rocks at the west end of the Santa Monica Mountains and on the north half of Santa Cruz Island, respectively. They erupted in the gaps created when the future Transverse Ranges were kidnapped by the Pacific Plate from the San Diego coastal region and began to rotate and slide away from the North American Plate about 19 to 17 million years ago.

The Conejo Volcanics consist of three eruptive suites ranging from basalt to dacite with minor rhyolite. Each suite contains massive basalt and andesite flows, tuff, dacite domes, volcaniclastic rocks, and hyaloclastite—lava that shattered when it flowed into water. Pillow lavas, which form when lava flows into seawater and cools in bulbous shapes, are present in the lower to middle members of the Conejo Volcanics, indicating an early submarine eruptive stage. The lava of later eruptions cooled on land. Feeder dikes intruded along high-angle normal faults, suggesting the eruptions occurred during the crustal stretching that formed the faults. Rocks of the same age and type as the Conejo Volcanics are also exposed deep beneath the Oxnard Plain and in the hills behind Laguna Beach in the Peninsular Ranges.

The Conejo Volcanics in this Santa Monica Mountains roadcut erupted about 18 to 16 million years ago. Red pocketknife for scale. (34°05.35N, 118°52.33W)

EASTERN TRANSVERSE RANGES

The San Gabriel Mountains are moving with a component of Pacific Plate motion, southwest of the San Andreas fault, whereas the San Bernardino Mountains and the Little San Bernardino Mountains, in the western part of Joshua Tree National Park, are northeast of the fault on the uplifted edge of the North American Plate. All three mountain ranges once formed a contiguous block of Proterozoic-age gneissic basement rocks, together with rocks and structures related to the younger Pelona and Orocopia Schists, 20 million years ago, before the San Andreas fault right-laterally separated them about 130 miles.

San Bernardino Mountains

The San Bernardino Mountains, a broad, strikingly flat plateau that drops off steeply on all sides, lies at an elevation of 5,000 feet or more, with meadows, lakes, and playas separated by smooth ridges. Streams meander through the uplands in the central part of the range, then plunge over falls into steep canyons. The mountains have risen so recently that the streams have not had time to erode gradual channels with uniform gradients.

The San Bernardino Mountains are a mix of Proterozoic metaplutonic rocks overlain by younger Proterozoic and Paleozoic metasedimentary rocks, originally deposited in a shallow sea covering a wide continental shelf. These older

Shaded relief image of the eastern Transverse Ranges. The San Andreas fault cuts diagonally from upper left to lower right.

rocks were intruded by Mesozoic dioritic to granitic rocks in three episodes, dated at about 255 to 225 million years, 150 to 145 million years, and 92 to 75 million years.

The San Andreas fault system bounds the southwest side of the San Bernardino Mountains. The Landers–Joshua Tree fault systems bound the east margin of the range, whereas impressive but less active thrust faults bound the north side. The northwestern San Bernardino Mountains had two distinct episodes of uplift, between 9.5 and 4.1 million years ago, and between 2.0 and 1.5 million years ago, possibly related to movements on low-angle faults beneath the range.

San Gabriel Mountains

The rugged, chaparral-covered San Gabriel Mountains are made of structurally complex Mesozoic plutonic and Proterozoic metamorphic rocks. They were uplifted en masse only in the last 5 million years by pushing and arching forces between the San Andreas fault on the northeast and the Sierra Madre and Cucamonga fault zones on the southwest. Their steep, south face is the fault-line scarp of those fault zones, where Proterozoic rocks of the range are thrust upward and southwestward over Quaternary gravel lying on the north edge of the Peninsular Ranges.

The deep interior of the San Gabriel Mountains exposes basement rocks separated into an upper and lower plate by the Vincent–Orocopia–Chocolate Mountains thrust fault, the fault along which the Farallon Plate subducted beneath the North American Plate. The older, upper plate consists of a mix of high-grade metamorphic rocks—San Gabriel Gneiss, migmatite, and amphibolite with predominant ages of 1,690 to 1,660 million years and 1,410 million years. A dome-shaped anorthosite-gabbro-syenite complex intruded the gneiss 1,410 to 1,220 million years ago. Anorthosite is a rare igneous rock consisting of almost entirely plagioclase feldspar. Several large and small bodies composed of

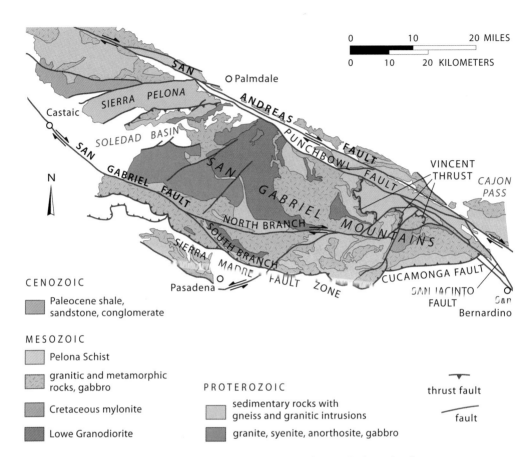

Geologic map of the San Gabriel Mountains with main faults and rock types.

the minerals apatite and ilmenite are genetically related to the complex. Biotite quartz diorite dikes and lamprophyric dikes—igneous rocks in which larger crystals of mafic minerals are imbedded in the finer-grained matrix—intruded all of these rocks in Proterozoic time. The entire rock complex is so unique that some authors believe they represent an exotic terrane—perhaps a small microcontinent—added to the North American Plate during the subduction of the Farallon Plate. All of these rock units were intruded by granitic rocks during three discrete episodes: about 215, 170 to 155, and 88 to 71 million years ago.

Beneath the Vincent–Orocopia–Chocolate Mountains thrust fault is a lower plate of mica-quartz-albite schist and greenschist collectively known as the Pelona Schist. These rocks formed by low-grade metamorphism of sandy graywacke, siltstone, shale, and basalt that were probably deposited upon oceanic crust of the Farallon Plate in Late Cretaceous time. The metamorphism occurred about 75 million years ago during subduction of the Farallon Plate beneath the North American Plate.

ROAD GUIDES FOR THE TRANSVERSE RANGES

INTERSTATE 5
SYLMAR—GRAPEVINE
60 miles

I-5, the primary highway between southern California and northern California, winds through Newhall and Tejon Passes, which separate the western Transverse Ranges from the San Gabriel Mountains. One of the earliest transportation routes, the Ridge Route, lies between these passes north of Los Angeles. The modern highway crosses the San Andreas fault in Tejon Pass—the saddle between the Tehachapi and San Emigdio Mountains—and continues down the Grapevine grade into the San Joaquin Valley.

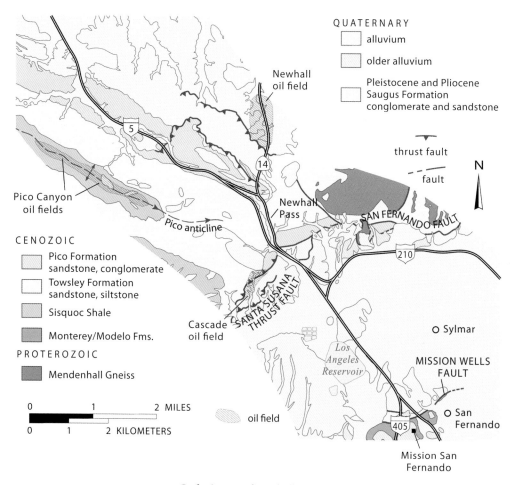

Geologic map of Newhall Pass.

Newhall Pass carries I-5 and CA 14 through deep roadcuts in marine sandstone of the Pliocene-age Pico Formation. The highway bridges in the distance collapsed during the 1971 San Fernando earthquake and again in the 1994 Northridge earthquake. See the discussion of the San Fernando earthquake in the road guide for I-405 in this chapter. (34°20.1N, 118°30.5W)

Newhall Pass to Castaic

Newhall Pass is one of the four major passes that are transportation and supply routes into and out of the Los Angeles Basin. Vice President Richard Nixon pointed out that fact to Russian president Nikita Khrushchev on their visit to Los Angeles in 1959. Khrushchev replied that the Russians had long known about the strategic importance of the passes in the region and had already targeted each one with intercontinental ballistic missiles.

The pass cuts across the Santa Susana Mountains and the southeast nose of the Pico anticline, an almost perfectly A-shaped fold in thick, marine sandstone beds of the Pliocene-age Pico Formation. The petroleum-rich anticline formed in the last 3 million years, indicating just how young the deformation is in this region. Native Americans used Pico Canyon oil for medicinal purposes. In September 1876 the California Star Oil Works drilled its Well No. 4 with steam and began pumping twenty-five barrels per day at 370 feet. The well turned out to be the first commercially successful oil well in the western United States, producing continuously for 114 years, until 1990.

North of Magic Mountain amusement park, I-5 passes through sandstone and gravel beds of the Pliocene and Pleistocene Saugus Formation. Late Pleistocene stream terraces, deposited after the Saugus was uplifted and tilted, are also warped and faulted in places, indicating that deformation continues today.

North of Castaic Junction (exit 172) are the Honor Rancho and adjoining Castaic Hills oil fields, both discovered in 1950. They may be identified from the highway by the presence of small storage tanks and pumpjacks. Production is from lenticular sandstone beds of Miocene age within faulted, en echelon anticlines partly cut off on their northeast ends by the San Gabriel fault.

Ridge Basin

The Ridge Route, followed by I-5 between Castaic and Lebec, was constructed in 1914–1915 by pick, shovel, and mule-drawn scrapers. It was so named because most of the road was placed on a 30-mile-long ridge west of Castaic Creek to avoid drainage problems and to reduce earthwork. The highway was realigned off the ridge in 1933 as part of US 99, widened and straightened in 1952, and then abandoned and reconstructed in 1968 as part of I-5. At that time it was the greatest earth-moving project in history, until the Aswan High Dam in Egypt was completed in 1976.

Between Castaic and Gorman (exit 202), I-5 proceeds along the axis of the Ridge Basin, a low-lying area formed along the San Gabriel right-slip fault. The basin is about 25 miles long and 7 miles wide, and accumulated clastic sediments, both marine and nonmarine, during late Miocene and early Pliocene time. The marine beds are in the south end of the basin, south of Templin Highway (exit 183). North of Templin Highway they are overlain by a great thickness of nonmarine sandstone, siltstone, and shale that crops out along I-5 between Templin Highway and Gorman.

The basin formed along the northeast side of the San Gabriel fault, the San Andreas system's principal active strand about 11 to 4 million years ago. During that time, the basin's depositional center slipped right-laterally along the fault relative to igneous and metamorphic rocks on the southwest side of the fault.

Coarse talus and debris-flow breccia were shed from those basement rocks northeastward across the fault into the basin to form the Violin Breccia, which extends laterally into the basin about 1 mile. It interfingers with stream and lakebed sandstone and shale in the main part of the basin. The Violin Breccia is unusual in that beds accumulated in an overlapping fashion, one after another, similar in form to overlapping slats in a Venetian blind. Deposition occurred in the way a coal train is loaded relative to a stationary tipple. As the coal train moves forward, a new load of coal is deposited into the next coal car. The aggregate thickness of breccia deposited in this way is 35,000 feet, but as with Venetian blinds, you cannot measure 35,000 feet of sedimentary rock in any single place.

The basin's stratigraphic succession is 45,000 feet thick, but like the Violin Breccia, the layers were deposited sequentially in an overlapping arrangement, also as a consequence of deposition in a strike-slip basin. The bulk of

The coal train, moving to the left as each car is loaded stepwise from a stationary source, is an analogy for how sedimentary layers are deposited in an overlapping arrangement on one side of a right-slip fault relative to a point source on the other side. —Modified from Crowell and Link, 1982

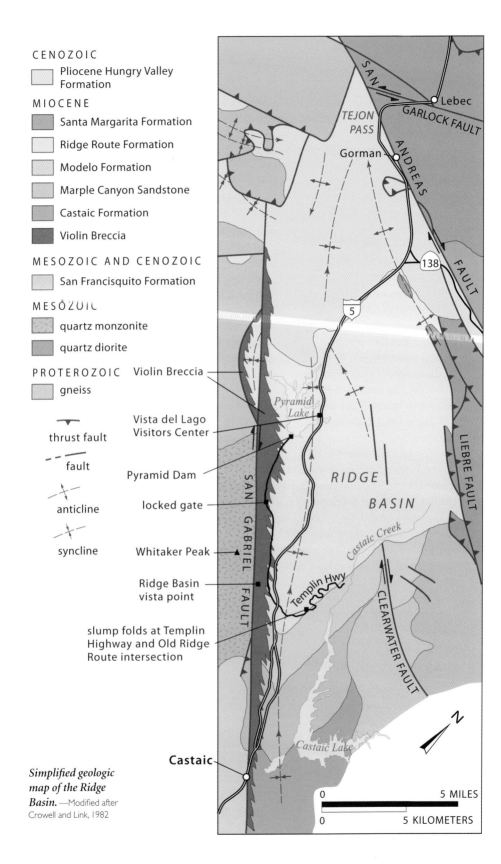

CENOZOIC

☐ Pliocene Hungry Valley Formation

MIOCENE

☐ Santa Margarita Formation

☐ Ridge Route Formation

☐ Modelo Formation

☐ Marple Canyon Sandstone

☐ Castaic Formation

☐ Violin Breccia

MESOZOIC AND CENOZOIC

☐ San Francisquito Formation

MESOZOIC

☐ quartz monzonite

☐ quartz diorite

PROTEROZOIC

☐ gneiss

⊢ thrust fault

– – fault

⤬ anticline

⤬ syncline

Violin Breccia

Vista del Lago Visitors Center

Pyramid Dam

locked gate

Whitaker Peak

Ridge Basin vista point

slump folds at Templin Highway and Old Ridge Route intersection

Lebec

GARLOCK FAULT

TEJON PASS

Gorman

SAN ANDREAS FAULT

138

5

SAN GABRIEL FAULT

Pyramid Lake

RIDGE BASIN

Castaic Creek

LIEBRE FAULT

Templin Hwy

CLEARWATER FAULT

Castaic Lake

Castaic

N

0   5 MILES

0   5 KILOMETERS

Simplified geologic map of the Ridge Basin. —Modified after Crowell and Link, 1982

the sediment in the Ridge Basin consists of shale-rich lakebeds and lesser sandy interbeds carried and deposited by streams from northern and northeastern sources that probably correspond today to the Lucerne Valley region of the Mojave Desert. That area has slipped right-laterally about 60 miles southeastward along the San Andreas fault relative to the northwest end of the Ridge Basin in the last 5 million years. The streams could flow from the Mojave region to the Ridge Basin because the San Gabriel Mountains had not yet been uplifted.

Ridge Basin Sedimentary Rocks along Old Ridge Route

You may obtain a safe and close look at the Ridge Basin rocks along Old Ridge Route south of its intersection with Templin Highway about 1 mile east of I-5 (exit 183). All of the sedimentary rock layers south of the intersection are deep-marine sandstone and siltstone beds. They shoal up-section from south to north to shallow-marine layers at the intersection. The marine-nonmarine transition is exposed in a deep roadcut 100 yards north of Templin Highway, where coarse sandstone beds contain channels and cut-and-fill structures filled with pebbly conglomerate, typical of stream flow deposits.

Climb the hill southeast of the intersection to obtain a view over the region. Stratigraphically you stand in the upper part of the shallow-marine section that is well exposed in the roadcut across Templin Highway. Notice that most of the beds are parallel to one another, as is common with marine sedimentary

View north across Templin Highway of a deep roadcut exposing tan, lenticular sandstone beds, folded by slumping, interbedded with undeformed gray mudstone. (34°35.6N, 118°40.3W)

rocks, but some interbeds are wavy and look as if they slumped. This deformation occurred when the beds slumped, or slid, on submarine slopes either during tectonic oversteepening of the depositional slope or during earthquake shaking. Some of the layers maintain their same stratigraphic position throughout the basin, suggesting that only an earthquake could have affected layers simultaneously over the entire basin. Subsequent deposits filled in the slumps, and deposition of flat, undeformed beds resumed.

Although most of the Ridge Basin to the northwest is out of sight from the hilltop, you can see the unconformable contact to the northeast between the San Francisquito Formation (Eocene) on the east edge of the basin and the rugged ledges of Ridge Basin conglomerate and sandstone (Pliocene) west of the big green surge tank in the middle distance. The zone of red-brown rocks in the middle distance marks the trace of the Clearwater fault. The northeast edge of the basin is near the point where power lines cross Liebre Mountain (elevation 5,768 feet), the whaleback ridge on the skyline.

Lakebeds and Sandstone in Piru Gorge

A great thickness of lakebeds was deposited in the lowest part of the Ridge Basin and is exposed along Old US 99 to Pyramid Dam. Drive west on Templin Highway (exit 183) beneath I-5 to its intersection with the old highway, turn right, and proceed north about 5 miles past spectacular exposures of basin shale to a big, locked gate. Unless an official is there who will let you through the gate, you'll have to walk 2 miles to the base of Pyramid Dam at the end of the road.

North of the gate, the canyon walls expose over 3,000 feet of a thick, northwest-dipping, thin-bedded sequence of siltstone and shale, soft mudstone, pyrite-rich shale and siltstone, and gypsum-rich siltstone. Here and there within this sequence are thin shale beds that contain beetle burrows, mud cracks, and wave ripples, characteristic of shallow-water deposits. The lake dried up periodically and then desiccation cracks would form on the surface of the muddy sediments.

Piru Gorge Sandstone is the best exposed of the stream and stream delta sequences in the lowest part of Ridge Basin. The formation is 600 feet thick at Pyramid Dam and consists of two sandstone beds separated by an interval of shale. A meandering stream deposited this sand in its delta in a shallow lake.

Vista del Lago

I-5 continues northwestward along the length of the Ridge Basin through stream-deposited sandstone with interbedded siltstone, all dipping northwestward. Along the way you'll pass an informative and highly recommended visitor center at Vista del Lago (exit 191), a splendid place to get a cool drink of state water on a hot day. Illustrative displays at the center tell how the California Aqueduct brings water 700 miles from northern California to southern California. Pyramid Lake is one of several water storage reservoirs that hold water for the Los Angeles metropolitan area. It takes its name from a pyramidal cut slope carved by road builders that stands adjacent to the dam, not the pyramidal island so visible in the middle of the lake.

Wave ripples in Piru Gorge Sandstone indicate that the sandstone was deposited in a shallow lake. (34°38.3N, 118°45.7W)

Stream, delta, and lake sandstone and shale beds in Piru Gorge Sandstone along Old US 99 at Pyramid Dam. (34°38.3N, 118°43.6W)

Sandstone and siltstone beds dip northward almost the entire length of I-5 in the Ridge Basin. (34°38.2N, 118°43.6W)

San Andreas Fault at Gorman

The Fort Tejon earthquake of January 9, 1857, was the strongest and latest "big one" on the San Andreas fault to hit southern California in recorded history. Seismographs didn't exist in those days to locate an earthquake epicenter or determine a magnitude, but personal letters, military reports, and scattered newspaper stories allow us to conclude the earthquake had an estimated magnitude of at least 7.9 and the epicenter was probably near Gorman. It was felt throughout southern and central California from the Colorado River to San Francisco and Sacramento. There was only one known fatality, probably owing to the sparse population and paucity of buildings in California at the time. A surface rupture, later realized to be the San Andreas fault, stretched 225 miles from Wrightwood, near I-15 in Cajon Pass, through Gorman, to Parkfield, in central California. The best indication of horizontal displacement associated with the earthquake comes from a Fort Tejon military report that the fault rupture passed through a circular corral, 30 feet in diameter, and displaced the two halves into an S shape.

One of the most accessible places to see the effects of San Andreas faulting on the land is along the Gorman Post Road (exit 202) at the north end of Ridge Basin. The valley lies along a 5-mile-long stretch of the Gorman Post Road between Gorman and its intersection with CA 138 about 1 mile west of Quail Lake (exit 198). It is a zone of faulting as much as 1,000 feet wide, with scarps and sag ponds that most likely formed or were freshened by surface rupturing accompanying the 1857 earthquake.

About one-quarter mile east of Gorman and then east over the next 2 miles of Gorman Post Road are roadcut exposures of highly fractured, dark lavender

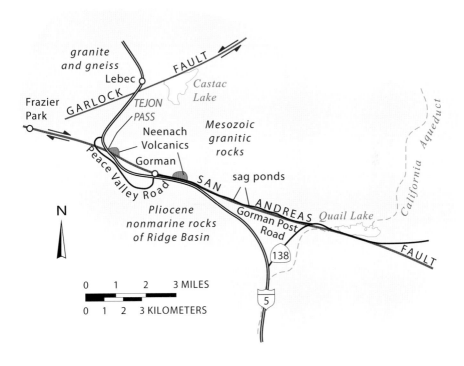

Gorman Post Road follows the San Andreas fault between Gorman and CA 138.

and dark gray andesite belonging to the Neenach Volcanics. These exposures lie in a thin fault sliver along the north side of the road. The main exposures are 15 miles farther southeast near the hamlet of Neenach, where they straddle Pine Canyon. The Neenach Volcanics are distinctive dark, red-brown andesitic lava flows and flow breccia, and light tan, hard, massive flow-banded rhyolite and dacite. These rocks erupted 23 million years ago from Pinnacles Volcano in central California over an area that was later transected by the San Andreas fault. The fault displaced the lava flows nearly 180 miles to Neenach, leaving slivers of rock along the way. The Neenach and Pinnacles Volcanics are the first rocks that were confidently correlated across the San Andreas fault and caused most of the doubters of great strike-slip movement on the fault to revise their thinking.

About 2.5 and 2.8 miles east of Gorman along Gorman Post Road, you will encounter several sags and undrained depressions with cottonwood trees and, in some, water and water-loving plants, including cattails. Together, they mark the trace of the fault just a few tens of feet north of the highway. Long, narrow ridges and cliffs parallel to the highway are fault scarps. Some gulches come south out of the hills and are displaced right-laterally as much as 1 mile. Crushed granite is exposed in roadcuts near the sag ponds.

A fault sliver of the Neenach Volcanics in a roadcut on the north side of Gorman Post Road between Gorman and the highway maintenance substation. (34°47.7N, 118°50.9W)

This sag pond was created when a block of ground sagged below the water table between two strands of the San Andreas fault. White salt deposits rim the shoreline. (34°46.0N, 118°48.4W)

Dark gray fault gouge separates tan, gravelly sandstone of Quaternary age next to the road from white and gray crushed granitic and gneissic rocks higher up the slope along the nearly vertical San Andreas fault at the crest of Peace Valley Road in Tejon Pass. (34°48.16N, 118°52.59W)

Tejon Pass

The main active strand of the San Andreas fault is exposed on the west side of the Peace Valley frontage road at the top of Tejon Pass (elevation 4,181 feet) about 2 miles west of Gorman. Over 3 feet of dark gray clay gouge separates sheared and crushed, white and gray Proterozoic gneissic rocks on the south from buff, gravelly sandstone of Pleistocene age on the north. The fault exposure is narrow enough that you may straddle this boundary between the North American and Pacific Plates. The fault, which last broke the surface here in the great 1857 earthquake, can be traced westward into the heart of the Big Bend, where the fault strikes almost exactly east-west.

Garlock Fault at Lebec and the Grapevine

I-5 crosses the Garlock fault in the vicinity of the Lebec Kern County Fire Station (exit 207), a few miles east of Frazier Park, where the fault branches off the San Andreas fault. The Garlock's main trace defines the straight, north shore of Castac Lake, which is a large sag pond east of the highway. The fault is a major, 160-mile-long left-slip fault that has accumulated about 40 miles of left-slip over the last 10 million years

North of Lebec, I-5 plunges steeply down Grapevine Canyon to the south edge of the San Joaquin Valley. The canyon is in a deep saddle between the Tehachapi Mountains to the east and the San Emigdio Mountains to the west. Soil, grass, grapevines, and landslides cover most of the steep canyon slopes and roadcuts in massive gneissic granitic rocks. The Grapevine fault, located on the north side of the little hill with a runaway truck ramp, separates the gneissic rocks in the mountains from Eocene marine sedimentary rocks in the valley. Large landslides abound in these Eocene rocks near the mouth of the canyon.

The Pleito thrust, marked by an 8-foot-high, north-facing scarp at the mouth of Grapevine Canyon, carries the San Emigdio Mountains northward over the south end of the San Joaquin Valley as part of the north-south squeezing of southern California in the region of the Big Bend. Two tan water tanks are on the uplifted side of the fault; a vineyard is on the down-dropped block. The fresh appearance of the scarp is a good indication of its youthfulness and therefore of the recency of fault displacement.

INTERSTATE 15 AND INTERSTATE 215
SAN BERNARDINO—CAJON SUMMIT
20 miles

Cajon Pass, between the San Bernardino Valley and the Mojave Desert, is one of the four main passes that bring rail and vehicular transportation, utilities, pipelines, and communications into the San Bernardino Valley and the greater Los Angeles region. While looking for Spanish army deserters, Pedro Fages, explorer and second Spanish military governor of California, became the first European to cross over Cajon Pass. Padre Francisco Garcés followed him in 1776 on his roundabout way from Yuma, Arizona, to the San Gabriel Mission. Jedediah Smith came through in 1826, Mormons settled the area between 1846 and 1851, and the Santa Fe railroad was completed through the pass in 1885.

Shaded relief image of Cajon Pass.

Formed by headward erosion of Cajon Creek along the San Andreas fault, the pass separates the San Gabriel Mountains to the west from the San Bernardino Mountains to the east.

San Jacinto Fault Overcrossing

The San Jacinto fault lies beneath the interchange of I-10 and I-215 in San Bernardino. From the San Timoteo Hills, southeast of the interchange and beneath the grain elevator, the fault passes northwestward beneath the northeast part of the graceful interchange, thence beneath an old motel northwest of the interchange, before continuing up Lytle Creek into the San Gabriel Mountains. This major right-slip fault has been very active in the twentieth century, having generated at least eight magnitude 6 or greater earthquakes since 1899. The segment through San Bernardino is considered especially worrisome, because it has not slipped in historic time. Microseismicity suggests that the San Jacinto fault zone, not the San Andreas, is presently the main locus of plate motion south of the Transverse Ranges.

The abundance of shallow groundwater contributed substantially to the founding of the city of San Bernardino. The groundwater is trapped beneath the city behind a subsurface zone of San Jacinto fault gouge, locally known as the Bunker Hill dike.

Shandin Hills

At the mouth of Cajon Creek, which flows out of Cajon Pass, landslide-prone Pelona Schist forms the low Shandin Hills at the north edge of San Bernardino (exit 48 on I-215). The flattened top of the hills is an old, abandoned stream terrace, the Muscoy terrace, which was beveled and then isolated by the lower reaches of Cajon Creek.

San Andreas Fault

The San Andreas fault lies at the sharp break in slope east of I-215 between low foothills and the steep front of the San Bernardino Mountains as far as Kenwood Avenue (I-15, exit 124). Pelona Schist is southwest of the fault in the San Gabriel Mountains; Proterozoic crystalline basement rocks crop out on the northeast side in the San Bernardino Mountains.

East of Palm Avenue (I-215, exit 50), the California Aqueduct exits from a tunnel through the San Bernardino Mountains and crosses the San Andreas fault. About 2 miles farther north on I-215 (PM 16), Cable Canyon flows southwest out of the San Bernardino Mountains and also crosses the fault on the northeast side of I-215. Look upstream the length of the wide canyon and see how it seems to come to an abrupt end about 1 mile from the highway. At that point the fault displaces the stream course a few hundred yards right-laterally.

Blue Cut

Cajon Boulevard (formerly Route 66) follows Cajon Creek upstream into the Blue Cut, where the creek, old highway, and railroads follow a 1-mile-long, right-lateral bend along the San Andreas fault. To get to Blue Cut, exit I-15 at

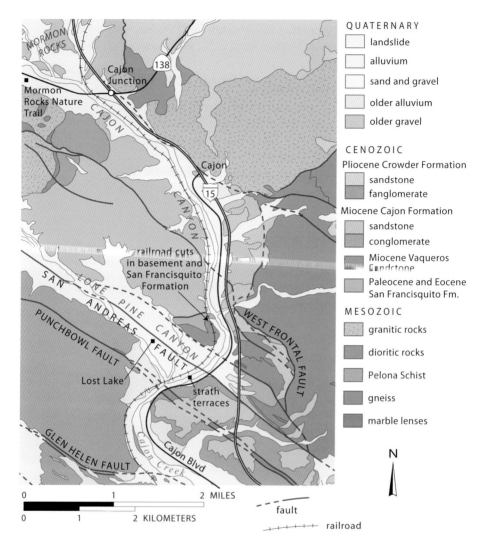

QUATERNARY
- landslide
- alluvium
- sand and gravel
- older alluvium
- older gravel

CENOZOIC
Pliocene Crowder Formation
- sandstone
- fanglomerate

Miocene Cajon Formation
- sandstone
- conglomerate

Miocene Vaqueros
- sandstone

- Paleocene and Eocene San Francisquito Fm.

MESOZOIC
- granitic rocks
- dioritic rocks
- Pelona Schist
- gneiss
- marble lenses

N

0   1   2 MILES
0   1   2 KILOMETERS

- - - fault
+++++ railroad

Geologic map of the Blue Cut area of Cajon Pass.

Kenwood Avenue (exit 124), proceed west from the I-15 overpass to the bottom of the hill, and turn right onto Cajon Boulevard. With Cajon Creek on your left, follow Cajon Boulevard about 4 miles north to where it takes a broad right bend to the east into the Blue Cut.

Numerous rockfalls have partly buried unmaintained lanes of the old highway. Stop at the wide turnout on the north side in the middle of the north-east-trending part of the highway and look between the highway and the several railroad tracks to see how Cajon Creek has cut deeply through flat terraces in Pelona Schist in just the last 8,000 years.

Cajon Boulevard bends back toward the north where it crosses the main, northwest-striking fault trace at the northeast edge of the gray-blue outcrops of schist in the canyon bottom. The fault continues northwestward up Lone Pine Canyon to Wrightwood.

Once you cross the San Andreas fault, you are on the west edge of the North American Plate. Upstream and north of the Blue Cut, look west at railroad cuts in gray granitic and gneissic basement rocks. They are overlain by a thin section of steep, north-dipping, brown marine sandstone and shale of the San

Blue Cut takes its name from the bluish-gray Pelona Schist so well exposed in this railroad cut north of Cajon Boulevard. (34°16.02N, 117°27.75W)

View west across Cajon Creek to railroad cuts in gray metamorphic and igneous rocks of Proterozoic age (P), overlain by steep, north-dipping, thin beds of brown marine sandstone and shale of the San Francisquito Formation (SFF) of Eocene age. These rocks are in fault contact with the pink and tan, nonmarine sandstone of the Cajon Formation (CF) of Miocene age. (34°16.6N, 117°27.4W)

Francisquito Formation (Eocene), which is in fault contact with pink and gray nonmarine Cajon Formation sandstone (Miocene). Proterozoic crystalline basement rocks of the San Bernardino Mountains form the slopes on the east side of Cajon Boulevard and I-15.

Mormon Rocks

More big, bold outcrops of Cajon Formation sandstone, the so-called Mormon Rocks, are west and north of the junction of I-15 and CA 138. These north-dipping, tan, feldspar-rich sandstone and pebbly sandstone beds of the Miocene Cajon Formation have brown interlayers, which represent soils formed on the sandstone beds when they were the land surface. Mormon Rocks are remarkably similar to outcrops on the opposite side of the San Andreas fault at Devils Punchbowl, 25 miles to the northwest, but surficial appearances of rock outcrops can be deceiving and lead to phony conclusions. Careful comparative studies of fossils and of the kinds of pebbles and cobbles in outcrops at each location prove that they are not exactly the same age and don't have the same clast assemblages.

The geology and natural history of Mormon Rocks are illustrated by educational signs along a trail starting at the US Forest Service trailhead near Mormon Rocks Fire Station, about 2 miles west of I-15.

Inface Bluffs of Cajon Summit

I-15 climbs a long grade to the top of Cajon Summit through steep cliffs to Oak Hill Road (exit 138). The steep, south face of these cliffs, called the Inface Bluffs, exposes the interior of the Victorville fan—gravelly beds of Pleistocene alluvium that slope gently northward beneath the desert floor toward Victorville. The fan sediments were shed from the San Gabriel Mountains across the San Andreas fault and built a broad bajada along the south edge of the Mojave Desert. The bajada lengthened intermittently as progressively younger fans were deposited and older fans were displaced right-laterally along the fault. Subsequent headward erosion by Cajon Creek, which flows into the Pacific Ocean, carved deeply into the fans, creating the Inface Bluffs and capturing the fan drainages that once flowed from the north flank of the San Gabriel Mountains into the Mojave Desert.

The upper gravels of the fans consist almost entirely of Pelona Schist clasts derived from the Wrightwood area. The lower part of the section contains clasts of rocks that crop out farther northwest in the central and western San Gabriel Mountains. Rare clasts of polka-dot granite, derived originally from the Devils Punchbowl area, show that from 20 to 30 miles of right-slip has occurred on this part of the San Andreas fault since deposition of the lower beds. The lowermost gravels in the oldest fan were eroded from the initial uplift of the San Gabriel Mountains during Pleistocene time.

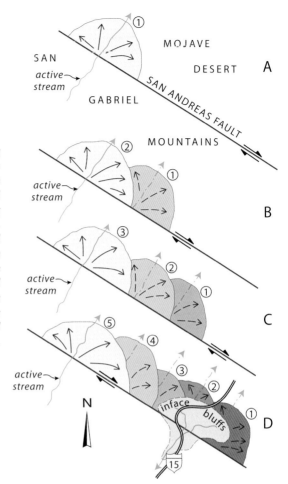

Alluvial fans spreading north from the San Gabriel Mountains were progressively displaced right-laterally along the San Andreas fault. Cajon Creek incised headward along the fault, separated the fans from their original sources, and eroded the steep cliffs, called the Inface Bluffs, at the head of the creek.

View north from Mormon Rocks across a broad amphitheater that Cajon Creek has eroded between the mountains and the Mojave Desert. The Inface Bluffs along the skyline reveal interiors of alluvial fans that make up the desert floor. (34°21.6N, 117°29.1W)

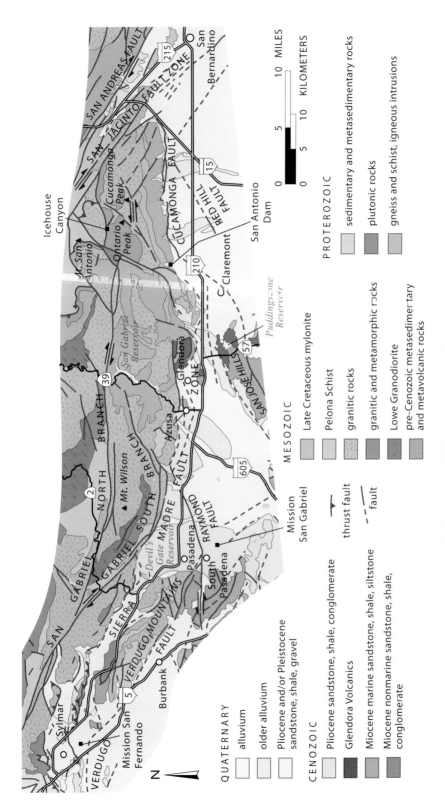

Geology along I-210 between Sylmar and San Bernardino.

N

QUATERNARY

alluvium

older alluvium

Pliocene and/or Pleistocene sandstone, shale, gravel

CENOZOIC

Pliocene sandstone, shale, conglomerate

Glendora Volcanics

Miocene marine sandstone, shale, siltstone

Miocene nonmarine sandstone, shale, conglomerate

MESOZOIC

Late Cretaceous mylonite

Pelona Schist

granitic rocks

granitic and metamorphic rocks

Lowe Granodiorite

pre-Cenozoic metasedimentary and metavolcanic rocks

PROTEROZOIC

sedimentary and metasedimentary rocks

plutonic rocks

gneiss and schist, igneous intrusions

Mission San Gabriel

thrust fault

fault

0   5   10   MILES

0   5   10   KILOMETERS

INTERSTATE 210
Sylmar—San Bernardino
75 miles

I-210 commences at its intersection with I-5 in Sylmar and follows the south front of the San Gabriel Mountains eastward to San Bernardino. Appropriately called the Foothill Freeway, most of the route lies upon great alluvial fans shed southward out of those mountains into the San Gabriel and San Bernardino Valleys.

San Fernando Fault Zone
The foothills between I-5 and Sunland are made of sandstone and shale of the Modelo Formation of late Miocene age. The Tujunga segment of the San Fernando fault zone lies at the base of these foothills and was the southernmost of several ground ruptures of the February 9, 1971, San Fernando earthquake (magnitude 6.6). As much as 4 feet of vertical displacement occurred on the north side of the fault, and part of the San Gabriel Mountains rose 8 feet as a result of the earthquake. The neighborhood between Polk Street (exit 3) and CA 118 was strongly damaged by the earthquake.

La Tuna Canyon and the Sierra Madre Fault Zone
I-210 slices through the north part of the Verdugo Mountains via La Tuna Canyon. Terraced roadcuts expose highly fractured gneiss of Proterozoic age intruded by Wilson Diorite of Early Cretaceous age.

As you drive eastward out of La Tuna Canyon, you are looking along the Sierra Madre fault zone and its nearly 1-mile-high fault scarp. The Sierra Madre fault zone extends along the south front of the San Gabriel Mountains from San Fernando east to Upland, where the name changes to the Cucamonga fault, to its junction with the San Jacinto fault north of San Bernardino. The fault zone consists of gently to moderately north-dipping thrust and reverse faults along the foot of the steep range front. Triangular ends of ridges, well-defined scarps, deeply incised alluvial fans, gouge and crushed bedrock, faulted alluvial terraces, and small historic earthquakes along the fault zone attest to the recency of geologic activity. Banded Proterozoic gneiss is thrust southward, up, and as much as 100 feet over unconsolidated bouldery deposits of Quaternary alluvium still containing tree stumps. Total vertical displacement along the fault is estimated to be as much as 10,000 feet. The steepness of the mountain slope and intensity of fracturing along the fault zone has spawned many landslides, large and small, on the mountain front.

Geologists regard the steep, south front of the San Gabriel Mountains as the type location for the Pasadenan orogeny, a term generally applied to the phase of mountain building that began about 4 million years ago, accelerated around 3 million years ago, and is still continuing. Some of the mountains are being uplifted at least as much as 25 feet per 1,000 years, and in one instance, perhaps 70 feet per 1,000 years. Their erosion rate is only about 7.5 feet per 1,000 years, so the mountains are rising faster than they are being eroded.

Mt. Lukens (elevation 5,074 feet) represents a small part of the steep south front of the San Gabriel Mountains. The Sierra Madre fault zone lies in and along the two rounded hills in front of the mountain mass. A major forest fire denuded the slopes in 2009. (34°16.2N, 118°14.8W)

I-210 curves around the north and east sides of the San Rafael Hills in Crescenta Valley to its intersection with CA 134. The hills are mainly chaparral-covered granitic rocks that are part of the Wilson Diorite, which has a radio-metric age of 122 million years (Early Cretaceous).

Devils Gate, Arroyo Seco, and Debris Flows

Arroyo Seco, a dry wash, is mentioned on TV every January first because the Rose Bowl lies in it about 2 miles south of the highway. I-210 crosses Arroyo Seco via a bridge directly in front of Devils Gate Dam, about 200 feet north of the highway (PM 22). The dam plugs a narrow water gap that Arroyo Seco has cut into a granite ridge. The stream could easily have avoided the ridge by meandering a half mile or so to the east, but it was able to downcut the ridge as fast as the land was uplifted. The dam can trap debris in the event of a debris flow and also allows water to seep into the subsurface and replenish the groundwater.

Huge, coalesced alluvial fans, which stretch from Pasadena to San Bernardino and are almost completely covered with urban development, were built by deposition of rock debris during past flash floods that emerged from the steep San Gabriel Mountain front. Future flash floods and debris-flow deposition are inevitable here. To mitigate flooding and consequent damage, many mountain drainages are dammed to trap debris while allowing water to run off quickly through concrete-lined flood channels. Debris basins not only have to be cleaned out periodically, but they also starve downstream basins of sediment. The Devils Gate debris dam has seventy years of sediment accumulation and should be cleaned out to regain its capacity and retain its effectiveness.

Gravel Mining in Alluvial Fans

The rock, sand, and gravel industry has dug huge gravel pits on many of the alluvial fans along the San Gabriel Mountains front, especially on the San Gabriel River fan, which ranges in thickness from 60 feet at its apex to 4,000 feet in its midsection. A large, deep pit on the north side of I-210 (PM 37.5) is active opposite a large beer brewery south of the highway. Then, between Vernon Avenue (exit 39) and Azusa Avenue (exit 40), I-210 goes through an abandoned gravel pit exposing abundant granitic and metamorphic cobbles that are typical components of alluvial fans along the San Gabriel Mountains front. A negative consequence of gravel mining in urban areas is that it lowers the erosional base level, so that floods scour more deeply upstream, and floodwaters may be diverted sideways out of the main channel. Also, residential areas built on unstabilized channel cutbanks may be destroyed by lateral scour of the stream channel.

Glendora Volcanics

The Glendora Volcanics, a heterogeneous series of extrusive volcanic rocks that intertongue with the Topanga Formation, are exposed in the hillsides north of I-210 at Sunflower Avenue (exit 43). They are among the several volcanic groups of middle Miocene age that are incompletely distributed around the Los Angeles Basin, the magma having oozed up through the crust during the opening of the basin. The Glendora Volcanics are extensively exposed in the eastern San Jose Hills around Puddingstone Reservoir, between I-210 and I-10. Puddingstone is another name for conglomerate, in this case consisting of pebbles and cobbles of Glendora Volcanics.

I-210 passes alongside a hill of Mesozoic granodiorite at the Claremont city limit. Claremont is the site of the Claremont Colleges, a consortium of five independent colleges and two graduate institutions, each with its own campus and faculty. The oldest is Pomona College, established in 1887 and sometimes called the Oxford of the Orange Groves. Sadly, few orange trees remain of once extensive and prolific groves, but the college still thrives.

East of Claremont and almost all the way to San Bernardino, I-210 lies between concrete block walls, so there isn't much geology to see. Here and there the highway emerges onto alluvial fan surfaces, with gravel quarries on the north side of the highway and shopping malls and residential areas on the south side. In the vicinity of Base Line Road (exit 52), I-210 breaks out of its trench long enough for travelers to look north and see three of the highest peaks in the San Gabriel Mountains: Mt. San Antonio (elevation 10,064 feet; aka Mt. Baldy), Ontario Peak (elevation 8,693 feet), and Cucamonga Peak (elevation 8,859 feet). You may also catch a glimpse of San Antonio Dam, below the peaks at the mouth of San Antonio Canyon, which carries Mt. Baldy Road up to Mt. San Antonio.

San Antonio Canyon

The high-grade metamorphic rocks of Proterozoic age that form the core of the San Gabriel Mountains are well exposed in San Antonio Canyon along Mt. Baldy Road. From I-210, take Mountain Avenue (exit 54) in Upland north about 3 miles through a residential area, where you'll pass by several retaining walls and house foundations built with cobbles and boulders of granite and gneiss. The road loops around the east edge of San Antonio Dam and intersects Mt. Baldy Road. San Antonio Dam is an earth-fill dam at the intersection of three major, active faults. It was built in 1956 to retain floodwater and debris. To date, floodwaters have not exceeded the height of the spillway, although they came within 10 feet of it in 1980. The underlying porous and permeable substrate provides groundwater recharge for wells in the city of Upland.

Cobbles and boulders from nearby washes are commonly used for residential construction in foothill communities alongside the San Gabriel and San Bernardino Mountains. (34°08.8N, 117°40.2W)

Mt. Baldy Road winds northward through a deep canyon with steep sides, many landslides, and great talus slopes, following the trace of the San Antonio Canyon fault. The creek has incised deeply along the fault through bedrock, old streambed deposits, and landslides that bury most of the fault, although here and there pulverized and hydrothermally altered bedrock marks its location. The fault separates Paleozoic metasedimentary rocks on the east side of the canyon from high-grade Proterozoic gneisses intruded complexly by quartz diorite, mafic diorite, and late Oligocene rhyolite sills and dikes west of the highway. Individual crystals are visible within the rhyolite. Left-lateral displacement along the fault is about 6.5 miles.

The road passes through the village of Mount Baldy, situated on an old landslide, to Icehouse Canyon, a prominent fault-controlled canyon carved along the north branch of the San Gabriel fault, which had about 13 miles of right-slip between 12 and 5 million years ago. Steep, north-facing walls along Icehouse Canyon prevent direct winter sunlight from reaching the lower parts—ideal conditions for preserving ice and snow. In the 1850s, local pioneers sold block ice from an icehouse in the lower part of the canyon. The canyon has had its share of catastrophic events since the early 1900s, when habitable vacation homes numbered around 120. Over the past century almost 100 homes have been destroyed by fire, flood, landslide, or snow avalanche.

According to *Minerals of California*, published in 1956, pale rose to deep lilac crystals of corundum were found in marble in Cascade Canyon, another branch of San Antonio Canyon. Corundum, an aluminum oxide rated as 9 on the Mohs hardness scale, is the second hardest mineral behind diamond. At the head of Cascade Canyon, one-eighth- to one-half-inch blue sapphire crystals, the gemstone variety of corundum, were also found in a small prospect pit disseminated with the semiprecious gemstone lapis lazuli in mica-diopside schist. The lapis lazuli was first found in boulders in the bed of San Antonio Creek and traced to the outcrop. The presence of corundum and sapphire indicates the extremely high metamorphic pressure the marble experienced.

North of Icehouse Canyon, Mt. Baldy Road climbs a series of steep switchback curves through a large landslide dissected by gullies. The road is on the relatively flat landslide surface at the top of the switchbacks. Mt. San Antonio, visible up the canyon at the north end of the flat, consists of Cretaceous quartz diorite, which is separated on its north and west sides from the underlying Pelona Schist by the Vincent–Orocopia–Chocolate Mountains thrust fault.

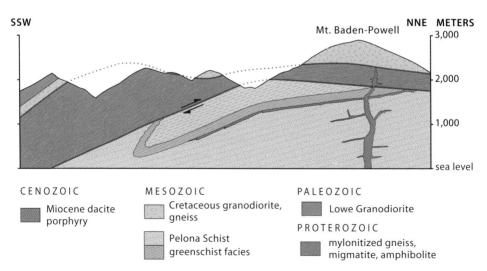

Vertical cross section of the Vincent segment of the Vincent–Orocopia–Chocolate Mountains thrust fault in the central San Gabriel Mountains, showing how Mesozoic Pelona Schist is overthrust by Proterozoic metamorphic rocks, which, in turn, are overthrust by Mesozoic granodiorite and gneiss.
—Modified from Ehlig, 1981

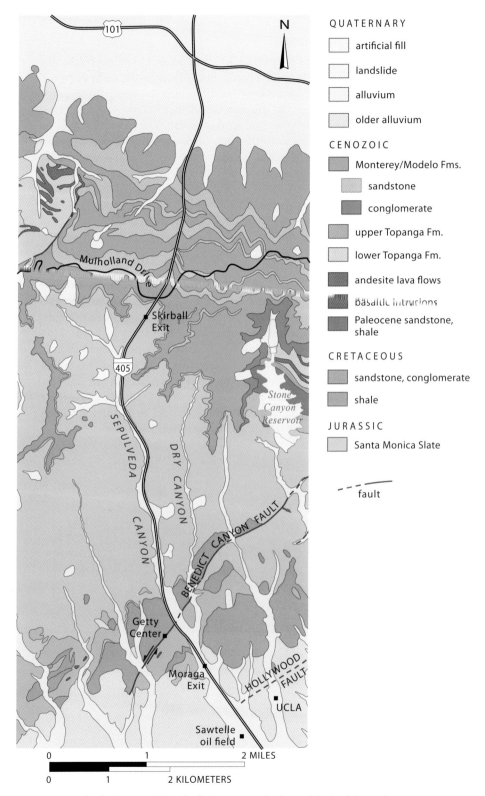

QUATERNARY

- [ ] artificial fill
- [ ] landslide
- [ ] alluvium
- [ ] older alluvium

CENOZOIC

- Monterey/Modelo Fms.
- sandstone
- conglomerate
- upper Topanga Fm.
- lower Topanga Fm.
- andesite lava flows
- basaltic intrusions
- Paleocene sandstone, shale

CRETACEOUS

- sandstone, conglomerate
- shale

JURASSIC

- Santa Monica Slate

- – – – fault

101

N

Mulholland Drive

Skirball Exit

405

Stone Canyon Reservoir

SEPULVEDA CANYON

DRY CANYON

BENEDICT CANYON FAULT

Getty Center

Moraga Exit

HOLLYWOOD FAULT

UCLA

Sawtelle oil field

0   1   2 MILES

0   1   2 KILOMETERS

Geologic map of Sepulveda Pass across the Santa Monica Mountains.

INTERSTATE 405
WEST LOS ANGELES—SYLMAR
20 miles

I-405 passes from the Los Angeles Basin into the western Transverse Ranges in West Los Angeles. The boundary between the two provinces is the Hollywood–Santa Monica fault, a broad zone of shallow and steep, north-dipping thrust faults that cross I-405 between Wilshire and Sunset Boulevards (exits 55B and 57A, respectively). The thrust faults carry the Santa Monica Mountains southward over the northwest edge of the Los Angeles Basin in such a way that oil wells drilled through the faults tap the Sawtelle oil field beneath at the northwest end of the Newport-Inglewood trend.

The Hollywood–Santa Monica fault is one of several east-west striking faults in the Southern Frontal fault system, a 150-mile-long complex of faults along the south edge of the Santa Monica Mountains. The system includes, from west to east, the Santa Cruz Island, Malibu Coast, Santa Monica, Hollywood, and Raymond Hill faults. The fault zone extends through the communities of Malibu, Santa Monica, Hollywood, and South Pasadena to the San Gabriel Mountains near Arcadia. Most of its west end lies offshore. Alluvium and dense urbanization bury much of the east half, but the location of the faults is known by mapping the scarps through urban neighborhoods and by subsurface geologic and geophysical studies.

Subsurface studies reveal that the Santa Monica and Hollywood faults dip steeply northward and have reverse and left-lateral components of displacement. Geologists have found paleoseismic evidence for a Santa Monica fault

This low hill is the scarp of the north strand of the Hollywood fault. View is northward up Vine Street from Hollywood Boulevard. (34°06.2N, 118°19.6W)

surface rupture between 17,000 and 10,000 years ago, and for a more recent event probably between 3,000 and 1,000 years ago. Its activity is sufficiently recent that a prominent south-facing scarp is easily traced through Santa Monica eastward through Hollywood.

Sepulveda Pass

Sepulveda Pass crosses the Santa Monica Mountains between the western Los Angeles Basin and the San Fernando Valley. The pass lies within a deep canyon lacking even the smallest creek to cut it. As discussed in depth in the Los Angeles Basin chapter, geologists think that the Los Angeles River formerly flowed across the Santa Monica Mountains but has since migrated progressively eastward, cutting canyons as the mountains rose faster than erosion could keep up. Today, the Los Angeles River flows from the San Gabriel and Santa Susana Mountains, crosses the San Fernando Valley, and loops around the east end of the Santa Monica Mountains into the Los Angeles Basin.

At the south end of Sepulveda Pass, between Sunset Boulevard (exit 57A) and Moraga Drive (exit 57B), look to the west and see a big, light yellow-brown outcrop of Cretaceous sandstone. It has been uplifted along the Benedict Canyon fault, which stretches about 7 miles northeastward from upper Brentwood, across I-405 to the mouth of Laurel Canyon, and thence along the north base of the Santa Monica Mountains to the Los Angeles River.

Perched partly on the sandstone foundation is the world-renowned Getty Center, which features not only a remarkable collection of artwork but also beautiful architecture, gardens, and panoramic views overlooking Los Angeles, Santa Monica, and Sepulveda Pass. Many of the center's exterior surfaces are covered by 1.2 million square feet of honey-colored travertine stone, totaling about 16,000 tons of rock. You can see fossilized leaves, feathers, and branches on some of the stone slabs that have split along natural surfaces. Other beautiful rock types have been used for floors and countertops in the Getty Center. It is well worth a side trip just to see the rock and stonework. Entrance to the center is free, but you will have to pay a parking fee.

The tan travertine was quarried at the Bagni di Tivoli springs, Italy, 15 miles east of Rome. Travertine consists typically of the mineral aragonite, which is deposited from mineral springwater (especially hot springs) or streams saturated with calcium carbonate. Travertine is a frequently used stone in modern architecture and a common facade material, wall cladding, and flooring. Because it is relatively soft and easily quarried and carved, the ancient Romans used Bagni di Tivoli travertine extensively for thousands of years for buildings all over Rome, including the Colosseum, Trevi Fountain, and the colonnades and facade of St. Peter's Basilica.

The Benedict Canyon fault is covered by dense brush on the north side of the I-405 sandstone roadcut west of Moraga Avenue. The fault separates Cretaceous sandstone from Santa Monica Slate, a rather crumbly, dull gray metamorphic rock of Jurassic age that forms the core of the Santa Monica Mountains. It's exposed in Sepulveda Pass roadcuts from Moraga Drive (exit 57B) to the Skirball Center (exit 61). Huge retaining walls cover many of the roadcuts to

The honey-colored travertine walls of the Getty Center contain fossils. (34°04.69N, 118°28.49W)

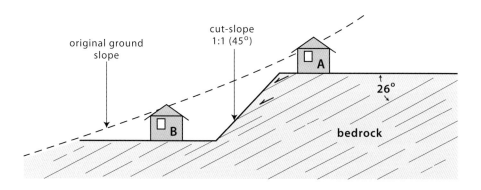

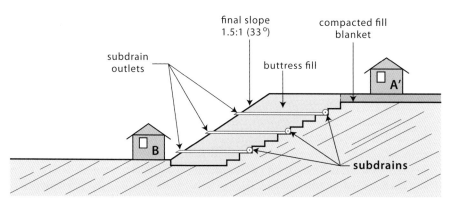

Unsupported rock layers of the Modelo Formation may slide and carry House A onto House B. To remediate the problem, House A must be moved onto a compacted blanket at position A′, slide layers must be removed and replaced with engineered buttress fill, and water must be kept out of the buttress with subdrains. —After Leighton, 1966

prevent the slate from sliding onto the highway, but it is well exposed in road-cuts along Sepulveda Boulevard south of the tunnel at the top of the pass.

At the top of Sepulveda Pass, you may have a fine view across the San Fernando Valley to the San Gabriel Mountains. Here, on the north side of the pass, a thin cover of weak, north-dipping sedimentary rock layers of Modelo Formation of Miocene age overlies the Santa Monica Slate. The Modelo Formation played a major role in the City of Los Angeles's strengthening of its grading ordinance in 1952. The weak formation is prone to landslides because its thin layers slope toward the San Fernando Valley, like roofing shingles, at an angle of about 25 degrees. Following heavy rains in January 1952, sections of the formation slid downhill, causing $7.5 million in damage to hundreds of recently built hillside homes. As a consequence, the city adopted a tough grading ordinance that required keying and benching of fill embankments for new homes on hillside lots and inspection of the work by a geologist certified by the city. Other agencies in southern California adopted similar statutes soon thereafter.

San Fernando Valley

The San Fernando Valley is a 200-square-mile, roughly triangular area surrounded by structurally complex mountains and bounded by faults. The Santa Susana and Sierra Madre fault zones are along its north edge, northeast-striking faults separate the basin from the Simi Hills to the west, and the buried Verdugo fault bounds the northeast edge of the basin. All of the faults are considered to be active. The basin's floor of basement rocks, beneath the thousands of feet of sediments filling the basin, slopes northward off the Santa Monica Mountains and then is displaced downward along the north-dipping Mission Wells fault into the 4,000-foot-deep Sylmar subbasin.

While the surrounding mountains rose over the last 3 million years, the valley subsided and filled with alluvial sediments brought by streams draining a large part of the western San Gabriel Mountains, particularly from Pacoima and Tujunga Washes, the main feeders for the Los Angeles River. The washes fed an alluvial fan complex, consisting of sand, silt, and gravel, that covers the east half of the valley. Clayey alluvium, derived from small drainages in the Santa Monica Mountains, Simi Hills, and Santa Susana Mountains, predominates in the west half of the valley.

Although not visible on the surface, an active thrust fault lies about 11 miles beneath the valley. It triggered a magnitude 6.7 earthquake on January 17, 1994. Known as the Northridge earthquake (even though the epicenter was beneath Reseda, about 4 miles west of I-405), it was felt as far away as Las Vegas, Nevada, and produced the highest ground acceleration ever recorded up until then in a North American urban area. Property damage was extensive throughout the San Fernando Valley and in parts of the Los Angeles metropolitan area, exceeding a total of $40 billion, making the earthquake one of the costliest natural disasters in United States history. Some freeway bridges and overpasses that collapsed in the 1971 San Fernando earthquake collapsed again. Eleven hospitals were damaged or unusable after the earthquake. As a result, the state legislature mandated that acute care and emergency units in

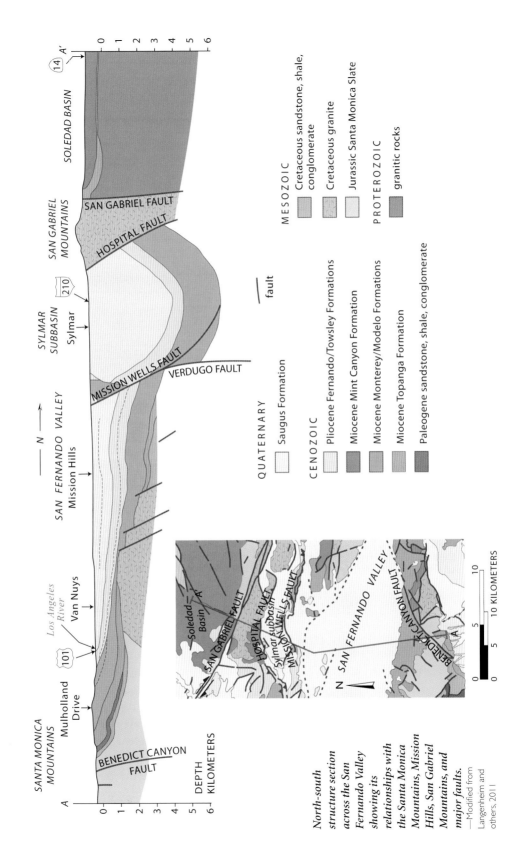

North-south structure section across the San Fernando Valley showing its relationships with the Santa Monica Mountains, Mission Hills, San Gabriel Mountains, and major faults.
—Modified from Langenheim and others, 2011

QUATERNARY

Saugus Formation

CENOZOIC

Pliocene Fernando/Towsley Formations

Miocene Mint Canyon Formation

Miocene Monterey/Modelo Formations

Miocene Topanga Formation

Paleogene sandstone, shale, conglomerate

MESOZOIC

Cretaceous sandstone, shale, conglomerate

Cretaceous granite

Jurassic Santa Monica Slate

PROTEROZOIC

granitic rocks

fault

This multistory parking structure caved in upon itself in the 1994 Northridge earthquake. (34°14.5N, 118°32.0W)

all California hospitals be housed in earthquake-resistant buildings, and major efforts were also made to reinforce highway bridges against seismic shaking.

San Fernando Earthquake of February 9, 1971

I-405 crosses the Mission Wells thrust fault along the south edge of the Mission Hills. North of the fault, a deep roadcut exposes thin beds of Modelo Formation of early Pliocene age folded into a complexly faulted anticline on the upper plate of the fault. After passing through a tunnel beneath I-5 north of the hills, I-405 crosses the San Fernando fault system in the vicinity of interchanges with I-5 and I-210 that collapsed in the 1971 San Fernando earthquake.

Ten million people felt the magnitude 6.6 San Fernando earthquake; one million people lived in the area of damage; sixty-four people died, and of those, forty were in an old hospital. The culprit was a 10-mile-long rupture on the Hospital segment of the San Fernando fault that dips 45 degrees north beneath the San Gabriel Mountains.

Perhaps because of their nearly obsessive fixation on the right-slip San Andreas fault and its potential for the "big one," many seismologists were startled

Several freeway bridges collapsed during the 1971 San Fernando earthquake, leading to a complete reevaluation of engineering practices and retrofitting of highway structures statewide. (34°19.0N, 118°29.5W)

by the earthquake's 6-foot, left-lateral displacement, which produced a 3-foot-high scarp through a San Fernando residential area and caused the central part of the western San Gabriel Mountains to flex upward 8 feet! But if the seismologists were startled, earthquake engineers were completely shocked by horizontal ground accelerations that were triple the prevailing design standard. Several hospitals were so badly damaged that they had to be razed, freeway bridges and interchanges collapsed, and many wood frame houses were knocked off their foundations. The Los Angeles Reservoir dam came within 3 feet of being overtopped by waves generated by the quake and possibly being washed away, putting eighty thousand people downstream at risk of inundation. The ground rupture also damaged underground utility lines and pipes. As a consequence of this earthquake, geologists focused much more attention on other southern California faults, although still with the San Andreas fault firmly in mind. Damaged structures were studied intensively, leading to adoption of tougher building codes and design specifications. Even with all of the earthquake damage, however, very little remains to be seen to indicate a major geologic event ever occurred here.

Blocks in the beds of slides break aqueduct water flow, thereby aerating the water as one of the first steps in its purification on its way to the Los Angeles Reservoir on the west side of I-405. (34°19.4N, 118°29.8W)

Los Angeles Reservoir

The Los Angeles Reservoir is one of several reservoirs along the route of aqueducts that bring water 338 miles from the east slopes of the Sierra Nevada to the Los Angeles metropolitan area. One mile north of the I-5 and I-405 interchange, big pipes and two long, concrete water slides are part of the aqueduct project.

US 101
HOLLYWOOD—VENTURA
70 miles
See map on page 288.

The Hollywood–Santa Monica fault separates the north edge of the Los Angeles Basin from the Santa Monica Mountains. Its buried trace lies along the base of the hills where US 101 crosses Vine Street. US 101 then enters the Hollywood Hills and crosses the east end the Santa Monica Mountains via Cahuenga Pass. You may catch a glimpse of the iconic Hollywood sign to the northeast on its foundation of Topanga Formation sandstone of Miocene age.

Cahuenga Pass

Vegetation obscures all but the most prominent sandstone beds on the east side of US 101 in Cahuenga Pass, but big roadcuts along Cahuenga Boulevard West, the frontage road west of the freeway, expose several hundred feet of black and brown lava flows and basalt sills in older, light brown or grayish, massive sandstone of the Miocene-aged Topanga Formation. The sandstone was baked and darkened at contacts with the hot basalt, much in the same way clay is fired and hardens into brick. Basalt in the pass is 17.4 million years old, one of the several early Miocene basalts on the periphery of the Los Angeles Basin. They erupted when the Transverse Ranges sheared off and rotated away from the Peninsular Ranges, with the consequent opening of the Los Angeles Basin.

Cahuenga Pass is another of several canyons carved by the Los Angeles River in the Santa Monica Mountains as it sought its way over the rising mountains to the Pacific Ocean. The pass is a wind gap now that the river has shifted eastward to its present position along I-5 at the east end of the mountains.

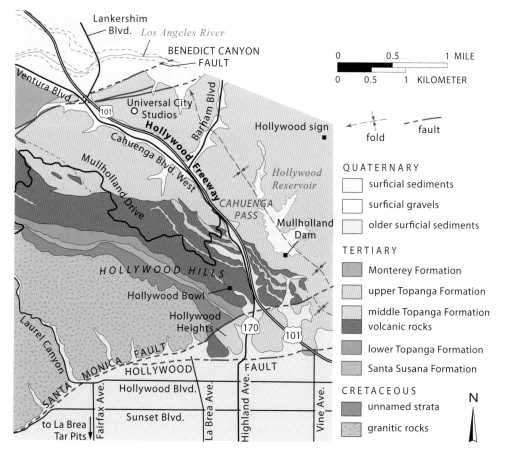

Geologic map of Cahuenga Pass.

In addition to rocks, cannonballs are occasionally found during excavations in the area. The pass was the site of two battles between unpopular nonlocal governors and forces assembled by wealthy local landowners: the Battle of Cahuenga Pass in 1831 and the Battle of Providencia or Second Battle of Cahuenga Pass in 1845.

San Fernando Valley to Camarillo

US 101 crosses the Benedict Canyon fault 1 mile or so north of Universal City at the south edge of the San Fernando Valley. The 15-mile-long stretch of US 101 west of Universal Studios is flat and straight until it enters the Chalk Hills between Winnetka (exit 25) and De Soto (exit 26) Avenues. The Chalk Hills are vaguely bedded, light gray claystone and siltstone of the upper Modelo Formation, which crops out over the next 20 miles and is exposed in big road-cuts at Las Virgenes Road (exit 32). Through Agoura Hills, Thousand Oaks, and Newbury Park, you'll see patches of Modelo, which are soft, do not resist erosion well, and are mostly covered with vegetation.

At Wendy Drive (exit 47C) look west and see the pyramid-like Conejo Mountain (elevation 1,814 feet), a big dacite intrusion in sundry extrusive and intrusive rock units of the Conejo Volcanics. These rocks crop out extensively in the western Santa Monica Mountains and are nicely exposed in deep road-cuts (PM 10.3) at the crest of the Conejo Grade in the vicinity of the truck weigh station. Look closely and see columnar-jointed dikes cutting volcanic breccia. The breccia is also exposed in four large roadcuts from the crest to the west base of the grade. One of the main dikes is exposed on Camarillo Springs Road (exit 50), about 1.5 miles northeast of its US 101 exit, in a roadcut where it is much safer to study than on the freeway.

Modelo Formation in a roadcut at US 101 and Las Virgenes Road. (34°09.0N, 118°41.9W)

This 1979 photo shows the style of folding in Modelo Formation shale and siltstone on US 101. The roadcut is now overgrown by vegetation except in drought years. (34°09.0N, 118°39.7W)

A thick, light gray, columnar-jointed dike cuts brown breccia of the Conejo Volcanics in a roadcut on the north side of US 101 on the west slope of the Conejo Grade. (34°12.1N, 118°58.5W)

On both sides of the road at the bottom of the Conejo Grade near Camarillo Springs Road is the old Conejo oil field, discovered in 1892 at a depth of just 70 feet. Extensive tar seeps at the surface led to the field discovery. The oil was found in sand interbedded with Conejo Volcanics and in fractures in the volcanic rocks. Around 110 wells were drilled, and windmills pumped most of the producing wells.

Cactus-covered volcanic breccia at the west base of the Conejo Grade near Pleasant Valley Road (exit 52) is the westernmost exposure of Conejo Volcanics on US 101. West of this point they are buried beneath the Oxnard Plain. US 101 flattens at the bottom of the grade as it traverses the Oxnard Plain to Ventura.

North of US 101 between Las Posas Road (exit 55) and Central Avenue (exit 57) are the Spanish Hills, a fault-bounded anticline in Pliocene and Pleistocene sedimentary rocks. An exclusive subdivision has been carefully laid out on the hills to avoid the surface traces of abundant faults within the anticline, especially the Springville fault along the south base of the hill. The Spanish Hills are the western extension of the Camarillo Hills, also a faulted anticline.

Oxnard Plain and the Santa Clara River

From Camarillo to Ventura, US 101 crosses the north part of the flat Oxnard Plain, the delta of the Santa Clara River. The rich delta soil forms a prime agricultural area, particularly for strawberries but also celery and onions. Here and there in the fields, you will see pumpjacks bringing up oil from beneath middle Miocene Conejo lava flows that overlie older, deeply buried, petroleum-bearing sedimentary rock. This is one of the few places in southern California where petroleum is produced from oil-bearing rock layers that have been buried and sealed by lava flows.

A long, wide bridge between Oxnard and Ventura carries US 101 across the Santa Clara River, the longest undammed river in southern California. It is 100 miles long and drops 6,000 feet from its headwaters in the San Gabriel Mountains, with an average gradient of about 70 feet per mile. Most of the river flows subsurface near Ventura, percolating through its sand and gravel bed. In years of heavy rainfall, however, the river may flow bank to bank. In 1969, an El Niño year, the river carried so much sediment to the sea that 1 square mile of new delta was built above sea level. Within two years, ocean waves had eroded the top of the delta back below sea level.

US 101 AND CA 1
Ventura—Buellton and Lompoc
76 miles

The coastline from Ventura to Gaviota is one of the most scenic routes in California because the sea is seldom far from sight. This stretch of US 101 includes a segment of the land route that Spanish commander Juan Bautista de Anza followed from colonial Mexico through the province of Las Californias in 1775–1776. Known as El Camino Real, or the Royal Highway, the route is marked

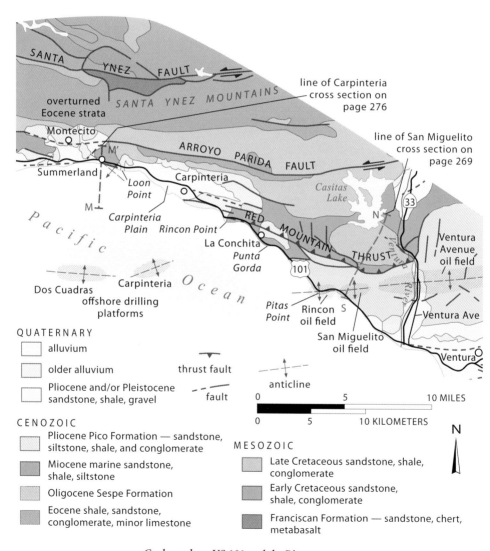

QUATERNARY

☐ alluvium

☐ older alluvium

☐ Pliocene and/or Pleistocene sandstone, shale, gravel

CENOZOIC

☐ Pliocene Pico Formation — sandstone, siltstone, shale, and conglomerate

☐ Miocene marine sandstone, shale, siltstone

☐ Oligocene Sespe Formation

☐ Eocene shale, sandstone, conglomerate, minor limestone

MESOZOIC

☐ Late Cretaceous sandstone, shale, conglomerate

☐ Early Cretaceous sandstone, shale, conglomerate

☐ Franciscan Formation — sandstone, chert, metabasalt

thrust fault

anticline

fault

0   5   10 MILES

0   5   10 KILOMETERS

N

Geology along US 101 and the Rincon.

by rusty brown mission bells on green standards. The original 700-mile-long El Camino Real linked California's twenty-one Catholic missions, which were spaced approximately one day's journey apart by horse.

In 1903, guidepost bells were placed 1 mile apart along El Camino Real to guide early travelers. Today, 555 such bells are situated along US 101 from Los Angeles to San Francisco.

Ventura Anticlinorium

An anticlinorium is a regional fold structure made up of smaller anticlines. The east-west-trending Ventura anticlinorium, which has been forming over the last 4 million years, is about 15 miles long and extends into the Santa Barbara Channel. Each of its anticlines is a major petroleum trap complexly faulted internally by thrust faults. The seaward extension of the Ventura anticlinorium is expressed by the alignment of pumpjacks north of US 101 at PM 39.6 through Rincon Island to four oil production platforms over the Dos Cuadras oil field in the Santa Barbara Channel. One of those platforms is the site of the Santa Barbara Channel oil spill in 1969, an event that spawned several environmental movements against offshore drilling. Dos Cuadras oil production is from turbidite sandstone beds of Pliocene to Pleistocene age.

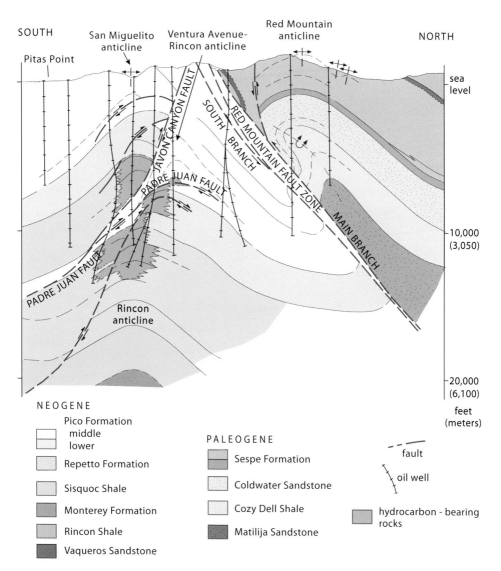

Structure section across the San Miguelito anticline, the subsurface extension of the Ventura Avenue anticline and the Red Mountain thrust fault. Location of cross section is shown on map on page 267. —Modified from Yeats and Grigsby, 1987, and Hopps and others, 1992

The anticlinorium is flanked on the north by the chaparral-covered Santa Ynez Mountains, which extend uninterruptedly from the town of Ojai to Point Conception and Point Arguello. The Red Mountain thrust fault carries older Monterey and Sespe Formation rocks onto the north flank of the anticlinorium at Punta Gorda, whereas the south-dipping Padre Juan fault carries the San Miguelito anticline onto the south flank of the subsurface extension of the Ventura Avenue anticline.

The San Miguelito anticline is one of a series of anticlines in the Ventura anticlinorium, which has produced over 1 billion barrels of oil since its discovery in 1888. (34°19.4N, 119°29.2W)

The Rincon

US 101 crosses the Ventura River and follows the base of a high sea cliff for 13 miles before it enters the Carpinteria Plain. This stretch of highway is locally known as the Rincon, Spanish for "corner." Geologically, the highway is in and nearly parallel to the south flank of the Ventura Avenue anticline, but the coastline sidesteps to the left, making corners, or points, such as Pitas Point, where cross faults displace the flank of the anticline left-laterally.

Steeply tilted, bouldery conglomerate, sandstone, and siltstone are in the first roadcuts you encounter along the Rincon west of the Ventura River. The rock layers were deposited in the sea and contain the 770,000-year-old Bishop Ash erupted from the Long Valley Caldera in eastern California. The ash, which is not visible from the highway, was deposited as a flat-lying bed, then was uplifted and tilted, eroded, and exposed, all within very recent geologic time.

Near exit 72, steep, south-dipping middle and late Pliocene shale and sandstone beds of the Pico Formation crop out on the south flank of the Ventura Avenue anticline. These 4-million-year-old beds are overlain conformably by soft clay of the 2-million-year-old Santa Barbara Formation. Numerous large landslides are present in these two units, and the highway is built on some of them. Large concrete buttresses have been constructed to prevent some parts of the hillslopes from sliding onto the highway.

Rincon Anticline

From exit 78 at Seacliff, drive north about 1 mile to the end of the old highway, where a pedestrian tunnel leads to the shoreline. You are on the crest of the Rincon anticline, one of several anticlines along the Ventura anticlinorium. Its east-west axial crest is marked by the onshore pumpjacks, on the north side of US 101, to a small island a half mile or so west, and then west through the line of offshore platforms. Rincon Island, the west extension of the field, is a man-made island connected to the mainland by a pier and was constructed in 1958 specifically as an oil well drilling platform. The Rincon oil field has produced 150 million barrels of oil since its discovery in 1927, mainly from the Pico Formation.

The folding and uplift of the Rincon anticline and the rest of the Ventura anticlinorium began about 4 million years ago and continues today. Geologically rapid uplift rates of between 0.1 and 0.8 inch per year and horizontal shortening rates of 0.8 inch per year have been calculated by several methods. One of the most rapid coastal terrace uplift rates along the California coast has been measured 2 miles north of the Seacliff ramp onto US 101 at Punta Gorda. Uplift of this 135-foot-high terrace of marine sandstone and conglomerate beds of Pliocene and Pleistocene age has been determined to be 0.2 inch per year. These layers dip steeply into the hill on the north flank of the Rincon anticline. They are beveled off near the top of the cliff and unconformably overlain by a flat marine terrace deposit containing 40,000-year-old shells of the sea snail *Olivella biplicata.*

View northwest of an uplifted marine terrace. This older photo shows the unconformity between the north-dipping Pliocene to Pleistocene sandstone and conglomerate beds of the main cliff, which are overlain by the flat-lying, 40,000-year-old sandstone of a coastal terrace at the very top. (34°21.5N, 119°25.0W)

La Conchita Area

La Conchita (exit 81) is the site of a shallow and massive, fluidlike landslide that slid into the north edge of the small community on January 10, 2005, killing ten people and destroying or damaging dozens of homes. An earlier and larger slide in 1995 prompted the County of Ventura to declare the entire community a geological hazards area. Geologic evidence indicates that landslides have occurred here for many thousands of years because of weak rocks. Deep infiltration of rainwater following prolonged or intense rainfalls triggers the slides.

The railroad was wary of the slide potential here in the late nineteenth century, when its tracks were overrun by small landslides. The railroad moved the tracks about 300 feet seaward from the base of the cliff, but even so, slides buried them in 1889 and 1909. Nevertheless, a land speculator acquired the land between the tracks and the hill and subdivided it into lots that are now occupied by homes. Lawsuits over the 2005 slide were flung back and forth between the homeowners and the owners of the avocado ranch above the community. The community said the ranch didn't provide adequate drainage for its orchards during torrential rains. Three years after the landslide, the ranch turned over all of its 700 acres and assets to settle the suit.

View north of the landslide and cliffs behind the community of La Conchita. The light-colored, exposed rock in the upper part of the photo is the main scarp of the 1995 slide. The southeast part of the 1995 deposit (right side of photo) remobilized in the January 10, 2005, slide. (34°21.9N, 119°26.7W)

About one-half mile west of La Conchita, a petroleum treatment plant separates oil from gas produced from the offshore platforms. The gas is vented and burns with a flame several feet high that is especially visible at night.

Notice the highway and railroad tracks are along the base of a steep cliff consisting of light gray, oil-saturated shale of the Monterey Formation. On the cliff at PM 42.8, 1 mile west of La Conchita, Monterey Formation organic material has undergone spontaneous combustion, probably caused by the oxidation of sulfides, cooking the gray shale to pink, red-brown, and brown colors. Now and then a strong odor of burning sulfur may be detected from points near the top of the cliff. At rare times, particularly after rains or on misty mornings, white smoke or condensation may rise from the outcrop, spawning reports in the early days of an active volcano here.

About 3 miles west of La Conchita, US 101 enters Santa Barbara County and bears right around a broad curve into a deep roadcut in folded and overturned Monterey Formation and Sisquoc Shale between exits 83 and 84. These formations have been thrust southward against unconsolidated Pleistocene sand. A thin veneer of Pleistocene marine terrace overlies the folded rock. About midway in the roadcut you may feel a bump in the highway where it is being uplifted on a strand of the Rincon Creek–Carpinteria fault system.

Carpinteria Oil Seeps

Spanish explorers found Chumash Indians building tar-caulked boats here and henceforth referred to the place as La Carpinteria, Spanish for "carpenter shop." The Carpinteria Oil Seeps were once one of just five natural asphalt lake areas in the world. Tar was mined here beginning in 1887 to pave streets of Carpinteria, Montecito, Santa Barbara, Goleta, and San Francisco. In 1915, crews mined the tar with furnace-heated shovels to pave the coast highway.

The tar oozes upward from shale of the Monterey Formation along a fault into the overlying, highly oil-saturated sandstone and conglomerate. As the oil nears the surface, its light fractions naturally evaporate, leaving the heavy tar residue and a pungent odor. Production from the offshore oil platforms has caused the natural seepage to decline considerably, as expected, since the late 1900s.

The tar pits have yielded an unusually rich collection of trapped Pleistocene vertebrate and plant fossils. Vertebrate remains include mastodons, saber-toothed cats, ground sloths, wolves, horses, camels, bison, deer, coyotes, foxes, skunks, mice, gophers, rabbits, and birds, including eagles, vultures, and hawks. Plant fossils include pine, cypress, fir, and redwood trees. Many fossils were removed from the pits before they became the site of a city dump.

To reach the tar seeps from US 101 in Carpinteria, take Casitas Pass Road (exit 86) south to Carpinteria Avenue and turn left (south). At Concha Loma Drive, turn right and follow its windings about one-half mile over the hill to Calle Ocho. Turn left and drive to the end of the road. Park and walk across the railroad tracks to view a series of black tar outcrops at the lookout point. Most of them are right on the beach.

Tar oozes from shale outcrops onto Carpinteria Beach on warm days. (34°24.2N, 119°30.8W)

Carpinteria Salt Marsh Reserve

Surrounding the town of Carpinteria is an alluvial plain covering part of the Carpinteria Basin, an east-trending faulted syncline filled with up to 4,000 feet of Pleistocene sediments deposited on previously folded pre-Pleistocene rock layers. During Miocene and Pliocene time, the Carpinteria area was the north margin of the offshore Ventura Basin. Subsequent uplift along the Red Mountain thrust fault isolated this part of the basin north of the fault during middle to late Pleistocene time. Frequency of activity along the geologically youthful main branch of the Red Mountain fault is indicated by displacement of a 45,000-year-old coastal terrace but not a 4,500-year-old terrace. The main trace of the fault lies offshore.

South and east of Carpinteria, the alluvial plain is cut by the Rincon Creek and Carpinteria faults, both of which are reverse faults that dip about 60 degrees seaward and steepen with depth. The Carpinteria fault can be traced from the deep US 101 roadcut between exits 83 and 84 westward and south of the freeway to the south part of town, where it merges with the Rincon Creek fault.

The 230-acre Carpinteria marsh formed by sagging downward along the north side of the Rincon Creek–Carpinteria reverse fault, which strikes along the shoreline. Monterey Formation shale has been thrust up along the south side of the fault, forming a reef that acts as a natural dam for slough sediments. The deposition rate is about 0.4 millimeter per year.

The Carpinteria salt marsh, or slough, one of the few relatively untouched salt marshes along the California coast, is an important ecosystem where

Aerial view westward of Carpinteria Salt Marsh Reserve. Houses along the shore in the middle distance are built upon an uplifted ridge of Monterey Formation that acts as a natural dam, preventing slough sediment from reaching the sea. (34°24N, 119°32W)

freshwater from the land meets saltwater from the sea. As Joan Lentz succinctly pointed out in *A Naturalist's Guide to the Santa Barbara Region*, salt marshes "dissipate rushing floodwaters after heavy rains; reduce erosion by slowing runoff; recharge groundwater and surface water; and absorb nutrients while removing toxic substances." They are especially important as layover sites for migrating and wintering waterbirds.

To reach the reserve from US 101, take exit 86 at Casitas Pass Road and head south toward the ocean. Turn west (right) on Carpinteria Avenue and then south (left) onto Linden Avenue and proceed almost to the end at the beach. Turn west (right) on Sandyland Road and proceed to its end at Ash Avenue, where informative signs and trails will guide you to various marsh features and viewpoints.

Summerland Village and Oil Field

Some houses in the village of Summerland are built on a slippery slope, the early Miocene Rincon Shale. The shale, consisting of clay, is notorious for expanding as much as 40 percent when wet, and that kind of expansion will ruin a building foundation. It is also very weak and can fail or slide on slopes with dips as low as 15 to 20 degrees. Permits to build homes on the hill of Rincon Shale overlooking Summerland were granted only after foundations were designed to be as much as 600 feet deep in some cases.

Between Evans Avenue (exit 91) and Sheffield Drive (exit 92), US 101 passes through Summerland and up and over Ortega Hill (PM 8.5) and descends into Montecito. The hill and its offshore extension is a southeast-plunging anticline,

Discovered in 1887, Summerland was the first offshore producing oil field in the world. Wooden piers extended as far as 700 feet into the open ocean before 1903, when a severe winter storm destroyed most of them. This oil field is one of the few known locations of oil production from nonmarine Pleistocene beds in California. (34°25.2N, 119°36.4W) —US Coast and Geodetic Survey Photo Archives

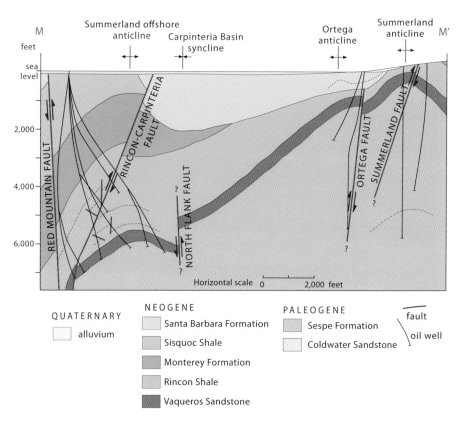

North-south structure section across the Carpinteria Basin, including the Red Mountain fault and Summerland offshore anticline. Location of cross section shown on map on page 267. —Modified from Jackson and Yeats, 1982

once the site of one of the earliest producing oil fields in California. Oil is trapped in the Pleistocene Casitas Formation beneath impermeable beds. A nearshore fault truncates the southeast end of the anticline.

In 1900, 300 wells produced an average of 500 barrels per well per day from depths of 100 to 800 feet. Peak production in 1899 amounted to a daily average of 571 barrels. Wells were drilled in 1928 to deeper zones in Miocene rock without economic success. Production gradually declined, and the field was eventually shut down in 1939 after yielding more than 3 million barrels of oil.

Santa Barbara

The rugged front of the Santa Ynez Mountains is readily visible from anywhere in Santa Barbara. The range continues unbroken westward beyond Santa Barbara until it disappears in the Pacific Ocean at Point Conception and Point Arguello. This section of coast is about the only east-west coastline in the continental United States besides the Louisiana to Florida Gulf Coast. It is also one

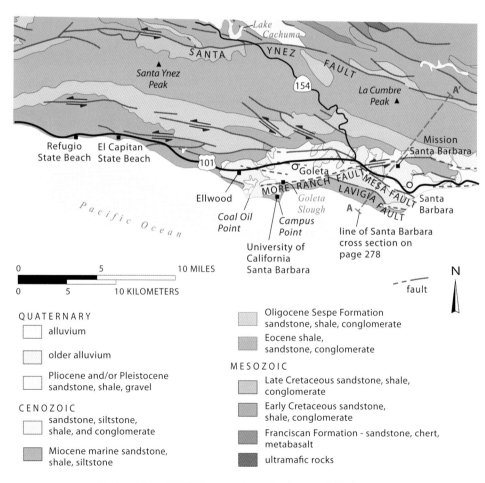

QUATERNARY
- alluvium
- older alluvium
- Pliocene and/or Pleistocene sandstone, shale, gravel

CENOZOIC
- sandstone, siltstone, shale, and conglomerate
- Miocene marine sandstone, shale, siltstone
- Oligocene Sespe Formation sandstone, shale, conglomerate
- Eocene shale, sandstone, conglomerate

MESOZOIC
- Late Cretaceous sandstone, shale, conglomerate
- Early Cretaceous sandstone, shale, conglomerate
- Franciscan Formation - sandstone, chert, metabasalt
- ultramafic rocks

Geology along US 101 between Santa Barbara and Gaviota.

of the few places in the world where the sun rises and sets over the same mountain range—in the summertime.

The seaward side of the range consists of a chaparral-veneered sequence of Eocene-age marine deposits and Oligocene-age river and lake deposits that dip seaward. The Eocene layers are steeply overturned behind Montecito and dip northward in a structure called the Montecito overturn.

The city of Santa Barbara mostly lies within a down-dropped block between the More Ranch–Mission Ridge–Arroyo Parida fault to the north and splays off this system to the south that include the Mesa and Lavigia faults. The Mesa fault lies near the base of the cliff southeast of the city. The hills north of town,

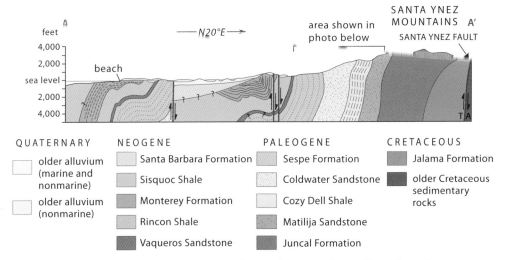

QUATERNARY

- older alluvium (marine and nonmarine)
- older alluvium (nonmarine)

NEOGENE

- Santa Barbara Formation
- Sisquoc Shale
- Monterey Formation
- Rincon Shale
- Vaqueros Sandstone

PALEOGENE

- Sespe Formation
- Coldwater Sandstone
- Cozy Dell Shale
- Matilija Sandstone
- Juncal Formation

CRETACEOUS

- Jalama Formation
- older Cretaceous sedimentary rocks

This structure section across Santa Barbara and the central Santa Ynez Mountains indicates how much the rocks in the western Transverse Ranges have been deformed during the immense crustal squeezing in last 6 million years.

Oligocene and Eocene sedimentary rocks in the Montecito foothills are overturned and dip from 60 to 70 degrees northward (to right in this image). (34°25N, 119°41W)

favored as residential building sites for ocean views, are a series of northwest-trending folds and faults.

Four geologically related sites in Santa Barbara are worth detours from US 101: Santa Barbara Harbor, Santa Barbara Mission, Monterey Formation exposures at Arroyo Burro Beach Park, and Goleta Slough.

SANTA BARBARA HARBOR

Santa Barbara's breakwater is an infamous engineering boondoggle. It was built in 1925 to provide a harbor close to the residences of the city's elite denizens, but the builders did not realize it would impede the normal longshore drift of sand. At first, sand accumulated at each end of the breakwater, making nice, wide, sandy Leadbetter and East Beaches. Eventually the city gave up trying to keep the west end open, so now sand drifts around the east end of the break-water, forming a spit that impedes entrance to the harbor. The city spends $1 million annually to dredge about 300,000 cubic yards of sand per year from the harbor entrance. The dredged sand is transferred through a pipe from West Beach to East Beach so that it may continue its natural journey eastward along the coast.

A splendid view across the harbor inlet and its breakwater may be obtained from the end of Stearns Wharf. Exit US 101 at Cabrillo Boulevard (exit 94C) and follow the road southwestward about 2 miles past the Andree Clark Bird Refuge and volleyball courts to State Street and turn left onto Stearns Wharf.

SANTA BARBARA MISSION

During the second half of the eighteenth century, Spanish Franciscans founded a string of twenty-one missions, each a day's walk apart, from San Diego to San Francisco. Mission Santa Barbara, known as the Queen of the Missions, was

Aerial view westward of Santa Barbara Harbor. The breakwater protects the boats, but sand drifts around the east end of it and impedes entry to the harbor. (34°24.4N, 119°41.5W)

Large buttresses were added to Mission Santa Barbara to support its damaged bell towers and facade following the 1925 earthquake. (34°26.3N, 119°42.8W)

established on December 4, 1786. Abundant, large boulders of Coldwater Sandstone littered the nearby alluvial slopes and were easily shaped into building blocks for the mission and many other projects in the city, including an aqueduct from Mission Creek, which supplied plentiful water to the mission.

The Santa Barbara Mission was about the only building of substance in Santa Barbara in 1812, when it was seriously damaged by an earthquake estimated to be magnitude 7. A 1925 earthquake also did extensive damage, especially to the bell towers, which weren't fully repaired until 1952. The original edifice was much smaller than that today, because each successive reconstruction was built around the former one.

The 1925 earthquake also caused considerable damage to downtown Santa Barbara. As the rebuilding process began, the city adopted a new building ordinance emphasizing the Spanish architectural style so evident in the city today, a move that aided a very necessary urban renewal.

Reach the mission by exiting US 101 at Mission Street (exit 99A) and following it about 1 mile toward the mountains. Turn left on Laguna Street.

MONTEREY FORMATION AT ARROYO BURRO BEACH PARK
The Monterey Formation and the slightly siltier Modelo Formation in the Los Angeles Basin are the major source rocks for petroleum in southern California. The Monterey consists of siliceous siltstone, shale, and diatomite that

formed from deposition of planktonic diatoms and coccoliths, both of which are microscopic marine critters. Over time, the rocks at Arroyo Burro Beach Park have been altered to porcellanite and chert by compaction and recrystallization. The rock layers are also strongly folded into various attitudes from a few degrees to vertical. Abundant fractures are filled with calcite, and some are filled with tar. In those places where the layers dip steeply seaward, yards and homes on the cliff edge slide onto the beach when the rock slips along the bedding planes.

You may reach the park by following Las Positas Road (exit 100) south to the T-intersection with Cliff Drive and then turning right and proceeding about one-fourth mile to the park entrance.

Faulted and irregularly folded Monterey Formation at Arroyo Burro Beach Park. (34°24.18N, 119°44.58W)

GOLETA SLOUGH

US 101 generally follows the railroad through the Santa Barbara urban area into Goleta Valley. The Santa Ynez Mountains north of the valley are drained by seven creeks that flow across the valley into Goleta Slough. Like Carpinteria Salt Marsh, Goleta Slough is an ecologically important area of estuary, tidal creeks, tidal salt marsh, and wetlands. Consideration was given to converting the slough into a harbor in the late eighteenth century. Heavy rainfall in 1861– 1862 caused so much flooding and erosion of the surrounding foothills and mountainsides already laid bare by heavy cattle grazing that sediment filled most of the slough, and before long it became a silt-filled salt marsh. Much of its area has been claimed by the Santa Barbara airport, which would be underwater today but for artificial fill trucked in during World War II to construct a US Marine air warfare training base. Visit the slough by taking CA 217 (exit 104B) south toward the airport and the ocean to Sandspit Road (exit 1), and exit straight ahead to a T-intersection and small viewing lot surrounded by airport security fencing.

Another one-quarter mile toward the sea from the slough viewing area is the county's Goleta Beach Park, which suffers coastal erosion due to the dearth of sand transported to the beach by longshore currents. The sea cliffs farther west consist mostly of Monterey and Sisquoc shales, which are not sources of beach sand. Instead, the Santa Ynez and Santa Maria Rivers once provided sand from the north slopes of the Santa Ynez Mountains, but the upper reaches of both rivers have been dammed since 1953, effectively blocking the transport of sand to the sea.

Goleta to Gaviota

Several oil and gas fields, large and small, are along the north edge of the Santa Barbara Channel. Offshore oil fields are marked by drilling platforms. Ellwood, located entirely offshore in the vicinity of Winchester Canyon (exit 110), was one of the largest oil fields. It was in production in 1928 and by 1930 accounted for 6 percent of all oil production in California. Much of the production was from wells located on wooden piers that extended several hundred feet offshore. When the piers were demolished, their timbers were used to build a large restaurant at Winchester Canyon. The field was abandoned in 1972.

Ellwood oil field gained considerable notoriety in World War II when a Japanese submarine shelled it on February 23, 1942, without causing much damage. This incident was the first direct naval bombardment on the US mainland by an enemy power since a German submarine attacked Orleans, Massachusetts, in 1918.

You may gain a royal impression of the rocks and ruggedness of the south flank of the Santa Ynez Mountains by taking a detour up Refugio Canyon (exit 120). It was during an unusually intense El Niño rainstorm in the winter of

Vegetation difference marks the contact between grass-covered Rincon Shale (early Miocene) and chaparral-covered Vaqueros Sandstone (middle Miocene). (34°28.7N, 120°11.5W)

1983 that President Ronald Reagan guided Queen Elizabeth II along this road up to his Rancho del Cielo at the crest of the range for lunch. The press corps considered it a hair-raising trip, but the queen had a grand time.

Sometimes rock formations may be distinguished from one another by the type of vegetation they support. That relationship is quite clear a few hundred feet north of the highway near Gaviota (PM 41.5–43.5). There the Rincon Shale, on which grass grows rather poorly, is in contact with the Vaqueros Sandstone, which supports a growth of chaparral, here mostly sage. The sharp contact is easily discerned for several miles along the highway.

Gaviota Pass

US 101 turns abruptly north at Gaviota, cuts down-section across grass- and brush-covered shale and sandstone to a rest stop (exit 130), and then passes through a tunnel in resistant Eocene marine sandstone of the Gaviota Formation. All of these sedimentary rock layers dip about 50 degrees south in this stretch of canyon. Several big bronze plaques at the rest stop commemorate the history of this route across the Santa Ynez Mountains, which follows the San Juan Bautista de Anza National Historic Trail, the 1775–1776 land route established by Spanish commander Juan Bautista de Anza.

About 1 mile north of the tunnel, the highway crosses the south branch of the Santa Ynez fault, one of the longest faults in southern California. Its official 65-mile length does not include its seaward extension. Little is known about the

Eocene sandstone of the Gaviota Formation at the Gaviota Pass tunnel dips steeply toward the viewer. (34°29.3N, 120°13.6W)

magnitude and direction of its displacement, because most of it is covered by chaparral, and because its strike is largely parallel to the enclosing formations. The vertical component of displacement is a few thousand feet, south side up. Tenuous geologic correlations of rock units across the fault suggest that about 30 miles of right-lateral displacement occurred after middle Eocene time, followed by 13 miles of left-lateral displacement before early Miocene time.

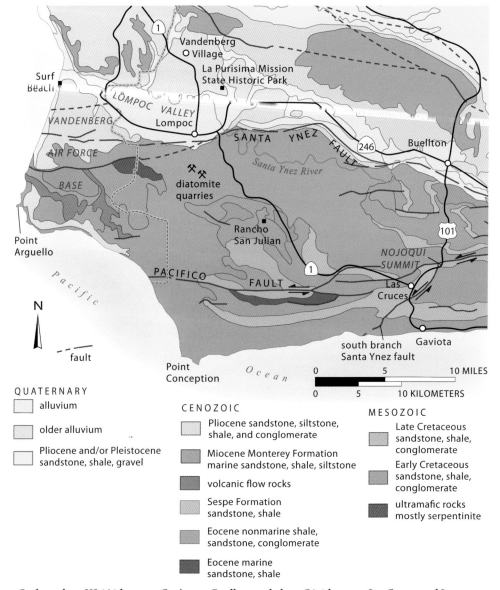

QUATERNARY
alluvium

older alluvium

Pliocene and/or Pleistocene
sandstone, shale, gravel

CENOZOIC
Pliocene sandstone, siltstone,
shale, and conglomerate

Miocene Monterey Formation
marine sandstone, shale, siltstone

volcanic flow rocks

Sespe Formation
sandstone, shale

Eocene nonmarine shale,
sandstone, conglomerate

Eocene marine
sandstone, shale

MESOZOIC
Late Cretaceous
sandstone, shale,
conglomerate

Early Cretaceous
sandstone, shale,
conglomerate

ultramafic rocks
mostly serpentinite

Geology along US 101 between Gaviota to Buellton and along CA 1 between Las Cruces and Lompoc.

The split of US 101 and CA 1 is at the hamlet of Las Cruces (exit 132). The surrounding grass- and tree-covered hills consist of complexly folded and faulted, easily eroded marine Eocene shale and siltstone beds as far north as the crest of US 101 at Nojoqui Summit. From there to the base of the grade, most of the highway lies upon stream-deposited alluvium until it reaches some deep roadcuts between PM 54 and PM 56 in Early Cretaceous turbidites in the core of the Nojoqui anticline. Turbidites are sedimentary rocks consisting of thin, interbedded layers of olive-gray feldspar-rich sandstone and hard, dark gray micaceous shale, deposited widely on the seafloors of sedimentary basins.

Early Cretaceous turbidites on US 101 a few miles south of Buellton are among the oldest rocks in Santa Barbara County. (34°35.2N, 120°11.5W)

California 1 to Lompoc

CA 1 west of US 101 proceeds through some deep, brush-covered roadcuts in rolling brown hills, with south flanks dotted with oak trees, north flanks blanketed with oak trees, and ridges capped by oak trees. If outcrops were to be seen along the first 6 miles west of US 101, they would be steeply dipping beds of the Sespe Formation. Elsewhere in the western Transverse Ranges, the Sespe Formation commonly crops out as thick, resistant beds of stream-deposited conglomerate and coarse reddish-brown sandstone, but out here at the west end of the Transverse Ranges, the Sespe transitions to marine sandstone, with a corresponding reduction of grain size and resistance to erosion.

On both sides of CA 1 in the vicinity of the headquarters for Rancho San Julian (PM 7.5), Eocene sandstone and shale are so fine-grained and friable that erosion has easily rounded them into barren hills. Rancho San Julian is an original Spanish land grant to the family of Thomas W. Dibblee, Jr., one of California's preeminent geologists. He mapped over 550 7.5-minute quadrangles —nearly 35,000 square miles of central and southern California—during his long career with two major oil companies and the US Geological Survey.

Fault contact between flat, thick-bedded, yellow Matilija Sandstone (younger) and thin-bedded, gray Cozy Dell Shale (older) that is bent downward against the fault, indicating that the Cozy Dell has been uplifted relative to the Matilija. (34°34.6N, 120°22.6W)

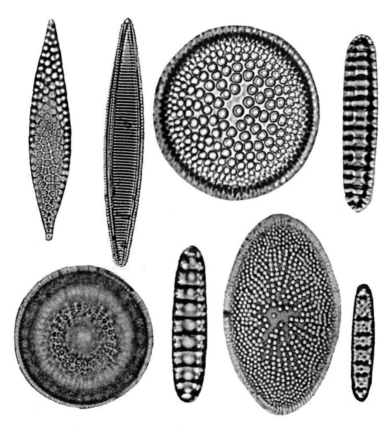

Some varieties of Monterey Formation diatoms. —Courtesy John Barron, US Geological Survey

The first real outcrop west of the CA 1–US 101 split is at Call Box 1 122—a big roadcut of yellow-brown Matilija Sandstone (Eocene). Farther north, 11.5 miles from US 101, a fault is clearly exposed in a magnificent roadcut across CA 1 from a big turnout with a sign: Caltrans Stockpile 20. The fault separates Matilija Sandstone on the south from the older Cozy Dell Shale, also of Eocene age. You can tell that the shale is uplifted relative to the sandstone by the way the Cozy Dell beds are dragged downward against the fault.

CA 1 cuts across a series of tight anticlines and synclines in white Monterey shale between Jalama and Santa Rosa Roads. North of the Salsipuedes Creek crossing, look to the west and see brush-shrouded quarry dumps of diatomaceous earth on the skyline, and look up some of the canyons to see the Monterey outcrops. These dumps were last used in the 1940s; the active quarry is located 2 miles south of Lompoc. Diatomaceous earth consists of fossilized remains of diatoms, a type of hard-shelled algae. It is used as a thermal insulator, a stabilizing component of dynamite, a mild abrasive in toothpaste, and a filtration aid, particularly for swimming pools and to filter not only drinking water and other liquids, such as beer and wine, but also syrup, sugar, and honey. One of its single greatest uses, because of its absorbent qualities, is for cat litter. One pound of the material has a surface area equivalent to about eight football fields.

CA 1

SANTA MONICA—OXNARD

45 miles

CA 1, more commonly known as the Pacific Coast Highway or just PCH, hugs the coast where it parallels the south edge of the Santa Monica Mountains, one of the most rugged and structurally complicated ranges in California. Its core consists of folded and faulted Santa Monica Slate of Jurassic age intruded by Cretaceous granodiorite. These rocks are draped by Paleogene and Neogene sedimentary and volcanic rocks. The Modelo Formation flanks the north edge of the range between its crest and the San Fernando Valley. Conejo Volcanics, which erupted in Miocene time as the Los Angeles Basin began to open, intruded the west half of the range. The Malibu Coast fault and a zone of complex thrust faults and landslides bound its south edge. Much of CA 1 is upon or close to the surface trace of the Malibu Coast fault.

Pacific Palisades

CA 1 was built on beach sand at the base of a cliff that has been eroded into fantastic palisades, and whose present height is a measure of coastal uplift in the last 40,000 years. At the north end of the Santa Monica Pier at the CA 1 intersection with I-10, the cliff consists of slightly consolidated, light brown, pebbly and sandy stream gravels derived from the Santa Monica Mountains in Pleistocene time. Thousands of years ago, the cliff deposits extended several miles out to sea, well beyond the present palisades. The shoreline retreated to its present

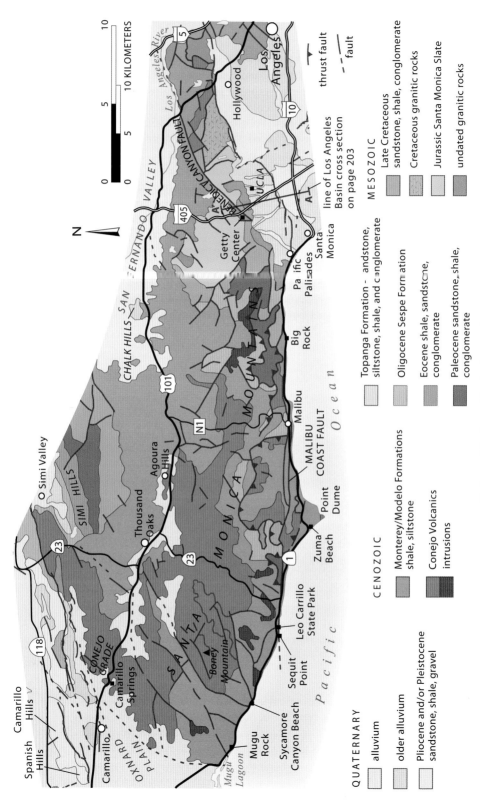

QUATERNARY

- alluvium
- older alluvium
- Pliocene and/or Pleistocene sandstone, shale, gravel

CENOZOIC

- Monterey/Modelo Formations shale, siltstone
- Conejo Volcanics intrusions
- Topanga Formation - andstone, siltstone, shale, and c nglomerate
- Oligocene Sespe Form ation
- Eocene shale, sandst ne, conglomerate
- Paleocene sandstone, shale, conglomerate

MESOZOIC

- Late Cretaceous sandstone, shale, conglomerate
- Cretaceous granitic rocks
- Jurassic Santa Monica Slate
- undated granitic rocks

— thrust fault

--- fault

Geology of the Santa Monica Mountains.

position as sea waves inexorably attacked, battered, and undermined the base of the cliffs, causing the upper part to collapse, maintaining a steep face.

Because of the height, steepness, and weak rocks, the Pacific Palisades section of the cliffs west of Chautauqua Boulevard is especially prone to land-slides. The largest historic slide swept across PCH in 1963 about three-fourths of a mile west of Chautauqua Boulevard. Eventually the slide was completely

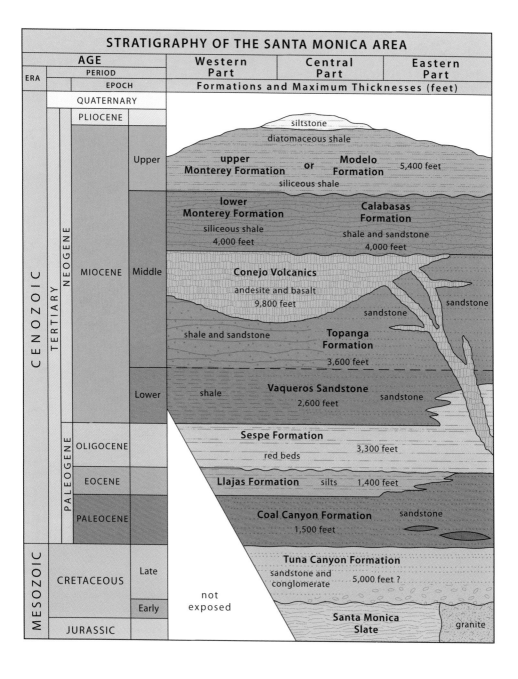

Landslides are common and frequent on the Palisade cliffs along PCH. Note how the fluted cliff face has broken off, exposing fresh surfaces. (34°01.8N, 118°31.2W)

Fence and steel netting prevent loose boulders from falling into passing automobiles and rolling into houses near Big Rock Beach. (34°02.3N, 118°27.2W)

removed, as were several damaged houses at the top of the cliffs, and the site was converted into Palisades Park.

Between Topanga and Las Flores Canyons, particularly at Big Rock Beach, (PM 43–44), the sea cliff rocks are mostly reddish sandstone and conglomerate. The layers are lenticular and crossbedded in places, and vary abruptly in color and texture over short distances. Although the rocks lack fossils, they are generally regarded as stream sediments belonging to the Sespe Formation and Vaqueros Sandstone. Every once in a while a boulder comes tumbling down the slope across the highway and slams into one of the houses along the beach, hence the heavy wall and netting.

Zuma Beach

PCH lies upon a coastal terrace as it crosses Point Dume before making a broad sweeping westward bend down to Zuma Beach and its many volleyball courts. Roadcuts on the north side of the highway expose thin, white beds of Monterey siliceous shale interbedded with light brown shale and cut by small normal faults.

One mile west of Zuma Beach, roadcuts and low hills to the north contain the San Onofre Breccia, with its clasts of glaucophane blueschist and riebeckite schist. Glaucophane and riebeckite are blue amphibole minerals that form in subduction zones under conditions of low temperature and high pressure. This middle Miocene sedimentary breccia is exactly the same as that exposed along the Peninsular Ranges coast between Dana Point and Newport Beach, providing additional evidence that the western Transverse Ranges were once connected to the Peninsular Ranges.

A normal fault in the Monterey Formation displaces white beds of siliceous shale at Zuma Beach. (34°01.0N, 118°49.4W)

Wave-Cut Coastal Terraces and Malibu Coast Fault

From Encinal Canyon (LA PM 58.5) west across the county line to Yerba Buena Canyon (VEN PM 1.2), PCH crosses two levels of coastal terraces cut by waves in Pleistocene time: one at 40 feet and an older, higher one at 200 feet above sea level. They consist of dissected, moderately consolidated, red-brown alluvial gravel, sand, and clay. The red-brown color is from oxidation of iron-rich minerals eroded from the Conejo Volcanics, which make up the highlands north of PCH. The terrace sediments were deposited upon the wave-eroded, upturned edges of the Topanga Formation, a marine deposit of interbedded sandstone and shale of early Miocene age.

Between Encinal Canyon Road (PM 59.4) and Decker Canyon Road (PM 59.9), the location of the Malibu Coast fault is marked by brown fault breccia with a chalklike matrix in roadcuts north of the highway. From Los Alisos Canyon westward, the fault strikes beneath the highway and terrace deposits and then goes offshore at Sequit Point at Leo Carrillo State Park.

Lower Topanga Formation

The coastal cliffs are steep and rugged west of Little Sycamore Canyon, with splendid exposures of interbedded sandstone and shale of the lower Topanga Formation. PCH hugs the cliffs in the south flank of the Sequit anticline, which trends east-west almost parallel to PCH and consists of south-dipping beds of lower Topanga Formation. The crest of the anticline lies about 2 miles north of PCH.

A magnificent cliff of interbedded Topanga sandstone and shale forms the west side of Big Sycamore Canyon. North of the cliff on the north side of the

Sand dune near Big Sycamore Canyon. (34°04.5N, 119°01.2W)

highway is a big sand dune, deposited by powerful local winds that blow sand off the beach up against the cliff. Once you are west of the sand dune, notice how the beds on the north flank of the Sequit anticline, west of the sand dune, dip northward.

Mugu Rock, Mugu Lagoon, and Port Hueneme

CA 1 crosses the west end of the Santa Monica Mountains through a deep roadcut at Mugu Rock. When the coastal highway was being contemplated in 1919, the resistant rock was a 150-foot-high, near-vertical cliff that plunged directly into the sea. Engineers blasted a narrow road around the base of the headland in 1923–1924 so motorists could at last make the trip from Santa Monica to Oxnard. It wasn't long, however, before it was dubbed Dead Man's Rock, because some drivers tended to pitch over the road's edge, often with fatal results. Not until 1937 did excavations begin to cut the present 200-foot-deep, 60-foot-wide roadway that was completed in 1940. The original road around Mugu Rock survived as a scenic byway until around 2010, when powerful sea waves eroded most of it away.

View west of the deep roadcut that separates Mugu Rock from the main mass of the Santa Monica Mountains. (34°05.1N, 119°03.6W)

Mugu Rock is made of turbidites—interbedded light gray sandstone and black shale of the Topanga Formation—intruded by 6- to 10-foot-thick diabase dikes of the Conejo Volcanics. The dikes dip south in north-dipping rock layers, indicating the dikes intruded vertically before they and their enclosing sedimentary rock layers tilted northward about 14 million years ago. The presence of *Turritella inezana* and *Pecten* species establish the early Miocene age for the Topanga Formation, which is about 2,500 feet thick here.

Mugu is derived from the Chumash Indian term *muwu*, meaning "lagoon," first mentioned by Spanish explorer Juan Cabrillo in his journals in 1542. Mugu Lagoon, home to large populations of fishes and invertebrates, is one of

Pecten *species are*
common clams
in early Miocene
marine rocks.
—Santa Barbara
Museum of Natural
History specimen

Turritella inezana *is a common gastropod in early Miocene marine rocks.*

the least disturbed and best protected estuaries and tidal marshes in southern California, and for that reason it serves as a baseline model for declining biodiversity in the region. Habitats within the Mugu Lagoon system include barrier beach, subtidal channels, creeks, ponds, intertidal flats, marsh, and salt pans. Nearly 75 percent of southern California's historic 77 square miles of coastal wetlands have been lost. Today, major efforts are being made to restore coastal wetlands, notably in Newport Beach, Mugu Lagoon, Carpinteria Salt Marsh, and Goleta Slough.

Naval Base Ventura County operates two runways at Point Mugu, together with a 36,000-square-mile sea test range anchored by San Nicolas Island. The US Navy uses the range to test and track weapons systems in restricted air- and sea-space without encroaching on civilian air traffic or shipping lanes. Port Hueneme (pronounced *Why-nee-mee*), operated by the US Navy, is the only deepwater port between Los Angeles and San Francisco.

CA 1 turns inland about 2 miles west of Mugu Rock and crosses the Oxnard Plain, the delta for the Santa Clara River. The delta sediments overlie Conejo Volcanics. One oil company bravely drilled through the hard volcanics and successfully encountered productive oil sands of early Cenozoic age beneath the lava flows.

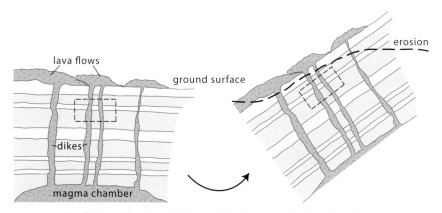

The diabase dikes intruded vertically, then were tilted northward during the uplift of the Santa Monica Mountains.

Brown, north-tilted diabase dikes cut light gray, north-dipping sandstone of the Topanga Formation near Mugu Rock. (34°05.12N, 119°03.20W)

CA 2
EAGLE ROCK—WRIGHTWOOD
65 miles

In his book, *The Mountains of California,* John Muir wrote that the San Gabriel Mountain range "is more rigidly inaccessible in the ordinary meaning of the word than any other I ever attempted to penetrate. The slopes are exceptionally steep and insecure to the foot, and they are covered with thorny bushes from 5 to 10 feet high. . . . When beheld from the open San Gabriel Valley, beaten with dry sunshine, all that was seen of the range seemed to wear a forbidding aspect. From base to summit all seemed gray, barren, silent, its glorious chaparral appearing like dry moss creeping over its dull, wrinkled ridges and hollows."

John Muir's "rigidly inaccessible" slopes and "glorious chaparral" have historically impeded detailed geologic studies of the San Gabriel Mountains. Most available geologic information is contained on 7.5 minute quadrangle maps made by Thomas W. Dibblee, Jr. Legend has it that he mapped much of the range on weekends and holidays after wildfires had cleared the chaparral. Highway roadcuts, carved since Muir's time, allow us to see several major igneous and metamorphic rock units, the complex relationships among them that characterize much of the range, and the trace of the San Gabriel fault, which forms a deep furrow along the length of the range. One of the salient geologic features to notice on your drive across the San Gabriel Mountains is how fractured, even shattered, the rocks are. That rock deformation is one of the manifestations of the enormous and pervasive internal strain suffered by crystalline rocks throughout the range during its uplift in the last 4 million years.

CA 2, known as the Angeles Crest Highway, is a sinuous US Forest Service scenic byway and California state scenic highway on the crest of the San Gabriel Mountains. It's a favorite location for car chase scenes and TV ads for high-performance automobiles and motorcycles. Be prepared for winding roads, breathtaking vistas, and shattered rocks prone to falling on the roadway. Watch out for bears on this tour, too, even though it is hard to imagine that wild bears and mountain lions inhabit these mountains just a few miles from downtown Los Angeles. In fact, more than 15 million people live within ninety minutes of the San Gabriel Mountains, which provide those same people with 70 percent of their open space and 30 percent of their drinking water.

Eagle Rock and the San Rafael Hills
This tour begins at Eagle Rock, which takes its name from the way a rock ledge projects a shadow of an eagle in flight on the side of an exposure of red-brown, crudely bedded conglomerate and sedimentary breccia. The rock, consisting of part of the Topanga Formation of Miocene age, is on the north side of CA 134 about 2 miles east of its junction with CA 2. The Eagle Rock fault places the north side of the rock in contact with various Cretaceous granitic rocks that are well exposed in CA 2 roadcuts in the San Rafael Hills between CA 134 in Eagle

Rock and I-210 in La Cañada Flintridge. Patches of Proterozoic gneiss were incorporated by the granitic magma as it intruded. The Eagle Rock fault is the southeast continuation of the Verdugo fault, which bounds the southwest side of the nearby Verdugo Mountains.

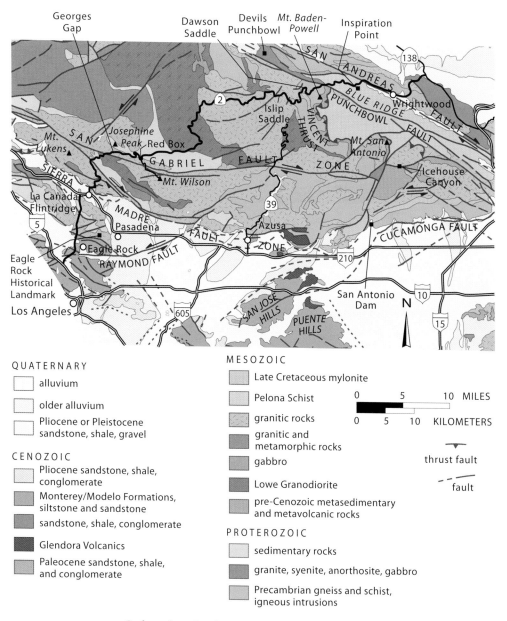

QUATERNARY

▢ alluvium

▢ older alluvium

▢ Pliocene or Pleistocene sandstone, shale, gravel

CENOZOIC

▢ Pliocene sandstone, shale, conglomerate

▢ Monterey/Modelo Formations, siltstone and sandstone

▢ sandstone, shale, conglomerate

▢ Glendora Volcanics

▢ Paleocene sandstone, shale, and conglomerate

MESOZOIC

▢ Late Cretaceous mylonite

▢ Pelona Schist

▢ granitic rocks

▢ granitic and metamorphic rocks

▢ gabbro

▢ Lowe Granodiorite

▢ pre-Cenozoic metasedimentary and metavolcanic rocks

PROTEROZOIC

▢ sedimentary rocks

▢ granite, syenite, anorthosite, gabbro

▢ Precambrian gneiss and schist, igneous intrusions

0   5   10 MILES

0   5   10 KILOMETERS

⊤ thrust fault

--- fault

Geology along CA 2 between Eagle Rock and Wrightwood.

The overhanging ledge on Eagle Rock makes the shadow of a flying eagle, giving the rock its name. The rock features some poorly defined, horizontal bedding layers in conglomerate and breccia of the Topanga Formation. (34°08.6N, 118°11.0W)

Clear Creek Vista at Georges Gap

CA 2 proceeds northward up a steep alluvial fan from Foothill Boulevard in La Cañada Flintridge. The first major curve bends southeastward along the base of a scarp of the Tujunga fault, a strand of the Sierra Madre fault zone. The highway winds northward again between a US Forest Service fire station (PM 27.65) and the Georges Gap vista stop (PM 32.8). Several roadcuts expose thin remnants of Proterozoic gneiss complexly intruded by the 122-million-year-old Wilson Diorite. Boulders of the diorite have been trucked in and placed at several of the stops along CA 2 for your close inspection, especially at the Red Box and the Switzer Picnic Area parking lots.

Georges Gap, with its concrete block walls and bronze plaques commemorating the establishment of Angeles National Forest, is on the crest of a ridge that divides Arroyo Seco to the south and Big Tujunga Canyon to the north and west, two of the main drainages in this part of the San Gabriel Mountains. On a clear day, you can see downtown Los Angeles skyscrapers, 18 miles to the south, from this vista point.

The highway in Clear Creek Canyon north of Georges Gap is Angeles Forest Highway (County Road N3), which terminates at Palmdale on the south edge of the Mojave Desert. The canyon contains the trace of the north branch of the San Gabriel fault, marked by a line of vegetation fed by springs that flow along the fault year-round. This right-slip fault displaces the vertical, west wall of the

Aligned vegetation about one-third the way up the side of Josephine Peak subtly marks the trace of the north San Gabriel fault as seen from Georges Gap. (34°16.4N, 118°09.3W)

Lowe Granodiorite 14 miles right laterally. The fault extends westward down Clear Creek Canyon, which formed, not by catastrophic rending of the Earth's crust, but by erosion along the fault. The San Gabriel fault was the principal active strand of the San Andreas fault system between 11 and 4 million years ago.

The prominent white-faced peak north of the Angeles Forest Highway junction, Josephine Peak (elevation 5,558 feet), is a biotite-muscovite granite of the Josephine Mountain intrusion. The same intrusive rocks also form Strawberry Peak (elevation 6,164 feet) 3 miles east of Josephine Peak, as well as nearly 30 square miles of country along the north side of the San Gabriel fault zone. At 80 million years old, the Josephine Mountain intrusion is one of the youngest in the San Gabriel Mountains.

Clear Creek to Red Box

The north branch of the San Gabriel fault passes through the intersection of CA 2 and Angeles Forest Highway at the Clear Creek ranger station and continues 4.2 miles eastward up the canyon to Red Box ranger station. Switchbacks between the Clear Creek and Red Box ranger stations expose complex intrusive relations between the Josephine Mountain granite and quartz- and feldspar-rich mafic gneisses. These rocks are sheared and oxidized to reddish brown along the San Gabriel fault. Dated at about 1,670 million years, these gneisses are the oldest rocks in the San Gabriel Mountains. Known as the

San Gabriel Gneiss, it is distinct from all other gneisses in these mountains in that it contains relict metamorphic minerals from some ancient mountain building event that occurred long before any other rocks in California existed. A complex series of anorthosite (a rare igneous rock of mostly plagioclase) and related gabbro, norite, and syenite, not exposed along CA 2, intruded the gneiss 1,410 to 1,220 million years ago. Norite is a pyroxene-bearing gabbro; syenite is a plutonic rock composed mainly of alkali feldspar.

Mt. Wilson

The Mount Wilson Observatory is a world-famous astronomical observatory with a 100-inch telescope, the largest in the world from its completion in 1917 until 1948, when the 200-inch Hale Telescope was placed upon Palomar Mountain in the Peninsular Ranges. Mt. Wilson is an ideal location for astronomy because the inversion layer over the Los Angeles region makes the air less turbulent on the mountain than anywhere else in North America, although increasing light pollution limits deep space observations here. Also nearby are solar observatories and a gaggle of TV transmitting antennas.

To reach the top of Mt. Wilson (elevation 5,710 feet), turn south at Red Box Station and proceed about 5 miles through roadcuts of gray, medium-grained Wilson Diorite with lenses of gneiss and complex intrusions of sills, dikes, and pods of granite. From the observatory parking lot atop Mt. Wilson, you may have a splendid view southward over the San Gabriel Valley, the Los Angeles Basin, and the Pacific coastline in the distance, unless an inversion layer has trapped smog.

Lowe Granodiorite

CA 2 proceeds from Red Box through a 6-mile-long stretch of gneiss to its contact with the Lowe Granodiorite, one of the principal and most distinctive rock types in the San Gabriel Mountains. Its 220-million-year-old (Late Triassic) age is older than most plutonic rocks in the western United States. Some geologists suggest the magma of the Lowe may have been generated at the beginning of subduction of the Farallon Plate beneath the North American Plate, perhaps 30 million years or so before the time other geologists have suggested the subduction began.

The Lowe Granodiorite is exposed over 120 square miles and is generally a very coarse-grained, feldspar-rich, white rock with 10 to 20 percent hornblende, about 10 percent biotite, and a trace to 25 percent quartz. Hornblende crystals up to 1 inch long within the finer-grained matrix give the rock a distinctive spotted texture like the back of a rainbow trout. It's so unique that if you put just one basketball-sized boulder into a truckload of similar-sized boulders from other plutonic rocks in the range, you could pick out the Lowe every time. Try it wherever you encounter a cobblestone wall on today's route. It is a good, durable building stone used locally in stone walls and foundations. Look for especially good in situ exposures in the large roadcut at PM 45.4, about 7 miles east of Red Box.

Lowe Granodiorite boulder (arrow) centered in wall among other San Gabriel Mountain rock types. (34°21.8N, 117°51.9W)

Chilao Flat to Inspiration Point on Blue Ridge

About one-half mile east of Chilao Flat, CA 2 passes into light-colored granitic rocks that intrude the Wilson Diorite. The geographic center of this complex granitic intrusion is Waterman Mountain (elevation 8,038 feet), 1 mile south of Camp Pajarito and Cloudburst Summit (PM 57.6). These rocks are exposed over the next 10 miles from Buckhorn Campground (PM 58.8) through Islip Saddle (elevation 6,670 feet, PM 64.0) to Dawson Saddle (elevation 7,943 feet, PM 69.5). Islip Saddle is located on the crest of a ridge separating drainages to the south that flow into the Pacific Ocean and those to the north that flow into the Mojave Desert. For that reason it is appropriate that the Pacific Crest Trail crosses this saddle.

CA 2 enters several miles of Proterozoic gneiss at Dawson Saddle, where you may have a good view of the Mojave Desert. On the south side of the highway is a splendid roadcut in Proterozoic gneiss cut by granitic dikes.

The Punchbowl fault separates red-brown sandstone and siltstone of Miocene age from Pelona Schist in Vincent Gap (elevation 6,593 feet, PM 74.8). CA 2 remains in Pelona Schist for the next 7 miles to the San Andreas fault zone at Wrightwood. The Punchbowl fault is an old, inactive strand of the San Andreas with about 30 miles of right-slip. It is not the northwest continuation of the young, highly active San Jacinto fault as is frequently mentioned in the older literature. The Punchbowl fault continues northwest, parallel to the San Andreas fault, toward Devils Punchbowl, a very scenic area where steeply tilted and folded sedimentary rocks form a big syncline in Miocene sandstone. The area is accessed from CA 138 on the north side of the San Gabriel Mountains.

Inspiration Point (elevation 7,381 feet, PM 78.0) on Blue Ridge has views to the southeast of Mt. San Antonio (elevation 10,064 feet), to the southwest of

Mt. Baden-Powell (elevation 9,399 feet), and to the south down the deep and rugged East Fork of the San Gabriel River.

The Vincent–Orocopia–Chocolate Mountain thrust, one of the fundamental structures in southern California, can be seen from Inspiration Point on the northeast flank of Mt. Baden-Powell. It is about eye level and 400 feet above a light-colored swarm of Miocene-age felsic volcanic sills. The fault separates Proterozoic gneiss of the upper plate from younger Pelona Schist of the lower plate. It dips down the East Fork and crosses the north flanks of Iron Mountain (elevation 8,007 feet) to the south and Mt. San Antonio to the southeast. The thrusting occurred during Late Cretaceous or early Cenozoic time, at the same time as the metamorphism of the Pelona Schist.

San Andreas Fault and Wrightwood

CA 2 intersects the San Andreas fault at an impressive stone lodge located at Big Pines (elevation 6,862 feet), the highest point along the fault's 800-mile length. The highway follows the fault southeastward down Swarthout Valley to Wrightwood, always with the Pelona Schist in the mountains to the south and Proterozoic gneiss and Mesozoic granite in the ridges to the north.

Wrightwood, a mountain resort community in Swarthout Valley, was not inhabited at the time of the 1857 Fort Tejon earthquake (magnitude 7.9), when the San Andreas fault broke the ground for about 200 miles northwest of San Bernardino. The earthquake shook the Wrightwood area with such force that tall, old pine trees whipped back and forth, and the tops snapped off several dozen of the largest trees. The roots of a few trees that grew directly on the fault were sheared, too, stunting their growth for many years after the earthquake.

Detailed geologic studies of the fault between Big Pines and Wrightwood revealed evidence that fourteen surface-rupturing earthquakes, similar in magnitude to the 1857 earthquake, occurred here in the last 1,500 years. A repeat of such an earthquake in the future would be a calamity not only for Wrightwood, but also for the San Bernardino–Riverside area.

Wrightwood was hit by a different kind of calamity in May 1941, when it was partly inundated by a series of surging flows of muddy, poorly sorted, fine to coarse rock debris and battered fragments of wood and pine cones. Flows occurred daily for more than a week. The immediate cause was rapid melting of winter snow in a large landslide scar at the head of Heath Canyon on the north side of Blue Ridge. Meltwater fluidized an intensely shattered mass of deeply weathered Pelona Schist that had accumulated at the base of the landslide scar. Debris flows originated at elevations between 7,250 feet and 8,250 feet on the mountain and descended through Wrightwood and out onto the floor of the Mojave Desert, 15 miles to the north. With the consistency of wet cement, the mudflows mostly followed preexisting channels, but overbank flows inundated and destroyed several houses.

Most of Wrightwood is built on mudflow deposits, evidence that the Heath Canyon slide has been the source of mudflows in the past—as it certainly will be in the future. Two large diversion channels have been built across the community and maintained for such an eventuality.

Wrightwood landslide scar on Blue Ridge overlooking the community of Wrightwood. (34°20.8N, 117°38.2W)

Little single crystals to basketball-size boulders of the fibrous, grass-green mineral actinolite, formed by metamorphism of basalt in the Pelona Schist, may be found in mudflow diversion channels in the Wrightwood area. (34°21.4N, 117°36.8W)

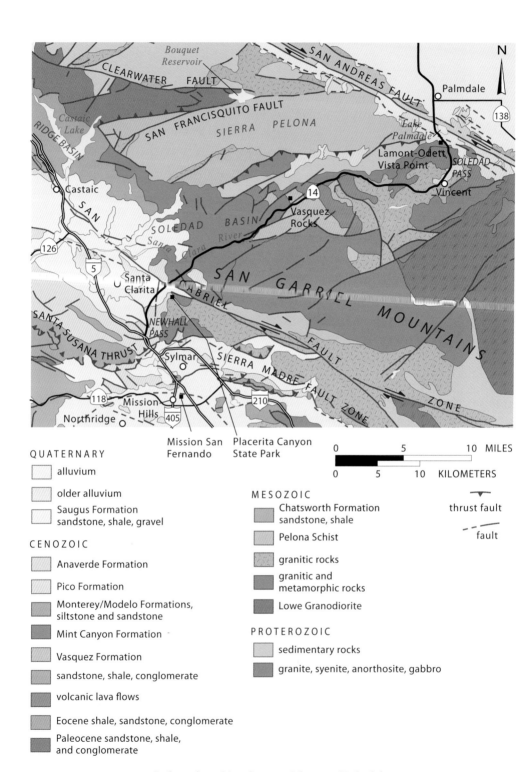

QUATERNARY

☐ alluvium

☐ older alluvium

☐ Saugus Formation
sandstone, shale, gravel

CENOZOIC

☐ Anaverde Formation

☐ Pico Formation

☐ Monterey/Modelo Formations,
siltstone and sandstone

☐ Mint Canyon Formation

☐ Vasquez Formation

☐ sandstone, shale, conglomerate

☐ volcanic lava flows

☐ Eocene shale, sandstone, conglomerate

☐ Paleocene sandstone, shale,
and conglomerate

MESOZOIC

☐ Chatsworth Formation
sandstone, shale

☐ Pelona Schist

☐ granitic rocks

☐ granitic and
metamorphic rocks

☐ Lowe Granodiorite

PROTEROZOIC

☐ sedimentary rocks

☐ granite, syenite, anorthosite, gabbro

⌄ thrust fault

– – – fault

0   5   10 MILES

0   5   10 KILOMETERS

Geology along CA 14 between Sylmar and Palmdale.

SYLMAR—PALMDALE
42 miles

CA 14, the Antelope Valley Freeway, heads northeast from I-5 across the north end of the San Gabriel Mountains. John C. Frémont led his forces along this same route in 1847 on his way to Los Angeles to sign a peace treaty with Mexico.

Newhall Pass
Complexly folded and faulted Pico Formation marine sandstone is in road-cuts at the junction of CA 14 and I-5. Just 2.5 miles farther north along CA 14, roadcuts expose younger, coarse, nonmarine Saugus Formation sandstone and conglomerate of Pliocene and Pleistocene age. The Saugus rocks may be studied more safely in roadcuts along the Sierra Highway, one-fourth mile west of CA 14 between the Old Road (near I-5) and Newhall Avenue.

Sierra Highway roadcut in Saugus Formation sandstone and conglomerate. (34°20.8N, 118°30.6W)

Placer Gold in Placerita Canyon
Francisco Lopez, a local rancher, made California's first commercially signif-icant gold strike in March 1842, six years before James Marshall made the discovery in northern California that spawned the California Gold Rush of 1849. Lopez found gold clinging to roots of wild onions around the base of a giant oak tree, hence today's name Oak of the Golden Dream. Only about $80,000 in gold was produced before the diggings quickly played out, but the tree still exists in Placerita Canyon State Park on Placerita Canyon Road (exit 3) about 4 miles east of CA 14. Between the park and CA 14, deep roadcuts in granitic basement rock are overlain by Saugus Formation fanglomerate. The fanglomerate is well exposed and accessible in a high roadcut along an extra wide CA 14 off-ramp at exit 3.

Placerita Oil Field

The relatively small oil field west of CA 14 and north of Placerita Canyon Road produces from steep, broadly warped, northwest-dipping sandstone and gravel beds of the upper Saugus Formation and Pico Formation sandstone, and even the underlying Modelo Formation. The eroded ends of these tilted beds at the land surface are sealed with tar, thus trapping oil and gas.

The active part of the Placerita oil field has been under development since 1948, when it was known as Confusion Hill for its crazy quilt of often conflicting oil claims. The land had been subdivided at the time into a large number of small "town lots," and because production was comparatively shallow and could be reached by relatively inexpensive wells, every lot owner wanted to recover as much oil as possible as fast as possible from his own land, as well as from his neighbor's! Soon after the discovery, a veritable forest of wooden derricks covered the hillsides, and wells produced splendidly by gas drive for about a year. Then, when the gas was bled off and pressure abruptly dropped as a consequence, the wells had to be pumped, necessitating an expense many well owners could not afford. Most wells ceased to pump enough oil profitably for each individual owner, and many wells were abandoned, leaving much more oil in the ground than was ever produced. Had the field been managed as a unit by a single entity from the beginning as it is today, ultimate production and recovery could have been much greater.

Santa Clara River

CA 14 crosses the Santa Clara River between Via Princessa (exit 6) and Sand Canyon Road (exit 9). At 100 miles in length, it is the longest undammed river in southern California. It drops 6,000 feet from its headwaters in the San Gabriel Mountains to the Pacific Ocean with an average gradient of about 70 feet per mile. Dry as it may seem when you drive across it, the river carries subsurface water for five large communities downstream. Although it floods infrequently, subdivisions recently built along its banks would seem to be at risk.

Sand and gravel quarries in the riverbed exploit a renewable resource. The pits refill with sediment during floods, so quarrying merely resumes after the water recedes. The river also carried and deposited much sediment in Quaternary time, as indicated by the sand and gravel river deposits now cropping out along CA 14, high above the present stream bottom. They lie unconformably upon the truncated edges of steeply dipping, gray and buff sandstones of the Mint Canyon Formation of Miocene age near PM 36.

Soledad Basin and the Mint Canyon Formation

CA 14 follows the axis of the Soledad Basin, going eastward and down-section stratigraphically into older rocks. This complex, northeast-trending basin began to open in Oligocene time with the eruption of basaltic lava flows. It then accumulated a 25,000-foot-thick, west-dipping succession of Oligocene and Miocene stream and lakebed sediments, most of which were shed from the ancestral San Gabriel Mountains to the south. Significant contributions of sediment also came from basement terranes now far removed by regional

Mint Canyon pebbly sandstone beds (1) are cut into and overlain unconformably by conglomerate and sandstone (2), deposited by a river in Quaternary time. (34°26.85N, 118°21.57W)

strike-slip faulting. The basin was folded into a broad syncline parallel to the Santa Clara River and subsequently uplifted in Pliocene and Pleistocene time and eroded to its present form.

The first and youngest stratigraphic unit you encounter upon entering the Soledad Basin is the Mint Canyon Formation of early to middle Miocene age, a widespread deposit of light tan, river-deposited conglomeratic sandstone, sandstone, and siltstone, and lake-deposited limestone. It is well exposed in roadcuts northeast of Sand Canyon Road (exit 9) for about 3 miles. At that point, CA 14 goes down-section into the slightly older, 22- to 18-million-year-old Tick Canyon Formation, which consists of light pinkish-brown sandstone, reddish silty claystone, and conglomerate having andesitic and basaltic volcanic pebbles and cobbles.

Vasquez Rocks

Nets cover deep and colorful roadcuts about 2 miles east of Agua Dulce Canyon Road (exit 15, PM 39.8) to prevent rockfalls onto the highway. This succession of red beds, sandstone, breccia, and conglomerate, known as the Vasquez Formation, is of Oligocene and early Miocene age and underlies the Tick Canyon Formation. It also contains a few interbedded basaltic andesite and dacite lava flows. Some boulders in the breccia and conglomerate are as much as 6 feet in diameter. They were deposited by debris flows originating from the

Vasquez Rocks, with its steeply tilted, colorful sandstone ridges of the Vasquez Formation, is one of the most recognized filming sites for TV series and commercials, still photography advertisements, and motion pictures. (34°29.1N, 118°18.8W)

Proterozoic anorthosite-gabbro complex and the Lowe Granodiorite pluton in the San Gabriel Mountains to the south. Finer-grained layers were deposited by streams on alluvial fans.

Several thousand feet of these sedimentary rocks are beautifully exposed in Vasquez Rocks Natural Area Park, reached via Agua Dulce Canyon Road. You may climb on and around the interbedded layers of coarse sandstone and pebbly conglomerate. Some rock layers are reddish brown because their iron-bearing minerals, biotite and hornblende, were oxidized to red hematite pigment.

Beneath the Vasquez Formation, a thick, monotonous sequence of Oligocene-age volcanic rocks crops out over a 13-mile-long stretch of CA 14 between Vasquez Rocks and Soledad Canyon Road (exit 27). These rocks are dark gray-brown basaltic andesite and dacite lava flows and sills. Their thickness in the central part of the Soledad Basin is about 3,700 feet. The base of the volcanic succession was deposited upon, and faulted against, Proterozoic gneiss and Mesozoic granitic rocks exposed in large roadcuts near exit 27 (PM 52). Plugs, domes, radial dikes, and abundant tuff breccia suggest that the eruption center was at or near Santiago Road (exit 26) about 24 million years ago.

A wide, dry canyon leads to the summit of Soledad Pass (exit 30) between the Santa Clara River drainage to the south and the dry gulch leading north into the Mojave Desert. The width of the canyon suggests a big river carved it, and its southward gradient suggests that the headwaters of the river would have been in the Mojave Desert to the north; those headwaters have now been displaced many miles southeastward along the San Andreas fault.

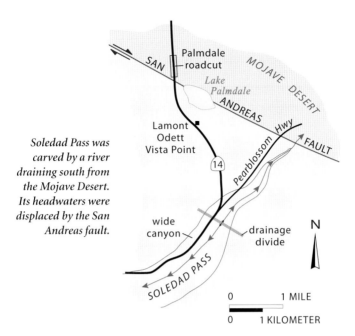

Soledad Pass was carved by a river draining south from the Mojave Desert. Its headwaters were displaced by the San Andreas fault.

Lamont Odett Vista Point

From the Lamont Odett Vista Point (PM 57, between exits 30 and 33), you can look across the San Andreas fault into Antelope Valley and the west end of the Mojave Desert. Directly in front of the vista point is the California Aqueduct, which has snaked its way 700 miles to southern California from the Feather River in northern California. It was one of the longest aqueducts in the world when built in the 1960s. The only break is where fourteen 80,000-horsepower pumps raise the water 1,926 feet in a single lift up and over the Tehachapi Mountains into the west end of Antelope Valley. Cost estimates to bring the water through a tunnel beneath the mountains are astronomical, so an enormous amount of California's electrical power is used just to pump water. Some of the expended power is recovered by three power plants situated where the water flows down the southeast side of the mountains.

The aqueduct is aboveground for much of its length, so that if an earthquake along the San Andreas fault should damage it, a couple of bulldozers and a few days are all that will be needed to make temporary repairs and resume service. If the aqueduct were in underground tunnels, it might take weeks or months to effect repairs.

Lake Palmdale, a few hundred feet north of the aqueduct, was once a large, natural sag pond on the San Andreas fault. Sag ponds form within a fault zone where elongate blocks of ground subside as a result of stretching between fault segments that are not exactly parallel to the main fault. An elongate depression becomes a swamp or sag pond when it fills with water. Around four hundred sag ponds exist along the San Andreas fault, and it is said that on a clear day, pilots can navigate from Los Angeles to San Francisco just by following the sag ponds one after another as they shimmer in the sunlight. Lake Palmdale was dammed in the 1890s to increase its capacity for water storage and recreation.

The San Andreas fault zone here is about 1 mile wide, extending from the Lamont Odett Vista Point to the north side of the low ridge north of Lake Palmdale. The most recently active trace of the fault is along the north shore of the reservoir. The last major surface rupture here was at the time of the Fort Tejon earthquake of 1857 (magnitude 7.9).

From the vista point if the visibility is good, you can see the south end of the Sierra Nevada to the north; Telescope Peak on the west edge of Death Valley is about 135 miles away to the northeast, at the crest of the Panamint Range. In the middle distance but still within the urbanized part of Palmdale, great warehouse-like workshops stand where stealth aircraft were designed and built. Rogers Lake playa, in the far distance to the north, is where NASA's Space Shuttle landed when unable to land at Kennedy Space Center in Florida or at Vandenberg Air Force Base in Santa Barbara County.

San Andreas Fault at Palmdale Roadcut

CA 14 crosses the San Andreas fault at the south entrance to the big roadcut west of Lake Palmdale (PM 58.5). An excavation across the fault, now covered, revealed a 10-foot-wide zone of dark gray clay gouge. Small drainages have been displaced about 50 feet right-laterally along the southwest side of the ridge west of the highway. Some of that displacement probably occurred at the time of the 1857 earthquake.

Since this photo was taken in January 1990, landslides and erosion have heavily degraded this roadcut in tightly folded Anaverde Formation within the San Andreas fault zone. (34°33.8N, 118°08.0W)

The large roadcut goes through a pressure ridge in the San Andreas fault zone, exposing highly folded and faulted lake evaporates, siltstone, sandstone, and gypsum-bearing shale of the Pliocene Anaverde Formation. The main fault is at the south end of the roadcut; a strand of the San Andreas fault, the Littlerock fault, lies at the north end of the roadcut. Extreme deformation of the sedimentary layers is a consequence of being squeezed between two faults.

CA 33
Ventura—Cuyama
71 miles

CA 33 is a winding, two-lane highway that trends generally north across the middle of the western Transverse Ranges to Cuyama Valley. Roadcuts along the highway expose a thick sedimentary succession of mainly Cretaceous and Eocene sandstone and shale, overlain in places by Pleistocene and Holocene stream and terrace deposits. To the untrained eye, the Eocene-age formations are monotonous and look quite similar to one another, consisting as they do of variable proportions of marine sandstone and shale beds, but geologists have separated them into discrete formations, based on fossils and stratigraphic position.

A word of caution: Poison oak is one of the chaparral plants, especially along streams and in heavily wooded areas. Be careful if you decide to wander out in the brush; know how to identify poison oak so that you can avoid it. Be aware also that CA 33 may be closed to traffic without warning, usually because of landslide or flood damage but also due to brush fires.

Oakview Terrace and Ventura Avenue Anticline

You can get a good view of the Oakview terrace and Ventura Avenue anticline by way of a detour up to the Serra Cross on the crest of the hill directly behind Mission San Buenaventura. You'll also see the city of Ventura, the hills on which it is built, the coastline in both directions, and the northern Channel Islands.

Roadcuts on the way to the Serra Cross expose a series of gravelly and sandy marine layers of the Las Posas Formation steeply inclined toward the coast. Waves and currents carved several benches into these Pleistocene-age rocks when the land was lower than it is today. Marine terrace deposits were laid down upon them and then the land was uplifted. Renewed wave erosion carved successively lower flats, now uplifted, including that upon which Ventura is built.

From the Serra Cross, look west across the Ventura River to see that the Oakview terrace was deposited unconformably upon south-tilted Pliocene-age sandstone beds that crop out along the riverbank. The terrace once sloped gently and consistently seaward but was warped over the Ventura Avenue anticline as it folded in late Pleistocene and Holocene time. In fact, leveling surveys indicate the anticline is still growing, rising at the rate of 2 millimeters per year.

CA 33, known here as the Ojai Freeway, proceeds north from US 101 up the Ventura River on the south-dipping, south flank of the Ventura Avenue

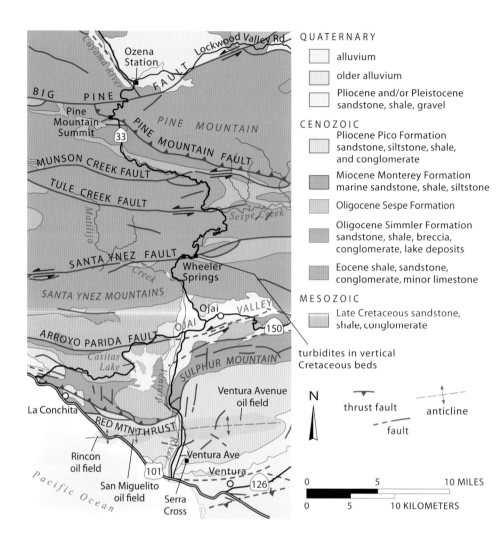

Geology along CA 33 between Ventura and Cuyama Valley.

anticline. The fold hinge is approximately at Shell Road (PM 2.8), where a multitude of pumpjacks lie on both sides of the highway. North of Shell Road, the height of the river levee decreases sufficiently to see tan sandstone beds of the Pico Formation in the west riverbank. Notice between PM 3.0 and PM 3.5 that the sandstone beds dip upstream and more steeply than those on the south limb of the anticline, and in places they are overlain unconformably by north-dipping terrace deposits folded over the rising anticline.

The Ventura Avenue anticline—7 miles long, 1 mile wide, and the largest of four anticlines on the Ventura anticlinorium—is fabled for the great quantity of petroleum it has yielded and for the remarkable youthfulness of its geologic development and accumulation of petroleum. Tuffaceous ash layers, blown here from titanic eruptions as far away as Yellowstone, are interbedded with layered marine rocks on the flank of the anticline. One of the ashes, the Bishop Ash, erupted 225 miles away in east-central California and was laid down as a flat-lying deposit 770,000 years ago—just a few geologic moments ago. The layers of rock were folded to their present 45-degree dips over the last 600,000 years. More than 1 billion barrels of oil were generated and migrated into the rising structure in just the last 250,000 years. That rapid rate of accumulation and enormous volume of oil astounds petroleum geologists, and that is just the amount of oil extracted since commercial production commenced in 1918. Much more is still in the ground.

W. C. Putnam's 1942 diagram of terraces folded over the Ventura Avenue anticline.
—From Putnam, 1942

Panoramic view west from the Serra Cross across the Ventura River to the Oakview terrace, covered by patches of green vegetation. Notice how the terrace surface rises upriver as the crest of the Ventura Avenue anticline is approached.

The Ventura Avenue oil field was discovered in 1885 during rotary drilling of a 200- to 300-foot-deep water well near the center of the anticline, a few hundred feet east of the Ventura River near Shell Road. Oil is produced from the Pliocene-age Pico Formation at depths ranging from about 3,000 to 12,000 feet. Peak production was 92,000 barrels per day in 1955. The prolific nature of the oil field has everything to do with the sedimentological architecture of the anticline. Sand was deposited along the length of the Ventura Basin, flanked by organic-rich shale. As the anticline rose and tightened, oil from the shale migrated up its shale flanks into the sandstone reservoir rock, now in the crest of the anticline.

Red Mountain Fault to Ojai Quarry

The Red Mountain thrust fault places Miocene-age Monterey Formation and Oligocene-age Sespe Formation onto the north flank of the Ventura Avenue anticline and its Pliocene sedimentary rocks. CA 33 crosses the fault trace about 2 miles north of Shell Road between the exits to Cañada Larga Road (PM 4.6) and Casitas Vista Road (PM 5.6), but typical of most faults in these mountains, it is not visible because of brush and soil cover. North of the fault, white shale beds of the Monterey Formation surround the red-brown Sespe Formation in the core of the great Red Mountain anticline. Contorted shale beds are exposed behind and east of the hamlet of Casitas Springs, home of Johnny Cash, noted country western singer and songwriter. Several white shale outcrops of Monterey Formation are in large and small roadcuts between Sulphur Mountain Road and Oak View. The Santa Ynez Mountains are on the skyline to the northwest.

About 3 miles north of the junction with CA 150 (PM 11), CA 33 passes some red-brown fault slices of Sespe Formation within older (Eocene-age) brown, layered rock (PM 14–14.5). About 4.5 miles north of the CA 150 junction, bold outcrops of thick, vertical sandstone beds in a roadside quarry (PM 15.5) are Eocene marine rocks. Like most of the pre-Miocene formations in the western Transverse Ranges, the sands were eroded from rocks in northern Mexico and the Peninsular Ranges and were deposited in the fore-arc basin created by the subduction of the Farallon Plate.

Marine sediments are deposited horizontally, but over the next 30 miles, you will see few flat-lying beds. Most are inclined, some vertically and even overturned, attesting to the intense folding that has occurred in the western Transverse Ranges since the end of Miocene time.

Wheeler Gorge

CA 33, known here as the Jacinto Reyes Scenic Byway, continues up the Ventura River through Eocene sandstone and shale and through the hamlet of Wheeler Springs (PM 17.5) to Wheeler Gorge, marked by three short tunnels. Outcrops along the stream in Wheeler Gorge (PM 18.84) expose vertical to overturned beds of Cretaceous marine cobble conglomerate in a hard, feldspar-rich sandstone matrix. When the cobbles were deposited, they scratched and scoured the underlying sediments, leaving magnificent scratches and grooves that are preserved as casts on the bottoms of beds. The sandstone beds are inversely graded, moreover, as is typical in turbidites, meaning that fine-grained sediment at the base of a bed grades upward into increasingly coarser sediment at the top—just the opposite of what one would expect. In normal graded bedding, the first influx of sediment is coarsest, but then as the strength of the current ebbs, the grain size decreases so that the last sediment deposited is the finest. The sedimentologic literature is full of arguments about the origin of inverse grading in sedimentary rocks, and some of the more credible explanations were developed from observations here in Wheeler Gorge. The prevailing explanation is that inverse grading occurs when a turbidity current containing a heterogeneous mix of sediment sizes undergoes downstream size segregation. Fine-grained fractions will arrive first and be deposited before the coarser fractions, which lag behind and are deposited upon the finer-grained fraction.

North of Wheeler Gorge, CA 33 enters a bewildering region of east-west striking marine formations of early and middle Cenozoic age that are faulted parallel to bedding. This geologic setting is difficult to interpret because the rocks offer little evidence of displacement along the faults. The main fault is the Santa Ynez fault, crossed by CA 33 about where the Wheeler Gorge Campground sign is located. This left-slip fault juxtaposes Cretaceous marine rocks on the south with a fairly monotonous section of broadly folded Eocene sandstone and shale beds to the north. Bold outcrops are generally sandstone, whereas stretches of road with little outcrop are mostly shale.

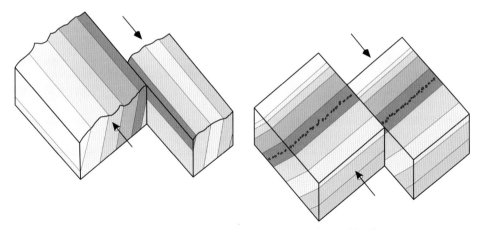

A right-slip fault parallel to bedding (left) has no evidence of displacement on the ground surface, in contrast to one perpendicular to bedding (right).

The Matilija Sandstone of Eocene age is well exposed for safe study in a big roadcut (near PM 27) at a wide turnout 8 miles north of the Wheeler Gorge Campground. Here the hard, tan sandstone is thick bedded with thin to thick interbeds of gray, micaceous shale. From the turnout, look north and see bold outcrops of pale pink sandstone of the Sespe Formation gently dipping into the Piedra Blanca syncline.

Low-angle crossbeds in the Matilija Sandstone in the roadcut indicate that the beds were deposited on a marine delta. (34°32.77N, 119°14.25W)

CA 33 crosses Tule Creek (PM 29) and the left-slip Tule Creek fault, another major east-west fault in this part of the Transverse Ranges. Very little is known about the timing or magnitude of displacement on the fault because, like the Santa Ynez fault, it is parallel to the strike of the beds on each side of it. Here it juxtaposes similar-looking Eocene rocks that differ greatly in their structural orientation.

Sespe Gorge

CA 33 winds through a spectacular gorge of vertical beds of Matilija Sandstone (PM 30.2) in the axis of a big syncline. You may see rock climbers testing their skills on the steep rock surfaces. The thin to thick shale interbeds in the sandstone are good gliding surfaces that allow coherent blocks of sandstone to slide onto the roadway. One such slide may be inspected (don't park your car under it!) about 1 mile north of the climbing rocks but south of the Potrero John Trailhead (PM 32).

About 1.5 miles west of the Potrero John Trailhead, CA 33 crosses the left-slip Munson Creek fault, which is also parallel to the general east-west grain of the Eocene rock formations, so that little is known about the magnitude and timing of its displacement. Eocene Cozy Dell Shale crops out in the long roadcut (PM 34) 2 miles west of the Potrero John Trailhead. The thin, rhythmic character of the bedding indicates that these layered rocks are turbidites, deposited bed by bed in a marine basin. Were it not for the chaparral, we might be able to trace individual thin beds over great distances, because each individual influx of sediment spreads out over a large area of the basin floor.

Steep bedding surface of Matilija Sandstone in Sespe Gorge. (34°34.7N, 119°15.5W)

Thick beds of Matilija Sandstone slide downhill on thin shale layers in this bedding surface landslide. (34°35.1N, 119°15.8W)

Thin, light gray to tan, feldspar-rich sandstone beds are interlayered with gray, clay-rich to silty, micaceous shale of the Eocene Cozy Dell Shale. (34°35.5N, 119°17.7W)

Pine Mountain Summit and Fault

Continue north on CA 33 through bold outcrops of Sespe Formation conglomerate mantled with piñon pines to a deep roadcut at Pine Mountain Summit (PM 42.8, elevation 5,084 feet). It is about 4 miles north of Pine Mountain Inn (PM 38.8), 300 feet north of the turnoff to Pine Mountain Recreation Area.

The summit is at the drainage divide between Sespe Creek to the south and the Cuyama River to the north. About 200 feet south of the crest of the summit (PM 42.73) is a contact between red beds at the top of the red-brown Sespe Formation and a thin bed of tan Vaqueros Sandstone. In the summit roadcut, thin siliceous shale beds of the Monterey Formation, which overlie the Vaqueros Sandstone, rise up to the crest of the roadcut then bend abruptly downward and northward where they are cut by a minor fault. If it is a clear day, walk through the roadcut to the vista point and look down the canyon far into the Cuyama Badlands, with their nonmarine rock layers ranging in age from Oligocene to Pleistocene.

CA 33 descends stratigraphically down-section, through gently folded shale beds of the Monterey Formation lying in a broad, east-west syncline, into Sespe Formation red beds, through a short stretch of Cozy Dell Shale, then across the Pine Mountain fault. This major thrust fault has several thousand feet of vertical displacement and an unknown amount of horizontal displacement. Gently south-dipping Matilija Sandstone beds north of the fault are thrust southward against vertical Cozy Dell Shale beds on the south. The fault can be traced along the south face of Pine Mountain Ridge for about 35 miles.

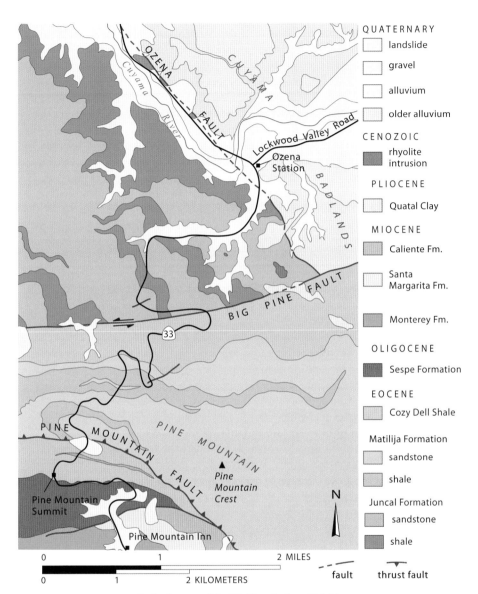

Geologic map of the Big Pine fault at PM 46.

Big Pine Fault to Cuyama Valley

North of the Pine Mountain fault, CA 33 passes through more Eocene marine rocks, and then crosses the main strand of the Big Pine fault at PM 46, where Cozy Dell Shale south of the fault is juxtaposed against Juncal Formation to the north. The Big Pine is a major east-west, left-slip fault that some geologists consider to be the north boundary of the western Transverse Ranges. The fault extends from its junction with the San Andreas fault at Lake of the Woods, east of Lockwood Valley, westward for 50 miles. Stream courses are displaced across the fault as much as 3,000 feet, whereas total left-slip is estimated to be between 8.5 and 18 miles.

Some of the shale formations in this area contain sulfide minerals that are prone to spontaneous combustion. Temperatures as high as 520°F have been measured where landslides have removed overlying rock layers, exposing the sulfide-bearing beds to air and oxidation.

CA 33 crosses the northwest-striking Ozena fault at the bottom of the grade between the turnoff to Lockwood Valley Road (PM 48.5) and the Corral Canyon bridge (PM 51.8). The thrust fault dips 45 degrees southwest, and it raised and shoved marine Eocene rocks northward over younger rock layers deposited on land. It is here, too, that the Cuyama River takes a northward course, and the fault is inferred to lie beneath the river and parallel to the highway almost to Apache Canyon. The normally dry river and the Ozena fault separate marine rocks of Eocene age on the west side of the highway from Quatal Clay of Pliocene age on the east.

Several hundred feet across the Cuyama River from the bridge over Apache Canyon (PM 44.5) is Morro Hill. It rises 500 feet and consists of conglomerate of the Miocene-age Caliente Formation. CA 33 heads northward about 10 miles from Burges Canyon to Ballinger Canyon Road, with Pleistocene and Holocene stream terraces west of the river and nearly flat-lying, nonmarine, pebbly sandstone of Pliocene age east of the highway. The pebbles are mostly plutonic and metamorphic clasts whose source is unknown. In the valley, terraces of older Quaternary alluvium support thriving vineyards and pistachio orchards.

CA 33 terminates at CA 166, but you may wish to visit the San Andreas fault zone by turning east onto CA 166 and driving about 4.5 miles to Reyes Station. Soda Lake Road and Cerro Noroeste Road follow the fault zone to the northwest and southeast, respectively. Cerro Noroeste Road, in particular, follows the San Andreas southeastward for 45 miles along a two-lane road through the Big Bend to I-5 at Frazier Park.

CA 38 AND CA 18
Redlands—Big Bear City—Lucerne Valley
60 miles

CA 18 ascends the San Bernardino Mountains, sometimes touted as the Alps of southern California, along a stretch of road known as Rim of the World Highway, hugging the sides of some of the steepest slopes in California. Engineering geologists speculate that these steep drop-offs are the head scarps of mega bedrock landslides. We'll avoid the incessant traffic that flies along this narrow, winding highway and instead follow CA 38 from Redlands on our traverse of the San Bernardino Mountains. CA 38, a designated National Forest Scenic Highway, intersects CA 18 in Big Bear.

Navigate your way to CA 38 in Redlands via Orange Avenue. Pass through a residential and commercial area in the community of Mentone with cross

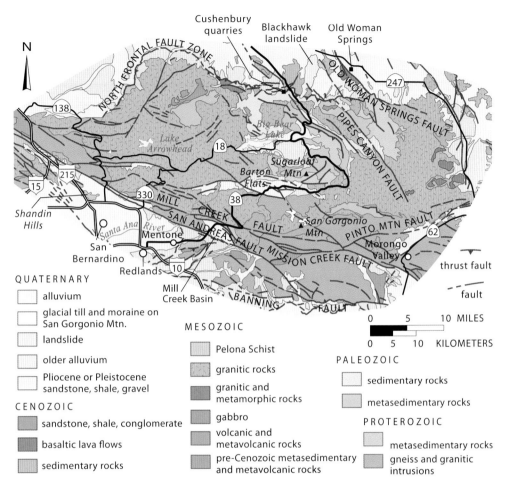

N

MESOZOIC

QUATERNARY

- alluvium
- glacial till and moraine on San Gorgonio Mtn.
- landslide
- older alluvium
- Pliocene or Pleistocene sandstone, shale, gravel

CENOZOIC

- sandstone, shale, conglomerate
- basaltic lava flows
- sedimentary rocks

MESOZOIC

- Pelona Schist
- granitic rocks
- granitic and metamorphic rocks
- gabbro
- volcanic and metavolcanic rocks
- pre-Cenozoic metasedimentary and metavolcanic rocks

PALEOZOIC

- sedimentary rocks
- metasedimentary rocks

PROTEROZOIC

- metasedimentary rocks
- gneiss and granitic intrusions

thrust fault

fault

0 5 10 MILES

0 5 10 KILOMETERS

Geology along CA 38 and CA 18 across the San Bernardino Mountains.

streets named after such gem minerals as beryl, tourmaline, olivine, sapphire, opal, and others. When you enter the rural area, notice how many retaining walls and older house foundations are made of rounded granitic and gneissic cobbles and boulders taken from the nearby creeks and washes. These are common building materials among all foothill communities on both sides of the San Gabriel and San Bernardino Mountains.

Mill Creek Basin

Mill Creek Basin, a small, elongate pull-apart basin, formed between the south and north branches of the San Andreas fault during Miocene time. You will encounter the basin after you cross the south branch of the San Andreas fault (PM 8.8) and enter the mouth of Mill Creek Canyon (PM 9.5). Alluvium buries the fault throughout most of its length in Mill Creek.

The basin sediments contain clasts from now-displaced sources on both sides of the San Andreas fault. The first roadcuts on the east side of the highway and the southwest side of the basin are in steep, north-dipping sedimentary breccia dominated by Pelona Schist clasts. Geologists believe these clasts were derived from the Mt. San Antonio area of the San Gabriel Mountains, approximately 35 miles to the northwest. Sediment debris along the northeast side of the basin has clasts characteristic of the Mojave Desert, brought here before the San Bernardino Mountains were uplifted.

A little farther up the canyon (PM 10.2) are nearly flat-lying, tan sandstone and gray siltstone layers deposited as turbidites in the center of the basin. From PM 11.0 to 11.5, you'll encounter steep, south-dipping sandstone on the northeast side of the basin. The north branch of the San Andreas fault, crossed by CA 38 at the intersection with Valley of the Falls Drive (PM 15), separates these rocks from the granite basement rocks exposed in roadcuts all the way to Barton Flats. The fault continues eastward along the long, east-trending segment of Mill Creek.

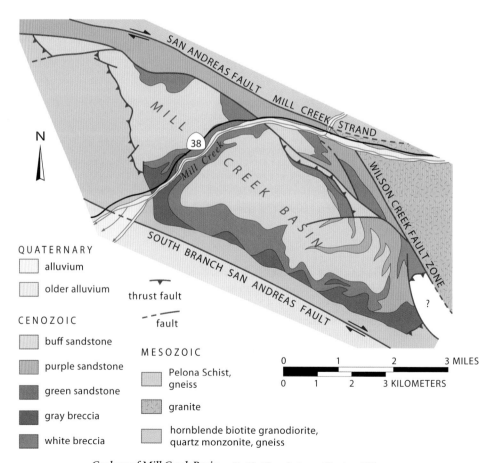

QUATERNARY
☐ alluvium

☐ older alluvium

CENOZOIC
☐ buff sandstone

☐ purple sandstone

☐ green sandstone

☐ gray breccia

☐ white breccia

▼ thrust fault

--- fault

MESOZOIC
☐ Pelona Schist, gneiss

☐ granite

☐ hornblende biotite granodiorite, quartz monzonite, gneiss

0   1   2   3 MILES
0   1   2   3 KILOMETERS

Geology of Mill Creek Basin. —Modified from Sadler and Demirer, 1986

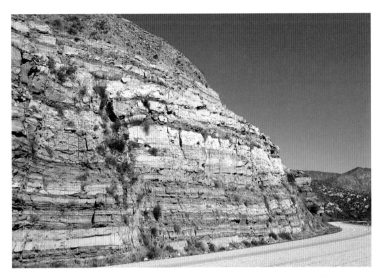

The remarkable continuity of each thin bed in the sandstone and shale in the Mill Creek Basin is characteristic of turbidites, in which each influx of sediment settles over a large area. That continuity is disrupted by a nearly vertical, minor fault (middle left). (34°05.8N, 117°01.8W)

Forest Falls Picnic Area

For a vivid demonstration of how rapid tectonic uplift is balanced by rapid and typically catastrophic erosion, turn east on Valley of the Falls Drive (PM 15) and proceed 4.3 miles to a picnic area. Forest Falls is located in a deep canyon that follows the San Andreas fault. The canyon slopes have 3,000 feet of relief, far exceeding the angle of repose, the maximum slope at which debris can be expected to remain stable. Bouldery debris-flow deposits underlie the community and are a sufficient clue to the potential landslide, avalanche, and flood hazards. Since the community was developed, flash floods and debris flows have struck the Forest Falls area about every four years. The flows are especially damaging when heavy rain falls on the sparsely vegetated, highly fractured bedrock on the surrounding ridges. The runoff picks up debris and roars down surrounding canyons, converging on Forest Falls. Over thirty homes were destroyed on July 11, 1999, after a short, intense summer monsoon dropped 1.5 inches of rain that triggered massive, high-velocity debris flows. Forest Falls was isolated for a day by a 6- to 8-foot-thick debris-flow deposit that blocked the main road into the community. Now widespread active debris flow channels and levees lessen the hazard.

The Climb to Barton Flats

Roadcuts expose granitic rocks for nearly 25 miles of winding switchbacks from Valley of the Falls Drive (PM 15) almost to Onyx Summit (PM 39). A complex system of dikes intrudes the granitic basement rock at PM 17. Most of the visible granitic basement in switchback roadcuts between PM 20 and PM 25 is decomposed into granular fragments by chemical weathering.

This fractured granite is crisscrossed by white, fine-grained felsic dikes and dark gray diabase dikes. (34°06.1N, 116°58.0W)

Decomposing granite in a CA 38 roadcut with pencil for scale. (34°09.6N, 116°55.5W)

The landslide scar on Slide Peak exposes crushed granite. (34°11.4N, 117°01.5W)

Some roadcuts are capped by thick debris-flow and stream deposits of boulders, sand, and gravel that originated from the north slope of San Gorgonio Mountain. They were deposited on an erosion surface that was once connected with the extensive surface of the Big Bear plateau but is now separated from it by a fault. From some turnouts are views to the north of extensive landslides along the south edge of the Big Bear plateau, especially the landslide scar below Slide Peak.

About 1 mile after passing the road to Jenks Lake (PM 25.6), CA 38 climbs up to Barton Flats, a prominent, flat to rolling landscape between San Gorgonio Mountain and the Big Bear plateau. The flats occupy a down-dropped fault block bounded on the north by a thrust fault, which carries the Big Bear plateau southward upon the north edge of the Barton Flats fault block.

Ancient landslide deposits at Barton Flats have been deeply incised by the headwaters of the Santa Ana River. You'll see several high roadcuts of these landslide deposits between PM 30 and PM 33. Slide movement is estimated to have happened 20,000 to 14,000 years ago. Some of the landslide detritus is crudely layered, indicating that the Santa Ana River reworked it.

Barton Flats landslide deposits settled onto an eroded surface of Santa Ana Sandstone, a 2,000-foot-thick Pliocene or older sedimentary formation. The age and type of sediments in the Santa Ana Sandstone indicate it accumulated on the Barton Flat fault block when the Big Bear plateau and the San Gorgonio blocks rose on either side of it.

Distinctive garnet-bearing clasts of gray schist are in Santa Ana Sandstone beds above the parking lot at Jenks Lake, a natural lake formed in the scooped-out depression left behind by a secondary landslide. The clasts resemble Pelona Schist, the nearest outcrops of which are in the San Gabriel Mountains. This correlation suggests the two areas have been displaced right-laterally along strands of the San Andreas fault system after Pliocene time during uplift of the San Bernardino Mountains.

Landslide deposits reworked by the Santa Ana River underlie Barton Flats at the river's headwaters. (34°10.2N, 116°53.2W)

Mafic gneiss cut by light-colored, fine-grained dikes. (34°11.2N, 116°43.0W)

Sugarloaf Mountain Roof Pendant

Sugarloaf Mountain (elevation 9,952 feet), the big, rounded peak north of Barton Flats, is Paleozoic metasedimentary rock, part of a large roof pendant within the Mesozoic granitic rocks. Other, lesser rock types in the pendant include Paleozoic marble and Proterozoic gneiss and schist. About 0.3 mile south of Onyx Summit (elevation 8,443 feet, PM 39.4), roadcut exposures of mafic gneiss are cut by light-colored felsic dikes between PM 38.7 and PM 39.0.

View southwest across Cienaga Seca Flat and over Heart Bar Peak to the barren slopes of San Gorgonio Mountain (elevation 11,499 feet), the highest peak in southern California. (34°06.0N, 116°49.4W)

Biotite schist interlayered with gneiss is sparsely exposed in one-half mile of roadcuts between PM 42.75 and PM 43.2, just south of Big Bear City.

San Gorgonio Mountain

Good views of San Gorgonio Mountain and other nearby high peaks may be had from highway turnouts around PM 39. Its south face is very rugged and steep, and its north flank slopes gently toward Barton Flats. The denuded appearance of several high peaks in the San Bernardino Mountains has been attributed to intensive logging at the turn of the nineteenth century, when twenty-two sawmills actively chopped up everything in sight.

Remnants of moraines and poorly developed cirques for seven valley glaciers have been mapped on San Gorgonio Mountain and are the southernmost indication of late Pleistocene glaciation in California. The largest glacier was nearly 2 miles long.

Baldwin Lake and Big Bear Lake

CA 38 enters Big Bear City at the west end of Baldwin Lake, a natural, intermittent, alkaline lake at the upper end of Bear Valley. At its widest, the lake is more than 1 mile across; its maximum depth is 25 feet. Cyclic drought keeps the lake dry about one-third of the time, but even so, vacation homes abound in the surrounding chaparral-covered terrain.

Big Bear Lake, a man-made reservoir, floods a long, flat valley near the top of the San Bernardino Mountains. The first dam across Bear Valley was built in 1884 to create a reservoir for downstream irrigation users in Redlands. At that time, the lake was the largest man-made body of water in the world. Subsequent higher dams created an even more extensive lake. Large irrigation demands during drought years in the late 1950s and early 1960s, however, reduced the lake to little more than a large mud puddle. Recreational interests on the lake required a reasonably stable lake level, so a municipal water district formed to manage the lake to meet both recreation and irrigation demands. Most of the lake covers granitic rock, which is well exposed in roadcuts and scenic boulders and cliffs around the west end of the lake, especially at Boulder Bay.

Gold Mountain

Placer and vein deposits of gold were discovered in the metasedimentary rocks of the Gold Mountain area in 1855 and prospected sporadically until the 1950s. Only a few of the prospects in the whole of the San Bernardino Mountains panned out, yielding a total of just about $20 million. A reddish streak of oxidized soil along quartzite on the northeast side of Gold Mountain (elevation 8,235 feet) marks the location of the Doble Mine, one of the original gold mines near Baldwin Lake and active for thirty-five years.

Cushenbury Canyon and Cement Quarries

Marble was originally prospected for its gold content at Cushenbury, but that gold was not worth nearly as much as the marble. During the 1940s, white marble was selectively mined for its high-grade calcite pigment. Kaiser Steel bought the workings in 1957 to use the marble in the manufacture of steel, and cement plant operations began the same year.

Today, the mines along the north slope of the San Bernardino Mountains are the largest producer of rare, high-brightness, high-purity limestone and one of the largest cement-grade limestone mining operations in North America. High-brightness, high-purity calcite marbles are relatively uncommon in nature because their formation requires the superposition of several independent geologic processes acting over a long period of time. Pure limestone must first be deposited in high-energy, agitated, shallow marine water, then metamorphism must bleach and recrystallize the rock to disperse impurities, and folding and faulting must place the rocks in a structural setting where they can be mined economically. The list of consumer goods made using the Cushenbury mines products is lengthy and includes acid-free art paper, paint, crayons, PVC pipe, styrofoam, toothpaste, buffered aspirin, chewing gum, Cream of Wheat, athletic field line marking, sugar, and glass.

Marble and associated quartzite are well exposed along CA 18 in Cushenbury Canyon. These metasedimentary rocks lie upon the Baldwin Gneiss of Proterozoic age and together are large blocks of the country rock that were intruded by Cretaceous-age granitic rocks throughout the eastern San Bernardino Mountains. Known as roof pendants, these blocks were completely surrounded by the granitic rocks and metamorphosed to a low grade by the intrusion. The presence of *Skolithos* tubes, fossilized burrows of marine worms, in the hard, vitreous

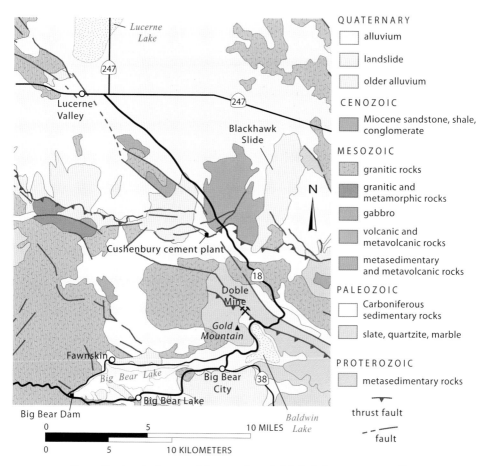

QUATERNARY
☐ alluvium
▦ landslide
▦ older alluvium

CENOZOIC
▦ Miocene sandstone, shale, conglomerate

MESOZOIC
▦ granitic rocks
▦ granitic and metamorphic rocks
▦ gabbro
▦ volcanic and metavolcanic rocks
▦ metasedimentary and metavolcanic rocks

PALEOZOIC
☐ Carboniferous sedimentary rocks
▦ slate, quartzite, marble

PROTEROZOIC
▦ metasedimentary rocks

▼▼ thrust fault
--- fault

Generalized geologic map of the route from Baldwin Lake to Lucerne Valley.

Aerial view south across CA 18 to a cement plant and quarry in Paleozoic marble along the north edge of the San Bernardino Mountains. (34°21N, 116°51W) —Photo by Mitsubishi Cement Corporation

Pink dikes of fine-grained, granular quartz and feldspar in gray Cretaceous granitic rock in Cushenbury Canyon. (34°20.0N, 116°50.0W)

quartzite suggests that it may correlate with the Neoproterozoic and Cambrian Zabriskie, Wood Canyon, Stirling, and Johnnie Formations—classic formations in the Basin and Range part of eastern California. Brachiopod and crinoid fossils in the dark gray to white marble suggest it may correlate with the Carrara and Kingston Peak Formations of Cambrian age or perhaps younger Mississippian formations also in eastern California. The light-colored granitic rock and its fine-grained felsic dikes are typical throughout much of the central Mojave Desert.

North Front of the San Bernardino Mountains

Along the base of the San Bernardino Mountains is an abrupt fault contact between the imposing north front of the range and the flat desert floor. That contact is a thrust fault zone 55 miles long and about 1 mile wide, known as the North Frontal thrust fault. It consists of multiple overlapping, discontinuous fault strands, shear zones in bedrock, and younger fault scarps and folds in Pleistocene alluvium. The uplift along the thrust fault zone is about 1 mile. The weight of great alluvial fans shed from the mountains has depressed the original basement surface, allowing even more alluvium to accumulate along the front of the range and extend north into the Lucerne Valley.

CA 126
VENTURA—SANTA CLARITA
40 miles

CA 126 proceeds eastward from Ventura, skirting the north edge of the Oxnard Plain and entering the Santa Clara River valley, which coincides with the deep Santa Clara syncline that trends roughly parallel to the Ventura Avenue anticline. The south side of the valley is bounded by South Mountain, Oak Ridge, and the Oak Ridge fault. Low hills, Santa Paula Ridge, and the San Cayetano fault bound the north side of the valley.

Only fragments of vast lemon groves, once the largest in the world, have survived urban development between Ventura and Fillmore. Orange and avocado trees predominate from Fillmore to Piru. Long rows of towering eucalyptus trees served as windbreaks for the orchards. The California Oil Museum at 1001 E. Main Street in Santa Paula provides very informative highlights of the region's petroleum exploration and production history.

Oak Ridge and Oak Ridge Fault

Oak Ridge bounds the south edge of the Santa Clara River valley between Ventura and Piru. Several small oil fields are along the north flank of the ridge within a series of anticlines. The oil is trapped by the Oak Ridge fault, a steep, south-dipping reverse fault that closely follows the locus of greatest thinning of beds in the south edge of the Santa Clara syncline. Rocks typically thin where folded, and faults typically follow zones of thinned, weakened rocks. Displacement on the Oak Ridge fault occurred mainly in Pleistocene time, with up to 23,400 feet of dip separation and 2 miles of left separation.

Rugged, chaparral-covered South Mountain (elevation 2,350 feet) surmounts Oak Ridge south of Santa Paula. The bulk of the mountain is the south-dipping limb of a big anticline in the Sespe Formation, whose red beds are exposed in the crest of the fold low in the north base of the mountain. South Mountain was a sea knoll in Pliocene time. Relatively uneroded fault scarps steeper than 40 degrees characterize the part of the knoll that was above sea level. The Pico Formation was deposited over the submerged slopes of the island. Numerous landslides scar the north face of South Mountain.

The Oak Ridge fault lies at the foot of South Mountain, almost right beneath the Santa Clara River. Oil is produced both above the fault in the anticline and below it from upturned Pico Formation in the Bridge Pool, which was discovered in 1955. The South Mountain oil field, discovered in 1914, has produced 150 million barrels of oil. Some geologists estimate that 300 million barrels of recoverable oil are still in place. Most of the oil is produced from wells in lenses of red-brown and yellow sandstone and shale of the Sespe Formation at depths ranging from 1,250 to 7,000 feet in a series of fault traps on the south flank of the anticline. Dozens of normal faults, believed to be extension fractures associated with the Oak Ridge thrust, are present on the south and west flanks.

On the north side of the valley between Santa Paula and Fillmore, well-bedded Eocene-age marine sandstone of Santa Paula Peak (elevation 4,957

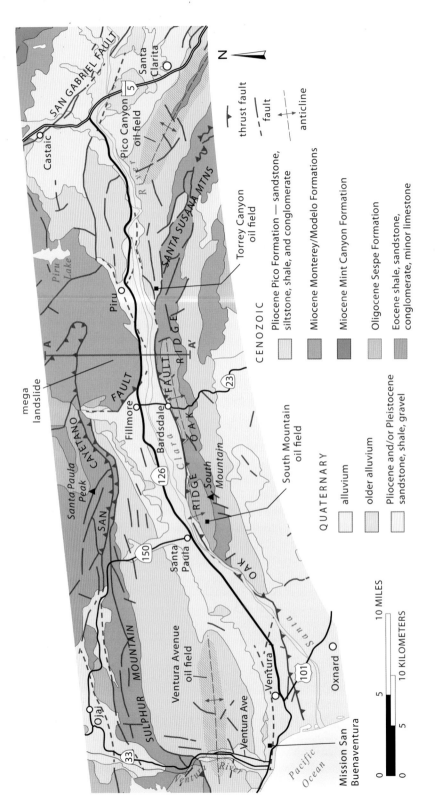

N

CENOZOIC

Pliocene Pico Formation — sandstone, siltstone, shale, and conglomerate

Miocene Monterey/Modelo Formations

Miocene Mint Canyon Formation

Oligocene Sespe Formation

Eocene shale, sandstone, conglomerate, minor limestone

thrust fault

— — — fault

↕ anticline

QUATERNARY

alluvium

older alluvium

Pliocene and/or Pleistocene sandstone, shale, gravel

Torrey Canyon oil field

South Mountain oil field

Ventura Avenue oil field

Mission San Buenaventura

mega landslide

Santa Clarita

Castaic

Pico Canyon oil field

SAN GABRIEL FAULT

Santa Clara River

Piru Lake

Piru

SANTA SUSANA MTNS

RIDGE

OAK RIDGE FAULT

Fillmore

Bardsdale

South Mountain

SAN CAYETANO FAULT

Santa Paula Peak

Santa Paula

SULPHUR MOUNTAIN

Ventura Ave

Ventura

Oxnard

Ojai

San Miguel

Pacific Ocean

Ventura River

0   5   10 MILES

0   5   10 KILOMETERS

Geology along CA 126 between Ventura and Santa Clarita. See cross section A-A' on page 334.

fcct) has been thrust southward over Pico Formation on the San Cayetano thrust fault. Whereas the Oak Ridge fault dips steeply south, the San Cayetano dips 60 to 65 degrees north, so that together the faults bound the deep Santa Clara syncline, as is shown in cross section A-A′ on page 334.

One mile west of Fillmore, CA 126 crosses Sespe Creek, which drains a large wilderness area north of the highway that contains the Sespe Condor Sanctuary. The condors give their name to the prominent thick, white Condor Sandstone of Eocene age, which is clearly seen from the highway on the skyline northeast

View east of the South Mountain anticline in the left center of the picture. South Mountain is entirely in the south-dipping flank of the anticline. The north flank is cut by the Oak Ridge fault, whose surface trace is at the base of the hills. (34°20N, 119°01W)

San Cayetano fault, a major thrust fault, lies between the lower grassy hillslope of Pliocene sedimentary rocks and the gray, brush-covered, north-dipping Eocene rock layers in the steep slope below Santa Paula Peak. (34°22N, 119°02W)

of the bridge that carries CA 126 over Sespe Creek. Also about 2 miles north of the highway, you'll see dark, red-brown beds of the Sespe Formation at creek level in the hills topographically below the Condor Sandstone. The creek floods bank to bank in torrential rainstorms, and overbank floods go into the houses and orange groves along the highway.

The Santa Clara syncline is narrow and deep in the Fillmore area, and its flanks are especially pinched. The valley is only about 1 mile wide a few miles east of Bardsdale and Fillmore, but the Pliocene and Pleistocene sediments that fill the valley are 22,000 feet thick. The smooth brown hills east of Fillmore are a huge, ancient landslide of rocks from the north side of the San Cayetano fault. The slide crossed at least 3 miles of the basin to the edge of CA 126. You'll see broken shale and sandstone in roadcuts in the toe of the slide north of the highway and the railroad tracks (PM 22.5).

The top of the marine Pliocene section is about 12,000 feet below sea level in the subsurface near Fillmore, yet the edges of the section curl up like the sides of a fishbowl and crop out as steep to overturned beds along the edge of the

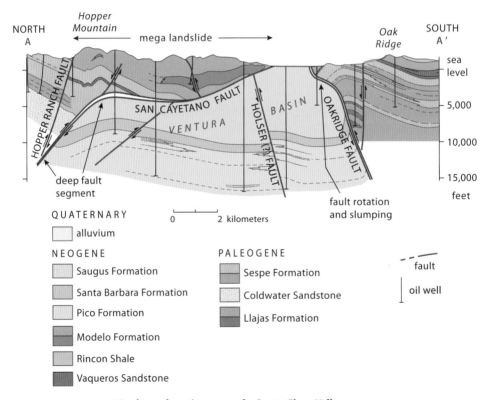

North-south section across the Santa Clara Valley.
—Modified from Hopps and others, 1992, and Nicholson and others, 2007

View north of Pliocene beds north of Piru that dip steeply north and are overturned. The San Cayetano fault lies directly behind these two pinnacles. (34°25.2N, 118°47.6W)

trough north of the village of Piru. Formations are much thicker in the basin than on Oak Ridge. The crust had to stretch to accommodate the formation of the basin in Miocene time, whereas the basin has continued to fill with sediments during the ongoing squeezing, folding, and faulting since Pliocene time.

Torrey Canyon Oil Field

High on the side of Oak Ridge across the valley from and south of Piru is the Torrey Canyon oil field, famous because the first oil tanker that ever broke up on the sea and caused a major oil spill was named the *Torrey Canyon*. The oil field was discovered in 1889, followed by the discovery of a deep zone of production in 1952. The oil is contained in the Sespe Formation within a faulted anticlinal dome, the easternmost of several en echelon anticlines along the Oak Ridge uplift. Three strands of the Oak Ridge fault cut the field into differing production zones.

San Martinez Grande Canyon to I-5

The river and hilly landscape on the south side of CA 126 between San Martinez Grande Canyon and I-5 along Castaic Creek has served as a backdrop for many TV series and movies, including *MASH* and *Apocalypse Now*. Pleistocene sandstone and siltstone beds of the nonmarine Saugus Formation overlie thick beds of Pliocene sandstone.

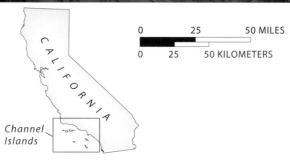

CHANNEL ISLANDS

A small rock holds back a great wave. —Homer, *The Iliad*

Islands have an aura of romance because of their isolation and being surrounded by the mysteries of the deep. The eight islands offshore of southern California are no exception. Only Santa Catalina Island is permanently inhabited today, although Native Americans lived on all of the islands for millennia and Spanish ranchers also occupied them. Spanish sailors named the islands in the sixteenth and seventeenth centuries. The four northern Channel Islands—San Miguel, Santa Rosa, Santa Cruz, and Anacapa, together with Santa Barbara Island to the south, are part of Channel Islands National Park. The western two-thirds of Santa Cruz Island are administered by the Nature Conservancy and may be visited only by permit. San Clemente and San Nicolas Islands, in the southern Channel Islands, are controlled by the US military.

The four northern Channel Islands, geologically part of the Transverse Ranges, have an east-west arrangement along the south edge of the Santa Barbara Channel and can be seen from the mainland. During the last glacial period of the Pleistocene epoch, about 110,000 to 12,500 years before present, sea level was as much as 400 feet lower than today, and the four islands constituted one huge island known as Santarosae. As the glacial period waned and ice melted, sea level rose and separated the mega island into four individual islands.

A unique layer of middle Eocene pebble conglomerate, correlated with the Poway Conglomerate in the San Diego area, crops out on San Nicolas, San Miguel, Santa Rosa, and Santa Cruz Islands. These exposures add evidence to the hypothesis that the south edge of the Channel Islands was once attached to the San Diego–San Clemente coastline, and that the islands, as well as the entire western Transverse Ranges, rotated 110 degrees clockwise from a northwest orientation to their present east-west orientation.

The southern Channel Islands are the exposed crests of fault-bounded mountains separated by deep basins. Together, they give glimpses of a 155-mile-wide region known to geologists as the Continental Borderland. These fault blocks are uplifted accretionary wedge and fore-arc basin rocks. Santa Catalina, San Clemente, and, less commonly, Santa Barbara are visible from the mainland.

Conglomerate clasts of metamorphosed rhyolite in lower Cañada de los Sauces, Santa Cruz Island. (34°00.74N, 119°52.82W)
—Andre Wyss photo

San Miguel Island

San Miguel, the westernmost of the four northern Channel Islands, with an area of only 14 square miles, is a barren 400- to 500-foot-high plateau with 26 miles of coastline and a high point of only 831 feet above sea level. Steep bluffs surround the island, particularly on its northwest and south sides. Several ships have snagged on jagged offshore rocks, giving the island its nickname the Graveyard of the Pacific.

Its rolling, low-relief surface is mostly covered by shifting sand. The prevailing northwest winds that blast the island most of the year, plus decades of overgrazing by sheep, have caused most of the topsoil to be blown away, exposing caliche (a calcareous soil layer) and eolianite (dune sand cemented by carbonate) at the surface. Vegetation began to recover when the sheep and burros introduced by the Spanish were removed. Because of their confined area, islands are particularly susceptible to overgrazing. Paleontologists have found evidence that pygmy mammoths also overgrazed the islands about 16,000 years ago.

Bedrock in the east half of San Miguel Island consists of middle Neogene sedimentary and volcanic rocks. Early Cenozoic and Late Cretaceous sedimentary rocks make up the west half. All formations dip to the west.

In a cave on the island, a unique sedimentary layer, just a few centimeters thick, contains iron-rich and alumina-silica-rich impact spherules, nanodiamonds, and other unusual features from a cosmic impactor, such as an asteroid or comet. Known as the Younger Dryas boundary layer, it has been dated by radiocarbon methods at 12,800 ± 150 years. James Wittke and others (2013) have documented similar impact spherules of the same age at eighteen sites spread over 20 million square miles on four continents. The age of this layer coincides with several major global catastrophes, including abrupt cooling of the Earth's atmosphere, extinction of some fauna at the end of the Pleistocene epoch, and widespread wildfires, probably all caused when a major cosmic impactor broke up in solar orbit near Earth.

Santa Rosa Island

Diamond-shaped Santa Rosa Island, with its 52 miles of coastline and 84 square miles of land, is the second largest of the five islands that make up Channel Islands National Park. It is 26 miles from the mainland, but that gap was only 5 miles when sea level was lower during ice age times. Vail Peak, at 1,589 feet, is the highest point, and steep cliffs border Santa Rosa on all but its eastern shore. The lower slopes of the island are covered by alluvium dissected by gullies. Several levels of Pleistocene terrace deposits cover the bedrock over much of this low-lying island.

The Santa Rosa Island fault strikes east, dividing the island into almost equal halves. About 300 feet of marine Cozy Dell Shale crop out south of the fault beneath about 700 feet of pink-gray and interbedded red claystone of the Sespe Formation. Vaqueros Sandstone and Rincon Formation overlie the Sespe, which is not present on the other islands. Volcanic rocks equivalent to the Santa Cruz Island and Conejo Volcanics overlie all these sedimentary units. Most of the island north of the fault exposes the Rincon Shale, medium- to coarse-grained sandstone rich in volcanic ash, and conglomerate with andesitic volcanic detritus assigned to the Beechers Bay Formation of middle Miocene age.

Winds, clocked up to 106 miles per hour, are so strong in this area that they carry sand from San Miguel Island onto Santa Rosa. Shifting white dunes at the west end of the island cover as much as 2 square miles, with a height of more than 400 feet. The greatest dune-building period commenced about 7,000 years ago and reached its peak 3,000 to 4,000 years before present.

Mammalian vertebrate fossils, including mastodons, have been found in the Pleistocene terrace deposits of Santa Rosa Island. The only complete skeleton of pygmy mammoth, descended from the great Columbian mammoth (*Elphas imperator*), which stood nearly 14 feet tall, was found on Santa Rosa Island. The skeleton was surprisingly intact, missing only a few toe bones and one tusk. It was lying in the position and location where it died some 12,840 years before present. Its progenitors swam to the islands from the mainland, and once established they gradually evolved into a smaller species, the Channel Islands pygmy mammoth (*Mammothus exilis*), which stood only 5 feet in height. Decreasing food supply and lack of predators may have favored a smaller size, and the rising sea isolated the islands into single entities, reducing the animals' foraging range.

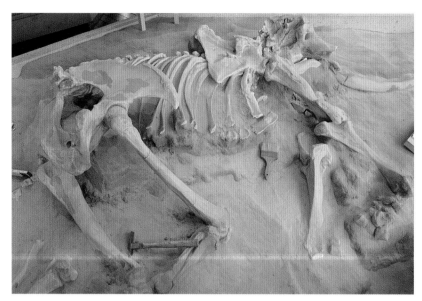

A replica of the pygmy mammoth skeleton found on Santa Rosa Island in 1994 is on display at Channel Islands National Park visitor center in Ventura.

Santa Cruz Island

Santa Cruz Island is the largest (96 square miles), longest, highest, ruggedest, and most geologically complex of the four northern Channel Islands. Steep cliffs with numerous caves bound its north side. Two main east-west ridges are separated by the Santa Cruz Island fault, which divides the island almost in half. The northern ridge, which is visible from the mainland, is surmounted by Devils Peak (elevation 2,450 feet). Most of the ridge has resistant Santa Cruz Island Volcanics correlated by age and rock type with the Conejo Volcanics in the western Santa Monica Mountains. The rest is Monterey Formation. The ridge south of the fault zone is lower than the north ridge, only about half as long, and not visible from the mainland. It consists of basement schist, igneous intrusions, and overlying, layered volcaniclastic rock of Miocene age. The Santa Cruz Island fault is part of a major east-west fault system that includes faults along the south margin of the Santa Monica Mountains. Sixteen small stream channels and minor ridges are consistently deflected about 50 feet left-laterally along the western 2 miles of the fault, indicating its Pleistocene and Holocene activity.

Santa Cruz is the only island among the northern Channel Islands with crystalline basement rocks, exposed mainly south of the Santa Cruz Island fault. The southern ridge consists of 150-million-year-old metamorphic rocks, weathered brick red and cut deeply by long, narrow, south-trending drainages. The basement rocks also include a 10-mile-long band of pre–Late Jurassic

View east of the Central Valley, which contains the Santa Cruz Island fault, on Santa Cruz Island. Brick-colored metamorphic rocks make up the weathered ridge in the foreground and south of the valley (right). Santa Cruz Island Volcanics form the ridge north of the valley (left). (33°59.5N, 119°41.7W) —Sophie Briggs photo

greenish-gray chlorite schist, and a complex mixture of plutonic rocks called the Willows Diorite that ranges from quartz diorite through diorite and gabbro to peridotite, all complexly injected by tonalite and diabase dikes. In addition, light gray tonalite, radiometrically dated as 141 million years old or Early Cretaceous, intruded the schist.

About 3,650 feet of Paleogene-age sedimentary rocks, mainly Eocene but including some of Paleocene age, crop out on the southwest side of Santa Cruz Island. The late Eocene Cozy Dell Shale correlates with the same formation on the mainland, whereas other older rock layers are local to the island.

Five major Neogene rock units on the islands correlate with the same formations on the mainland: Rincon Shale and Vaqueros Sandstone (early Miocene), San Onofre Breccia (Miocene), Conejo Volcanics (middle Miocene), and the Monterey Formation (late Miocene). Pliocene rock layers do not crop out on Santa Cruz or any of the other islands but are present beneath the Santa Barbara Channel.

Anacapa Island

From the mainland, Anacapa looks like a low, 5-mile-long ridge east of Santa Cruz Island, but it is really three separate islands. The narrow, cliff-bounded islands are rugged erosional remnants of resistant gray andesite and basaltic andesite flows and volcaniclastic rocks of the 16-million-year-old Conejo Volcanics. The western island is a steep ridge, 930 feet above sea level, whereas the other two islands are narrow walls of volcanic rock with flat, beveled tops rising to a maximum elevation of 325 feet. Beds of San Onofre Breccia crop out on Middle and West Anacapa, consisting of blocks up to 3 feet across of glaucophane schist, hornblende schist, chloritic and talc-rich schist, and pink quartzite interbedded with pink and green sandstone. This assemblage of rocks is much like the bedrocks exposed on Santa Catalina Island and the Palos Verdes Hills, as well as the breccia at Dana Point near San Juan Capistrano. The blocks of rock in the breccia were eroded from or tumbled in rockfalls from a now-submerged bedrock source west of the present California coast and south of the northern Channel Islands.

Aerial view of Anacapa Island looking east. (34°00.6N, 119°25.5W)
—Photo courtesy DX News.com

Waves have excavated more than one hundred sea caves of various sizes along faults and joints along the Anacapa shore. Where excavation occurs from one or both sides of a narrow headland, a sea arch may eventually form. Arch Rock is an 80-foot-high arch at the east end of East Anacapa that gives a distinguishing touch to the island's silhouette. It is large enough to see from the mainland on days with clear visibility from a rise in US 101 (PM 32) about 1 mile west of the Ventura River crossing.

Santa Barbara Island

Sometimes called the Rock, Santa Barbara is the smallest island, a gently rolling tableland of about 1 square mile located about 38 miles off the southern California coast from Palos Verdes Peninsula. It is the southernmost island in Channel Islands National Park and the northernmost of the southern Channel

Islands. The island is visible on clear days from high points on the mainland. Its highest peak is Signal Hill, at 634 feet. Cliffs from 200 to 600 feet high almost completely encircle the island.

Most of Santa Barbara Island is flat-topped because ocean waves in Pleistocene time eroded six distinct coastal terraces, the highest of which is 250 feet above sea level. The island's bedrock consists of about 1,000 feet of tilted pillow basalt flows of Miocene age with interbedded volcaniclastic beds and lenses of shale, claystone, and ash-rich siltstone.

Santa Catalina Island

Situated about 20 miles south-southwest of the Palos Verdes Peninsula, Santa Catalina is the largest of the southern Channel Islands, with an area of 75 square miles. This rugged, mountainous island has steep, precipitous shores notched by narrow, dry ravines and a few wide stream valleys. The island is an elevated, northwest-trending fault block whose highest peak, Mt. Orizaba, is 2,125 feet above sea level. There is no evidence that the island was ever connected to the mainland or to any of the other islands.

The northwest half of Santa Catalina Island is made of blueschist, greenschist, and amphibolite of the Catalina Schist, all of which were mafic igneous and sedimentary rocks before being metamorphosed during subduction of the

The Shark Harbor sea cliffs on Santa Catalina Island expose several different types of metaconglomerate, metagraywacke, and greenstone in a mélange—all metamorphosed to blueschist facies. Numerous landslides are evident, and the relatively flat-lying surfaces are likely wave-cut terraces. Shells and shell debris on these surfaces were originally thought to be beach deposits but are now considered midden deposits that accumulated over a long period of human habitation. (33°23.1N, 118°28.5W) —AT International photo

Farallon Plate. The blueschist was broken into a chaotic mixture of rock fragments and blocks of all sizes, called a mélange, whereas the greenschist and amphibolite facies rocks are relatively coherent tectonic units. Each rock unit is separated from the others by poorly exposed zones of thrust faults: greenschist rocks are thrust upon blueschist, and the amphibolite is thrust upon the greenschist. Serpentinite is widely distributed on the island and was used by Native Americans for making stone bowls.

Miocene-age plutonic and volcanic rocks make up most of the south half of the island. The oldest of these is quartz diorite of the Catalina pluton, about 19 million years old. Its intrusion is thought to be the first among several diorite-dacite dome and dike intrusions that culminated about 15 to 12 million years ago. Andesitic and basaltic andesitic flows and flow breccias are over 1,200 feet thick in the center of the island. Within this section are several middle Miocene volcaniclastic breccias, ash-rich shales, and claystones in beds up to 60 feet thick in places. Some of the breccias have been extensively quarried and transported to the mainland to construct jetties and seawalls.

Coastal terraces, which are so well developed on some of the other islands, are conspicuously lacking on Santa Catalina, perhaps owing to the hardness of its bedrock. Various geomorphic features, such as benches on ridges, leveled summits, and an elevated embayment in Little Harbor, however, do record successive episodes of marine beveling and pulses of uplift.

San Clemente Island

San Clemente, the second largest and southernmost of the southern Channel Islands, is about 75 miles west of San Diego and entirely owned and operated by the US Navy. The low, long and narrow island has an area of 56 square miles. The island is the exposed part of a tilted and gently arched, northwest-trending

San Clemente Island. —Phillip Colla photo/Oceanlight.com

fault block bounded on its northeast side by the submerged San Clemente fault. The steep fault scarp on the northeast side of the island is about 1 mile high from the seafloor to the top of the island. The fault is parallel to other faults in the San Andreas fault system. Twenty unfaulted coastal terraces have been recognized on San Clemente below an elevation of 1,500 feet. They are some of the best-developed coastal terraces in southern California and clearly indicate that the island is rising.

About 95 percent of the island consists of as much as 2,000 feet of pyroxene andesite and basalt lava flows and volcaniclastic rocks yielding ages of about 15.5 million years old. Dacite and rhyolite have also been mapped on the island. From 250 to 300 feet of marine siltstone, sandstone, diatomite, and ash-rich claystone of middle Miocene age generally overlie the volcanic rocks, but in places they are interbedded with the upper part of the volcanic rocks. A one-quarter square mile of brilliant white sand dunes consisting of marine shells has accumulated at the north end of the island.

San Nicolas Island

With an area of 22 square miles, San Nicolas Island is the fifth largest of all the offshore islands, the most isolated of the southern Channel Islands, and the only one surrounded by sandy beaches. The beaches are present here because the main rocks on the island—about 3,550 feet of alternating sandstone, siltstone, conglomerate, and cobble-bearing mudstone of late Eocene age—are easily eroded. The rocks are part of a broad, complexly faulted anticline that plunges southeast, roughly parallel to the long dimension of the island. A few small igneous dikes cut these rocks in the southeast part of the island. Pleistocene marine terrace deposits are on much of the island, and the entire west half is covered with reddish-brown dune deposits as much as 30 feet thick, deposited in Holocene time.

NATURAL HISTORY MUSEUMS AND EXHIBITS IN SOUTHERN CALIFORNIA

MOJAVE DESERT

MOJAVE RIVER VALLEY MUSEUM
270 E. Virginia Way, Barstow
The museum is dedicated to the preservation and promotion of the scientific, historical, and cultural heritage of the Mojave Desert.

DESERT DISCOVERY CENTER
831 Barstow Road, Barstow
Displays include extinct animal tracks, the famous Old Woman Meteorite, paleontology, and geology.

CALICO EARLY MAN SITE
Minneola Road (exit 198 off I-15), about 15 miles northeast of Barstow
The alluvial fan deposits in this area may contain the oldest evidence of human occupation in the Americas. Tool fragments were embedded in the sediments of the shoreline of ancient Pleistocene Lake Manix. Guided tours only.

RED ROCK CANYON STATE PARK VISITOR CENTER MUSEUM
25 miles northeast of Mojave on CA 14
A small museum featuring some of the Pliocene and Pleistocene vertebrate fossils found in the park. Closed winter and summer months.

MATURANGO MUSEUM
100 East Las Flores Avenue, Ridgecrest
Exhibit galleries feature the natural and cultural history of the northern Mojave Desert. The museum includes tours to the world-famous Coso petroglyphs and is an information center for Death Valley and the northern Mojave Desert. Open daily.

BORAX VISITOR CENTER
Borax Road (exit 196 off CA 58), Boron; go left and follow the signs
The Borax Visitor Center overlooks the largest open-pit mine in California and has displays of minerals, mining operations, and mining products. The visitor center is open seven days a week, excluding major holidays and weather permitting. Entry fee.

CALIFORNIA ROUTE 66 MUSEUM
16825 South D Street, Victorville
The museum features US 66 in both historic and contemporary exhibitions.

ROUTE 66 MOTHER ROAD MUSEUM
681 North First Avenue, Barstow

The museum, located in the historic Casa del Desierto Harvey House, displays historic photographs and artifacts related to the development of US Route 66.

CALICO GHOST TOWN
Ghost Town Road (exit 191 off I-15) in Yermo, northeast of Barstow
This former silver mining town was founded in March 1881. One-third of the town is original, and the rest is reconstructed.

KELSO DEPOT VISITOR CENTER
90942 Kelso Cima Road, Essex
The renovated Kelso Depot is now the primary visitor center for Mojave National Preserve. Former dormitory rooms contain exhibits describing the cultural and natural history of the surrounding desert.

SALTON TROUGH

SANTA ROSA AND SAN JACINTO MOUNTAINS NATIONAL MONUMENT VISITOR CENTER
51500 Highway 74, Palm Desert
The visitor center features exhibits on desert wildlife and cultural history.

LIVING DESERT ZOO AND GARDENS
47900 Portola Avenue, Palm Desert
The exhibits and gardens are focused on animals, birds, and vegetation of the Sonoran Desert, including an 8-foot-tall giant ground sloth skeleton. Replica bones and skulls of Pleistocene animals are presented on a fossil wall, where visitors can feel and touch the remnants of life that once inhabited Coachella Valley.

SONNY BONO SALTON SEA NATIONAL WILDLIFE REFUGE
906 W. Sinclair Road, Calipatria
The visitor center has an exhibit on migratory birds, a bookstore, and a walking trail to one of the rhyolite domes at the south end of the Salton Sea.

PENINSULAR RANGES

EAGLE AND HIGH PEAK MINES TOUR
2320 C Street, Julian
The mine tour boasts 1,000 feet of hand-dug tunnel, authentic tools, machinery of the period, and gold-bearing quartz veins.

ANZA-BORREGO DESERT STATE PARK
200 Palm Canyon Drive, Borrego Springs
Anza-Borrego has an exceptional fossil record. Over five hundred different types of organisms have been identified, ranging from microscopic plant pollen and spores to the largest of mammoth elephants.

SAN BERNARDINO COUNTY MUSEUM
2024 Orange Tree Lane, Redlands
The Division of Geological Sciences holds more than a half million fossils of extinct vertebrates and invertebrates, primarily from the southwestern United

States with an emphasis on San Bernardino and Riverside Counties. There is a nice display of minerals.

MISSION TRAILS REGIONAL PARK
1 Father Junipero Serra Trail, San Diego
The interpretative center features the park's geology, plants, animals, and history. The park offers campsites and panoramic views.

JURUPA MOUNTAINS DISCOVERY CENTER
7621 Granite Hill Dr., Riverside
The Ruth and Sam Kirkby Earth Science Museum houses unique exhibits of local rocks and minerals with one of the largest collections of Chinese dinosaur eggs for public display in North America.

RIVERSIDE METROPOLITAN MUSEUM
3580 Mission Inn Avenue, Riverside
The museum's Geologic and Earth Science collection has approximately 3,500 specimens, including rare minerals from the Crestmore Quarry contact metamorphic complex. The S. M. Purple Fossil Collection has type specimens of giant prehistoric California sharks.

LOS ANGELES BASIN

NATURAL HISTORY MUSEUM OF LOS ANGELES COUNTY
900 Exposition Boulevard, Los Angeles
The Gem and Mineral Hall displays more than two thousand specimens and is considered one of the finest exhibits of gems and minerals in the world. The dinosaur gallery features a baby, a juvenile, and a subadult Tyrannosaurus rex.

GEORGE C. PAGE MUSEUM AT LA BREA TAR PITS
5801 Wilshire Boulevard, Los Angeles
One of the world's most famous fossil localities, this on-site museum displays over one million ice age fossils from 650 species—including saber-toothed cats, dire wolves, and mammoths—found in 10,000- to 40,000-year-old asphalt deposits.

CABRILLO MARINE AQUARIUM
3720 Stephen M. White Drive, San Pedro
The aquarium offers interpretive displays and museum collections exhibiting southern California's rich biodiversity and adaptations of local sea life.

AQUARIUM OF THE PACIFIC
100 Aquarium Way, Long Beach
The world-class Aquarium of the Pacific is southern California's largest aquarium and the fourth largest in the nation, with over eleven thousand animals in more than fifty exhibits. The aquarium also has outdoor exhibits, including the Shark Lagoon, the Lorikeet Forest aviary, and Our Watersheds: Pathway to the Pacific.

BOLSA CHICA CONSERVANCY INTERPRETIVE CENTER
3842 Warner Avenue, Huntington Beach

The center's main exhibits include three saltwater aquaria containing marine species native to the Bolsa Chica wetlands and the southern California coast.

OCEAN INSTITUTE
24200 Dana Point Harbor Drive, Dana Point
This marine education facility features programs on marine science, the environment, oceans, and maritime history.

RALPH B. CLARK REGIONAL PARK
8800 Rosecrans Avenue, Buena Park
The park's extensive fossil collection displays marine fossils dating from about 1 million years ago to fossils of more recent mammals that walked the Earth tens of thousands of years ago. These specimens were recovered inside the boundaries of Clark Park and from the development of the Coyote Hills area in northern Orange County. Visitors can also view a working, on-site paleontological laboratory.

UCLA METEORITE COLLECTION
Room 3697 Geology Building, UCLA campus, 595 Charles E. Young Drive E., Los Angeles
The UCLA collection of meteorites is the largest on the west coast and contains over 2,400 samples from about 1,400 different meteorites.

TRANSVERSE RANGES

CALIFORNIA OIL MUSEUM
1001 E. Main Street, Santa Paula
Workings and history of the oil and gas industry are explained through video programs, interactive models, computer displays, artifacts, and photographs. The 1890 museum building, the original headquarters of Union Oil Company of California, is included in the National Register of Historic Places because of its exceptional Victorian–Queen Anne architecture.

SANTA BARBARA MUSEUM OF NATURAL HISTORY
2559 Puesta del Sol, Santa Barbara
The museum has a splendid Geology and Paleontology Hall and Mineral and Gem Gallery. Informative exhibits feature birds, insects, mammals, marine life (including a 74-foot blue whale skeleton), fossils, and Native Americans.

MOUNT WILSON OBSERVATORY
Access via the Angeles Crest Highway (CA 2) from I-210 at La Canada Flintridge
The observatory, an astronomical research facility in the San Gabriel Mountains, is located on the summit of Mount Wilson at 5,715 feet. Open to visitors every day from April 1 through December 1 weather permitting. Ticket fees for guided tours.

VISTA DEL LAGO VISITORS CENTER
I-5 between Castaic and Gorman
This wonderful information center offers exhibits pertaining to water, water in California, and the California State Water Project. Open daily.

GLOSSARY

aa. A Hawaiian term for a lava flow that has a rough, jagged, spinous, clinkery surface.

actinolite. A greenish amphibole mineral that grows as needles or fibrous crystals in metamorphic schist and altered mafic and ultramafic igneous rocks.

alluvial fan. A gently sloping, fan-shaped deposit of loose rock detritus bordering the base of a steep slope and deposited by a stream or debris flow at the mouth of a canyon.

alluvium. Sediment deposited by rivers, streams, or wind.

amphibolite. A dark, fine-grained metamorphic rock derived from metamorphism of basalt or diabase and composed almost entirely of the mineral amphibole. The **amphibolite facies** grade of metamorphism of mafic rocks is represented by the minerals amphibole and plagioclase, an assemblage typical of regional metamorphism under moderate to high pressure and temperature.

andesite. A gray to dark gray volcanic rock, made mostly of plagioclase and lesser amounts of dark minerals. Intermediate in composition and color between rhyolite and basalt; the plutonic equivalent of diorite.

anticline. An arch-shaped fold in layered rocks with the oldest rocks toward the core. Opposite: syncline.

anticlinorium. An anticlinal structure of regional extent consisting of smaller folds.

aplite. A fine-grained, light-colored intrusive igneous rock, usually dikes or veins, with a sugary texture, consisting of quartz, potassium feldspar, and sodic plagioclase. **Aplitic** pertains to igneous rocks having a fine-grained, sugary texture.

aquifer. A porous, permeable rock or layer of sediment from which water may be obtained.

arkosic. Said of sandstone that contains more than 25 percent feldspar grains.

asthenosphere. The ductile part of the Earth's upper mantle, about 60 miles beneath the lithosphere. It is the zone upon which tectonic plates move.

badlands. Stream-dissected topography, commonly barren of vegetation, characterized by a very fine drainage network and short steep slopes with narrow ridges.

bajada. A broad, continuous alluvial slope or gently inclined detrital surface extending from the base of mountain ranges out into and around an inland basin, formed by the lateral coalescence of a series of separate but confluent alluvial fans.

basalt. A fine grained black or very dark gray volcanic rock consisting mainly of micro scopic crystals of plagioclase feldspar and usually olivine, sometimes pyroxene.

basement. The deepest crustal rocks of a given area, typically granitic and metamorphic rocks.

basin. A broad, enclosed depression, commonly with no drainage to the outside.

Basin and Range. A physiographic province in the western United States characterized by long, linear, fault-block mountains separated by intervening fault-block valleys; developed as a result of crustal extension.

batholith. A mass of coarse, granular granitic igneous rock exposed over an area greater than about 30 square miles and consisting of two or more plutons.

bedding. The layering structure in sedimentary rocks. A single layer is a bed. Several interlayered beds or rock types are said to be interlayered or interbedded.

bedrock. Solid rock exposed in place or that underlies unconsolidated superficial sediments.

biotite. Black or brown mica, a flexible platy mineral. It is a minor but common mineral in igneous and metamorphic rocks.

blueschist. A schistose metamorphic rock with a blue color imparted by the presence of the blue metamorphic mineral glaucophane. Also **glaucophane schist**, wherein glaucophane rather than hornblende is the predominant amphibole mineral.

boulder. A rounded rock fragment larger than 10 inches in diameter.

braided stream. A stream that divides into or follows an interlacing or tangled network of branching and reuniting shallow channels separated from each other by branch islands or bars. Such a stream usually indicates an inability to carry all of its sediment load.

breccia. A coarse, clastic sedimentary rock consisting of angular to rounded rock fragments held together by a fine-grained matrix. Applied to broken rock along faults and in landslides, debris from volcanic eruptions, and sedimentary deposits.

calcareous. Pertains to a rock containing more than 50 percent calcium carbonate.

calcite. A widespread, abundant mineral composed of calcium carbonate ($CaCO_3$). The major component of limestone, most marble, and many marine fossils; a common cement binding sediment in sedimentary rocks.

caldera. A large, steep-walled, circular or oval basin formed by collapse into an evacuated or partially evacuated magma chamber following voluminous volcanic eruption.

carbonate rock. A sedimentary rock composed of carbonate minerals such as calcite and dolomite.

chaparral. A thicket-like vegetative complex of scrubby bushes densely cloaking hilly areas in semiarid regions.

chert. A hard, dense, dull to partly glassy sedimentary rock composed mainly of microcrystalline quartz.

chlorite. A green, platy mineral characteristic of low-temperature metamorphism of mafic rocks—rocks with iron and magnesium.

cinder cone. A steep-sided, cone-shaped accumulation of volcanic ejecta erupted from a central vent.

clast. An individual grain or rock fragment produced by disintegration of a larger rock mass. A **clastic rock** consists of broken rock fragments, such as sand, derived from preexisting rocks.

clay. Rock or mineral particles smaller than 0.00016-inch; plastic when wet.

coarse-grained. A relative term used to describe the size of constituents in a rock. Said of an igneous rock with crystals larger than 0.2 inch in diameter. Said of sedimentary rocks with particles larger than 0.08 inch in diameter.

cobble. A rounded rock fragment larger than a pebble and smaller than a boulder, having a diameter in the range of 2.5 to 10 inches, or between that of a tennis ball and a volleyball.

colluvium. A general term applied to any loose, heterogeneous, and incoherent mass of soil and rock fragments accumulated on gentle hillslopes.

conglomerate. A coarse-grained sedimentary rock composed of rounded pebbles, cobbles, or boulders set in a fine-grained matrix of sand or silt.

convergence. The process of two lithospheric plates moving toward each other, resulting in collision and subduction.

country rock. The preexisting bedrock intruded by or surrounded by igneous rocks.

craton. A part of the Earth's crust that has attained stability and has been little deformed for a prolonged period of time. The Colorado Plateau and the midwestern United States are good examples of cratonal parts of the North American Plate.

crust. The uppermost, hardened layer of the Earth's lithosphere, 3 to 25 miles thick. Continental crust consists mainly of granitic rocks and metamorphic rocks; oceanic crust consists of basalt and peridotite.

crystal. A many-faced solid bounded by smooth planar surfaces that reflect an orderly internal arrangement of atoms.

crystalline. Said of a rock formed of interlocking mineral crystals, usually igneous or metamorphic.

dacite. A medium light–colored, fine-grained volcanic rock with a composition intermediate between andesite and rhyolite; the extrusive igneous rock equivalent in composition to the intrusive rock granodiorite.

debris flow. A jumbled mass flow of sediment and rock fragments moving downslope.

deformation. Any process by which preexisting rocks are bent, broken, or uplifted.

delta. A nearly flat accumulation of clay, sand, and gravel deposited into a standing body of water, ocean, or lake.

desert pavement. A mosaic of tightly packed stone fragments one layer thick that mantles the surface of flat or gently sloping areas in deserts.

desert varnish. A distinctive, usually shiny dark brown surface coating of manganese and iron on rocks. It may be related to the presence of organic acids formed by the decomposition of lichen.

detachment fault. A complex, low-angle, large-scale normal fault with displacement measured in miles, associated with crustal extension. The huge slab of the upper plate is displaced on a very gently inclined, smooth surface across the underlying rock body of the lower plate.

detritus. Loose, disintegrated particles of rock.

diabase. An intrusive igneous rock with the composition of basalt but which cooled beneath the surface of the Earth. Finer-grained than gabbro, its compositional intrusive equivalent.

diatom. A microscopic, single-celled plant that grows in both marine and freshwater environments. Diatoms secrete a great variety of walls of silica called frustules. Frustules may accumulate in sediments in enormous numbers.

diatomaceous. Pertaining to a sediment or rock composed of or containing numerous diatoms or their remains.

diatomite. A light-colored, soft, friable, siliceous sedimentary rock consisting chiefly of opaline silica secreted by diatoms.

dike. A tabular igneous intrusion that cuts across the grain of its host rock, generally through a fracture in solid rock. Opposite: sill.

diorite. A plutonic igneous rock intermediate in composition between granite and gabbro in color and silica content. Its volcanic equivalent is andesite.

dip. The downsloping angle of any planar surface in rocks, such as a sedimentary bed or metamorphic foliation. The dip angle is measured from the horizontal.

divergence. The process of two lithospheric plates moving away from each other (spreading) with volcanic activity along the mutual boundary.

dolomite. A carbonate mineral with the formula $CaMg(CO_3)$; the term is also applied to a sedimentary rock composed of the mineral dolomite.

earthquake. The shaking caused by abrupt displacement along a fault. See also **magnitude.**

en echelon. An adjective describing geologic features, especially faults or fractures, that have a staggered or overlapping arrangement. Collectively they form a linear zone.

epicenter. The point on the Earth's surface directly above the point of origin, or focus, of an earthquake.

epidote. A pistachio-green mineral formed in low-grade metamorphic rocks. It also forms in mafic rocks altered by hydrothermal activity.

erosion. The process of removal of rock material by any natural process, such as wind, water, gravity, or ice.

evaporite. A nonclastic sedimentary rock composed of minerals produced from a saline solution as a result of extensive or total evaporation of the solvent. Evaporite minerals include rock salt, gypsum, anhydrite, and various nitrates and borates.

extrusive igneous rocks. Rocks that solidify from magma on the Earth's surface.

fanglomerate. A solid rock originally deposited as an alluvial fan and cemented together since deposition.

Farallon Plate. An ancient oceanic plate located originally between the Pacific and North American Plates. It subducted beneath the west edge of the North American Plate during the Jurassic Period. It is named for the Farallon Islands about 30 miles west of San Francisco, California

fault. A fracture in the Earth's crust along which blocks of the crust have slipped past one another. A **normal fault** forms under crustal extension, and one side drops down relative to the other side. A **reverse fault** forms under crustal shortening, and one side is pushed up and over the other side. A **strike-slip fault** is one where one side slips sideways relative to the other side.

fault block. A body of rock adjacent to a fault.

feldspar. The most abundant rock-forming mineral group, making up 60 percent of the Earth's crust and consisting of calcium, sodium, or potassium with aluminum silica. Includes plagioclase feldspars (albite and anorthite) and alkali feldspars (sanidine, orthoclase, and microcline).

felsic. Said of igneous rocks that are composed of light-colored minerals, such as feldspar, quartz, and muscovite.

fine-grained. A relative term used to describe the size of constituents in a rock. Said of igneous rocks with minerals too small to see with the unaided eye. Said of sedimentary rocks with silt-size or smaller particles.

fold. A bent or warped rock layer or layers shortened by compressive tectonic stress.

foliation. A textural term referring to planar arrangement of minerals or structures in any kind of rock and formed primarily by solid-state metamorphism.

formation. A distinct body of sedimentary, igneous, or metamorphic rock that can be recognized, correlated, and mapped over a large area. It is the basic stratigraphic unit in geologic mapping. Formations are named after places where they are best recognized and can either bear the term *Formation* (for example, Mecca Formation) or the name of a rock type (for example, Vaqueros Sandstone). A formation may be part of a larger group and may be subdivided into members.

fossil. The remains of a plant or animal preserved in a rock. A **trace fossil** is a structure, such as a track or a burrow that is left by the activity of a plant or animal.

fossiliferous. Containing fossils.

fracture. Any break in rocks caused by natural mechanical failure under stress, including cracks, joints, and faults.

gabbro. A dark intrusive igneous rock consisting mainly of plagioclase and pyroxene, but also olivine, in crystals large enough to be seen with a simple magnifier. Gabbro is the plutonic equivalent of basalt but contains much larger crystals than its compositional equivalents, intrusive diabase and extrusive basalt, because it cooled at depth over a long period of time.

garnet. A family of red or brown silicate minerals with widely varying chemical compositions. Garnet is common in metamorphic rocks, less common in igneous rocks.

geomorphic. The form of the Earth or its surface features.

geothermal. Pertaining to heat released from within the Earth. **Geothermal power** is energy derived from the internal heat of the Earth.

glaciation. The formation and movement of glaciers or large ice sheets.

glaucophane. A bluish-black or grayish-blue mineral of the amphibole group. It is a fibrous or prismatic mineral in schist resulting from regional metamorphism of sodium-rich igneous rocks, such as ocean floor basalt.

gneiss. A regionally metamorphosed rock characterized by alternating, irregular bands of coarse minerals grains and finer, flaky mica minerals. Mineral composition is not an essential factor in its definition; varieties are distinguished more by texture and origin.

gouge. Soft, earthy, or claylike fault-crushed rock material along a fault.

grain size. The size of mineral fragments that make up a rock.

granite. A plutonic igneous rock composed mostly of orthoclase feldspar, plagioclase, and quartz in crystals large enough to see without using a magnifier. The intrusive equivalent of rhyolite.

granodiorite. A coarse-grained intrusive plutonic rock intermediate in composition between granite and diorite. Its volcanic equivalent is dacite.

gravel. An unconsolidated natural accumulation of rounded rock fragments, most of particles larger than sand, such as cobbles, pebbles, granules, or any combination thereof.

graywacke. A sedimentary rock made primarily of mud and sand, commonly deposited by turbidity currents.

greenschist. A schistose metamorphic rock whose green color is due to the presence of chlorite, epidote, or actinolite. **Greenschist facies** include rocks that have undergone conditions of low-grade regional metamorphism: relatively low pressure and temperatures in the range of 570°F to 930°F.

greenstone. A dark green, altered or metamorphosed basalt or gabbro. The green color is imparted by the mineral chlorite or epidote.

groundwater. Subsurface water that fills spaces in rock or sediment.

gypsum. A common evaporite mineral, calcium sulfate; usually colorless to white.

high-grade. Said of an ore with a relatively high ore-mineral content. Also pertains to rocks metamorphosed under conditions of high pressure and temperature.

hornblende. The most common rock-forming silicate mineral of the amphibole group. It commonly forms needle-shaped or stubby, dull black, brick-shaped crystals in igneous and metamorphic rocks.

hydrothermal. Pertaining to geothermally heated water.

ice ages. Poplar name for a period of Earth history, mainly during the Pleistocene epoch, when continental ice sheets periodically advanced and retreated over North America and Europe.

igneous rock. Rock formed from the crystallization and solidification of molten magma.

inselberg. An isolated, steep-sided, generally bare and rocky residual knob, hill, or small mountain, usually smoothed and rounded, rising abruptly from and surrounded by an extensive lowland erosion surface or alluvium, characteristic of an arid or semi-arid landscape in a late stage of the erosion cycle.

intrusive igneous rocks. Rocks that cool from magma beneath the surface of the Earth. The body of rock is called an intrusion. Opposite: extrusive.

joint. A planar fracture or crack in a rock along which insignificant displacement has occurred.

landslide. The downslope movement of soil and rock under the force of gravity.

lava. Molten rock erupted on the surface of the Earth.

left-slip fault. A fault along which the opposing block appears to be displaced sideways to the left.

limestone. A sedimentary rock composed of the mineral calcite ($CaCO_3$).

lineation. Any penetrative linear structure or alignment of constituents in a rock.

lithospheric plates. Large, rigid units of the crust and upper mantle of the Earth (60 to 150 miles thick) that consist of continental and/or oceanic crust and are broken into plates. These plates are defined by the Earth's major earthquake zones at their margins and move slowly relative to each other owing to inexorable plastic flow of the Earth's mantle.

longshore drift. Current that flows near and parallel to the shore and moves sand.

low-grade. Said of an ore with a relatively low ore-mineral content. Also pertains to rocks metamorphosed under conditions of low pressure and temperature.

mafic. Said of a dark-colored igneous rock that contains more iron, magnesium, and calcium and less silica and sodium than a felsic rock. Mafic rocks contain abundant dark minerals, such as hornblende, biotite, and pyroxene.

magma. Molten rock within the Earth.

magmatic arc. The zone of magma production that stretches in an arc-like fashion above and parallel to a subduction zone.

magnitude. A measure of strain energy released during an earthquake. A Richter magnitude is measured on a logarithmic scale corrected for a standard seismograph at a standard distance of 100 kilometers from the epicenter. Each tenfold increase on the Richter scale is 30 times greater than the previous one. Thus a M6 releases 30 times more energy than a M5 and 900 times more energy than an M4. Moment magnitude is a very different measure of earthquake strength that factors in the length of the surface rupture and the hypocenter, or depth of the origin point of rupture. Richter magnitude is used in this book.

mantle. The largest subdivision of the Earth's interior (80 percent), which lies between the lithosphere and the very dense core.

marble. Metamorphosed limestone or dolomite, usually coarsely crystalline.

marine. Pertaining to sedimentary rocks formed in the sea or ocean, and to oceanic environmental conditions or realms. **Nonmarine** pertains to sedimentary rocks formed on land, and to on-land environmental conditions or realms.

massive. Said of a rock layer or rock type lacking evident internal layering or structure.

megawatt. A measure of the electrical output of a power plant. One megawatt = 1,000 kilowatts = 1,000,000 watts. A typical coal plant is about 600 megawatts in size. The average American household residence uses 0.01 megawatts per year.

mélange. A heterogeneous mixture of rocks.

metamorphic rock. A rock derived from preexisting rock that changes mineralogically and texturally in the solid state in response to changes in temperature and/or pressure, usually deep within the Earth. The change occurs without melting of the preexisting rock.

metamorphism. Recrystallization of an existing rock due to heat and pressure within the Earth but without the rock having melted.

metasedimentary rock. A sedimentary rock that has been metamorphosed.

metavolcanic rock. A volcanic rock that has been metamorphosed.

mica. A family of silicate minerals, including biotite and muscovite, that crystallizes into thin flakes with perfect platy cleavage. Micas are common in many kinds of igneous and metamorphic rocks.

micaceous. Containing mica, such as muscovite and biotite.

migmatite. A composite of metamorphic rock, commonly gneissic, mixed with igneous rock crystallized from magma that has partially melted out of or has injected into the gneiss.

mineral. A naturally occurring, inorganic solid substance of specific chemical composition and physical properties, or ones that varying within fixed limits.

mudstone. A fine-grained sedimentary rock consisting of silt or clay.

muscovite. A common, colorless to light brown mineral of the mica group. It is present in many igneous and metamorphic rocks, and much less commonly in sedimentary rocks.

mylonite. A microbreccia with flow structure, formed by ductile "smearing out" of rock within a shear zone between two blocks of crust.

normal fault. An inclined fault along which the overhanging rocks have moved down the inclined surface relative to the underlying rock. Forms as a result of crustal extension, or stretching. Opposite: reverse fault.

North American Plate. One of seven huge moving plates that make up the outer, solid part of the Earth.

obsidian. Volcanic glass; lava that cooled too quickly to form crystals; commonly rich in silica.

oil field. Two or more subsurface accumulations of petroleum in a single geologic structure that will yield oil in economic quantities.

olivine. An iron and magnesium silicate mineral that typically forms pale green to pistachio green crystals in gabbro, basalt, and peridotite.

orogeny. The process of building mountains.

orthoclase. A potassium-rich alkali feldspar, a common rock-forming mineral.

outcrop. An exposure of bedrock at the surface. The rock is said to "crop out."

Pacific Plate. One of the Earth's seven major contemporary plates, lying west of the North American Plate and consisting of oceanic crust and upper mantle under the Pacific Ocean.

pahoehoe. A Hawaiian term for basaltic lava with a relatively smooth, undulating surface of small-scale bulbous, ropy, corded, drapery-like features.

paleontology. The study of ancient life in past geologic time, largely by means of plant and animal fossils.

pebble. A small stone, usually worn and rounded, between 0.17 and 2.5 inches in diameter.

pediment. A broad, usually bare, gently sloping, bedrock-floored erosion surface or plain of low relief in an arid or semiarid region at the base of an abrupt and receding mountain front or plateau. Commonly partly mantled with a thin, discontinuous veneer of alluvium.

pegmatite. An exceptionally coarse-grained igneous rock, generally granitic, with interlocking crystals, usually found as irregular dikes or veins at the margins of batholiths and usually intruded after the surrounding rock has cooled.

peridotite. A coarse-grained, ultramafic, low-silica igneous rock consisting mainly of olivine. Earth's mantle consists of peridotite.

plagioclase. A feldspar mineral rich in sodium and calcium. One of the most common rock-forming minerals in igneous and metamorphic rocks.

plate. In a tectonic sense, one of seven large drifting crustal slabs composing the Earth's solid outer part. Plates are roughly 60 miles thick.

plate tectonics. A theory of global tectonics in which Earth's lithosphere is divided into seven huge plates that move slowly and interact with one another upon a ductile asthenosphere, with seismic, tectonic, and volcanic activity along the edges of the plates.

playa. A smooth, fine-grained lakebed in a desert valley, normally dry but may be flooded.

pluton. A large intrusion of igneous rock into solid, overlying country rock. Two or more plutons make up a batholith.

plutonic rock. Intrusive, coarse-grained igneous rock that formed underground when magma cooled and solidified; usually of a grainy, granitic texture. Opposite: volcanic rock.

pumice. Silicic, bubble-filled volcanic glass, often light enough to float on water.

pumpjacks. A mechanical pump to lift oil or water out of the ground where bottom hole pressure is insufficient for the fluid to flow to the surface.

pyrite. A common, pale-bronze or brass-yellow iron sulfide mineral (FeS_2). Also commonly called "fool's gold."

pyroclastic. Pertaining to an explosive volcanic eruption, and to all sizes and shapes of lava fragments, such as ash, cinders, blocks, and bombs, ejected in such an eruption.

pyroxene. An iron- and magnesium-bearing silicate group of minerals that occur mostly in dark, mafic igneous and metamorphic rocks.

quartz. A mineral form of silica (SiO_2). Quartz is one of the most abundant and widely distributed minerals in the Earth's crust. It comes in a wide variety of forms, including clear crystals, sand grains, and chert. It is hard and chemically resistant.

quartz diorite. A medium- to light-colored plutonic rock. Composed mostly of plagioclase feldspar and from 5 percent to 20 percent quartz. Quartz diorite grades into granodiorite as the alkali feldspar content increases. Similar to tonalite, which is generally more mafic. Approximate volcanic equivalent: dacite.

quartzite. A metamorphic rock composed of mainly quartz and formed by recrystallization of quartz-rich sandstone.

quartz monzonite. A granitic rock in which quartz constitutes 10 to 50 percent of the felsic constituents and alkali feldspar is 35 to 65 percent of the total feldspar.

radiometric dating. The calculation of rock age from the measured ratios of one or more radiometric elements and their decay products in minerals.

resistant. Said of a rock that withstands the effects of weathering or erosion.

reverse fault. An inclined fault with relative upward movement of the overhanging rocks relative to the underlying rocks. Forms as a result of crustal shortening. Opposite: normal fault.

rhyolite. A felsic volcanic rock, the extrusive equivalent of granite, commonly tan or reddish brown, depending upon impurities. It contains quartz and feldspar in a very fine-grained, crystalline or glassy matrix.

rift. A long, narrow belt where the Earth's crust is separating. A rift basin is the trough, or valley, formed by the rifting.

right-slip fault. A fault with sideways displacement where the opposite block appears to be displaced sideways to the right.

rock. Any naturally formed, consolidated aggregate of minerals or natural glasses. The most important rock-forming minerals are quartz, feldspars, micas, amphiboles, pyroxenes, olivine, calcite, and dolomite.

rock varnish. A patina or thin coating of dark material abnormally rich in iron and manganese on the exposed surface of a rock. See also **desert varnish**.

roof pendant. Country rocks that are completely encased in a younger pluton or batholith.

sag pond. A small body of water occupying an enclosed depression, typically along a strike-slip fault where recent fault-related activity has impounded drainage.

San Andreas fault. California's longest fault, along the junction of the Pacific and North American Plates.

sand. Weathered mineral grains, most commonly quartz, between 0.0025 and 0.08 inches in diameter. Larger than silt, smaller than pebbles.

sandstone. A sedimentary rock made primarily of sand-sized particles of rock or mineral.

scarp. A steep cliff face from a few feet to thousands of feet high, formed by faulting or erosion.

schist. A metamorphic rock with well-developed, thin foliation due to an abundance of oriented, platy minerals.

sediment. Unconsolidated rock fragments.

sedimentary rock. A rock formed from the consolidation, cementation, or compaction of loose sediment or organic material.

sedimentation. The process of sediment settling out of wind or water.

seismicity/seismic. Pertaining to earthquake activity.

serpentine. A hydrated iron- and magnesium-rich mineral with a long fibrous shape. **Serpentinite** is California's state rock, whereas gold is the state's mineral.

shale. A sedimentary deposit of clay, silt, or mud solidified into more or less solid rock.

shear zone. The zone in which deformation occurs when two bodies of rock slide past each other, resulting in crushed and brecciated rock with parallel fractures due to shear strain.

silica. Silicon dioxide (SiO_2); occurs naturally as quartz and as a component of many rock-forming minerals.

siliceous. Said of a rock or plant rich in silica.

sill. A tabular igneous intrusion that parallels the planar structure of the enclosing rock.

siltstone. A sedimentary rock made primarily of silt to dust size particles of rock.

slate. Slightly metamorphosed shale or mudstone that breaks easily along parallel surfaces.

slip. The actual amount of horizontal or vertical displacement across a fault.

stratigraphy. Pertaining to the stacking or sequence of deposition of sedimentary rocks. Multiple layers of sedimentary rock are called **strata**.

strike. Compass bearing of a horizontal line on the face of an inclined planar surface.

strike-slip fault. A fault along which the relative displacement is sideways rather than up or down; displacement is parallel to the fault's strike.

subduction zone. A type of convergent plate tectonic boundary where oceanic crust of one plate descends beneath another plate.

syenite. Intrusive igneous rock similar to granite but with less quartz and a predominance of orthoclase feldspar over plagioclase.

syncline. A downfold in layered rocks with younger beds toward the core, limbs inclined inward.

talus. Accumulation of coarse, angular blocks of rock at the base of a cliff or other steep bedrock slope.

tectonic. Pertaining to the deformation of the Earth's surface, including plate movements, due to internal Earth forces. See also **lithospheric plates**.

terrace. Steplike landform consisting of a flat tread and a steep riser, commonly shaped by the running water of rivers or the waves along the shores of lakes and oceans, and standing above the present river or coast.

thrust fault. A fault that dips less than 45 degrees, upon which the older, upper block of rocks moves up and above the younger rocks beneath the fault. Typically forms in crustal shortening.

tonalite. A plutonic igneous rock synonymous with quartz diorite and composed mostly of plagioclase feldspar and from 5 to 20 percent quartz. Tonalite grades into granodiorite as the alkali feldspar content increases.

transform fault. A plate tectonic boundary where two plates slide horizontally past one another.

Transverse Ranges. A geologic province of southern California with east-west structural grain, thus transverse to the prevailing north-northwest trend.

tufa. Rock composed mainly of calcium carbonate or silica deposited from water and found at spring sites and along shorelines of saline lakes.

tuff. A volcanic rock made mostly of consolidated pyroclastic volcanic ash and pumice.

turbidite. A sedimentary bed, or sandstone and shale interbeds, formed by deposition from a turbidity current, irrespective of water depth.

turbidity current. A dense slurry of sediment that moves down an underwater slope.

ultramafic rocks. Black to dark green igneous rocks, which are more mafic than basalt, consisting mainly of iron- and magnesium-rich minerals, such as hypersthene, pyroxene, and olivine. The mantle consists of ultramafic rocks, and most ultramafic rocks formed originally in the mantle.

unconformity. A surface of erosion and/or nondeposition separating younger deposits from underlying older rocks, and across which the rock record is missing.

vein. A sheetlike deposit of minerals in a fracture in a rock. Quartz and calcite are the most common vein minerals.

volcanic arc. An arcuate chain of volcanoes, usually in oceanic crust, that formed above an ocean floor subduction zone.

volcaniclastic. Pertaining to a clastic rock containing volcanic rock fragments in any proportion and without regard to origin or environment.

volcanic rock. Extrusive, fine-grained igneous rock, cooled and solidified after eruption onto the surface of the Earth. Opposite: plutonic rock.

water gap. A deep gorge or ravine cut through resistant rocks by a stream that existed prior to the uplift of land and is still flowing through it today.

weathering. The mechanical breakdown or chemical decomposition of rocks and minerals at the Earth's surface in response to atmospheric agents such as air and rain.

welded tuff. A glassy pyroclastic volcanic rock that has been hardened by the fusing together of its glass shards under the combined action of heat, weight of overlying rocks, and hot gases.

wind gap. A shallow notch or ravine in the crest or upper part of a ridge of resistant rocks. It may have been a former water gap or a pass that is not now occupied by a stream.

zircon. $ZrSiO_4$. A common accessory mineral, especially in siliceous igneous rocks, schist, and gneiss. It survives high-grade metamorphism, so it is a good mineral for determining radiometric ages of metamorphic rocks.

FURTHER READING
AND REFERENCES

Unless otherwise noted, geologic maps were obtained in 2013 from the California Geological Survey and modified with permission from a digital version of 2010 *Geologic Map of California,* originally compiled by C. W. Jennings (1977) and updated in 2010 by Carlos Gutierrez, William Bryant, George Saucedo, and Chris Wills. It can be downloaded in various formats from http://www.consrv.ca.gov/cgs/cgs_history/Pages/2010_geologicmap.aspx.

Regional Overviews of Southern California Geology

Bilham, R., and P. Williams. 1985. Sawtooth segmentation and deformation processes on the southern San Andreas fault, California. *Geophysical Research Letters* 12 (9): 557–60.

Fairbanks, H. W. 1907. The great earthquake rift of California. In *The California Earthquake of 1906,* ed. D. S. Jordan, p. 319–38. A. M. Robertson.

Glazner, A. F., J. D. Walker, and J. M. Bartley, eds. 2002. *Geologic Evolution of the Mojave Desert and Southwestern Basin and Range.* Geological Society of America Memoir 195.

Gutierrez, C., W. Bryant, G. Saucedo, and C. Wills. 2010. *Geologic Map of California.* Originally compiled by C. W. Jennings, 1977. California Geological Survey.

Hall, C. A., Jr. 2007. *Introduction to the Geology of Southern California and Its Native Plants.* University of California Press.

Harden, D. R. 2004. *California Geology,* 2nd ed. Pearson/Prentice Hall.

Hill, M. L., ed. 1987. *Centennial Field Guide, Volume I, Cordilleran Section of the Geological Society of America.* Geological Society of America.

Hill, M. L., and T. W. Dibblee, Jr. 1953. San Andreas, Garlock, and Big Pine faults, California: A study of the character, history, and tectonic significance of their displacements. *Geological Society of America Bulletin* 64 (4): 443–58.

Hough, S. E. 2004. *Finding Fault in California.* Mountain Press Publishing Company.

Irwin, W. P. 1990. Geology and plate-tectonic development. In *The San Andreas Fault System, California.* USGS Professional Paper 1515, ed. R. E. Wallace, p. 61–81.

Jahns, R. H., ed. 1954. *Geology of Southern California.* Bulletin 170, California Division of Mines and Geology.

Leighton, F. B. 1966. Landslides and hillside development. In *Engineering Geology in Southern California,* p. 149–200. Association of Engineering Geologists Special Publication.

Lung, R., and R. J. Proctor, eds. 1966. *Engineering Geology in Southern California.* Association of Engineering Geologists Los Angeles Section Special Publication.

Lynch, D. K. 2009. *Field Guide to the San Andreas Fault.* Thule Scientific.

Meldahl, K. H. 2011. *Rough-Hewn Land: A Geologic Journey from California to the Rocky Mountains.* University of California Press.

Mehldahl, K. H. 2015. *Surf, Sand, and Stone: How Waves, Earthquakes, and Other Forces Shape the Southern California Coast.* University of California Press.

Morton, D. M., and F. K. Miller, eds. 2014. *Peninsular Ranges Batholith, Baja California and Southern California.* Geological Society of American Memoir 211.

Muir, J. 1921. *The Mountains of California.* Century.

Murdoch, J., and R. W. Webb. 1956. *Minerals of California.* Bulletin 173, California Division of Mines and Geology.

Norris, R. M. 2003. *The Geology and Landscape of Santa Barbara County, California, and Its Offshore Islands.* Santa Barbara Museum of Natural History.

Norris, R. M., and R. W. Webb. 1990. *Geology of California,* 2nd ed. John Wiley & Sons.

Sharp, R. P., and A. F. Glazner. 1993. *Geology Underfoot in Southern California.* Mountain Press Publishing Company.

Stock, J. M., and K. V. Hodges. 1989. Pre-Pliocene extension around the Gulf of California and the transfer of Baja California to the Pacific Plate. *Tectonics* 8: 99–115.

Sylvester, A. G., and J. C. Crowell. 1989. *The San Andreas Transform Belt.* 28th International Geological Congress Field Trip Guidebook T309.

Yerkes, R. F., T. H. McCulloh, J. E. Schoellhamer, and J. G. Vedder. 1965. *Geology of the Los Angeles Basin, California: An Introduction.* USGS Professional Paper 420-A.

Mojave Desert

Burnett, J. L., and J. Brady. 1990. Cactus Gold Mine. *California Geology* 43 (4): 85–88.

Casebier, D. G. 1987. *Guide to the East Mojave Heritage Trail.* Tales of the Mojave Road Publishing Company.

Casebier, D. G. 2010. *Mojave Road Guide: An Adventure Through Time* 4th ed. Mojave Desert Heritage and Cultural Association.

Decker, B., and R. Decker. 2006. *Road Guide to Joshua Tree National Park.* Double Decker Press.

De Kehoe, J. 2007. *The Silence and the Sun.* Trails End Publishing Company.

Dillon, J. T., G. B. Haxel, and R. M. Tosdal. 1990. Structural evidence for northeastward movement on the Chocolate Mountains thrust, southeasternmost California. *Journal of Geophysical Research* 95 (B12): 19,954–19,971.

Dokka, R. K., et al. 1991. Aspects of the Mesozoic and Cenozoic geologic evolution of the Mojave Desert. In *Geological Excursions in Southern California and Mexico,* eds. M. J. Walawender and B. B. Hanan, p. 1–43. Guidebook, 1991 Annual Meeting, Geological Society of America, Department of Geological Sciences, San Diego State University.

Fackler-Adams, B. N., C. J. Busby, and J. M. Mattinson. 1997. Jurassic magmatism and sedimentation in the Palen Mountains, southeastern California: Implication for regional tectonic controls on the Mesozoic continental arc. *Geological Society of America Bulletin* 109: 1464–84.

Fife, D. L., and A. R. Brown, eds. 1980. *Geology and Mineral Wealth of the California Desert,* Dibblee Volume. South Coast Geological Society.

Force, E. R. 2001. *Eagle Mountain Mine: Geology of the Former Kaiser Steel Operation in Riverside County, California.* US Geological Society Open-File Report 01-237.

Frost, E. G., and D. L. Martin, eds. 1982. *Mesozoic-Cenozoic Tectonic Evolution of the Colorado River Region, California, Arizona, and Nevada.* Cordilleran Publishers.

Glazner, A. F., J. D. Walker, J. M. Bartley, J. M. Fletcher, M. W. Martin, E. R. Schermer, et. al. 1994. Reconstruction of the Mojave Block. In *Geological Investigations of an Active*

Margin, eds. S. F. McGill and T. M. Ross, p. 3–30. Geological Society of America Cordilleran Section Guidebook, San Bernardino County Museum Association.

Greely, R. 1990. Amboy, California. In *Volcanoes of North America: United States and Canada*, eds. C. A. Wood and J. Kienle, p. 243–45. Cambridge University Press.

Hamilton, W. 1987. Mesozoic geology and tectonics of the Big Maria Mountains region, southeastern California. In *Mesozoic Rocks of Southern Arizona and Adjacent Areas*, Arizona Geological Society Digest 18, p. 33–47.

Ingersoll, R. V., et al. 2014. Paleotectonics of a complex Miocene half graben formed above a detachment fault: The Diligencia Basin, Orocopia Mountains, southern California. *Lithosphere* 6 (3): 157–76.

Lancaster, N. 1994. Studies of Quaternary eolian deposits of the Mojave Desert, California. In *Geological Investigations of an Active Margin*, eds. S. F. McGill and T. M. Ross, p. 172–75. Geological Society of America Cordilleran Section Guidebook, San Bernardino County Museum Association.

Martin, M. W., A. F. Glazner, J. D. Walker, and E. R. Schermer. 1993. Evidence for right-lateral transfer faulting accommodating en echelon Miocene extension, Mojave Desert, California. *Geology* 21 (4): 355–58.

McKinney, C. R., and J. McKinney. 2004. *Mojave National Preserve, A Visitor's Guide*, 2nd ed. Olympus Press.

Miller, D. M., R. J. Miller, J. E. Nielsen, H. G. Wilshire, K. A. Howard, and P. Stone. 2007. Geologic map of the East Mojave National Scenic Area, California. In *Geology and Mineral Resources of the East Mojave National Scenic Area, San Bernardino County, California*, ed. T. G. Theodore. US Geological Survey MF 2414.

Orme, A. R. 2008. Lake Thompson, Mojave Desert, California: The late Pleistocene lake system and its Holocene desiccation. *GSA Special Papers* 439: 261–78.

Phillips, F. M. 2003. Cosmogenic ^{36}Cl ages of Quaternary basalt flows in the Mojave Desert, California, USA. *Geomorphology* 53: 199–208.

Rummelhart, P. E., and R. V. Ingersoll. 1997. Provenance of the upper Miocene Modelo Formation and subsidence analysis of the Los Angeles Basin, southern California: Implications for paleotectonic and paleogeographic reconstructions. *Geological Society of America Bulletin* 109 (7): 885–99.

Schmidt, R. J. 1996. *A Field Guide to Motion Picture Locations at Red Rock Canyon, Mojave Desert, California*. Canyon Two Publications.

Seiple, E. 1994. Plant and animal life of Pleistocene Lake Manix. *California Geology* 47 (2): 50–57.

Shreve, R. L. 1987. Blackhawk landslide, southwestern San Bernardino County, California. In *Centennial Field Guide, Volume I, Cordilleran Section of the Geological Society of America*, ed. M. L. Hill, p. 109–14.

Stone, P. 2006. *Geologic Map of the West Half of the Blythe 30′ by 60′ Quadrangle, Riverside County, California and La Paz County, Arizona*. US Geological Survey, Scientific Investigations Map SIM-2922, scale 1:100,000.

Stone, P., and M. M. Kelly. 1989. *Geologic Map of the Palen Pass Quadrangle, Riverside County, California*. USGS, Miscellaneous Field Studies Map MF-2070.

Trent, D. D. 2006. *Mines and Geology of the Randsburg Area*. San Diego Association of Geologists, Sunbelt Publications.

Trent, D. D., and R. W. Hazlett. 2002. *Joshua Tree National Park Geology*. Joshua Tree National Park Association.

Weber, F. H. 1976. Geology of the Calico Silver District, San Bernardino County, California. In *Geologic Guidebook to the Southwestern Mojave Desert Region, California*, ed. M. S. Woyski, p. 83–94. South Coast Geological Society Guidebook No. 4.

Wells, S. G., W. J. Brown, Y. Enzel, R. Y. Anderson, and L. D. McFadden. 1994. A brief summary of the Late Quaternary history of pluvial Lake Mojave, eastern California. In *Geological Investigations of an Active Margin*, eds. S. F. McGill and T. M. Ross, p. 182–88. Geological Society of America Cordilleran Section Guidebook, San Bernardino County Museum Association.

Wells, S. G., J. C. Tinsley, L. D. McFadden, and N. Lancaster. 1994. Quaternary stratigraphy and dating methods: Understanding geologic processes and landscape evolution in southern California. In *Geological Investigations of an Active Margin*, eds. S. F. McGill and T. M. Ross, p. 120–40. Geological Society of America Cordilleran Section Guidebook, San Bernardino County Museum Association.

Woyski, M. S., ed. 1976. *Geologic Guidebook to the Southwestern Mojave Desert Region, California*. South Coast Geological Society Guidebook No. 4.

Salton Trough

Abbott, P. L., D. R. Kerr, S. E. Borron, J. L. Washburn, and D. A. Rightmer. 2002. Neogene sturzstrom deposits, Split Mountain area, Anza-Borrego Desert State Park, California. *Reviews in Engineering Geology* 15: 379–400.

Baldwin, J., L. Lewis, M. Payne, and G. Roquemore, eds. 1997. *Southern San Andreas Fault: Whitewater to Bombay Beach, Salton Trough, California*. Field Trip Guidebook No. 25, South Coast Geological Society.

Bock, C. G. 1977. Martinez Mountain rock avalanche. *Reviews in Engineering Geology* 3: 155–68.

Crowell, J. C., and A. G. Sylvester, eds. 1979. *Tectonics of the Juncture between the San Andreas Fault System and the Salton Trough, Southeastern California*. Department of Geological Sciences, University of California, Santa Barbara.

Dorsey, R. J., A. Fluette, K. McDougall, B. A. Housen, S. U. Janecke, G. J. Axen, and C. R. Shirvell. 2007. Chronology of Miocene–Pliocene deposits at Split Mountain Gorge, southern California: A record of regional tectonics and Colorado River evolution. *Geology* 35 (1): 57–60.

Fattaruso, L. A., M. L. Cooke, and R. J. Dorsey. 2014. Sensitivity of uplift patterns to dip of the San Andreas fault in the Coachella Valley, California. *Geosphere* 10 (6): 1235–46.

Frost, E. G., L. Heizer, R. Blom, and R. Crippen. 1996. Western Salton Trough detachment system: Its geometric role in localizing the San Andreas system. In *The San Andreas Fault System: A guidebook for the 1996 Annual Meeting of the American Association of Petroleum Geologists Annual Meeting*, trip leader F. V. Corona, p. 163–78.

Guptill, P. D., R. W. Ruff, and E. M. Gath, eds. 1986. *Geology of the Imperial Valley, California*. Field Trip Guidebook No. 14, South Coast Geological Society.

Hudnut, K. W., L. Seeber, and J. Pacheco. 1989. Cross-fault triggering in the November 1987 Superstition Hills earthquake sequence, southern California. *Geophysical Research Letters* 16 (2): 199–202.

Hudnut, K. W., L. Seeber, J. Pacheco, J. Armbruster, L. Sykes, G. Bond, and M. Kominz. 1988. Cross faults and block rotation in southern California: Earthquake triggering and strain distribution. *Lamont Research Annual*: 44–49.

Massini, A., H. Svensen, G. Etiope, N. Onderdonk, and D. Banks. 2011. Fluid origin, gas fluxes, and plumbing system in the sediment-hosted Salton Sea geothermal system (California, USA). *Journal of Volcanology and Geothermal Research* 205 (3–4): 67–83.

Nicholson, C., L. Seeber, P. Williams, and L. R. Sykes. 1986. Seismic evidence for conjugate slip and block rotation within the San Andreas fault system, southern California. *Tectonics* 5 (4): 629–48.

Oskin, M., and J. Stock. 2003. Pacific–North American plate motion and opening of the Upper Delfín Basin, north Gulf of California, Mexico. *GSA Bulletin* 115 (10): 1173–90.

Sylvester, A. G. 1979. Earthquake damage in Imperial Valley, California, May 18, 1940, as reported by T. C. Clark. *Seismological Society of America Bulletin* 69 (2): 547–68.

Sylvester, A. G., and R. T. Clarke. 2012. *Rifting, Transpression, and Neotectonics of the Salton Trough, Southern California.* American Association of Petroleum Geologists and Society for Sedimentary Geology, 2012 AAPG/SEPM Annual Convention, Long Beach.

Sylvester, A. G., and R. R. Smith. 1976. Tectonic transpression and basement-controlled deformation in the San Andreas fault zone, Salton Trough, California. *American Association of Petroleum Geologists Bulletin* 60 (12): 1415–34.

Sweet, M. L., G. Kocurek, and K. Havholm. 1991. A field guide to the Algodones Dunes of southeastern California. In *Geological Excursions in Southern California and Mexico*, eds. M. J. Walawender and B. B. Hanan, p. 171–85. Guidebook, 1991 Annual Meeting, Geological Society of America, San Diego State University.

Peninsular Ranges

Abbott, P. L. 1999. *The Rise and Fall of San Diego.* Sunbelt Publications.

Abbott, P. L., and J. A. May. 1991. *Eocene Geologic History, San Diego Region.* Pacific Section of the Society of Economic Paleontologists and Mineralogists.

Birnbaum, B. B., and K. D. Cato, eds. 2000. *Geology and Enology of the Temecula Valley, Riverside County, California.* Sunbelt Publications.

Bonsangue, J., and R. Lemmer, eds. *Geology of the Orange County Region, Southern California.* Field Trip Guidebook No. 33, South Coast Geological Society.

Brown, J. D. Geologic Formations of Western San Diego County. http://www.geiconsultants.com. Accessed 23 April 2013.

Camacho, H., C. J. Busby, and B. Kneller. 2002. A new depositional model for the classical turbidite locality at San Clemente State Beach, California. *American Association of Petroleum Geologists Bulletin* 86 (9): 1543–60.

Clifford, H. J., F. W. Bergen, and S. G. Spear. 1997. *Geology of San Diego County: Legacy of the Land.* Sunbelt Publications.

Elliott, W. J. 1987. The Silver Strand: A unique tombolo, San Diego, California. In *Centennial Field Guide, Volume 1, Cordilleran Section of the Geological Society of America*, ed. M. L. Hill, p. 169–70. Geological Society of America.

Gastil, R. G., and R. H. Miller, eds. 1993. *The Prebatholithic Stratigraphy of Peninsular California.* Geological Society of America Special Paper 279.

Germinario, M. 1993. The early Mesozoic Julian Schist, Julian, California. In *The Prebatholithic Stratigraphy of Peninsular California.* Geological Society of American Special Paper 279, eds. R. G. Gastil and R. H. Miller, p. 107–18.

Grine, D. 2014. Geology of Torrey Pines State Reserve. http://www.torreypine.org/geology. Accessed 11 February 2014.

Hertlein, L. G., and U. S. Grant. 1944. *The Geology and Paleontology of the Marine Plio-cene of San Diego, California.* San Diego Society of Natural History Memoir 2.

Imlay, R. W. 1963. Jurassic fossils from southern California. *Journal of Paleontology* 37 (1): 97–107.

Kimbrough, D. L., D. P. Smith, J. B. Mahoney, T. E. Moore, M. Grove, R. G. Gastil, A. Ortega-Rivera, and D. M. Fanning. 2001. Forearc-basin sedimentary response to rapid Late Cretaceous batholith emplacement in the Peninsular Ranges of southern and Baja California. *Geology* 29 (6): 491–94.

Kuhn, G. G., and F. P. Shepard. 1984. *Sea Cliffs, Beaches, and Coastal Valleys of San Diego County: Some Amazing Histories and Some Horrifying Implications.* University of California Press.

Lindsay, L., and D. Lindsay. 2006. *The Anza-Borrego Desert Region: A Guide to the State Park and Adjacent Areas of the Western Colorado Desert.* Wilderness Press.

Morton, J. B., ed. 2014. *Coast to Cactus: Geology and Tectonics, San Diego to Salton Trough, California.* San Diego Geological Society.

Remeika, P., and L. Lindsay. 1992. *Geology of Anza-Borrego: Edge of Creation.* Sunbelt Publications.

Shlemon, R. J. 1987. The Christianitos fault and Quaternary geology, San Onofre State Beach, California. In *Centennial Field Guide, Volume I, Cordilleran Section of the Geological Society of America*, ed. M. L. Hill, p. 171–74. Geological Society of America.

Todd, V. R. 2004. *Preliminary Geologic Map of the El Cajon 30′ x 60′ Quadrangle, Southern California.* US Geological Survey Open-File Report 2004-1361, scale: 1:100,000.

Walawender, M. J. 2000. *The Peninsular Ranges: A Geological Guide to San Diego's Back Country.* Kendall/Hunt Publishing Company.

Walawender, M. J., and B. B. Hanan, eds. 1991. *Geological Excursions in Southern California and Mexico.* Department of Geological Sciences, San Diego State University.

Woodford, A. O., R. A. Crippen, and K. B. Garner. 1941. Section across Commercial Quarry, Crestmore, California. *American Mineralogist* 26: 351–81.

Woyski, M. S., and A. H. Howard. 1987. A section through the Peninsular Ranges Batholith, Elsinore Mountains, southern California. In *Centennial Field Guide, Vol. I, Cordilleran Section of the Geological Society of America*, ed. M. L. Hill, p. 185–90.

Los Angeles Basin

Bjorklund, T., K. Burke, H. Zhou, and R. S. Yeats. 2002. Miocene rifting in the Los Angeles basin: Evidence from the Puente Hills half-graben, volcanic rocks, and P-wave tomography. *Geology* 30 (5): 451–54.

Crouch, J. K., and J. Suppe. 1993. Late Cenozoic tectonic evolution of the Los Angeles Basin and inner California borderland: A model for core complex–like crustal extension. *Geological Society of America Bulletin* 105 (11): 1415–34.

Dibblee, T. W., Jr. 1999. *Geologic Map of the Palos Verdes Peninsula and Vicinity, Redondo Beach, Torrance, and San Pedro Quadrangles, Los Angeles County, California.* Dibblee Geological Foundation Map DF-70, scale 1:24,000.

Dolan, J. F., K. Sieh, T. K. Rockwell, P. Guptill, and G. Miller. 1997. Active tectonics, paleoseismology, and seismic hazards of the Hollywood fault, northern Los Angeles Basin, California. *Geological Society of America Bulletin* 109: 1595–1616.

Dolan, J. F., D. Stevens, and T. K. Rockwell. 2000. Paleoseismologic evidence for an early to mid-Holocene age of the most recent surface rupture on the Hollywood fault, Los Angeles, California. *Bulletin of the Seismological Society of America* 90 (2): 334–44.

Higgins, J. W., ed. 1958. *A Guide to the Geology and Oil Fields of the Los Angeles and Ventura Regions.* Pacific Section American Association of Petroleum Geologists.

Hill, Merton. 2013. Crystal Cove State Park Beach Geology. http://www.everytrail.com/guide/crystal-cove-state-park-beach-geology. Accessed 13 December 2013.

McCullough, T. H., R. J. Fleck, R. E. Denison, L. A. Beyer, and R. G. Stanley. 2002. *Age and Tectonic Significance of Volcanic Rocks in the Northern Los Angeles Basin, California.* US Geological Survey Professional Paper 1669.

Merriam, R. 1960. Portuguese Bend landslide, Palos Verdes Hills, California. *Journal of Geology* 68 (2): 140–53.

Miller, G. A., and R. Bielefeld, eds. 1974. *Guidebook to Selected Features of Palos Verdes Peninsula and Long Beach, California.* South Coast Geological Society Field Trip Guidebook No. 3.

Sharp, R. P., and L. H. Nobles. 1953. Mudflow of 1941 at Wrightwood, southern California. *Geological Society of America Bulletin* 53 (5): 547–60.

Stille, H. 1935. *Der Derzeitige Tektonische Erdzustand.* Preussische Akademie der Wissenshaften.

Stille, H. 1938. The present tectonic state of the earth. *American Association of Petroleum Geologists Bulletin* 20 (7): 849–80.

Stout, M. L. 1972. Regional geomorphology of San Juan Capistrano–Laguna Niguel area. In *Geologic Guidebook to the Northern Peninsular Ranges, Orange and Riverside Counties, California,* ed. P. K. Morton, p. 85–91. South Coast Geological Society.

Tsutsumi, H., R. S. Yeats, and G. J. Huftile. 2001. Late Cenozoic tectonics of the northern Los Angeles fault system, California. *GSA Bulletin* 113 (4): 454–68.

Weaver, K. D., and J. F. Dolan. 2000. Paleoseismology and geomorphology of the Raymond fault, Los Angeles County, California. *Bulletin of the Seismological Society of America* 90: 1409–29.

Wright, T. L. 1991. Structural geology and tectonic evolution of the Los Angeles Basin, California. In *Active Margin Basins,* ed. K. T. Biddle, p. 35–134. AAPG Memoir 52.

Yerkes, R. F., T. H. McCulloh, J. E. Schoellhamer, and J. G. Vedder. 1965. *Geology of the Los Angeles Basin, California: An Introduction.* USGS Professional Paper 420.

Transverse Ranges

Barth, A. P., and P. L. Ehlig. 1989. Geology of Mesozoic plutonic rocks, central and western San Gabriel Mountains, Southern California. In *Geologic Excursions in the Greater Los Angeles Area,* ed. L. G. Collins, p. 20–37. Far Western Section, National Association of Geology Teachers Spring Conference Guidebook, April 21–23, 1989.

Blakley, E. R. 2004. *A Traveler's Guide to California's Scenic Highway 33 from Ojai to Cuyama.* Shoreline Press.

Brown, G. C., and A. G. Sylvester. 1980. *Geologic Field Guide of Santa Maria Basin and Western Transverse Range.* Unpublished Guidebook for the Triton Energy Corp.

Brown, H. 2008. High brightness, high purity limestone and cement grade limestones in the San Bernardino Mountains of southern California, updated geology, genesis, and mining. In *Geology and Hydrology of the Big Bear Valley and San Bernardino*

Mountains, Transverse Ranges, California, eds. T. Devine and V. Talbott, p. 359–70. South Coast Geological Society Field Trip Guidebook No. 35.

Crowell, J. C., ed. 2003. *Evolution of Ridge Basin, Southern California: An Interplay of Sedimentation and Tectonics.* Geological Society of American Special Paper 367.

Crowell, J. C., and M. H. Link, eds. 1982. *Geologic History of Ridge Basin, Southern California.* Pacific Section Society of Economic Paleontologists and Mineralogists.

Devine, T., and V. Talbot, eds. 2008. *Geology and Hydrology of the Big Bear Valley and San Bernardino Mountains, Transverse Ranges, California.* Field Trip Guidebook No. 35, South Coast Geological Society.

Dibblee, T. W., Jr. 1966. *Geology of the Central Santa Ynez Mountains, Santa Barbara, County, California.* Bulletin 186, California Division of Mines and Geology.

Dibblee, T. W., Jr. 2006. *Geologic Map of the Frazier Mountain and Lebec Quadrangles, Los Angeles and Ventura Counties, California.* Dibblee Geological Foundation Map DF-198, scale 1:24,000.

Ehlig, P. L. 1981. Origin and tectonic history of the basement terrane of the San Gabriel Mountains, central Transverse Ranges. In *The Geotectonic Development of California: Rubey Volume*, ed. W. G. Ernst, p. 253–83. Prentice-Hall.

Fife, D. L., and J. A. Minch, eds. 1983. *Geology and Mineral Wealth of the California Transverse Ranges, Mason Hill Volume.* South Coast Geological Society.

Hendrix, E. D., R. B. Cole, and R. V. Ingersoll. 2010. Soledad and Plush Ranch Basins: mid-Tertiary extensional terrane dismembered by the San Andreas fault system. In *Geologic Excursions in California and Nevada: Tectonics, Stratigraphy and Hydrology*, eds. H. E. Clifton and R. V. Ingersoll, p. 103–71. The Pacific Section Society for Sedimentary Geology, Book 108.

Higgins, J. W., ed. 1958. *A Guide to the Geology and Oil Fields of the Los Angeles and Ventura Regions.* Pacific Section American Association of Petroleum Geologists.

Hitchcock, C. S., and C. J. Wills. 2000. *Quaternary Geology of the San Fernando Valley, Los Angeles County, California.* California Division of Mines and Geology Map Sheet 50, scale 1:48,000.

Hopps, T. E., H. E. Stark, and R. J. Hindle. 1992. Subsurface geology of Ventura Basin, California. *Ventura Basin Study Group Report.* Rancho Energy Consultants.

Jackson, P. A., and R. S. Yeats. 1982. Structural evolution of Carpinteria Basin, western Transverse Ranges, California. *AAPG Bulletin* 66 (7): 805–29.

Kerr, P. F., and H. G. Schenck. 1928. Significance of the Matilija overturn, Santa Ynez Mountains, California. *Geological Society of America Bulletin* 39 (4): 1087–1102.

Langenheim, V. E., T. L. Wright, D. A. Okaya, R. S. Yeats, G. S. Fuis, K. Thygesen, and H. Thybo. 2011. Structure of the San Fernando Valley region, California: Implications for seismic hazard and tectonic history. *Geosphere* 7 (2): 528–72.

Lentz, J. E. 2013. *A Naturalist's Guide to the Santa Barbara Region.* Heyday Press.

Matthews, Vincent, III. 1973. Pinnacles-Neenach correlation: A restriction for models of the origin of the Transverse Ranges and the big bend in the San Andreas fault. *Geological Society of America Bulletin* 84 (2): 683–88.

Matthews, Vincent, III. 1976. Correlation of Pinnacles and Neenach volcanic formations and their bearing on San Andreas fault problems. *American Association of Petroleum Geologists Bulletin 60 (12): 2128–41.*

McCulloh, T. H., R. J. Fleck, R. E. Denison, L. A. Beyer, R. G. Stanley. 2002. *Age and Tectonic Significance of Volcanic Rocks in the Northern Los Angeles Basin, California.* US Geological Survey Professional Paper 1669.

Meisling, K. E., and R. J. Weldon. 1989. Late Cenozoic tectonics of the northwestern San Bernardino Mountains, southern California. *GSA Bulletin* 101 (1): 106–28.

Miller, W. J. 1934. Geology of the San Gabriel Mountains of California. *University of California Publications in Mathematical and Physical Sciences* 1: 1–114.

Nicholson, C., M. J. Kamerling, C. C. Sorlien, T. E. Hopps, and J. P. Gratier. 2007. Subsidence, compaction, and gravity sliding: Implications for 3D geometry, dynamic rupture, and seismic hazard of active basin-bounding faults in southern California. *Bulletin of the Seismological Society of America* 97 (5): 1607–20.

Nicholson, C., C. C. Sorlien, T. Atwater, J. C. Crowell, and B. P. Luyendyk. 1994. Microplate capture, rotation of the western Transverse Ranges, and initiation of the San Andreas transform as a low-angle fault system. *Geology* 22 (6): 491–95.

Norris, R. M. 2003. *The Geology and Landscape of Santa Barbara County, California, and Its Offshore Islands.* Santa Barbara Museum of Natural History.

Putnam, W. C. 1942. Geomorphology of the Ventura region, California. *California Geological Society of America Bulletin* 53 (5): 691–754.

Sadler, P. M., and A. Demirer. 1986. Pelona Schist in the Cenozoic of the San Bernardino Mountains, southern California. In *Neotectonics and Faulting in Southern California,* compiler P. L. Ehlig, p. 129–46. 82nd Cordilleran Meeting, GSA.

Sadler, P. M., A. Demirer, D. West, and J. M. Hillenbrand. 1993. The Mill Creek Basin, the Potato Sandstone, and fault strands in the San Andreas fault zone south of the San Bernardino Mountains. In *The San Andreas Fault System: Displacement, Palinspastic Reconstruction, and Geologic Evolution,* eds. R. F. Powell, R. J. Weldon, II, and J. C. Matti, p. 289–306. Geological Society of America Memoir 178.

Saint, P., M. Herzberg, and B. Zaprianoff, eds. 2010. *Geology and Hydrology in the Eastern San Gabriel Mountains Through the River of Time.* Field Trip Guidebook No. 36, South Coast Geological Society.

Stout, M. L. 2008. Barton Flats landslide. In *Geology and Hydrology of the Big Bear Valley and San Bernardino Mountains, Transverse Ranges, California,* eds. T. Devine and V. Talbott, p. 357–58. South Coast Geological Society Field Trip Guidebook No. 35.

Sylvester, A. G., and G. C. Brown, eds. 1988. *Santa Barbara and Ventura Basins, Tectonics, Structure, Sedimentation, Oilfields along an East-West Transect.* Coast Geological Society Guidebook 64.

Sylvester, A. G., and S. H. Mendes. 2011. *A Case Study of Earthquake Damage and Repair: The Santa Barbara Earthquake of 1925.* Prepared for the Network for Earthquake Engineering Simulation (NEES) Young Researchers, August 20, 2011, and the Fourth Symposium on Effects of Surface Geology on Ground Motion, August 27, 2011.

Trent, D. D., and R. W. Hazlett. 2002. *Joshua Tree National Park Geology.* Joshua Tree National Park Association.

US Geological Survey. 1987. *Recent Reverse Faulting in the Transverse Ranges, California.* US Geological Survey Professional Paper 1339.

Vaughn, F. E. 1922. Geology of San Bernardino Mountains north of San Gorgonio Pass. *Bulletin of the Department of Geological Sciences* 13 (9): 319–411.

Weigand, P. W., A. P. Barth, and P. L. Ehlig. 1989. Field trip guide to a portion of the western San Gabriel Mountains, Los Angeles County, California. In *Geologic Excursions in the Greater Los Angeles Area*, ed. L. G. Collins, p. 38–44. Far Western Section, National Association of Geology Teachers Spring Conference Guidebook, April 21-23, 1989.

Woodring, W. P., and M. N. Bramlette. 1950. *Geology and Paleontology of the Santa Maria District, California.* US Geological Survey Professional Paper 222.

Yeats, R. S. 1978. Large-scale Quaternary detachments in Ventura basin, southern California. *Journal of Geophysical Research: Solid Earth* 88 (B1): 569–83.

Yeats, R. S. 2004. Tectonics of the San Gabriel Basin and surroundings, southern California. *Geological Society of America Bulletin* 116 (9–10): 1158–82.

Yeats, R. S., and F. B. Grigsby. 1987. Ventura anticline: Amphitheater locality, California. In *Decade of North American Geology Centennial Field Guide*, Volume I, ed. M. L. Hill, p. 219–23, Geological Society of America.

Yerkes, R. F., and R. H. Campbell. 1980. *Geologic Map of East-Central Santa Monica Mountains, Los Angeles County, California,* scale 1:24,000.

Yerkes, R. F., and S. E. Graham, compilers. 1997. *Preliminary Geologic Map of the Beverly Hills 7. 5′ Quadrangle, Southern California: A Digital Database.* US Geological Survey Open-File Report 97-430.

Yule, D., and J. Spotila. 2010. Quaternary geology of the San Bernardino Mountains and their tectonic margins. In *Geologic Excursions in California and Nevada: Tectonics, Stratigraphy, and Hydrology*, eds. H. E. Clifton and R. V. Ingersoll, p. 273–322. Pacific Section Society for Sedimentary Geology Book 108.

Channel Islands

Dibblee, T. F. W., Jr. 2001. *Geologic Map of East Santa Cruz Island, Santa Barbara, California.* Dibblee Geological Foundation Map DF-78, Santa Cruz Island Foundation Occasional Map 5, Part B, scale 1:24,000.

Dibblee, T. F. W., Jr. 2001. *Geologic Map of West Santa Cruz Island, Santa Barbara, California.* Dibblee Geological Foundation Map DF-77, Santa Cruz Island Foundation Occasional Map 5, Part A, scale 1:24,000.

Dibblee, T. F. W., Jr., J. J. Woolley, and H. E. Ehrenspeck. 1998. *Geologic Map of Santa Rosa Island, Santa Barbara, California.* Dibblee Geological Foundation Map DF-68, Santa Cruz Island Foundation Occasional Map 2, scale 1:24,000.

Gleason, D. 1958. *The Islands and Ports of California: A Guide to Coastal California.* Devin-Adair Company.

Kamerling, M. J., and B. P. Luyendyk, 1985. Paleomagnetism and Neogene tectonics of the northern Channel Islands, California. *Journal of Geophysical Research: Solid Earth* 90 (B14): 12,485–502.

Lamb, S. 2000. *Channel Islands National Park.* Western National Parks Association.

Legg, M. R., P. Davis, and E. Gath, eds. 2004. *Geology and Tectonics of Santa Catalina Island and the California Continental Borderland.* South Coast Geological Society Field Trip Guidebook No. 32.

Norris, R. M. 1995. Little Anacapa Island. *California Geology* 48 (1): 3–9.

Norris, R. M. 2003. *The Geology and Landscape of Santa Barbara County, California, and Its Offshore Islands.* Santa Barbara Museum of Natural History.

Weaver, D. W., D. P. Doerner, and B. Nolf, eds. 1969. *Geology of the Northern Channel Islands.* Pacific Section, AAPG/SEPM Special Publication.

Weigand, P. W., ed. 1998. *Contributions to the Geology of the Channel Islands, Southern California.* Pacific Section AAPG, Miscel-laneous Publication 45.

INDEX

Page numbers in bold indicate photographs.

aa lava, 62, 67
Abalone Cove landslide, 223
accretionary wedge, 6, 14
actinolite, 152, **303**
Afton Canyon, 49, 50–52, 95
agates, 78, 86
Agoura, 264
Agua Hedionda, 168
alabaster, 128
Alamitos Heights, 209
Alamitos No. 1, 207
Alamo River, 105, 130
Alberhill, 193
albite, 116, 156
Alegria Formation, 226
Algodones Dunes, 109, 110–11, **111**, 130–31
Alisitos volcanic arc, 154
alkali feldspar, 3, 300
All American Canal, 130, 150
alluvial fans, 8, **9**, 141; coalescing, 48, 103, 183, 250; deposits of, 110, 114, 115, 123, 125, **125**, **126**, 182; displaced, 246–47; dissected, 48, 63, 249; of Eocene time, 165–66; gravel pits in, 42, 251; headward erosion of, 247; infiltration of water in, 183; interfingering with lakebeds, 53, 108, 110; sand from, 37, 91, 110, 137; from San Bernardino Mountains, 330; from San Gabriel Mountains, 41, 180, 246, 249, 251, 298
alluvium, 9, **24**, **76**, **171**
Alpine pluton, 173–74, **175**
Alpine Village, 142
aluminum oxide, 253
aluminum silicate, 132, 173
Amargosa River, 41, 49
Amboy, 61, 67
Amboy Crater, 66–68
amphibolite, 12, 15, 73, 74, 214, 229, 343, 344
Anacapa Island, 337, 341–42, **342**
Anaverde Formation, **310**, 311
andalusite, 156

andesite: basaltic, 17, 27, 308, 341, 344; breccia, 49, 50; of Cretaceous time, 156; dikes of, 132; lava flows of, 62, 74, 179, 255, 307; mineralization with, 48; of Miocene time, x, 17, 61, 62, 180, 220, 227, 239, 289, 341, 344, 345; pebbles of, 307, 339
Angeles Crest Highway, 296
Angeles Forest Highway, 298, 299
angular unconformity, 114, **115**
Anita Formation, 226
anorthosite, x, 37, 121, 229, 300
Antelope Valley, 25, 34, 77, 84, 309
Antelope Valley California Poppy Reserve, 34, 77
Antelope Valley Freeway, 305
anticlines, **23**, **333**; currently forming, 44, 104, 137, 211, 232, 311; crystalline core of, 37, 222; en echelon, 232, 335; faulted, 260, 266, **333**, 345; in Mecca Hills, 115, **116**, 119, **119**, 120; oil in, 207, 209, 232, 268, 269, 270, 271, 275, 276, 313–14, 331; in Split Mountain Gorge, 124, 125, **127**; in turbidites, 285, 292
anticlinoriums, 227, 268–70, 271, 313
Anza–Borrego Desert State Park, 199
Apache Canyon, 320
apatite, 230
aplite dikes, **32**, 33. *See also* dikes, felsic
aqueducts, 79, 83, 130, 236, 243, 262, **262**, 309
aragonite, 256
Ararat, Mt., 186
Arcadia, 255
Arch Rock, 342
Arguello, Point, 269
Arica Mountains, 92
Arroyo Burro Beach, 281
Arroyo Parida fault, 267, 278
Arroyo Seco, 250, 298
Arroyo Trabuco, 214
Arthur B. Ripley Desert State Park, 34
ash-flow tuff, 81. *See also* tuff
ash. *See* volcanic ash

asphalt, 212, 273
asteroid, 339
Atchison, Topeka & Santa Fe Railroad, 44, 63, 64
Atolia granodiorite, 87
autunite, 86
Aztec Sandstone, 73
Azucar Mine, 61

Baden-Powell, Mt., 15, 302
badlands, 51, 127, 128, 139, 167, 318
Baja California, 17, 105, 155, 157, 177
bajada, 9, 246
Baker, 41, 53, 54, 97
Baker Hill, 54
Balboa Peninsula, 220, 221
Baldwin Gneiss, 103, 328
Baldwin Hills, 207–8
Baldwin Lake, 327
Ballena River, 20, 158, 159, 174, 185
Ballona Creek, 211
Banner Canyon, 194, 196–97, **197**
Banning fault, 89, 106, 108, 135, 139, 140
Banning Pass, 105
Bardsdale, 334
Barstow, 27, 39, 44, 46, 61, 69
Barstow anticline, 44
Barton Flats, 322, 325, 326
basalt, 3; columnar jointed, 218, 219, **220**; of Cretaceous age, 156; cobbles of, 307; crystals in, 67; dike and sills of, 216, 218, 263; of Holocene age, 61, 62, 66; lava flows of, **54**, **99**; metamorphosed, 4, 14, **31**, 303, **303**; of Miocene age, 28, 61, 74, 77, 84, 99, 180, 189, 216, 227, 263, 289, 345; of ocean floor, 6, 14, 230; of Oligocene age, x, 306; olivine in, 81, 99, **99**; pillows of, 6, 227, 343; of Pleistocene age, x, 54, **54**, 59, 66, 97; of Pliocene age, 85, 101
basaltic andesite, 17, 27, 308, 341, 344
Basin and Range, x, 17, 25, 28
bastnaesite, 58
Bat Caves Buttes, 151
batholiths, 13–14, 27; erosion surface on, 155, 158, 160, 177, **177**, 185. See also Peninsular Ranges Batholith; Sierra Nevada Batholith
Batiquitos lagoon, 168
Bay Point Formation, 162, 167, **167**
beach bars, 50, **51**, 97, 164
Bear Valley, 327, 328
Beaumont, 133
Bedford Canyon Formation, x, 156, 186, 189, 193

Beechers Bay Formation, 339
Bell Mountain, 43, **43**
Bell Mountain Wash, 42
Benedict Canyon fault, 203, 256, 264
bentonite, 62
Berdoo Canyon, 33
Bernardo Mountain, 186
beryl, 156, 188
Beverly Glen, 210
Big Bear City, 101, 327
Big Bear Lake, 328
Big Bear plateau, 325
Big Bend, 21, 225, 241, 242, 320
Bigelow Cholla Garden Wilderness, 64
Big Maria Mountains, 38, 72–73, **73**
Big Morongo Canyon Preserve, 90
Big Pine fault, 319–20
Big Pines, 302
Big Rock Beach, 290, 291
Big Sycamore Canyon, 292
Big Tujunga Canyon, 298
biotite: in dacite, 46; in diorite, 230; in gneiss, 12, 31, 90, 92, 120, 146; in granitic rock, 61, 156, 173, **174**, 175, 176, 177, 179, 299, 300; oxidized, 308; in schist, 3, 52, 141, 327
Bishop Ash, 112, 189, 270, 313
Black Butte, 61
Blackhawk landslide, 101–3, **102**
Black Hill, 99
Black Lava Butte, 99
Black Mountain, 186
Blue Cut, 243–46, **245**
Blue Cut fault, 33, 90
Blue Ridge, 302, 303
blueschist, 291, 343, 344
Blythe, 37
Blythe intaglios, 70–71, **72**
Bolsa Chica Lagoon, 222
Bombay Beach, 106, 149–50
borate (borax), 63, 83, 85–86
boron, 188
Boron, 86
Borrego Mountain, 199
Borrego Springs, 158
Boulder Bay, 328
boulder-pile topography, 10–11, **10**, 31, **32**, 92, 99, 179, 188, 195
Box Canyon, 113–18, 157
brachiopods, 330
braided stream deposits, 110, 124, **125**, **126**
Brawley, 144, 146
Brawley Seismic Zone, 106, 107, 150, 151
breccia: debris flow, 233, 307; fault, 74, 87, 292; landslide, 74, 101, 125, **127**,

180; sedimentary, 33, 120, 214, 233, 291, 296, **298**, 322; tuff, 61, 77, 84, 308; volcanic, 47, 49, 50, 53, 62, 74, 77, 84, 152, 156, 239, 264, **265**, 266, 344. *See also* San Onofre Breccia; Violin Breccia
Brentwood, 256
Bridge Pool, 331
Bristol Lake playa, 66, 68
Bristol Mountains, **24**, 68
Brown Butte, 84
Buckhorn Campground, 301
Buckhorn Lake playa, 77
Buellton, 285
Buena Vista lagoon, 168
Bullion fault, 63
Bullion Mountains, 62
Bunker Hill dike, 243
Buried Mountain, 34
burrows, 236, 328
Buzzard Peak, 46, **46**

Cabazon, 133, 135
Cabezon Formation, 135, 137
Cable Canyon, 243
Cabrillo Formation, 162
Cabrillo National Monument, 165
Cactus Mine, 78
Cadiz Lake playa, 91
Cadiz Summit, 68
Cadiz Valley, 91, **91**
Cady Mountains, 50, 62
Cahuenga Pass, 210, 263–64
Cahuilla, Lake, 109–10, 123, 142–44, **143**, 149, 150, 151
Cajon Creek, 243, 244, 246, 247
Cajon Formation, 244, 245, 246, **247**
Cajon Pass, 238, 242, 244
Cajon Summit, 39, 41, 246–47
Calabasas Formation, 289
calcite, 87, 95, 132, 219, 281, 328
calcium silicate, 132, 137
caldera, 78, 101, 270
Calexico, 130, 144, 145
caliche, 338
Calico, 47–48
Calico Early Man Site, 48
Calico fault, 27, 47, 48, 61
Calico Mountains, 46–47
Caliente Formation, 320
California Aqueduct, 236, 243, 309
California Condor Reserve, 333
California Oil Museum, 331
California Route 66 Museum, 64
California Star Oil Works, 232

californite, 182
Calipatria, 147
Calumet Mountains, 91
Camarillo, 266
Camarillo Hills, 266
camels, 273
Camp Pajarito, 301
Camp Pendleton training center, 169–70
Camp Pendleton terrace, 169–70
Capistrano Bay, 217
Capistrano Formation, 214, 216, 217, **217**
carbonate, 4, 37, 95, 96, 104, 143, 146, 256
carbonatites, x, 57, 58
carbon dioxide, 146, 149
Cargo Muchacho gold district, 146
Cargo Muchacho Mountains, 132–33
Carlsbad, 167, 168
Carpinteria, 273, 274
Carpinteria Basin, 274, 276
Carpinteria fault, 273, 274, 276
Carpinteria Oil Seeps, 273
Carpinteria Salt Marsh, 274–75, **275**
Carrara Formation, 330
Carrizo Creek, 178
Carrizo Gorge, 177
Cascade Canyon, 253
Cascade oil field, 231
Casitas Formation, 226, 277
Casitas Springs, 314
cassiterite, 95
Castac Lake, 241
Castaic, 233
Castaic Formation, 234
Castaic Creek, 335
Castaic Hills oil field, 232
Castle Butte, 84
Catalina Island, 216
Catalina pluton, 344
Catalina Schist, x, 14, 201, 203, 209, 214, 215, 216, 222, 343
Cave Mountain, 52, **52**, 95
caves, 62, 124, 339, 340, 342
cement industry, 42, 83, 156, 182, 328, **329**
Cenozoic time, x, 16–20
chalcedony, 78
chalcopyrite, 95
Chalk Hills, 264
Chambless, 68
Chambless Limestone, 68
Channel Islands, 2, 17, 20, 159, 165, 225, 337–45
Channel Islands National Park, 337, 339, 340, 342
channels, submarine, **217**
Chemehuevi Mountains, 74, **76**

Chemehuevi Valley, 74
Cherry Hill fault, 206
chert, 14, 62, 204, 219, 281
Chilao Flat, 301
Chino Basin, 194
Chino Canyon, 137
Chino fault, 157, 194
Chino Hills, 180
Chiriaco fault, 34, 90
Chiriaco Summit, 36
chlorite, 74, 116, 120, 132
Chocolate Mountains, 15, 133, 146, 150
cholla, **30**, 64
Chuckwalla Complex, 114
Chuckwalla Mountains, 37
Chuckwalla Valley, 37
Chumash Indians, 273, 293
Cienaga Seca Flat, **327**
Cigarette Hills, 197
Cima Dome, 56–57, **57**
Cima volcanic field, 97
Cinder Cone National Natural Land-
    mark, 95, 97
cinder cones, 61, 62, 66, 97, **97**
cirques, 327
clams, 53, **294**
Claremont, 251
Clark Mountain, 57
Clarks Pass, 91
clasts, 4, 42, 141, 158, 322
clay, 85, 103, 123, 127, 186, 193, 219, 270,
    320; in alluvium, 258, 292; expansion
    of, 275; along faults, 119, 241, 310; in
    shale, 180, 226, 318
claystone, 114, 137, 156, 226, 264, 307,
    339, 343, 344, 345
Clear Creek Canyon, 298, 299
Clear Creek Ranger Station, 299
Clearwater fault, 236
climate: arid, 9, 12, 84, 141; in Miocene
    time, 204–5; in Pleistocene time, 48, 141
climbing dunes, 52, 53
clinopyroxene, 97
Clipper Mountains, 69
Cloudburst Summit, 301
Coachella, 140, 141
Coachella Canal, 113
Coachella Valley, 33, 105, 107, 113, 133,
    136, 138, 141
Coachella Valley–Banning fault, 106, 108,
    135, 139, 140
coal, 193
Coal Canyon Formation, 289
coastal terraces. See terraces, coastal
Coast Ranges, 14

coccoliths, 281
Coldwater Canyon, 210
Coldwater Sandstone, 226, 280
Colorado Desert, 2, 8, 25, 105
Colorado River, 17, 22, 72, 105, 108, 109,
    110, 113, 130, 131, 133, 144, 146, 192
Colorado River Extensional Corridor,
    70, 74
Colton, 182
columnar jointing, 46, 218, 219, 264, **265**
Conception, Point, 269
concretions, 219
Condor Sandstone, 333
Conejo Grade, 264–66
Conejo Mountain, 264
Conejo oil field, 266
Conejo Volcanics, 17, 227–28, **228**,
    264–66, **265**, 287, 289, 341; dikes of,
    293, 295; iron in, 292; oil below, 295
Confusion Hill, 306
conglomerate, 4, 226; of alluvial fans,
    108, 114; of Cretaceous age, 37, **164**,
    314; of Eocene age, 337, **338**, 345; of
    Miocene age, 74, 77, 120, 218, 307, 320,
    339; oil in, 273; of Pleistocene age, 165,
    270, 271, **305**; of Pliocene age, 180,
    183, 236, 305; of stream deposits, 235,
    251, 285, 291, 296, **307**, 308, 318. See
    also Ocotillo Conglomerate; Poway
    Conglomerate; Stadium Conglomerate
Continental Borderland, 2, 337
continental shelf, x, 13, 87, 92, 95, 156,
    160, 221, 228
copper, 92, 132
corals, 54
cordierite, 156
core-stones, 10–11, 174, **175**, 188
Corona, 183, 193, 220
Corona Del Mar, 220, 221
Coronado Island, 164
Coronado Islands, 165
corundum, 253
Cottonwood Mountains, 34
Cottonwood Springs, 31
Cottonwood Valley, 176
Covina, 182
Cowles Mountain, 173
Coxcomb Mountains, 91
Coyote Mountains, 130
Cozy Dell Shale, 226, **286**, 287, 316, 318,
    318, 319, 339, 341
Crafton Hills, 183
Crescenta Valley, 250
Crespi, Juan, 183
Crestmore, 182

crestmoreite, 182
Crestwood, 177, 179
crinoids, 330
Cristianitos fault, 170–71, **171**
Cronise Lake, 52
Cronise Mountains, 52–53, **53**
Cronise Valley, 41
crossbedding, 167, 291, **316**
cross faults, 107, 144, 270
Crowder Formation, 244
Crowell, John, 36, 121
Crucifixion Thorn Natural Area, 128
crust, 4
Crystal Cove, 220
Crystal Cove State Park, 218–20
crystals, 3, 31, **132**, 156, 177, **188**, 197, 230, 252, 253, 300, **303**; in lava, 62, 67, 156; in pegmatites, 33, 188, 197–98, **198**; visible, 3, 42, 46, 252
Cucamonga fault, 21, 229, 230, 249
Cucamonga Peak, 251
Cushenbury cement quarries, 328–29
Cushenbury Canyon, 328–30
Cuyama Badlands, 318, 319
Cuyamaca-Laguna Mountains, 176; shear zone in, 154
Cuyamaca Rancho State Park, 195
Cuyama River, 36, 318, 320

dacite: cobbles of, 160, 171; of Miocene age, 46, 59, 62, 63, 74, 220, 227, 239, 264, 307, 344, 345; of Oligocene age, 308; ore associated with, 48, 78–79; porphyry, 253; volcanism of, x, 17
Daggett, 46, 59
Daggett Ridge, 104
Dale Lake playa, 90, 91
Dana Cove fault, 217
Dana Point, 170, 214–17
Dawn Mine, 78
Dawson Saddle, 301
Dead Man's Rock, 293
Dead Mountains, 63, 70
Death Valley, 41, 44, 49, 63, 79
Death Valley fault zone, 83
debris flows, 8, 250–51, 302, 323; deposits of, **126**, 233, 307, 325; submarine, 123
Del Cerro, 186
Del Mar, 168, 169
Delmar Formation, 167, **167**
Del Mar Race Track, 169
deltas, 22, 108, 109, 115, 144, 146, 160, 165, **192**, 236, 266, 295, 316; fan, 49, 109, 160
deserts, 8–12, 25; vegetation, 128

Desert Center, 37
Desert Discovery Center, 69
Desert Hot Springs, 89
desert pavement, 11, **11**, 72
Desert Training Center, 36, 69
desert varnish, 11–12, 52, 54, 101, 143, **179**
Desert View Tower, 179
detachment faults, 17, 28, 63, 70, 74, 76, 92, 140
Devers Hill, 89
Devils Gate Dam, 250–51
Devils Peak, 340
Devils Playground, 53, 54, 94
Devils Punchbowl, 246, 301
diabase, 121, 293, **295**, **324**, 341
diatomite, 280, 287, 345
diatoms, 16, 204, 205, 219, 281, **286**, 287
Dibblee, Thomas W., Jr. , 20, 285, 296
dikes: basaltic, 216, 218, 227; dacitic, 264, **265**, 344; diabase, 121, 216, 293, 295, **324**, 341; felsic, **32**, 33, **324**, 326, **326**, 330, **330**; granitic, **176**, **295**, 300, 301; lamprophyric, 230; mafic, 174, **175**, **176**; radial, 308; rhyolite, 114, 120, 252; swarms of, 75; volcanic, 78, 132. *See also* pegmatites
Diligencia Formation, x, 16
dinosaurs, 164
diopside, 182
diorite, 3, 103, 104, 121, 137, 252, 341. *See also* Wilson Diorite
dip-slip faults, 7
Discovery Well Park, 207
Dish Hill, 66, **66–67**
divergent plate boundaries, 5, 105
Doble Mine, 328
dolomite, 37, 72, 73, 83, 87, 95, 141, 219
domes: granitic, 31, 56–57; volcanic, 22, 78, 79, 146–47, **148**, 227, 308, 344
Dos Cuadras oil field, 268
Dove Spring Formation, 81, **81**
Dume, Point, 291
dunes. *See* sand dunes
Durmid, 147
Durmid Hill, 106, 109, 151–52

Eagle and High Peak Mines, 196
Eagle Mountain Mine, 37
Eagle Mountains, 152
Eagle Rock fault, 296
Earp, 92
earthquakes, 5, 6–8, 21, 22, 27; of 1812, 213, 280; Borrego Mountain, 199; in Brawley Seismic Zone, 107; on Calico fault, 48; El Centro, 106, 108, 145;

Fort Tejon, 238, 241, 302, 310; Hector Mine, 63; Landers, 100–101; Long Beach, 201; on Manix fault, 51–52; Northridge, 258, 260; in Peninsular Ranges, 157, 158; in Salton Trough, 108–9, 148; San Fernando, 249, 258, 260–61; San Francisco, 20; on San Jacinto fault, 243; Santa Barbara, 280; Whittier Narrows, 180; first written record of, 183; uplift during, 170
Earthquake Valley fault, 198
East Beach, 279
East Mesa Geothermal Field, 130
East Pacific Rise, 5, 18, 22, 105, 107, 146
Edom Hill, 138–39
Edwards Air Force Base, 84–85
elbaite, 188
El Cajon pluton, 173
El Cajon Valley, 160, 173, 174
El Camino Real, 267–68
El Capitan Dam, 165
El Centinela, **129**, 130
El Centro, 107, 146
El Centro earthquake, 106, 108, 145
Elephant Mountain, 59
Elephant Trees Formation, 124, 125
ellestadite, 182
Ellwood oil field, 282
El Mayor–Cucupah earthquake, 145, 157
El Modeno Volcanics, 17, 200, 215
Elmore Ranch fault, 144
El Paso fault, 80
El Paso Mountains, 80
Elsinore, 191–92
Elsinore fault, x, 6, 7, 107, 157, 158–59, 160, 189, 191–92, 193, 194, 196–97, **197**
Elsinore, Lake, 191–92, **192**
Elsinore Mountains, 189
El Toro Plain, 201
Elysian Park anticline, 210, 211
Encinal Canyon, 292
enclaves, 173, **174**, 175
Eocene time, x, 16, 20; erosion surface of, 155, 158, 160, 171, 176, 177, **177**, 185
eolianite, 338
epidote, 74, 95, 104, 116
erosion: along coast, 161, 164, 165, 168, 219, 282, 311; of Eocene surface, 16, 155, 158, 160, 171, 176, 177, **177**, 185; along faults, 299; of granitic rock, 9, 10–11, 42, 56, 173; headward, 144, 243, 246; man-caused, 251, 281; rates of, 99–100, 249; resistance to, 32, 186, 341; susceptibility to, 264, 285; triggered by uplift, 227, 323. *See also* topographic inversion; weathering

Escondido, 186, 194
Essex, 69
evaporite deposits, 4, 8, 53, 68, 85, 127, 128, 311

Fages, Pedro, 242
Fairbanks, H. W., 20
falling dunes, 52, 53
fan delta, 49, 109, 160
fanglomerate, 8, 49, 61, 90, 97, 135, 137, 305
Farallon Islands, 13
Farallon Plate: fore-arc basin of, 14, 227, 314; remnants of, 17–19; schist of, 14–15, 36, 111, 116, 152, 183, 200, 216, 230; subduction of, x, 1, 6, 13–14, 17, 27, 30, 72, 153, 229, 300
faults, 6–8; as barrier to groundwater flow, 63, 89, 90, 108, 139, 140, 201, 243; breccia, 74, 87, 292; en echelon, 107, 199; recent signs of, 26, 90, 108, 238, 249, 330. *See also* gouge; scarps; *specific fault names*
feeder dikes, 227
feldspars: in igneous rock, 3, 31, 37, 42, 58, 229, 300; in gneiss and schist, 12, 14, **31**, 92, 299; in sand, 53; in sandstone, 226, 246, 285, 314, 318; in veins, **32**, 33, 197, 330; weathering of, 11
Fenner, 63, 64
Fenner Hills, 70
Fenner Valley, 69
Ferrum, 37, 152
Fillmore, 331, 333, 334
fire clay, 193
Fish Creek, 123, 124
Fish Creek Gypsum, 124–25
Fish Creek Mountains, 120, 125
flash floods, 8, 96, 123, 250, 323
Flat Top, 99
flooding, 49, 110, 113, 144, 165, 169, 189, 210, 220, 281, 306, 334; of playas, 41, 53, 77. *See also* flash floods
fluoride, 192
folding, 47, **47**, 121, **127**, 219, 225, 232, **265**, 268, 271, 287, 314. *See also* anticlines; slumping; synclines
Fontana, 37
Foothills Freeway, 249
forams, 108
fore-arc basin, 1, 14, 153, 162, 165, 227, 314
Forest Falls, 323
Fort Irwin National Training Center, 50
Fort Tejon earthquake, 238, 241, 302, 310
fossils, 189, 256; brachiopods, 330; clams, 294; corals, 54; crinoids, 330; diatoms, 287; dinosaurs, 164; forams, 108;

gastropod, 294; mammals, 213, 339; Miocene, 81, **257**; plants, 213, 273; Pleistocene, 97, 218, 223, 271, 273; snails, 34; trace, 328; trilobites, 68
Franciscan Formation, 226
Frazier Park, 241
Friars Formation, 173
Fry Mountains, 103

gabbro, 3, 27, 137, 156; intruding marble, 103, **103**, 104; olivine-hypersthene, 156; of Peninsular Ranges Batholith, 156, 173, **174**, 186, **187**, 189; of Proterozoic age, 229, 300, 308; pyroxene-bearing, 300; soils on, 188; in Willows diorite, 341
Garces, Pedro Francisco, 242
Garlock fault, 6, 25, 27, 79, 80, 83, 241
garnets, 74, 95, 104, 156, 182, 325
Garnet Hill, 136, 137
Garnet Hill fault, 135, 137
gastropod, **294**
Gaviota, 283
Gaviota Formation, 226, 283
Gaviota Pass, 283–84, **283**
Gem Hill Formation, 78
geodes, 78
geoglyphs, 70
Geology Road, 30
George C. Page Museum, 48, 212
Georges Gap, 298, 299
geothermal power, 22, 130, 147
Getty Center, 256, 257
glaciation, 23, 327. *See also* Pleistocene time, lakes of; sea level, Pleistocene time
Glamis, 146
glaucophane, 214, 215, 218, 222, 291, 342
Glendora Volcanics, 17, 180, 182, 200, 251
Glen Ivy fault, 191, 192
Glen Helen fault, 244
gneiss, x, 12, 14–15, 300, 301; banded, 249; brecciated, 12, **12**; cobbles of, 252, 321; granitic, 241; in lower plate, 64, 74, 92; mafic, **31**, 63, 90, 146, 299, 326, **326**; with metasedimentary rocks, 52, 87, 137, 153; in upper North American Plate, 36, 116, 132, 146, 152, 183, 253, 302. *See also* Baldwin Gneiss; Pinto Gneiss; San Gabriel Gneiss; Waterman Gneiss
Goffs, 70
gold mining, 17, 42, 61, 78–79, 86–87, 101, 132–33, 146, 147, 195–96, 305, 328
Gold Basin, 146
Gold Mountain, 328

Goleta, 273
Goleta Beach Park, 282
Goleta Slough, 281–82
Gorman, 77, 233, 238
Gorman Post Road, 238, 239, 240
gouge, 119, 140, 201, 241, **241**, 243, 249, 310
graded bedding, 315
Granite Mountain, 197
Granite Mountain pluton, 176
Granite Mountains Reserve, 92
Granite Pass (Kelbaker Road), 92
granitic rock, 3, 26, 27, 31, **32**, **174**, **176**; biotite-muscovite, 156, 299; boulder piles, 10–11, **31**, **44**, 99; clasts of, 246; cobbles of, 252; of Cretaceous age, 52, 74, 91, 193, 296, **330**; jointed, **10**; landslides in, 179, 199; of Mesozoic age, 34, 36, 43, 52, 54, 68, 70, 86, 91, 95, 120, 230; pediment of, 42–43, 84, 92, 99; of Proterozoic age, 37, 68, 120; quarry, 194; sills of, 37; true, 178; water gap through, 41, **41**; weathering of, 9, 10–11, 56, 84, 92, 157, **175**, 323, **324**; veins in, 12, 31, 32, 33. *See also* granodiorite; pegmatite; tonalite
granodiorite, 3, 27, 31, 87, 91, 137, 156, 173, **174**, 179, 186–88, 189, 251, 287, 300. *See also* Lowe Granodiorite
Grapevine, 233
Grapevine Canyon, 241–42
Grapevine fault, 241–42
Grapevine Mountain, 198
gravel pits, 165, 251, 306
graywacke, 116, 152, 193, 226, 230, 343
Great Valley, 14
Green Rock Mine, 103
greenschist, 14, 116, 214, 230, 343, 344
greenschist facies, 15, 91, 253
Grossmont Summit, 173
groundwater: basins of, 59, 103, 201; contamination of, 87; fault barrier to, 63, 89, 90, 108, 139, 140, 201, 243; landslides caused by, 186; near surface, 99, 243; overdrafting of, 77, 103, 189; recharge of, 250, 252, 275; weathering by, 10. *See also* subsidence, land
grus, 56, 324
gryphons, 148, 149, **149**
Gulf of California, x, 5, 17, 18, 19, 105, 108, 123
gypsum, 124, 127, 128

Hale telescope, 300
Halloran Springs, 54, 56

Hancock Park, 212
Harvard Hill, 49
head scarp, 141, 142, 272, 320
Heath Canyon slide, 302
hectorite, 62
Hector Mine, 62; earthquake, 27, 63
Helendale, 43
Helendale fault, 27, 43, 103
Helix, Mt., 173
hematite, 95, 308
Henshaw, Lake, 196
Hermit Shale, 73, 92
Hidden Spring fault, 115, **117**
Hill, Mason, 20
Hilltop Park, 207
Hinkley, 87
Hinkley fault, 104
Hodges, Lake, 186
Hollywood, 255, 256, 262
Hollywood fault, 255
Hollywood Freeway, 263
Hollywood Hills, 262
Hollywood fault, 202, 203, 255, 262
Homestead Valley, 100
Honor Rancho oil field, 232
hornblende, 3, 12, 58, 74, 103, 137, 176,
    177, 300, 308, 342
hornitos, 62
Horse Hills, 92
horses, 189, 273
Hospital fault, 259
hot springs, 62, 89, 150, 191, 192
Hugh T. Osborne Lookout Park, 110
Huntington Beach, 183, 209, 222
Huntington Beach oil field, 204, 208–9
hyaloclastite, 227
hydrothermal, 47, 50, 77, 103, 156
hypersthene, 155

Ice Age, 23
Icehouse Canyon, 253
idocrase, 182
igneous rocks, 3
ilmenite, 95, 230
impact spherules, 339
Imperial fault, 107, 108, 144, 158
Imperial Formation, 22, 127, 137, 139
Imperial Valley, 105, 108, 110, 130,
    144–46; faults in, 144
Indian Canyons, 137
Indio, 109, 133, 141
Indio Hills, 106, 139–40, 151
Inface Bluffs, 242, 246–47, **247**
Inglewood oil field, 207–8
In-Ko-Pah Gorge, 179–80

In-Ko-Pah Mountains, 177, 179
inselbergs, 9, 70, 84, **91**, 92
Inspiration Point, 301
intaglios, 70
iron, 3, 4, 11, 37, 70, 95, 152, 188, 193,
    292, 339
Iron Mountain, 302
Iron Mountains, 91, **91**, 92
iron oxides, 4, 11, 120, 308
Irvine Cove, 218
Islip Saddle, 301
Ivanpah Valley, 58

Jacinto Reyes Scenic Byway, 314
Jacumba Volcanics, 177–78
Jacumba Valley, 177
Jamul, 186
jasper, 86
Jawbone Canyon, 79
Jenks Lake, 325
jetties, 165, 221, 223
Johannesburg, 86
Josephine Mountain intrusion, 299
Josephine Peak, 299, **299**
Joshua Tree (town), 90
Joshua Tree National Park, 12, 28–34,
    90, 228
Juan Bautista de Anza Trail, 199
Julian, 195–96, 197
Julian Schist, x, 156, **157**, 173, 176, 194,
    195, 196, 199; quartzite with, 156, **157**
Jumbo Rocks, 31
Juncal Formation, 226, 279, 319
Jurupa Mountains, 182
Jurupa Valley, 182

kaersutite, 66
Kearny Mesa, 185
Kelbaker Road, 92–97
Kelley Mine, 87
Kellogg Hill, 180
Kelso, 96
Kelso Dunes, 94–95, **94**
Kelso Mountains, 97
Kenneth Hahn State Recreation Area, 208
kernite, 85
Keys Canyon, 188
Keys View, 30
Kilbeck Hills, 91
Kingston Peak Formation, 330
Kitchen Creek, 177
Kramer deposit, 85
Kramer Hills, 86
Kramer Junction, 86
kurnakovite, 85

kyanite, 132, **132**

La Brea Tar Pits, 212–13
La Cañada Flintridge, 297, 298
La Conchita, 272–73
La Cresta pluton, 173–76, **175**
lagoons, 168–69, 221–22, 293–94
Laguna, 216
Laguna Beach, 214, 218, 227
Laguna Diversion Dam, 131
Laguna Salada fault, 145, 157
lahar deposits, 178
La Jolla, 20, 158, 165
lakebeds, 108, 113, 235, 236
Lake of the Woods, 319
Lakeside, 165, 166
La Mesa, 173
Lamont Odett Vista Point, 309
lamprophyric dikes, 230
Lancaster, 77
Landers, 100, 101
Landers earthquake, 8, 27, 100–101
Landers–Joshua Tree fault systems, 229
Landing Hill, 209
landslides, 101–3, 141–42, 179–80,
    223, 242, 302–3, 334; along bedding
    planes, 186, 210, 258, 281, 316, **317**;
    breccia of, 74; coastal, 165, 170, 223,
    270, 272, **272**, 287, 289, **290**, 343; de-
    posits of, 108, 110, 123, 125, 126, 176,
    199, 325, **326**; head scarp of, 141, 142,
    272, **303**, **325**, 331; in San Gabriel and
    San Bernardino Mountains, 249, 252,
    253, 320, 325; triggered by quakes, 63
lapis lazuli, 253
La Posta Creek, 177
La Posta pluton, 154, **157**, 176–77, 178, 179
Las Cruces, 285
Las Flores Canyon, 291
Las Posas Formation, 311
Las Posas Hills, 266
Latham Shale, 68, 69
Latrania Formation, 124
La Tuna Canyon, 249
Laurel Canyon, 256
Lava Bed Mountains, 62
lava flows: andesite and dacite, 179, 239,
    307, 308, 345; basalt, 54–55, 61–62, 67,
    81, 84, 97, 99, 178, 189, 219, 263, 306; of
    Early Cretaceous age, 186; oil trapped
    by, 266, 295; pillows of, 227, 343
Lavic Lake fault, 63
Lavic Lake Volcanic Field, 61
La Vida Member, 180
Lavigia fault, 278

Leadbetter Beach, 279
Lebec, 25, 241
left-slip faults, 6, 79, 90, 241, 261, 315,
    316, 319. *See also* Garlock fault; Santa
    Ynez fault
Lenwood, 44
Lenwood fault, 27, 44, 101, 104
lepidolite, 156
Leucadia, 168
Leuhman Ridge, 85
Liebre Mountain, 234, 236
limestone, 4; gold in, 101; of Miocene age,
    204, 307; of Paleozoic age, 13, 54, 57,
    58, 68, 73, 83, 92, 95, **96**, 137; quarry
    in, 42, 79, 83, 182, 328; skarn in, 95; of
    Tertiary age, 49; tungsten in, 87
limonite, 95
Lindavista Formation, 162, 167, **167**
Lindavista terrace, 185–86
lithium, 62
Little Maria Mountains, 38
Littlerock fault, 311
Little San Bernardino Mountains, 28,
    224, 225, 228
Little Sycamore Canyon, 292
Little Treasure Cove, 219
Llajas Formation, 289
Lobecks Pass, 76
Lockwood Valley, 320
Loma, Point, 164–65
Lompoc, 287
Lone Pine Canyon, 245
Long Beach, 158, 205, 209, 211, 212, 221
Long Beach earthquake, 201
Long Beach oil field, 205–7
longshore drift, 163, 165, 169, 220, 221,
    279, 282
Long Valley Caldera, 270
Los Alisos Canyon, 292
Los Angeles, 6, 21, 37, 83, 146, 200, 258
Los Angeles Aqueduct, 79, 83
Los Angeles Basin, x, 2, 17, 200–203, 255;
    oil fields in, 202, 204–10; volcanism
    upon opening of, 17, 182, 251, 263
Los Angeles Museum of Natural History, 212
Los Angeles Narrows, 210, 211
Los Angeles Pueblo, 211
Los Angeles Reservoir, 261, 262
Los Angeles River, 210–12, 221, 256,
    258, 263
Lowe Granodiorite, x, 230, 253, 299,
    300, **301**
Lucerne fault, 191, 192
Lucerne Lake playa, 103
Lucerne Valley, 103, 235, 330

Ludlow, 63, 64
Ludlow fault, 63
Lukens, Mt., 250
Lusardi Formation, 162
Lycium Sandstone, 124
Lytle Creek, 243

mafic, 3
Magic Mountain, 232
magmatic arc, 1, 5, 14, 153
magnesium silicate, 95, 173
magnetite, 37, 95
Malibu, 170, 255
Malibu Coast fault, 255, 287, 292
mammoths, 213; pygmy, 338, 339, **340**
Mancos Shale, 108, 146
Mandeville Canyon, 210, 211
manganese oxide, 11
Maniobra Formation, 36
Manix earthquake, 27
Manix fault, 27, 49, **50**, **51**, **51**
Manix, Lake, 48–49, 51
mantle, 4, 22, 66, 97, 146
marble, 4, 13; calc-silicate, 132; corundum in, 253; dolomitic, 87, 141; with Pelona schist, 15; metamorphosed Grand Canyon strata, 72, 73, 92; quarries in, 42, 79, 83, 103–4, **103**, 156, 182, 328–29; roof pendant in, 326, 328
Marble Mountains, 59, 68, 69
Marina del Rey, 211, 223
Marl Mountains, 97
Marple Canyon Sandstone, 234
marsh, salt, 222, 274, 281
Martinez Mountain rockslide, 141–42, **142**
mastodons, 189, 273, 339
Matilija Sandstone, 226, **286**, 287, 315, 316, **316**, **317**, 318
Matthews, Vince, 20
McCoy Mountains, 37–39
McCoy Mountains Formation, 91
Mecca, 107, 112, 113, 141
Mecca Formation, 114, 119, 120, 121, **122**
Mecca Hills, 106, 111–22, 151
mélange, 343, 344
Mendenhall Gneiss, 231
Mentone, 320
Mesa de Burro, 189
Mesa fault, 278
Mesa Grande mining district, 156, 188
Mesonacis, **69**
Mesozoic time, x, 13–15
Mesquite Mine, 146, **147**
metabasalt, 4, 14, **31**, **303**
metachert, 15

metamorphic core complexes, 17, 28
metamorphic rocks, 4, 228, 229. *See also* Bedford Canyon Formation; gneiss; marble; metasedimentary; metavolcanic; quartzite; schist
metamorphism, 4, 153, 230
metasedimentary rock, 4, 11, 25, 30, 37, 42, 73, 87, 92, 103, 141, 228, 252, 326, 328
metavolcanic rock, 4, 25, 50, 52, 53, 54, 73, 86, 153. *See also* metabasalt
meteorite, **69**
Mexico, 105, 129, 130, 158, 162, 185
micas. *See* biotite; muscovite; schist, mica
midden deposits, 343
Middle Butte, 78
mid-ocean ridge, 6
migmatite, 57, 229, 253
military activities, 36, 59, 62, 337
Mill Creek Basin, 321–22, **323**
mineralization, 17, 48, 57, 87, 132, 146
minerals, 3, 57–58, 182, 188. *See also* specific mineral names
mining: copper, 32, 92; gold, 42, 61, 78–79, 86–87, 101, 132–33, 146, 147, 195–96, 305, 328; hectorite, 62; iron, 37; rare earth, 57–58; silver, 42, 46–48, 78, 87, 101, 132; tungsten, 87
Mint Canyon Formation, 306–7
Miracle Hill, 89
Miramar Marine Corps Air Station, 185
Mission Bay, 158, 164, 165
Mission Creek fault, 89, 90, 106, 108, 139, 140
Mission Gorge, 174, 185
Mission Hills, 259, 260
missions, 213, 279, **280**, 311,
Mission San Buenaventura, 311
Mission San Juan Capistrano, 213, **213**
Mission Santa Barbara, **280**
Mission Trails Regional Park, 165, 185
Mission Valley, 160, 165, 171, 183, 185
Mission Valley Formation, 186
Mission Viejo, 216
Mission Wells thrust fault, 231, 258, 259, 260
Modelo Formation, 203, 204, 234, 249, 257, 258, 260, 264, **264**, **265**, 287, 306
Modjeska Peak, 193
Mojave (town), 78, 79, 83–84
Mojave Desert, 2, 8, 24, 25–34; basalt volcanism in, x, 23; core complexes in, 17; earthquakes in, 63, 100; faults in, 27; granitic complexes in, 27, 56; ice age lakes in, 23; mineralization in,

17; Paleozoic rocks in, 13; vegetation in, 34, 64; volcanic rocks of, 27
Mojave, Lake, 49, 53, 97
Mojave National Preserve, 25
Mojave River, 41, **41**, 44, 46, 48, 49, 50, 94
monazite, 95
Monolith, 83
Montebello Hills, 180
Montecito, 273, 275, 278
Monterey Formation, x, 204–5, **205**, 216, 226, 289; in Channel Islands, 340, 341; along coast, 214, 218–20; concretions in, 219; diatoms in, 286, 287; faulted, 170, **171**; folds in, **23**, **219**, 269, 280–81, **281**, 287, 314; natural dam of, 274–75; oil in, 204, 227, 273, **274**; siliceous shale of, 180, 205, 219, 291, **291**, 318; in Ventura Basin, 227, 269, 314
Monterey Hills, 180
monticellite, 182
monzogranite, 31
moraines, 327
Morena tonalite, 176
More Ranch–Mission Ridge–Arroyo Parida fault, 278
Mormon Rocks, 246, **247**
Morongo Valley, 33, 90
Morongo Valley fault, 90
Morro Hill, 320
Mountain Pass Mine, x, 57–58, **57**
Mountain Springs, 179
Mt. Baldy Road and Village, 252, 253
Mt. Wilson Observatory, 300
Mt. Soledad, 158
mud balls, 119
mud cracks, 8, 236
mudflows, 178, 302
mudstone, 4, 116, 152, **164**, 180, 186, 204, 226, 236, 345
mud volcanoes, 148
Mugu Lagoon, 293
Mugu Rock, 293, **293**
Munson Creek fault, 316
Murray, Lake, 159, 165, 186
Murrieta, 158, 189, 191
muscovite, 3, 132, 156, 179, 299
Muscoy terrace, 243

nanodiamonds, 339
National Trails Highway, 64
Native Americans, 71, 129, 232, 273, 337, 344
Naval Base San Diego, 183
Naval Base Ventura County, 294
Needles, 64, 74

Neenach Volcanics, 20, 239, **240**
Newberry Mountains, 59, 61
Newberry Springs, 59, 61
Newbury Park, 264
Newhall Pass, 232, **232**, 305
Newport Bay, 220–21
Newport Beach, 201, 221
Newport-Inglewood fault zone (trend), 158, 201, 206, 207, 208, 209, 255
Newport Submarine Canyon, 221
New River, 105, 130, 144, 146
Nickel Mountain, 54
Nojoqui Summit, 285
norite, 137, 300
normal faults, 7, 28, **33**, 80, 227, **291**, 331
North American craton, 12, 13, 73, 92
North American Plate, x, 1, 5, 6, 13, 14, 15; boundary of, 241, 245; jamming of Pacific Plate into, 1, 21, 225; juxtaposition with Pacific Plate, x, 1, 6, 17, 18–20, 63, 105, 107, 153, 200, 227; microcontinent added to, 230; relict subduction zone of, 14, 15, 36, 183, 229; subduction of Farallon beneath, x, 1, 6, 13, 14, 15, 30, 72, 116, 152, 153, 227, 230, 300; tectonic window in, 15
Northeast Flank fault, 206
North Frontal thrust fault, 330
North Island, 164
North Palm Springs, 89
Northridge earthquake, 21, 232, 258, 260
North Shore, 149, 152

Oak of the Golden Dream, 305
Oak Ridge, 331–33
Oak Ridge fault, 227, 331–33, 335
Oakview terrace, 311, **313**
oases, 139–40, **139**, **140**
oblique-slip faults, 7
obsidian, 146–48, **148**
Ocean Beach, 164, 171
Oceanside, 170, 216
Ocotillo, 128
Ocotillo Conglomerate, 112, 114
Ocotillo Wells, 123, 124, 199
Ogilby, 131, 132
oil, 17, 202, 204; claims for, 306; fields, 202, 204–10; in Los Angeles Basin, 201, 202, 203, 204–10, 255; museum about, 331; in Pico anticline, 232; from Pleistocene beds, 276; along Santa Barbara Channel, 282; seeps of, 212, 223, 273, **274**; spills of, 335; trapped by lava, 266, 295; unsuccessful exploration for, 36, 110, 139; in

Ventura Basin, 227, 268, 269, 270, 271, 273, 275–77, 313–14, 331, 335. *See also specific oil field names*
Ojai, 269
Ojai freeway, 311
Old Plank Road Historic Site, 130
Old Ridge Route, 235
Old Woman meteorite, **69**
Old Woman Mountains, 69
Old Woman Sandstone, 103
Old Woman Springs fault, 101
Old Woman Springs Road, 99
Olivella biplicata, 271
olivine, 58, 66, 67, 81, 97, 99, 137, 156
Onyx Pass, 326
opal, 78
opalite, 86
open-pit mining, 37, 57, **57**, 62, 78, 85, **85**, 87, 95, **96**, 146, **147**
Orange County, 183, 194
ore deposit. *See* copper; gold; iron; silver; rare earth
organic matter, 16–17, 204, 205, 227, 273, 314
Orocopia Mountains, 36, 152
Orocopia Schist, x, 14, 15, 36, 112, 114, 116, **117**, 120, 121, 152, 228
Oro Grande, 42
Ortega anticline, 276
orthoclase feldspar, 58
orthopyroxene, 97
Otay Formation, 162
oxides, 4, 11, 120, 253
Oxnard, 266, 293
Oxnard Plain, 227, 266, 295
Ozena fault, 320

Pacific Coast Highway, 214, 287
Pacific Palisades, 287, 289, 290
Pacific Plate, 1, 5, 6, 17, 18–20, 105, 107, 153, 225
Pacoima Wash, 258
Page Museum, 212
pahoehoe lava, 62, 67
Painted Canyon, 118–22
Painted Canyon fault, 112, 113, 115, 118, 120, **120**, **121**
Pala mining district, 156, 188
Palen Mountains, 37
Paleozoic time, x, 13, 92
palisades, 287, 289–90
Palisades Park, 291
Palmdale, 77, 152, 298, 310
Palmdale, Lake, 309–10

Palm Spring Formation, 113, 114, 115, **116**, 119, **119**, 121, 139
Palm Springs, 17, 105, 137; tramway at, 137, **138**
Palomar Mountain, 300
Palos Verdes Hills, 201, 216, 222–23, **222**
Parkfield, 238
Pasadena, 180, 250
Pasadenan orogeny, 1, 21, 249
Pauba Formation, 189
Peace Valley, 241
Pecten species, 293, **294**
pediments, 9, 25, 42, 84, 92
pegmatite dikes, 33, 137, 156, 157, 179, 182, 188–89, 197–98, **198**, 199
Pelona Schist, x, 14–15, 244–45, **245**, 301, **303**; clasts of, 246, 322, 325; landslides in, 243, 302; thrust fault and, 183, 230, 253, 302
peneplain, x, 153, 155, 158
Peninsular Ranges, 2, 18, 153–61; core complexes in, 17; faults of, 157; uplift of, 160; Paleozoic rocks in, 13; plutons of, 153, 155–57, 173–77, 186–88
Peninsular Ranges Batholith, x, 14, 16, 153, 154, 155–57, 160, 173–77, 186–88, 195
peridot, 86
peridotite, 341
Perris Plain, 158–60, 191
Peterman Hill, 103–4
petrified wood, 86
petroleum. *See* oil
phyllite, 92
physiographic provinces, 2
Picacho Peak Volcanics, 133, 146
Picacho State Recreation Area, 133
Pickhandle Formation, 46, 47, **47**
Pico anticline, 231, 232
Pico Formation, 203, 226, 231, 232, 270, 271, 305, 306, 313, 314, 331, 333
Piedra Blanca syncline, 315
pillow lava, 6, 227, 343
Pilot Knob, 131
Pine Canyon, 239
Pine Mountain fault, 318, 319
Pine Mountain Ridge, 318
Pinnacles National Park, 20
Pinnacles Volcano, 239
Pinto Gneiss, 12, 31, **31**, 89–90, **89**, 112, 120, **122**
Pinto Mountain fault, 33, 90, 99
Pinyon Flat landslide, 142
Pioneertown, 99
Pipes Wash, 99

Piru, 331, 335
Piru Gorge Sandstone, 236, **237**
Pisgah Crater, 61–62, 63
Pisgah fault, 27
Pitas Point, 270
Pitas Point fault, 269
Piute Mountains, 70
placer deposits, 86, 87, 305, 328
Placerita Canyon State Park, 305
Placerita oil field, 306
plagioclase feldspar, 3, 37, 46, 67, 229, 300
plank road, 130–31
Plaster City, 128
plate tectonics, 4–6
Playa del Rey, 223
playas, 8, 9, 25, 41, 52, 53, 77, 79, 84, 91, 103. *See also* Bristol Lake; Rogers Lake; Soda Lake; Troy Lake
Pleistocene time, x; alluvial fans of, 53, 95, 97, 193, 246; basalt of, 54; climate of, 77; deposits of, 135, 137, 139, 165, 167, 185, 201, 218, 274, 287, 334, 339; drainages during, 41, 99, 210; faulting in, 41, 50, 90, 101, 108, 112, 115, 241, 330, 331, 340; folding in, 116, 209, 211, 232, 266; fossils of, 212–13, 273, 339; glaciation of, 327; lakes of, 48–49, 50, 52, 77, 84, 97, 109, 110; mammals, 48; oil deposits of, 268, 276, 277; sea levels of, 161, 337; terraces cut in, 292, 311, 320, 343, 345; uplift during, 21, 201, 206, 271, 307. *See also* Cabezon Formation; Casitas Formation; Santa Barbara Formation; Saugus Formation
Pleistocene Lake Manix, 48–49, 50, 51
Pleito thrust fault, 242
plugs, 14, 46, 54, 59, 63, 84, 308
plutonic rocks, 14, 26, 153, 154, 156, 186
plutons, 56, 74, 153, 155, 156, 173–77. *See also specific pluton names*
Point Arguello, 269
Point Conception, 269
Point Dume, 291
Point Loma, 164–65
Point Loma Formation, 162, 164
Point Mugu, 294
porcellanite, 204, **205**, 219, 281
Porcupine Hill, 206
Port Hueneme, 295
Portuguese Bend landslide, 223
Poway, 160
Poway Conglomerate, x, 20, 158–60, **159**, 162, 165–66, **166**, 337
Poway Group, 160, 171

Poway terrace, 186
Prado Dam, 194
Prospect Mountain Quartzite, 68
Proterozoic time, x, 12. *See also* gneisses
Providence Mountains, 59, 95
Puddingstone Reservoir, 251
Puente Formation, 180, 194, 204
Puente Hills, 180, 194
Puente Hills thrust fault, 194
pull-apart basin, 191, 192, 321
pumice, 147
Punchbowl fault, 230, 244, 301
Punta Gorda, 269, 271
Pyramid Lake, 236
pyrite, 37, 95, 132, 236

Qualcomm Stadium, 173
quarries: cinders, 61, 62, 97; carbonates, 42, 83, 103, 156, 182, 328; diatomaceous earth, 287; granite, 193–94; gravel, 165, 251, 306; gypsum, 128; pegmatite, 188; sand and clay, 193. *See also* open-pit mining
quartz, 3, 33, 46, 52, 74, 132, 156, 197, 300, 330; veins of, **32**, 78, 87, 152
quartz diorite, 3, 50, 74, 87, 230, 252, 253, 341, 344
quartzite, 4, 37, 132, 141; carbonate-bearing, 156; clasts of, 160, 342; similar to that in Great Basin, 87, 330; Paleozoic, 13, 73, 92; quarried, 42. *See also* Bedford Canyon Formation; Prospect Mountain Quartzite
Quartzite Mountain, 42
quartz monzonite, 3, 27, **32**
Quatal Clay, 319, 320

radial dikes, 308
radioactive minerals, 78
Ramona mining district, 188
Rancho Bernardo, 186
Rancho San Julian, 285
Rand Mountains, 86
Randsburg, 86–87
Randsburg granodiorite, 87
Rand Schist, x, 14, 87
rare earth deposits, 58
Raymond Hill fault, 255
red beds, 70, 74, 289, 307, 318, 323, 331
Red Box, 298
Red Box Ranger Station, 299, 300
Red Hill rhyolite dome, 148
Redlands, 320, 328
Red Mountain anticline, 269, 314

Red Mountain thrust fault, 227, 269, 274, 276, 314
Redondo Beach, 223
Redondo Submarine Canyon, 223
Red Rock Canyon State Park, 80–81, **81**
Redwall Limestone, 73, 92
Refugio Canyon, 282
Repetto Formation, 203, 204
Reseda, 258
reverse faults, 7, 135, 225, 249, 274, 331
rhyolite: clasts of, 159, **159**, 160, **338**; of Cretaceous age, 156; dikes of, 114, 120, 252; domes of, 146–48; flow-banded, 239; Holocene volcanism of, 22, 147, **148**; Miocene volcanism of, x, 77–78, 133, 227, 239, 345
Rice, 92
Ridge Basin, 227, 233–36, 238
Ridge Route, 231, 233, 235–36
Ridge Route Formation, 234
riebeckite, 291
rift basin, 105
rifting, 4, 5, 6, 17, 22, 105, 155
right-slip faults, 6, 157, 158, 192, 233, 315. See also Elsinore fault; San Andreas fault; San Jacinto fault
Rim of the World Highway, 320
Rincon, 270
Rincon anticline, 269, 271
Rincon Creek–Carpinteria fault system, 273, 274, 276
Rincon Island, 268, 271
Rincon mining district, 188
Rincon oil field, 271
Rincon Shale, 226, 275, **282**, 283, 339, 341
Rio Hondo River, 180
ripples, 236, **237**
river deposits, 16, 83, 104, 110, 113, 115, 125, 135, 151, 183, 227, 236, 285, 306, 325
Riverside, 155, 156, 158, 182, 302
Riverside Mountains, 73, 74
riversideite, 182
Rock, the, 342
rockslides, 141. See also landslides
rock types, 3–4
Rodriguez Canyon, 196, 197, **197**
Rogers Lake playa, 77, 84, 310
roof pendants, 326, 328
Rosamond Hills, 77–78
Rosamond Lake playa, 77, 84
Rose Canyon fault, 158
Round Mountain, 178
Route 66, 39, 46, 64–70
Royal Highway, 267
Rubidoux, Mt., 182

Ruby Mountain, 101
rutile, 95

saber-toothed cats, 213, 273
Sacate Formation, 226
Sacramento Mountains, 63–64
Saddleback Basalt, 85
Saddleback Ridge, 193
sag ponds, 90, 238, 239, **240**, 241, 309, 310
Salinian Block, 26
salt, 53, 68
Salt Creek Wash, 152
Salton City, 142
Salton Sea, 105, 107, 109–10, 147, 149, 150
Salton Sink, 105, 110
Salton Trough, 2, 17, 105–10; alluvial fans in, 141; depth of, 107; earthquakes in, 106, 108–9; faults in, 106, 108; marine incursion in, 127; rifting in, 22; San Andreas fault in, 18, 107–8; subsidence of, 123; world-class sites in, 111–28
saltwater marshes, 222, 274, 281
San Andreas fault, x, 1, 6, 17–22, 105–7, 229, 238–41, **241**, 243, 320, 345; Big Bend of, 21, 225, 241, 242, 320; development of, 1, 17–22; discovery of, 20; displacement along, 14, 26, 36, 37, 41, 121, 152, 228, 235, 239, 246, 247, 308, 309, 322, 325; earthquakes along, 109, 238, 302; gouge zone in, 119; Garlock fault and, 25, 27, 83, 241; passes formed by, 133; predecessor of, 201; pressure ridge of, 310–11; pull-apart basin along, 321; road crossing of, 34, 77, 113, 119, 245, 310; rocks folded along, 34, 111–13, 138, **310**; rocks tilted by, 34; sag ponds along, 240, 309; south end of, 105–7, 144, 150; strands of, 33, 89, 106, 135, 157, 189, 233, 299, 301; transform shearing along, 20; uplift along, 111, 113, 139, 151, 229
San Antonio Canyon, 251, 252–53
San Antonio Canyon fault, 252
San Antonio Dam, 251, 252
San Antonio, Mt., 251, 253, 301, 302, 322
San Bernardino, 180, 183, 243, 250, 302
San Bernardino Mountains, **41**, 135, **135**, 224, 225, 228–29, 320–30; drainages from, 41, 49, 53, 99, 105, 136, 182, 183; earthquakes in, 101; faults in, 90, 101; logging in, 327; mining in, 101; roof pendants in, 328; San Andreas fault and, 27, 243; uplift of, 135
San Bernardino Valley, 242

San Cayetano thrust fault, 227, 331, 333, **333**, 334, 335
San Clemente fault, 345
San Clemente Island, 161, 165, 337, 344–45, **344**
San Clemente State Beach, 170
sand, 91, 92, 164, 279, 282, 338; silica, 193
sandbars, 142, 220, 221
sandblasting, 136, **136**
sand dunes: desert, 8, 37, 49, 52–53, **53**, 72, 91, 92, 94–95, **94**, 103, 110–11, 130–31, 136, 138; coastal, 223, **292**, 293, 338, 339, 345
San Diego, 20, 158, 163, 183, 185
San Diego Bay, 158, 162–64, 165, 174
San Diego Formation, 162, 183
San Diego River, 158, 165, 171, 185
San Dieguito River, 168, 169
sandstone, 4, 226, 289; alluvial fan, 108; ash-rich, 47, 77, 81; for building stone, 280; coarse, 308, **308**; in coastal terrace, 270, 271; of Cretaceous age, 39, 256; cross-bedded, 167, 291, 316; delta, 115; of Eocene age, 34, 36, 160, 186, 283, **283**, 285, 314, 311, 331, 345; feldspar-rich, 246, 285; in breccia, 214, 342; lakebed, 233; marine, 137, 170, 171, 183, 185, 227, 232, 235, 245, 271, 305; of Mesozoic age, 37; of Miocene age, 81, 103, 180, 194, 262, 263, **282**, 301, 307, 345; nonmarine, 189, 233, 246, 305, **305**; oil in, 204, 206, 208, 232, 268, 273; oxidized, 70; of Paleozoic age, 13, 92; pebbly, 217, 246, 307; of Pleistocene age, 165, 270, 271, 335; of Pliocene age, 113, 114, 115, 137, 151, 232, 236, 270, 271, 311, 313, 335; quartz, 156; stream-deposited, 81, 124, 151, 235, **236**, **238**, 285, 307; thick-bedded, 315. *See also* turbidites
San Elijo lagoon, 168
San Emigdio Mountains, 241, 242
San Felipe Creek, 123, 198
San Fernando earthquake, 21, 232, 249, 258, 260–61
San Fernando fault zone, 249, 260
San Fernando Valley, 21, 210, 211, 256, 258–61, 264
San Francisco, 6, 21, 26; earthquake, 20
San Francisquito Formation, 234, 236, 244, 245, 246
San Gabriel fault, 135, 139, 140, 201, 230, 232, 233, 253, 296, 298, 299, **299**
San Gabriel Gneiss, 12, **12**, 229, 300
San Gabriel Mountains, 224, 225, 228, 229–30, **250**, 259, 296; alluvial fans

from, 41, 180, 246 47, 250, 251, 258; anorthosite in, 37; displaced rocks in, 36, 121; drainages of, 41, 182, 210, 258, 266, 298; faults of, 107, 158, 243, 249, 253, 260; intrusions in, 299; metamorphic rocks of, 252, 296; uplift of, 235, 246, 249
San Gabriel River, 180, 209, 221, 302; fan of, 251; valley of, 180, 296
San Gorgonio Mountain, 23, 105, 189, 325, 327, **327**
San Gorgonio Pass, 105, 133–35, **135**
San Jacinto fault, x, 6, 106, 107, 108, 141, 144, 157–58, 199, 243, 301
San Jacinto Mountains, 133, 135, 182
San Jacinto Peak, 105, 137
San Jacinto pluton, 137
San Jacinto River, 192
San Joaquin Hills, 214, 220
San Joaquin Valley, 242
San Jose Hills, 180, 251
San Juan Bautista National Historic Trail, 283
San Juan Capistrano, 168, 213
San Juan Valley, 213–14
San Luis Rey River, 188
San Marcos gabbro, 186, **187**, 188
San Margarita Formation, 234
San Martinez Grande Canyon, 335
San Mateo Formation, 170, **171**
San Miguel Island, 165, 337, 338–39
San Miguelito anticline, 269
San Miguel Mountain, 186
San Nicolas Island, 337, 345
San Onofre, 170
San Onofre Breccia, x, 162, 214, **214**, 216, 218, 291, 341, 342
San Onofre nuclear plant, 170–71
San Onofre State Beach, 170
San Pedro Bay, 207, 212
San Rafael Hills, 250, 296
San Sebastian Marsh, 123
Santa Ana Mountains, 157, 158, 182, 189, **192**, 193, 194
Santa Ana River, 182–83, 194, 220, 221, 325, 326
Santa Ana Sandstone, 325
Santa Barbara, 205, 273, 277–82, **279**
Santa Barbara Channel, 268, 282, 337, 341
Santa Barbara Formation, 226, 270
Santa Barbara Island, 337, 342–43
Santa Barbara Mission, 279–80
Santa Catalina Island, 337, 343–44
Santa Clara River, 225, 266, 295, 306, 331, 334
Santa Clara syncline, 331, 333, 334

Santa Cruz Island, 165, 227, 337, **338**, 340
Santa Cruz Island fault, 255, 340–41, **341**
Santa Cruz Island Volcanics, 227, 339, 340, 341
Santa Fe gold mine, 101
Santa Fe Springs oil field, 204
Santa Margarita River, 189
Santa Maria River, 282
Santa Monica, 211, 255, 256, 287, 289, 293
Santa Monica Bay, 223
Santa Monica fault, 202, 203, 255–56, 262
Santa Monica Mountains, 224, 225–27, 259; Conejo volcanics in, 17, 227–28, 264; core of, 256, 287; southward thrusting of, 201, 203, 255; uplift of, 211, 256; wind gaps through, 210–11, **211**, 263
Santa Monica Slate, x, 203, 255, 256, 287, 289
Santa Paula, 227, 331
Santa Paula Peak, 331, 333
Santarosae, 337
Santa Rosa Island, 165, 167, 337, 339, 340
Santa Rosa Island fault, 339
Santa Rosa Mountains, 140, 141, 142
Santa Rosa Plateau, 189
Santa Rosa–San Jacinto Mountains National Monument, 137
Santa Susana fault zone, 231, 258
Santa Susana Formation, 263
Santa Susana Mountains, 210, 224, 225, 232, 258
Santa Ynez fault, 6, 283, 284, 315
Santa Ynez Mountains, 16, 224, 225, 269, 277, **278**, 281, 282, 283
Santa Ynez River, 282
Santiago Peak, 193
Santiago Peak Volcanics, 14, 155, 156, 173, 186, 193
San Timoteo Hills, 243
sapphires, 253
Saugus Formation, 231, 232, 305, **305**, 306, 335
Sawtelle oil field, 202, 203, 255
scarps, fault, 43, 140, 238, 239, 242, 255–56, **255**, 331; forming mountain face, 21, 78, 191, 193, 229, 249, 298, 345; of historic earthquake, 261; impounding of water by, 48; in young alluvium, 26, 90, 108, 330
scarps, landslide, 141, 142, 272, 320
schist, 4, 13, 14, 15; calcium-silicate, 137; chlorite, 341; clasts of, 325; glauco-phane, 214, 222, 342; mafic, 14, 132; mica, 137, 156, 179, 194, 230, 253,

327; riebeckite, 291. *See also* Catalina Schist; Julian Schist; Orocopia Schist; Pelona Schist; Rand Schist
schorl, 156, 188, 198, **198**
Scripps, 165, 166
Seal Beach oil field, 209
sea level, Pleistocene time, 161, 168–69, 186, 201, 211, 223, 292, 337
Searles Lake playa, 79
sedimentary rocks, 4
sedimentation, 16–17, 162, 225, 227
Sentenac Canyon, 198–99; marsh at, 198
Sentenac Mountain, 199
Sepulveda Canyon, 210
Sepulveda Pass, 211, **211**, 256–58
Sequit anticline, 292, 293
Sequit Point, 292
sericite, 132
serpentine, 95
serpentinite, 226, 284, 344
Serra Cross, 311, 313
Sespe Creek, 318, 333, 334
Sespe Formation, x, 16, **16**, 216, 226, 227, 289; claystone of, 339; conglomer-ate of, 318; faulted, 269, 314; oil in, 331, 335; red beds of, 318, 331, 334; sandstone of, 285, 291, 315
Sespe Gorge, 316–17, **317**
Shadow Valley, 56
shale, 4; diatomaceous, 204; Eocene marine, 285, 311; expansion of, 275; gypsum-bearing, 311; of lakebeds, 236; marine, 227, 245; metamor-phosed, 156; micaceous, 214, 315; of Miocene age, 343; oil from, 204; organic, 227, 273; phosphatic, 204, 205, **205**; pyrite-rich, 236; siliceous, 180, 219, 280, 291, **291**, 318; sulfides in, 320; tar in, 273; in turbidites, 285, 293, **318**, **323**
Shandin Hills, 243
Shark Harbor, **343**
Shavers Valley, 34
Shavers Well, 116, 117
shear zone, 176
sheelite, 87
Sheep Hole Mountains, 90
shells, 97, 218, 271. *See also* fossils
Ship Mountains, 68
shonkinite, 58
shorelines, 77, 109, 142, **143**, 144
Siberia Crater, 66
Sidewinder Volcanics, x, 14, 42–43
Sierra Highway, 305
Sierra Madre fault zone, 21, 229, 230,

249, **250**, 258, 298
Sierra Nevada Batholith, x, 14, 16, 26, 83, 153, 155
Sierra Pelona, 152
Signal Hill oil field, 204, 205–7
silica, 3, 4, 37, 193, 204, 219
sillimanite, 156
sills, 37, 216, 252, 263, 300, 302, 308
siltstone, 4, 47, 185, 226; ash-rich, 343; with borate, 85; of delta, 115; of Eocene age, 285, 345; gypsum-rich, 236; of lakebeds, 113, **115**, 236; marine, 194, 235, 264, **265**, 270, 280, 345; metamorphosed, 156, 230; of Miocene age, 194, 301, 307; nonmarine, 233; of Pleistocene age, 335; of Pliocene age, 180, 311; of red beds, 70; siliceous, 280; in turbidites, 194, 217, 322
Silurian Lake, 41, 49
silver, 17, 42, 46–48, 78, 87, 101, 132
Silverado Formation, 193, 194
Silver Lake, 49
Silver Queen Mine, 78
Silver Strand, 163–64
Simi Hills, 258
Sisquoc Formation, 226, 231, 273, 282
skarn, 37, 95
Skeleton Canyon, 119
Skolithos, 328
slate, 186, 193, 258. *See also* Santa Monica Slate
slickenlines, 115, **117**, 125
Slide Peak, 325, **325**
sloths, 273
Slover, Mountain, 182
slumping, 219, **235**, 236, 334
smectite, 123
Snaggletooth, 76
Soda Lake playa, 41, 49, 53–54, 94
soils, 135, 162, 173, 176, 188, 246, 338
Solana Beach, 168
solar energy, 58, 59, 86, 130
Soledad Basin, x, 17, 227, 259, 306–7, 308
Soledad Mountain, 77–78, **79**
Soledad Pass, 308, 309
Sonny Bono Salton Sea Refuge, 147
Sonoran Desert, 105, 128
Southern California Logistic Airport, 42
Southern Frontal fault system, 255
South Mountain, 331, 333, **333**
South Mountain oil field, 331
South Pasadena, 255
South Pass fault, 135
spatter, 62
spessartine, 188

spherules, impact, 339
spinel, 97
spit, 164
Split Mountain Gorge, 123–28, **123**
spodumene, 156, 188
springs, 59, 63, 101. *See also* hot springs
Springville fault, 266
Stadium Conglomerate, x, 160, 171, 173
Stille, Hans, 21
Stoddard Mountain, 43
Stoddard Valley, 104
Stone Canyon, 210, 211
Stonewall Mine, 195
strath terraces, 194, 244
Strawberry Peak, 299
stream deposits. *See* river deposits
stream terraces, 232, 243, 320
strike-slip faults, 6–7. *See also* left-slip faults; right-slip faults; *specific fault names*
sturzstrom, 125, 127
subduction zone, 1, 5, 6, 13, 14, 15, 153, 201; minerals formed in, 291
submarine canyon channels, 217, **217**
submarine debris flows, 123
submarine fan, 160, 165, 166
subsidence, land, 77, 130, 189, 210
Sugarloaf Mountain, 326
sulfides, 132, 273, 320
Summerland oil field, 275–77, **276**
Sun City, 158
Sunland, 249
Superstition Hills, 144
Superstition Hills fault, 106, 107, 108, 144
Superstition Mountain, 144
Swarthout Canyon, 302
Sweetwater Formation, 162
Sweetwater River Canyon, 174
Switzer Picnic Area, 298
syenite, 58, 229, 300
syenogranite, 31
Sylmar, 233, 249
Sylmar subbasin, 259
synclines, 72, **73**, 164, 214, 269, 274, 287, 301, 307, 315, 316, 318; in Mecca Hills, 115, **116**, 119, **119**, 120, 121; Santa Clara syncline, 331, 333, 334

Table Mountain, 179
tailings (waste dumps), 78, 85, 96
talc-rich schist, 342
talus, 54, 233, 252
Tamarisk Grove campground, 199
tar, **212**, 213, 266, 273, **274**, 281, 306
tectonic plates, 4–6
tectonic windows, 14, 15

Tehachapi, 79, 83
Tehachapi Mountains, 79, 241, 309
Tehachapi Pass, 83
Tejon Pass, 241
Temblor Formation, 218
Temecula, 189, 191
Temecula Canyon, 189
Temecula Valley, 189–91
Temescal Valley, 189, 193
Templin Highway, 233, 235
terraces, coastal, 155, 161, **160–61**, 169–70, 271; deposits of, 161, 167, 170, 185, 218, 222, 271, 273, 311, 313, 339, 345; faulting of, 274; formation of, 223; locales with multiple, 167, 185, 201, 220, 222–23, **222**, 292, 339, 343, 345; uplift rates of, 271
terraces, stream, 232, 243, 311–12, **312**, 320. *See also* strath terraces
terrane, exotic, 230
Teutonia Batholith, 56
Teutonia Peak, 56, **57**
Thompson, Lake, 77, 84
Thousand Oaks, 264
Thousand Palms Oasis, 140
thrust faults, 7, 14, 21, 26, 194, 242, 255, 258, 318, 320, 330, 333. *See also* Mission Wells thrust fault; Red Mountain thrust fault; San Cayetano thrust fault; Vincent–Orocopia–Chocolate Mountain thrust fault
Tick Canyon Formation, 307
Tiefort Mountains, 50
Tijuana River, 162, 164
tin, 193
tombolo, 142
tonalite, 31, 137, 156, 173–77, **174**, **175**, **179**, 182, 186, **187**, 188, 189, 341
Tonopah & Tidewater Railroad, 63
Topanga Canyon, 210, 291
Topanga Formation, 216, 289, 292–93, **293**; oil in, 204; sandstone of, 262, 263, 296, **298**; volcanics with, 218, 220, 251, 293, **295**
topaz, 156
topographic inversion, 56
Toro Peak, 141
Torrey Canyon oil field, 335
Torrey Pines State Reserve, 167–68
Torrey Sandstone, 162, 167, **167**
tourmaline, 156, 188, 197–98, **198**
tramway, aerial, 137
transform faults, 6, 17, 18, 19, 105
Transverse Ranges, 2, 224–30; basins in, 225; deformation of rocks in, 278;

eastern, 225, 228–30; Eocene rocks in, 311; extent of, 337; gneiss in, 12; left-slip faults in, 225; Pelona Schist in, 15; relation to Peninsular Ranges, 225; rotation of western, x, 20, 159, 165, 200, 225, 337; uplift of, x, 1, 21, 135, 201, 225, 229, 246, 249; volcanics in, 227–28; western, 225–27
travertine, 62, 256, **257**
Travertine Rock, 142, 143
trilobites, 68–69, **69**
Trona, 79, 83
Tropico Group, 77, 78
Tropico Hill, 78
Troy Lake playa, 59, 61
tufa, 142, 143, **143**
tuff, 62, 77, 81, 84, 227; breccia, 61, 84, 308; welded, 74, 156
Tujunga fault, 249, 298
Tujunga Wash, 258
Tule Creek fault, 316
tumuli, 62
Tuna Canyon Formation, 289
tungsten, 87
turbidites, 123, 127, 194, 204, **217**, 268, 285, **285**, 293, 315, 316, 322, **323**
Turritella, 34, 293, **294**
Turtle Mountain, 43
Turtle Valley, 43
Twentynine Palms, 90
Twentynine Palms Marine Corps Center, 62, 63, 90
Twentynine Palms quartz monzonite, 31
Two Hole Spring, 101

ulexite, 85
ultramafic rocks, 97
unconformity, 120, **122**, 164, 167, **167**, 219, 270, 271, **307**, 311; angular, 114, 115
Universal City, 264
Universal Studios, 264
Upland, 252
uplift, 1, 13, 16; coastal, 160, 169, 170, 222, 271, 287; with detachment faulting, 28; along faults, 44, 80, 90, 104, 111, 139, 151, 194, 198, 206, 227; of Peninsular Ranges, 153, 160; of Transverse Ranges, x, 1, 21, 135, 201, 225, 229, 246, 249

Vail Peak, 339
Vallecito Mountains, 125, 199
Vallecitos, 177
Valley of the Falls Drive, 323
Vaqueros Sandstone, 216, 218, 226, 244,

282, 283, 289, 291, 318, 339, 341
varnish, desert, 11–12
Vasquez Formation, x, 16, 17, 307–8, **308**
Vasquez Rocks, 307–8, **308**
Vasquez Rocks Natural Area Park, 308
veins, 31, 32, 33, 47, 78, 87, 152, 153, 156, 189, 328
Ventura, 170, 266, 267, 311, 331, 340
Ventura anticlinorium, 227, 268–69, 271, 313
Ventura Avenue anticline, 269, 270, 311–14, 331
Ventura Avenue oil field, 314
Ventura Basin, x, 16, 17, 225–27, 274, 314, 334
Ventura River, 270, 311, 313, 314
Verdugo fault, 258, 297
Verdugo Mountains, 249
Victorville, 41, 42, 49, 64
Victorville fan, 246
Victorville pediment, 42
Vidal Junction, 11, 74
Vidal Valley, 74, 92
Vincent–Orocopia–Chocolate Mountains thrust fault, 14, 36, 122, 132, 146, 152, 183, 229, 230, 253, 302
Violin Breccia, 233, 234
Vista del Lago, 234, 236
Vitrefax Mine, 132, 133
volcanic ash, 47, 77, 81, 97, 179, 339, 343, 344, 345; layers of, 62, 112, 189, 270, 313
volcanic bombs, 66, 97
volcaniclastic rocks, 4, 62, 156, 160, 173, 227, 340, 341, 343, 344, 345
volcanic rocks, 3. *See also* andesite; basalt; dacite; lava flows; metavolcanic; rhyolite
Volcan Mountain, 196
volcanoes, 5, 6, 95, 97, 146–48; necks of, 54, 152, 178. *See also* calderas; cinder cones; plugs
volcanoes, mud, 148
Vulcan Mine, 95, **96**

Ward Valley, 91
water gap, 41, **41**, 80, 180, 198
Waterman Gneiss, 47
Waterman Mountain, 301
wave-cut platforms. *See* terraces, coastal
weathering, 4, 9, 10–11, 56, 84, 92, 120, 157, 173, 174, **175**, 186, 193, 323, **324**

welded tuff, 74, 156
West Covina, 180
West Frontal fault, 244
West Los Angeles, 201, 255
Westmorland, 144
wetlands: coastal, 165, 281, 294; mountain, 199. *See also* lagoons; marshes
Wheeler Gorge, 314–15
Wheeler Springs, 314
Whipple Mountains, 28, 74, **76**
White Tank, 31
Whitewater River, 105, 133, 135, 136
Whittier fault, 157, 194, 201
Whittier Narrows, 180
Wildomar, 189
Wildomar fault, 192
wilkeite, 182
Willard fault, 191, 192
Willis Palms, 140, **140**
Willows Diorite, 341
Willow Springs fault, 78
Wilmington oil field, 204, 207, 209
Wilson Diorite, 249, 250, 298, 300, 301
Wilson, Mt., 300
Winchester Canyon, 282
wind: energy from, 83, 133–35, **135**; blasting by, 136–37, **136**; desert varnish and, 11; on playas, 84. *See also* sand dunes
Wind Caves, 124
wind gaps, 180, 210, 263
Wister, 149
Witch Creek, 194
wollastonite, 132, 182
Wonderland of Rocks, 31
Wrightwood, 238, 245, 246, 297, 302, 303
Wynola, 194

Yaqui Well, 199
Yerba Buena Canyon, 292
Younger Dryas, 339
Yucaipa Plain, 183
Yucca Valley, 90, 99
Yuha Basin, 130
Yuha Desert, 128

Zabriskie Formation, 330
Zaca Lake, 23
zircon, 95
Zuma Beach, 291
Zzyzx, 53

—MOLLY GANS

Arthur Sylvester is a native southern Californian whose eyes were opened to geology by high school biology class trips to the Colorado Plateau. He earned a BA in liberal arts at Pomona College. Graduate study at UCLA was interrupted by a one-year Fulbright Fellowship in Norway, where he studied the emplacement of the Vrådal granitic pluton. He returned to UCLA to write an MA thesis about the pluton and then a PhD dissertation about the emplacement of Papoose Flat pluton in eastern California. Afterward, he joined a team of Shell Development Company research geologists and geophysicists to study the tectonic history of the Pacific margin of the United States. UC Santa Barbara lured him from Shell to teach courses in structural geology, field geology, and petrology. His academic research focused on structural, seismic, and igneous rock problems in the Colorado and Mojave Deserts, the Transverse Ranges, and the Lake Tahoe region, as well as in Norway and southern Italy. He received the UC Presidents Award for Excellence in Undergraduate Research Mentoring in 1994, the UCSB Academic Senate Distinguished Teaching Award in Mathematical, Life & Physical Sciences 1996–97, and the Dickson Emeriti Fellowship 2015–2016. He retired from active teaching in 2003.

Elizabeth O'Black Gans, Libby to most, holds a BS in geology from UC Santa Barbara, where she was introduced to plenty of great southern California geology, as well as to the art of map making. Shortly after graduation, Libby started Gans Illustrations and began working on maps and scientific illustrations for publication, eventually becoming the first digital artist of the Dibblee Geological Foundation. It was there, with Helmut Ehrenspeck, that she pioneered the transition to digital drafting of the Dibblee maps. While Libby's main vocation of the last fifteen years has been raising a family, she continues to work on geologic map making and scientific illustration projects, with her work most recently appearing in *Science*, in *Tectonics*, and in *Geochemistry, Geophysics, Geosystems (G-Cubed)*, as well as in posters at AGU and GSA national meetings. Libby is currently employed at Santa Barbara City College in the Department of Earth and Planetary Sciences.